The Peoples of
Southeast Asia Today

BOOKS BY ROBERT L. WINZELER

Anthropology and Religion: What We Know, Think, and Question, 2008

The Architecture of Life and Death in Borneo, 2004

Indigenous Architecture in Borneo: Traditional Patterns and New Developments, editor, 1998

Indigenous Peoples and the State: Politics, Land, and Ethnicity in the Malayan Peninsula and Borneo, editor, 1997

Latah in Southeast Asia: The History and Ethnography of a Culture-Bound Syndrome, 1995

The Seen and the Unseen: Shamanism, Mediumship and Possession in Borneo, editor, 1993

Ethnic Relations in Kelantan: A Study of the Chinese and Thai as Ethnic Minorities in a Malay State, 1985

The Peoples of Southeast Asia Today

Ethnography, Ethnology, and Change in a Complex Region

Robert L. Winzeler

ALTAMIRA
PRESS

A division of
ROWMAN & LITTLEFIELD PUBLISHERS, INC.
Lanham • New York • Toronto • Plymouth, UK

Published by AltaMira Press
A division of Rowman & Littlefield Publishers, Inc.
A wholly owned subsidary of The Rowman & Littlefield Publishing Group, Inc.
4501 Forbes Boulevard, Suite 200, Lanham, Maryland 20706
http://www.altamirapress.com

Estover Road, Plymouth PL6 7PY, United Kingdom

British Library Cataloguing in Publication Information Available

Library of Congress Cataloging-in-Publication Data
Winzeler, Robert L.
   The peoples of Southeast Asia today : ethnography, ethnology, and change in a
complex region / Robert L. Winzeler.
      p. cm.
   Includes bibliographical references and index.
   ISBN 978-0-7591-1862-1 (cloth : alk. paper) — ISBN 978-0-7591-1863-8 (pbk. :
alk. paper) — ISBN 978-0-7591-1864-5 (electronic)
   1. Ethnology—Southeast Asia. 2. Human geography—Southeast Asia.
3. Southeast Asia—Social conditions. 4. Southeast Asia—Economic conditions.
5. Southeast Asia—Social life and customs. I. Title.
GN635.S58W46 2011
305.800959—dc22
                                                                2010043849

♾™ The paper used in this publication meets the minimum requirements of
American National Standard for Information Sciences—Permanence of Paper
for Printed Library Materials, ANSI/NISO Z39.48-1992.

Printed in the United States of America

For Lisa, Alice, Josh, Emma, and Rachel

Contents

Maps and Photos

MAPS

PHOTOS

Preface and Acknowledgments

Books that offer an overview of the peoples of Southeast Asia have been few and far between. Robbins Burling's *Hill Farms and Padi Fields* is probably the most successful of such efforts. It was published in 1965, and, while still in print, has never been revised, though great changes have taken place in the ensuing forty-five years. And like several other older books that offer an introduction or overview, it is concerned only with the mainland half of Southeast Asia. Moreover, treatments of the insular region have mainly concerned the country of Indonesia. Going beyond these limits is one place where this book aims to make a contribution.

Any book offering a worthwhile anthropological treatment of the peoples of Southeast Asia should do certain things. I think it should make clear that—the great diversity and variation notwithstanding—there are important commonalities or continuities across the region. It should also include some background on geography, prehistory, languages, and history, or what we know of these. It should further offer a meaningful treatment of the ethnology and ethnography of the region, and it should deal with what has happened to people in recent decades and what they are like today.

How all of this is done is another matter. This book certainly expresses my own prejudices and experiences—where I have been, and what I have done, what I have read, and how I have reacted to it. The book is somewhat more reflective of my recent interests, enthusiasms, and efforts in Southeast Asia than my more ancient ones. I have a longstanding concern with matters of religion that shows in the three chapters devoted to this general topic, including one on indigenous patterns of belief and practice, a second on religion, society, and the state, and a third on patterns of conversion. The latter chapter also reflects the particular interest I have taken in indigenous peoples and ethnic minorities and their problems over the past several decades, an interest also developed in the chapters on hunter-gatherers and tribal cultivators and in several other sections of the book. My discussions of religion and the state as well as of agrarian transformations and problems of development also pay a lot of attention to differences in patterns of change in the socialist and nonsocialist countries.

ACKNOWLEDGMENTS

My debts are multiple and deep. I owe my original interest in Southeast Asia to several talented teachers and experts on the region I encountered as a graduate student at the University of Chicago. As I see it, the development of my own orientation and theoretical prejudices has diverged rather sharply from theirs but the influence has remained. I have also benefited over the years from the largess of various institutions, including the Fulbright Program, the National Science Foundation, the National Institute of Mental Health, the Luce Foundation, and the University of Nevada, Reno. The friends, colleagues, informants, guides, and casual acquaintances I have made in Southeast Asia have made possible whatever I have accomplished, greatly enriched my life, and made me want to return time and again.

As for this book, however much I have learned firsthand about some regions of Southeast Asia over the years, what I have written here depends heavily on the work of others. I owe a great debt to the scholars and researchers on whose accounts I have relied, and I hope I have done them justice. Writing a book is always a voyage of discovery, but the general orientation of this one as well as the motivation to write it owes much to the course on Southeast Asia I have been fortunate to be able to teach every several years over a long period of time.

The editors at AltaMira Press and Rowman & Littlefield have again been a pleasure to work with, highly professional, and very responsive to my preferences and suggestions. The book itself had its origin in a conversation over breakfast several years ago with Alan McClare, the editor of my previous book published by AltaMira. I am deeply saddened that he is not here to see its publication. The book has also benefited from the criticisms of two anonymous readers for the press, although I have not been able to incorporate all of the good advice provided. Kris Pizarro drew the maps that appear in chapter 1. An earlier version of chapter 10 ("Religious Conversion on the Ethnic Margins") was presented at a conference on "Mainland Southeast Asia at Its Margins: Minority Groups and Borders," at the Center for Khmer Studies, Siem Reap, Cambodia, on March 14, 2008.

Of those who have contributed to the book I am by far most indebted to my wife, Judy, who has been a part of it all. She read, criticized, advised, and helped me edit the several drafts of the book. Beyond this she was with me during my earliest stay in Southeast Asia, on many of the subsequent trips, and all of the recent ones.

1

Introduction

The Peoples of Southeast Asia Today is chiefly about living peoples and their cultural ways and patterns of adaptation rather than geography, history, or prehistory, although much will be said about these as well. Southeast Asia forms the southern and eastern corner of the Asian continent, plus the great adjacent Philippine and Indonesian archipelagoes that lie just beyond it. The modern countries of Southeast Asia include the Philippines, Indonesia, Malaysia, Thailand, Cambodia, Burma (or Myanmar), Laos, and Vietnam, plus the small nations of Brunei, Singapore, and Timor. The Southeast Asian countries are the creation of European colonialism rather than a reflection of natural geographical, cultural, or linguistic boundaries. Most importantly, a map of the ethnic groups or languages of Southeast Asia does not fully match a political map of the eleven countries listed above. For one thing, the modern country of Indonesia includes the eastern half of the great island of New Guinea (second only to Greenland in size) that, along with various adjacent islands, is considered a part of the Melanesian culture area of Oceania. And for another, various essentially Southeast Asian peoples and languages extend well beyond the named Southeast Asian countries, especially in northern Southeast Asia. Here, many of the indigenous minorities or tribal groups are also spread over southern or southwestern China, where they are in some instances much more numerous than in the northern Southeast Asian countries themselves. This kind of overlapping also occurs in the northwestern region, where a number of ethnically and linguistically Southeast Asian peoples dwell in India and Bangladesh as well as in Burma.[1]

But is Southeast Asia real or invented? Recently, there has been some concern among Southeast Asianist scholars about whether Southeast Asia

1

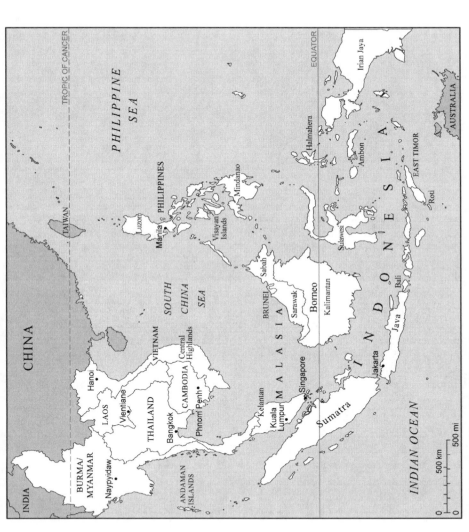

Map 1.1. Countries of Southeast Asia

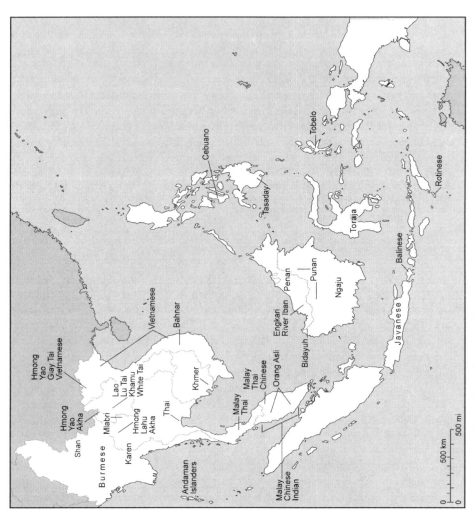

Map 1.2. Locations of peoples in Southeast Asia

is a real place or a cultural construction. I would urge the reader not to be overly concerned with this issue. All of the identified regions of the world, including Europe, Asia, Oceania, and the Americas, are cultural constructions. All came into existence as concepts or "imagined places" at various points in human history, mainly as Europeans, Middle Easterners, Asians, and others gained an ever-widening knowledge of the world through exploration, trade, conquest, religious proselytization, and colonialism. It is true that many other places have been named for a much longer time than Southeast Asia, which came to be imagined in its present form only in the mid-twentieth century. Though recently constructed, the identity of Southeast Asia as a major area of the world now seems firmly established, even if it has been "South-East Asia" in British usage and "Southeast Asia" in American. In 1967, the governments of Southeast Asia created an organization called the Association of Southeast Asian Nations, or ASEAN, whose purpose is to advance what they perceive to be their common interests and solve problems in the region. There are also a great many university and college courses in the United States and elsewhere that concern Southeast Asia, presumably based on the assumption that something is there. The present book proposes that, while a great deal of human diversity exists in Southeast Asia, there are also impressive continuities, several of which will be mentioned below and throughout the book.

Both the variations and the continuities within Southeast Asia have to do with geography. Most of Southeast Asia lies within the Northern Hemisphere, and nearly all of it is tropical or subtropical. Thus, weather patterns are based largely on the monsoons. The English term monsoon comes from (probably by way of Malay) the Arabic word *musin*, or "season." There are two monsoons, one sometimes referred to as the Winter Monsoon because it occurs or reaches its peak during the winter months and the other as the Summer Monsoon because it takes place in the opposite part of the year. Again, such phrases can seem misleading. For one thing, applying terms that refer to temperate seasons seems inappropriate, especially regarding the year-round hot and humid equatorial tropics. For another, the summer and winter referred to in the names of the two monsoons are based on the seasons of the Northern Hemisphere, even though the "summer" monsoon actually blows from the Southern Hemisphere when it is actually winter. (Or to put it slightly differently, both weather patterns are actually "winter monsoons" in terms of their places of origin.) A more accurate set of names for the two monsoons is based simply on their directions, that is, the northeast monsoon blows from the northeast and the other from the southwest.

Regardless of what they are called, the two monsoons do not usually have the same strength throughout Southeast Asia. Rather, one affects some areas more strongly than others. Overall, the northeast monsoon has the greater effect in that more of Southeast Asia is in the Northern than the Southern Hemisphere. But exposure to the force of the monsoons—including storms, rough seas, and heavy rainfall—is also affected by other geographic factors, especially landmasses and mountains. Today, the monsoons are most commonly associated with rainfall and storm patterns. They are also linked to prevailing seasonal winds that were for a long period the basis for trade and for the introduction of religious and cultural influences from India and the Middle East. The northeast monsoon produces easterly winds, and the southwest monsoon creates westerly ones, enabling sailing vessels to move easily and reliably from India and Middle Eastern lands to Southeast Asia during one season and in the opposite direction in the other.

There are also differences involving latitude. There is first an equatorial zone sometimes defined as the region extending from five degrees north to five degrees south latitude. This region of year-round high heat and humidity is seasonally differentiated mainly into periods of greater and lesser rainfall linked to the monsoons. Note that "greater" and "lesser" do not mean a dry period followed by wet one, for it tends to rain at least periodically (and often frequently) year-round throughout most of equatorial Southeast Asia, and prolonged periods of drought are rare. It has sometimes been said that the dry season here is when it only rains once a day. Although this is an overstatement, during the rainy season it can rain off and on for days at a time, and flooding is a frequent occurrence in many places. The natural vegetation of much of the humid tropical zone is luxuriant rain forest, marked by high species variability. Though much of it has now been cleared for various purposes, equatorial Southeast Asia still has the second-most extensive tropical forest in the world.

The climate of the more northerly areas of Southeast Asia is more distinctly seasonal, which means marked differences throughout the year in rainfall (that is, a marked dry season rather than simply one of less moisture), temperature, and wind patterns. The climate of the northern mainland is often referred to as monsoonal, although this is misleading insofar as it implies that this term does not apply to the equatorial region as well. Here the weather is also affected by the monsoons though somewhat less markedly in terms of seasonal differences in rainfall, wind velocity, and storm patterns. Typhoons (as hurricanes are known in Asia) or even strong winds are rare on or near the equator but common over the seas and coastal areas to the north. The natural vegetation in the north is also generally less dense or luxuriant than in the equatorial zone. Monsoon forests in the northern regions are dryer. Here the leaves of some types of trees change color and fall during the dry season so that such forests sometimes resemble those of temperate regions. As is also true in the equatorial zone, mountains and elevation also affect climate and vegetation.

MAINLAND AND INSULAR SOUTHEAST ASIA
AND OTHER CONTRASTS

Several important characteristics of Southeast Asia can be introduced as a series of contrasts. Some of these are natural, such as the two monsoons that have already been noted. Others refer to language, history, and culture. Some of these contrasts will need to be qualified as we go along but are useful for getting an initial grasp on the region.

The most important of the natural contrasts is the division of the region into insular and mainland zones. The mainland includes those lands that are physically part of the Asian continent, while the insular part consists of the vast intersecting Indonesian and Philippine archipelagoes. All but one of the eleven countries lie entirely within either mainland or insular Southeast Asia, and as we shall see, the languages spoken in each part belong mainly to different language groups. The mainland countries include Vietnam, Laos, Cambodia, Thailand, and Burma, and the insular ones include Indonesia and the Philippines as well as the smaller countries of Singapore, Brunei, and Timor. The exception is Malaysia, which is divided between the mainland and insular regions—specifically, the western part of the country consists of the Malay Peninsula, which is the southern extremity of the continent, while the eastern part (the states of Sabah and Sarawak) consists of the northern one-third of the great island of Borneo. In cultural and historical terms, peninsular Malaysia belongs more to insular than to mainland Southeast Asia. In linguistic terms, the Malays speak an Austronesian language, as do the native occupants of the insular countries (except for the Papuan speakers of Indonesian New Guinea). In contrast, nearly all of the other peoples of the mainland speak non-Austronesian languages belonging to one of four major language families. The exceptions here are the remnant Chams of Vietnam and Cambodia and some of the highland ethnic minorities of the central highlands of southern Vietnam, who also speak Austronesian languages.

Lowland and Highland and Coastal and Interior Peoples

The indigenous peoples of Southeast Asia are also commonly described in terms of a geographical contrast. For the mainland, this contrast is phrased in terms of elevation. Specifically, there are the "lowland" peoples, on the one hand, and "highland" ones, on the other. The distinction between lowlanders and highlanders refers not simply to whether people live in the valleys and plains or in the hills and mountains. It also embraces other important characteristics, ones involving ecology, history, political organization and power, ethnicity and culture, languages, settlement patterns and stability, population size and density, and religion. The lowlanders are generally cultivators of wet rice, live in more permanent towns and villages, have state political organization, and adhere to Buddhism or Islam. The highlanders, by contrast, mainly practice shifting or swidden cultivation of dry rice, live in more scattered and less permanent settlements (ones occupied for a few years, though now often much longer than formerly), have local or "tribal" political organization, and generally adhere to animistic religious practices or, more recently, to Christianity.

In terms of power and numbers the lowland groups include the dominant, majority peoples of the various countries of the region. The modern countries of mainland Southeast Asia are named for these lowlanders: the Vietnamese of Vietnam, the Lao of Laos, the Thai of Thailand, and the Malays of Malaysia. Cambodia and Burma are exceptions, though not really important ones. The dominant people of Cambodia are known as Khmer rather than Cambodians, and the dominant people of Myanmar, as Burma now calls itself (though not everyone else in the world agrees to do so), are still known as Burmese (or Burmans) rather than Myanmarese. However, not all of the lowland peoples are dominant majorities everywhere they are found. The Vietnamese who are the dominant majority in Vietnam are a minority in Cambodia, while the Khmer who dominate in Cambodia are a minority in Vietnam. The Malays dominate Malaysia but form an important (and very dissatisfied) minority in southern Thailand, and so on. In addition, there are also lowland peoples that are not demographically or politically dominant in any of the present-day Southeast Asian countries— the Shans in Burma, the Chams in Cambodia and Vietnam, and the Mons in Thailand, for example.

The highland peoples of mainland Southeast Asia are all ethnic minorities. (Many in the past were sufficiently autonomous that the term "minority" did not really fit.) The highland groups have been referred to by the lowlanders in various ways, including some very negative ones meaning savage or slave. The modern, official, ethnological labels vary from one country to another but include "indigenous ethnic minorities" (to distinguish them from "immigrant" or "overseas" minorities, especially the Chinese) or "hill tribes." Whatever they are called exactly, the highland peoples are an important part of most of the countries in mainland Southeast Asia. In Laos, the various indigenous ethnic minorities form about half of the total population, while at the opposite extreme in neighboring Cambodia such groups amount to only a few percent of the national population. In the other countries of mainland Southeast Asia, the size of the indigenous ethnic minority populations varies between these two extremes. In most cases, the overall percentages are at the lower end of the range, but keep in mind that in most cases the highland peoples tend to be located in particular regions (mountainous ones, of course) rather than distributed throughout the entire country. This is so in Thailand, for example, where the hill

tribes are highly concentrated in the northern part of the country. It is also
the case in Cambodia, where the indigenous upland minorities are to be
found in the northeastern corner of the country. The same can be said of
Burma and Vietnam. Only in Laos, which is mainly mountainous, are the
highland peoples distributed over much of its entire territory, from the far
north to the far south and from east to west.

Finally, many of the highland minority peoples in the mainland are
spread over several modern countries. While often known by different local names in different places, the widespread groups are basically the same
or closely related in terms of language and culture, and often in terms of
identity as well. Of these groups, the Hmong are by far the best known to
westerners because of the recent large-scale movement of many of them to
the United States, France, Australia, and elsewhere as a consequence of the
American wars in Laos and Vietnam. There are many varieties of Hmong to
be found throughout southern China, northern Vietnam, Laos, and Thailand (locally identified in terms of the colors of their traditional clothing).
However, the commonalities in their traditional lifeways and material culture are obvious to anyone who has visited their villages in different places.
Other widely dispersed indigenous minorities include the various Akha
groups of southern China (where they are known as Hani), northern Laos,
Thailand, and Upper Burma; the Tai peoples of northern Vietnam, Laos,
and Thailand; and the Yao (including Mien, Dao, and Lantien) groups
of Vietnam, Laos, Thailand, and China. We will be discussing all of these
peoples in more detail in later sections of this book.

In turning to insular Southeast Asia, we find the same general kind of
distinction, though it has not always been phrased in the same way. At
the present time, the preference appears to be for lowland and highland
(or upland).[2] In the past, however, the main distinction usually made was
between coastal and interior peoples.[3] The general assumption here has
been that coastal peoples have the same general characteristics attributed
to the lowlanders of the mainland, while the interior groups have the same
ones as the highlanders. The interior regions of most of the islands and
the Malay Peninsula are mountainous and until recently at least mainly
covered by dense forests, with the regions between the mountains and the
coast sometimes containing nearly impenetrable swamps. Such conditions
made overland travel and therefore communication difficult, and this, in
turn, made for the creation and perpetuation of linguistic and ethnic differentiation (and beyond this frequent intergroup hostility). The great rivers
that also occur in the larger islands and the Malay Peninsula provide easier
travel and communication between the interior and the coast, or between
upstream and downstream areas, but the difficulties of movement from one
river system to another remain.

By contrast, movement by sea, both along the coasts and from one body of land to another, is relatively easy for people who long ago developed the use of boats. Such conditions and such developments in turn made for the often-striking spread of language and culture between distant points and over large areas. They also made for maritime trade and economic integration and lesser amounts of political integration based on trade, alliance, and conquest. These conditions and developments occurred to the greatest extent across the large area of western insular and peninsular Southeast Asia that includes the Malay Peninsula and the great islands of Sumatra and Borneo. But they extended from there to the southern Philippines and eastern Indonesia. The main exception to this general pattern is the island of Java and the smaller island of Bali at its eastern end. Here, the interior is formed by volcanic mountains, between which are sloping plains and basins with extremely rich soils and, consequently, much denser interior populations. There is also much greater traditional political and economic integration and cultural similarity than found in the neighboring large islands of Sumatra or, especially, Borneo. Put differently, the human ecology and cultural development of Java and Bali is more like that of some of the interior areas of mainland Southeast Asia (for example, Cambodia, central Thailand, Lower Burma, or the delta of northern Vietnam) than is much of the rest of the insular world.

The highland-lowland dichotomy has also been phrased in part in terms of a contrast between tribes and states—the generalization being that the highland peoples are tribally organized while the lowland ones are encompassed in states.

Indic and Sinitic Influences

Another distinction concerns patterns of external cultural influence. The archaeologist Peter Bellwood (1997) points out that throughout the prehistoric period the main influences on Southeast Asia came from the north, from present-day China. But for the past two thousand years the patterns of outside influence have been more complicated. Some regions of Southeast Asia have been much more strongly influenced by India than China and developed civilizations that reflected this influence in their government, religion, and architecture. In earlier periods the notion of "India" in Western thought included the lands and waters of Southeast Asia as well as the Indian subcontinent, as reflected in the name "The Dutch East Indies" for present-day Indonesia. In the insular realm, Indic influence extended from Sumatra and the Malay Peninsula to Borneo, Java, Bali, and perhaps beyond, though it was confined mainly to the coastal zones of this region. In the Southeast Asian mainland, Indian influence prevailed in the lowland regions of present-day Burma, Thailand, Laos, Cambodia, and in earlier times, southern Vietnam. Throughout this region, Indic influence was, so far as we know, based on peaceful contact and interaction, involving trade and the spread of Hinduism and Buddhism. Southeast Asian rulers and courts imported and synthesized versions of Indian cosmology, and states built some of the finest Indic temple cities ever created, above all at Angkor in Cambodia.

The influence of China has been different in several ways. To begin with material culture and commerce, Chinese goods (especially jars and other ceramics) have been imported and traded throughout much of Southeast Asia, including the insular region, for probably as long as Indian influence has been exerted. Beyond trade goods, Chinese influence has been limited in geographical terms. In lowland Southeast Asia, Chinese influence was most pervasive among the Vietnamese, which in the earlier period meant the northern part of present-day Vietnam and in the later period the central and southern parts of the country as well—that is, as these were later brought under control and settlement by the ethnic Vietnamese. In the second century BCE Vietnam became a province of China and remained so for the next thousand years. During this time, the government, class system, and many dimensions of Vietnamese religion and culture—from the adoption of Chinese characters to chopsticks, social organization, and ritual practices—became Sinitic. The Vietnamese eventually threw off Chinese rule and became an independent state, but they never rejected Chinese religion and culture. They carried it with them as they expanded southward and gained control of the coastal region and Mekong Delta at the expense of the Indic-oriented Cham and Khmer (Cambodians) who had previously held these regions.

The indigenous tribal peoples of the northern highland ethnic frontier of Southeast Asia have also been influenced by China, though for somewhat different reasons and in different ways. Some of these groups originated in present-day China, from which they have been moving southward as a result of the expansion of the ethnic Han Chinese. And, as noted above, all of these peoples include populations that currently exist in China as well as in Burma, Laos, Vietnam, and Thailand. Most of these groups have forms of kinship and patrilineal (through the male line) descent that link them to China (including Tibet), though whether this is more a matter of ancient cultural sharing or of influence by the ethnic Chinese is another matter. In any case, the forms of social organization that prevail among the northern highland peoples generally distinguish them from those groups farther south. Even the bulkier and more fully body-covering traditional clothing styles of the northern highland peoples seem to reflect links to the north and northwest, although such styles are also suited to the cooler part of the year, especially at higher elevations, in northern Southeast Asia.

Austronesian and Non-Austronesian Languages

A final division in Southeast Asia that is worth noting is between Austronesian and non-Austronesian languages. The complexity or variation in the Southeast Asia linguistic landscape is as great as that of any comparable region in the world, and probably more than most. Perhaps the simplest way to get an initial hold on this complexity is to divide the indigenous languages into those that are Austronesian and those that are not. Nearly all of the various Austronesian languages occur in insular and peninsular Southeast Asia, while most of the non-Austronesian ones are in the mainland. So the simple equation of Austronesian languages with insular and peninsular Southeast Asia and of the non-Austronesian languages with mainland Southeast Asia is very largely accurate and a good generalization to keep in mind to understand the big picture. Malay and other Malayic languages of the Malay Peninsula are Austronesian. There is also a cluster of Austronesian languages in southern Vietnam and Cambodia (Lebar, Hickey, and Musgrave 1964; see also Benjamin and Chou 2002).

Also, the general equation of Austronesian languages with insular Southeast Asia and non-Austronesian ones with the mainland does not mean that either are limited to Southeast Asia, which is definitely not so in either case. The Austronesian family is the most geographically widespread in the world and includes most of the languages of the Pacific Islands.[4] The situation is more complicated in the case of the non-Austronesian languages of the mainland, for here we do not have a single language family or super family but (depending on how you slice and group them) four or five of these. Like the Austronesian languages, most of the non-Austronesian ones extend far beyond Southeast Asia but, in this case, into the heart of the Asian continent, including the Himalayas (Lebar, Hickey and Musgrave 1964).

The exceptions to the general equation of the non-Austronesian languages with the mainland and the Austronesian ones with insular Southeast Asia are not accidents of prehistory. None of the non-Austronesian languages of the mainland are found anywhere in the islands of Southeast Asia beyond the Malay Peninsula (where the Aslian languages spoken by some of the indigenous interior people are Mon-Khmer, which is a branch of Austroasiatic). If any of these languages (and it would most likely have been Mon-Khmer) ever extended into the present-day islands of Southeast Asia, they have been completely replaced by Austronesian ones. It is tempting to say that the non-Austronesian peoples of the mainland were mainly land-based peoples whose movement into and throughout the insular world was inhibited by the seas. The only problem with this explanation is that, until ten or eleven thousand years ago, the Malay Peninsula was a part of Sunda Land, that is, connected to Sumatra, Java, and Borneo, and to much of the rest of what became insular Southeast Asia before the sea level rose at the end of the Pleistocene. However, even during the Pleistocene, the land corridor that connected the bulk of the Southeast Asian mainland (that is, the modern countries of Vietnam, Laos, Cambodia, Burma, and most of Thailand) to the Sunda landmass (present-day Borneo, Sumatra, Java, and the Malay Peninsula) was narrow and rugged.

Nevertheless, the Austronesians were or became primarily a maritime people who began to spread into Southeast Asia some five thousand years ago. Two different proto-Austronesian origins have been suggested. Based on the general historical linguistic theory that the homeland of a language family is found at the point of its greatest diversity, the first view is that this would be Melanesia, from which diverse branches spread both westward into the Southeast Asian islands and then eastward into the Pacific Islands. The other view places the proto-Austronesian home in southwestern coastal China or the island of Taiwan, where the indigenous peoples speak diverse Austronesian languages. The evidence for this view is based in part on culture history, especially the assumption that rice was introduced into the Southeast Asian Archipelago with the Austronesian expansion, for rice is lacking in Melanesia. For this and other reasons, it is the southeast coastal China–Taiwan place of origin that is now accepted (Bellwood 1997).

Continuities across Southeast Asia

The forgoing discussion of geographical, cultural, and linguistic dichotomies may sound like an argument for separate treatments of mainland and insular Southeast Asia. In the past, this was a popular approach and in some ways makes things easier. Until recently, textbooks and other comparative studies were usually focused on one or the other of the two regions. But this has begun to change since there are compelling reasons for a unitary approach. There are widespread commonalities throughout Southeast Asia. Moreover, some of these contrast remarkably with cultural patterns characteristic of other regions of Asia and therefore make Southeast Asia not just a region on the map but also a real cultural area with defining characteristics. One of these is the way that houses are commonly built (see photo 1.1). Most indigenous houses are customarily built entirely of organic materials, including wood, leaves, grass, and very often a lot of bamboo, which is commonly used for flooring, siding, and some structural elements (and in some areas for roofing as well). Brick or cement block and mortar are used extensively today but not traditionally, especially outside of lowland Vietnam. Houses vary in design, but again there are widespread continuities that span the mainland and insular areas and often the highland and lowland peoples as well. The most important such feature is placing houses (and usually also other buildings) on posts or piles, sometimes a few feet

Photo 1.1. Khamu house, Ban Keo village, Luang Prabang Province, Lao People's Democratic Republic (PDR), 2005.

but very often the height of a person or more so that the space underneath can be used for work, leisure, or the keeping of animals or storage. Far less pervasive but also not uncommon in Southeast Asia is the traditional practice of building multifamily dwellings, especially in the form of longhouses. Such dwellings are, or were, especially common in Borneo, but they can also be seen in some areas in the mainland, including the central highlands of southern Vietnam and in adjacent areas of northeastern Cambodia in Ratanakiri Province. Formerly, they were more widespread.

Social organization, especially matters of gender, is even more important as a defining contrast that sets Southeast Asia apart from adjacent regions of Asia, that is, China, India, and elsewhere. Although there are exceptions, the traditional culture of most of the peoples of both South Asia and East Asia are marked by a strong male bias. Women are usually formally subordinated to men. Descent is typically patrilineal, or traced through the male line, and the relatives of the husband are emphasized. Residence after marriage is usually virilocal—that is, with or near the family and kin of the husband rather than the wife, which along with patrilineal descent, tends to weaken the social position of women relative to men. Women inherit less property than men or receive a dowry instead. Sons are preferred to daughters, and fewer daughters survive, either as a consequence of female infanticide or of unequal nourishment and support. Marriages are usually arranged by parents, and virginity in girls is stressed. These are traditional (and probably ancient) practices that have now often changed in favor of greater gender equality and posttraditional lifestyles. There is also considerable variation according to social status in stratified societies and according to religion.

These typical South Asian and East Asian traditional cultural patterns in gender and in other areas of social organization are not simply reversed in Southeast Asia. And there is again variation in stratified societies and according to different religious traditions. But overall, family, marriage, kinship, descent, and social behavior in Southeast Asian are much closer to equality or balance in gender than those in South and East Asia. The social customs of the Vietnamese and of some of the northern highland peoples of the mainland, including the Hmong and the Yao, reflect the influence of China and are male oriented. Elsewhere in the Southeast Asian countries, instances of both female-oriented matrilineal and male-oriented patrilineal descent and kinship can be found. But among both highland or tribal and lowland or state-organized societies across both mainland and insular Southeast Asia, the main pattern of descent and kinship is bilateral. And in keeping with this, residence after marriage is often with or near the family of the wife or in a new location; families have little if any preference for sons over daughters; and female sexual purity is overall of less concern as a matter of family or male honor—and in some places premarital sexual activity forms a normal part of traditional courtship. Again, there are important differences according to religious traditions, but the overall contrast with South and East Asia remains striking.

In terms of religion, Southeast Asia is one of the most diverse regions in the world. However, we also find broad continuities—to be discussed in more detail in chapters 8, 9, and 10. The world religions that today predominate in Southeast Asia are not spread equally across mainland and insular regions. Mass popular adherence to Buddhism is presently limited to mainland countries, but in earlier periods it was not. Formal adherence to Hinduism is today limited to a small area of Indonesia centering on Bali. But formerly Hindu cults extended over a much larger region of insular and mainland Southeast Asia, where their remains are widely evident in both archaeological sites and popular beliefs and practices. Islam predominates in the lowlands and coastal zones of the insular realm but also extends to the southern region of the mainland. Christianity dominates only in the Philippines but is distributed widely as a minority religion in both insular and mainland Southeast Asia. Outside of the Philippines and a few other places, moreover, Christianity is generally recent, and the pattern of conversion is similar in mainland and in insular Southeast Asia—involving in both places mainly the highland and interior peoples who formerly adhered to indigenous animist religions. And when we look beyond the world religions to the indigenous traditions of supernaturally oriented belief and practice, we also find continuities across Southeast Asia. To take one example that will be treated in some detail in chapter 8, beliefs and practices involving inauspicious and dangerous "bad death" have a notably wide distribution over both insular and mainland Southeast Asia. Two-stage funeral practices are less common but also have an interesting distribution in both the islands and continental regions.

RESOURCES FOR THE STUDY OF SOUTHEAST ASIAN PEOPLES

In the earliest periods of contact by the West, written knowledge (there are also earlier Indian and Chinese accounts and other sources) about Southeast Asia was produced mainly by missionaries, ship captains, explorers, adventurers, traders, and at least one literate English pirate (William Dampier). Such works often had titles beginning with phrases like "The Voyages (or Travels) of . . . ." Later information came from sojourning natural scientists (most notably Alfred Wallace, author of *The Malay Archipelago*) and colonial empire builders and administrators, including Thomas Raffles (who wrote the classic two-volume *History of Java*) and John Crawfurd (the three-volume *History of the Indian Archipelago*). Such individuals often combined an interest in geography and exploration, archaeology, linguistics, ethnology, and collecting. In the case of the colonial scholars, such interests were mixed with practical matters of expanding the bounds of empire and pacifying, subduing, settling, controlling, and administrating local peoples. Some missionary and colonial knowledge was based on long experience ("on the ground") in dealing with local peoples in vernacular languages, and some of it was based on more superficial contact gained through expeditions using guides and translators; these expeditions were aimed at showing or planting the flag, treaty making, pacification, punishment, exploration, or various combinations of these. Such information was turned into notes and journal accounts and published as reports, books, and articles. As photography developed in the latter part of the nineteenth century, this was added to the older techniques of information gathering, including note taking, drawing, and mapping. The information produced about Southeast Asian peoples in these ways is vital. That is all there was until historians and epigraphers began to translate vernacular documents and inscriptions. Beginning in the nineteenth century (in the case of the Dutch) and in twentieth (in the case of the British, French, and Americans), some officials took courses in ethnology as well as local languages but seldom pursued full professional programs leading to graduate degrees.

Professional anthropologists or other social scientists in Southeast Asia carried out few studies in the period before World War II. British social anthropology was by then well established on the basis of research done mainly in Africa, the Pacific Islands, and Australia. Early in the twentieth century, A. R. Radcliffe-Brown did a famous study of the hunter-gatherers of the Andaman Islands, but most other studies did not come until the close of the prewar period. The Englishman Gregory Bateson collaborated with the American Margaret Mead (his wife at the time) in research on the Balinese in the late 1930s that led to *Balinese Character* (1942), a classic study in psychological anthropology and a pioneering work in the anthropological use of photography. A few other studies by professional British anthropologists can also be mentioned, but not many. Raymond Firth did a study (set in the state of Kelantan in northeastern Malaya in 1939–1940) of the economics of Malay coastal fishermen on the eve of the Japanese invasion (Firth [1946] 1966).[5] And a little later, Edmund Leach began his very influential research on Kachin political systems, ecology, and kinship in northern Burma (Leach 1954). Also, there were not many studies by noncolonial professional ethnologists from Europe—the few examples include the Swedish scholar Karl Izikowitz ([1951] 1979), who studied the Lamet in highland Laos, and the Austrian Hugo Bernatzik, who pursued the elusive Phi Tong Luang hunter-gatherers in the mountainous forest of northern Thailand, also in the 1930s (Bernatzik [1938] 1951). For their part, while American professional anthropologists assumed a very large role in Southeast Asian studies from the 1950s onward, their interests in the prewar period involved only a few research projects. In addition to Mead's study of Bali, Cora Dubois did culture-and-personality research on the people of Alor, a small island in the eastern Netherlands Indies (Indonesia). This was done also in the 1930s and produced another classic in psychological anthropology (Du Bois [1944] 1960). In addition, some American anthropologists, including A. L. Kroeber, took some interest in the Philippines in the prewar period while it was still a colony (Kroeber 1919).

Noncolonial anthropological research in Southeast Asia increased vastly after the war but has been much more extensive in some countries than others. Malaysia, Indonesia, and the Philippines have generally been open to anthropological and other forms of social science research by outside scholars in the post–World War II period. In part because of its great size and ethnic variation, Indonesia in particular has been the focus of many famous postwar studies. In contrast, large areas of the mainland above Malaysia were closed throughout much of the second half of the twentieth century. Burma became an early focus of research involving both the highland groups and the lowland Burmese, but this was closed off after the military takeover in 1962. With a military dictatorship still in power in Burma, research based on sustained fieldwork has never been fully resumed except with refugee populations living outside the country. In Indochina, there were a few studies in the 1950s and early 1960s (the Americans Gerald Hickey in Vietnam and Joel Halpern in Laos and the French scholar Georges Condominas in Vietnam and Laos), but after this the Indochinese wars in Vietnam, Laos, and Cambodia put an end to most research for the next several decades (Hickey 1964; Halpern 1964; Condominas [1957] 1994). The Southeast Asian peoples in Yunnan and other areas of southern China were also not accessible following the revolution in 1949 until late in the twentieth century.

In contrast to these other mainland countries, Thailand and peninsular Malaysia have remained open. It is therefore not surprising that far more research has been done in these countries on a wide range of anthropological and other topics than in Burma, Laos, Cambodia, or Vietnam. These two countries also have the largest numbers of universities, research institutes, and scholars and publishers concerned with the region. As Thailand has become more economically developed it has become less similar to the countries that surround it. But Thailand has also been an important window on the neighboring countries. Populations of many of the ethnic groups that live in Burma, Laos, and Cambodia (and farther away in Yunnan China and northern Vietnam) also live in Thailand, especially northern Thailand. Such groups include the Karen, Hmong, Yao, Akha, Lisu, Lahu, various Tai groups, and many others. Such groups vary from one place to another, but there are also similarities in traditional clothing, house types, religious practices, and modes of cultivation that are obvious to anyone who visits them in different places (for example, northern Thailand, Laos, and northern Vietnam, in the case of the Hmong, Akha, and Yao), as can now be readily done. While many ethnic minority populations have a long history in Thailand, many others—including some from groups not known to have resided there in the past—have entered Thailand as refugees from Burma (from which many still come), Cambodia, Laos, and Vietnam over the last six decades. For this reason, northern Thailand in particular has become even more ethnically diverse than it formerly was. And more of our information on some groups (for example, the Hmong) has come mainly from those living in Thailand rather than in the surrounding countries.

ETHNOGRAPHY AND ETHNOLOGY

As in other regions of the world, anthropological research and knowledge about Southeast Asia has generally been reported in ethnographic accounts, on the one hand, and ethnological ones, on the other. While the distinction between ethnography and ethnology is not absolute or necessarily always clear, it is worth some discussion at this point. Both kinds of accounts may be published in shorter and longer versions ranging from notes, articles, or book chapters to entire books or dissertations. Both may also appear as stand-alone accounts or as parts of collections.

Ethnography

Traditional ethnographies are accounts of particular groups, usually in particular places or at least regions. Formerly, such accounts were occasionally combined with travel narratives, which are structured as a story of the writer's movement in time and place—notable events experienced; the strange, horrible, or beautiful things seen; difficult developments overcome; amusing or otherwise memorable characters met with; and so on. One example to be discussed below is Bernatzik's *Spirits of the Yellow Leaves*, named after a little-known group of hunter-gatherers in the deep forest of northern Thailand. Most of the book is a travel narrative of the author's search for and eventual encounter with some members of the group and his efforts to learn about them. But it also includes an ethnographic section titled a "Monograph of the Phi Tong Luang" that attempts to summarize what the author has found. Such travel narratives are usually written in the first person ("I left at dawn by small native boat for upriver and soon saw my first crocodile of the day"). Ethnographic accounts also contain some information about the movements and other activities of the writer that are written in the first person. But this is usually confined to an initial preface or introduction and limited to a brief account of what is most relevant to understanding, explaining, or validating what is to follow. Otherwise, first-person perspectives are usually limited to an occasional observation ("It was only after many months that I began to understand the ritual.").

While containing more general background material, ethnographies usually focus on some topic such as kinship, ecology, economy, religion, or political organization. The specific topic is often mentioned in the title. Several well-known examples (of books) include Firth's *Malay Fishermen: Their Peasant Economy*, Clifford Geertz's *The Religion of Java*, Leach's *Political Systems of Highland Burma*, Bateson and Mead's *Balinese Character: A Photographic Analysis*, and Melford Spiro's *Burmese Supernaturalism*. While ethnographic accounts must contain considerable descriptive information, all are written from some point of view. Those that become most important or influential involve an argument about something and are generally innovative in this or some other respect. For example, *Balinese Character* was innovative both in terms of its arguments about the formation and expression of Balinese character in art and religion and in its extensive use of photography as a research technique. And *Political Systems of Highland Burma* was innovative in arguing that the traditional political organization of the Kachin of northern Burma was not static but fluctuated between hierarchical and egalitarian forms in response to various influences, and in arguing against a view of ethnic groups as real, enduring cultural entities (Leach 1954).

Ethnographies may be written in several different ways. One older (but still used) approach is to simply make them about some ethnic group. Here we have examples such as Karl Izikowitz's *Lamet: Hill Peasants of French Indochina*, Robert Jay's *Javanese Villagers: Social Relations in Rural Mojokuto*, F. K. Lehman's *Structure of Chin Society*, and Carl Hoffman's *Punan: Hunters and Gatherers of Borneo*. Less often, ethnography may be about a set of groups, as is Jane Richardson Hanks and Lucian Hanks's *Tribes of the North Thailand Frontier*. Alternatively, some ethnographies take the form of community studies, which typically cover a range of topics for some specific named community, usually a village. If this is done, it is again usually signaled in the title—for example, *Bang Chan: Social History of a Rural Community in Thailand*, by Lauriston Sharp and Lucian Hanks; *Treacherous River: A Study of Rural Chinese in North Malaya*, by William Newell; and *Rusembilan: A Malay Fishing Village in Southern Thailand*, by Thomas Fraser.

Ethnographic writing changes over time. In the 1950s and 1960s, village studies such as those mentioned above were very common. But then they went out of fashion and by now seem to have disappeared entirely, at least where Southeast Asia is concerned. Anthropologists still do in-depth research on particular villages, and the value of doing so remains unquestioned, but particular communities are seldom the explicit focus or topic of written accounts, and the names of villages no longer appear in book titles. Instead, ethnographic writing has become more explicitly concerned with wider issues, with broader regions and history, and often with indigenous peoples and the state. Recent examples include *Mien Relations: Mountain People and State Control in Thailand*, by Hjorleifur Jonsson; *After the Massacre: Commemoration and Consolation in Ha My and My Lai*, by Heonik Kwon; and *Redefining Nature: Karen Ecological Knowledge and the Challenge to the Modern Conservation Paradigm*, by Pinkaew Laungaramsri.

No matter how ethnography is organized or exactly what it is about, time presents a problem. If ethnographic accounts concern particular places, they also tend to be concerned with particular times. They show explicit concern with change and with the correct use of "traditional" and other such adjectives to avoid misleading terminology for what people are like or doing "today," "now," or "at the present time." The results of ethnographic research are usually published some years (several years is usually the minimum before a book-length account appears, and a decade is probably more typical) after the research has been done or the ethnographer last visited the place in question. This raises the issue of when or whether to use the present or the past tense (strictly speaking, by the time anything is written, it is already in the past). The customary way of dealing with this was to make reference to the "ethnographic present" as the period concerned, to write in the present tense, and not qualify for in the past, only in the past, or still there and going on. Here there are no perfect solutions.

Ethnology

While the term ethnology is sometimes used very broadly to mean cultural anthropology in general, it is used here in the more restricted sense to refer to the comparative study of ethnic groups or "peoples and cultures," as it is sometimes put. Ethnologies are by our definition about more than one group, but beyond that the number of groups or the size of the region involved may vary. This makes for a certain amount of ambiguity about whether a study is to be considered ethnography or ethnology. *Tribes of the North Thailand Frontier* was referred to above as ethnography, but it could also be called ethnology. A work such as Bernard Sellato's *Nomads of the Borneo Rain Forest* might be labeled either way as well. It has specific, detailed ethnographic information about some groups, but its main purpose is to make broader comparisons and generalizations about a variety of nomadic hunting and gathering peoples in Borneo, especially regarding the process of settling into permanent villages and adopting cultivation. In contrast (and to stay in Borneo for a moment), Jérôme Rousseau's *Central Borneo* is less ambiguously an ethnological study, whereas his *Kayan Religion* is unquestionably ethnography. The first book delineates a culture area (that he calls "Central Borneo"), in terms of its common cultural characteristics (including elaborate patterns of social stratification) and then attempts to sort out the various and very complex ethnic groups that dwell there. The second is a detailed study of the pre-Christian religious beliefs and practices of the Bungan (a religious movement) among the Kayan, a specific people of central Borneo at one point in time (the 1970s).

The most comprehensive of all the ethnological works in Southeast Asia is a three-volume series covering all of the peoples of the region, or rather all of those about which information was available—which varied greatly from one group to another. This was a project of the Human Relations Area Files (HRAF), the main archival base of anthropological knowledge. It was published over a period of time beginning in 1964 with the volume on mainland Southeast Asia (edited by Frank Lebar, Gerald Hickey, and John Musgrave), followed by two others on insular Southeast Asia (both edited by Lebar), including one covering Indonesia, Andaman Islands, and Madagascar published in 1972 and another on the Philippines and Formosa published in 1974 (Lebar, Hickey, and Musgrave 1964; Lebar 1972; Lebar 1975).

Though now dated, this series remains the most authoritative general compendium of the ethnology of Southeast Asia. The main principle of organization and classification used in the first volume is language, supplemented in some instances by geographical distinctions (e.g., highland and lowland, northern and southern, and eastern and western). By the 1960s, the naming and classification of ethnic groups by linguistic criteria was well known to be problematic. The editors, however, evidently regarded this as the most objective and reliable approach to organizing information in general comparative terms. The volume on mainland Southeast Asia is organized in four parts, each referring to a language family or super family: part 1 is Sino-Tibetan divided into Sinitic, Tibeto-Burman, Karen, and Miao-Yao branches, each divided in turn into geographically defined subgroups, under which a series of local groups are listed. For example, the Tibeto-Burman division of the Sino-Tibetan super family is divided into Eastern Upland groups (sixteen entries), Central Lowland groups (the Burmese), and Western Upland groups (the Nagas, Chins, and Garos). The remaining three great language divisions are Austroasiatic, Tai-Kadai, and Malayo-Polynesian (now Austronesian). All of these also have two sublevels of classification, the second being some sort of geographical reference. The specific groups listed under the lowest or geographical divisions are usually simple proper ethnic names that have no recognizable meaning (at least for most nonspeakers of the languages involved), although the Central Upland Tai groups include the Black Tai, White Tai, and Red Tai, the color references being translations of local terms for these groups, based on clothing colors.

The content for each specific ethnic group is organized under six general headings: Orientation, Settlement Patterns and Housing, Kin Groups, Marriage and Family, Sociopolitical Organization, and Religion. These are followed by various subheadings—for example, Orientation includes the subheadings of identification, location, demography, linguistic affiliation, history, and culture and religion. Subheadings may vary somewhat depending on the characteristics of the group in question and on how much is known, which varies greatly. Long entries in general indicate greater knowledge and short ones, less, although the complexity of some practices (such as kinship) is also involved. In other words, the entry for each specific ethnic group is a compendium of ethnological information in categories created by the editors and assumed to be generally or cross-culturally significant. The descriptions for the various groups commonly refer to traditional or customary cultural practices and institutions rather than necessarily present-day ones. However, descriptions of particular practices (for example, headhunting) may be qualified by statements such as "in the past," "no longer practiced," "in decline," "dying out," "in more recent times," and so forth. References to the amount and quality of information are also often given. The reliability of information provided in the various sources is not necessarily noted but can usually be judged from the quantity and sometimes by the presence of dubious or obviously incorrect statements. For example, the entry for the Saoch, an obscure group of hunter-gatherers of Cambodia, begins with reference to an 1830 traveler's account that the Saoch had tails and could not therefore sit down (in Borneo, similar things were also reported). Needless to say, Lebar, Hickey, and Musgrave did not intend for such observations to inspire confidence in the original source.

In the two subsequent volumes on insular Southeast Asia the principles of ethnic classification followed in the mainland volume are abandoned. The two later works are primarily organized simply by country (e.g., Indonesia and the Philippines), islands (e.g., Madagascar, Sumatra, and Borneo), or groups of islands (e.g., the Andamans). The subdivisions are usually more specific places, including smaller groups of islands, while the linguistic relationships among ethnic groups are generally not considered. The language grouping or affiliation is simply reduced to one of the categories organized by ethnographic information, where available. However, Madagascar, an island off the east coast of Africa, is included. The assumption here is that Madagascar is an important outlier of insular Southeast Asia. This is because linguistic and cultural evidence indicates it was colonized some two thousand years ago from Borneo (making it the greatest westward extension of Austronesian-speaking peoples) with which it continues to show affinities (e.g., in mortuary practices).

The differences between the earlier HRAF volume on mainland Southeast Asia and the later ones on insular Southeast Asia notwithstanding, the general approach is ethnological realism. The identified ethnic groups are assumed to be real ethnolinguistic groups, that is, discrete groups of peoples who speak the same language or closely related dialects; who are recognized as such by themselves and others (if often by different terms in different places); who share other concrete cultural characteristics, or at least did so in the past; and who endure over time unless destroyed by war, disease, or assimilation into another group. This realistic view of ethnic groups had already been challenged by Leach (1954) regarding Upper Burma, and it was soon followed by others. These accounts showed that culturally and linguistically different groups sometimes got put in the same ethnic class, while groups of people who actually spoke the same language and followed the same cultural practices were not always included in a common ethnic category. Also, the names for ethnic groups often change, and sometimes one group decided for some reason to change its ethnic identity. For example, it has been noted since the nineteenth century that some local Mon-Khmer groups in northern mainland Southeast Asia become Tai (Black Tai, White Tai, etc.), a process referred to by Condominas and others who have written about it as "Tai-ization" (Evans 1999, 126–28). Naive ethnological realism has also been a common problem in the naming of peoples in Borneo, as anthropologists concerned are well aware. Governments in

Southeast Asia continue to adhere to ethnological realism in compiling official or semiofficial lists of the ethnic makeup of the population and in classifying peoples in various ways, as will be discussed later on. Today, most anthropologists familiar with Southeast Asia would probably regard ethnological realism as problematic. This is perhaps part of the reason the HRAF volumes have never been updated and republished. Yet, their flaws and somewhat outdated nature notwithstanding, these volumes remain very useful and perhaps essential as ready and generally (if often incomplete) reliable sources of ethnological and ethnographic information on the peoples of Southeast Asia.[6]

2

Prehistory and Languages

Fossil evidence indicates that humans or protohumans have been in Southeast Asia for a million or more years, though not necessarily everywhere or continuously. At the end of the nineteenth century, the first of a series of fossil finds were made in eastern Java that became an important part of the general record of human evolution. First named *Pithecanthropus erectus* (but commonly referred to as Java Man), and now known as *Homo erectus*, the discoveries of these early hominids established one of the first points of dispersal outside of Africa (Bellwood 1997, 39–69). The earliest direct evidence of fully modern humans in Southeast Asia dates to about forty thousand years ago. This involves the discovery of a single "deep skull" at Niah Cave in northern Sarawak in Borneo. Although the accuracy of this date has been questioned, evidence from Australia (which could have been reached only via Southeast Asia) would indicate an even slightly earlier date. Regardless of the exact date of their first appearance, whether there is any genetic connection between modern humans in Southeast Asia and the much earlier *Homo erectus* forms has long been debated (Bellwood 1997).

Several years ago the prehistory of early hominids in Southeast Asia became further complicated by the discovery of *Homo floresiensis*, the so-called hobbit fossil skeletons on the small island of Flores in central Indonesia. In addition to being very small in comparison to both modern and earlier humans, these fossil forms showed a variety of characteristics that linked them with much earlier hominid or even prehominid types. The particular significance of the hobbit skeletons lies in the incongruity of their apparently primitive characteristics and their evidently very recent date—only about seventeen thousand years ago, when fully modern humans undoubtedly had occupied much of Southeast Asia for many thousands of years. There are currently several competing solutions to the hobbit problem (neither of which involves issues of dating). One is that they represent the very remarkable survival until very recently of a comparatively much earlier human or protohuman form, perhaps to be explained as an isolated adaptation to a limited and resource-poor small island environment. The other and less exciting solution is that the hobbits represent a pathologically malformed local population of modern humans. In the latter case, unless further examples are found elsewhere, the hobbit fossils (for all of their inherent fascination) would seem to have little bearing on the broader human prehistory of Southeast Asia (Brown et al. 2004; Wilford 2009).

The earliest modern humans in the region are generally referred to as Australoids, part of a much larger population that may have extended from southern India through Southeast Asia, New Guinea, and Australia. Australoid physical characteristics have undoubtedly survived widely in Southeast Asia, especially throughout the insular region. But the vast majority of peoples of both mainland and insular Southeast Asia today form the southern part of a larger East Asian group and are therefore commonly referred to as southern Mongoloids. This means the main affinity of most Southeast Asians is with the Chinese, Japanese, and Koreans to the north, although there are differences. In contrast to these northern East Asians, Southeast Asians tend to be darker in skin color, to often have wavy rather than straight hair, and to lack the eye fold. These differences probably reflect the survival of Australoid characteristics, although the darker skin color of Southeast Asians is also probably a matter of continuing selection. The predominance of East Asian physical features is mainly accounted for by population numbers and southward movements over time. East Asians have been moving into Southeast Asia over at least the last five or ten thousand years, both by water (as in the case of the Austronesians into the insular realm) and along the rivers that flow from southwestern China into present-day Burma, Thailand, Laos, Cambodia, and Vietnam. The movement of people out of China—both ethnic (or Han) Chinese and highland minority peoples, including the Hmong, Yao, Akha, and many others—has continued into the present.

THE NEGRITO ISSUE

There are several exceptions to this general pattern of physical characteristics. One is the peoples of eastern Indonesia who show Melanesian physical features that generally become more pronounced over a west-to-east gradient. This is to be expected, especially given the extensive human mobility characteristic of the region. Another exception has gained more attention and has been controversial, for it goes against the tendency for anthropologists to consider questions of ethnography and ethnology separately from those of physical anthropology—specifically of human physical types. However, some of the hunter-gatherer groups of Southeast Asia are physically distinct to varying degrees from surrounding southern Asian populations. Most notably, these distinctive groups include hunter-gatherers of the Philippines, Malay Peninsula, and Andaman Islands. These are groups of people who tend to have frizzy or peppercorn hair, dark skins, and a short stature, although such characteristics are mixed in some regions. Because of their relatively small size, in the past they have been called pygmies or forest dwarfs. Today, such groups in the Philippines, Malaya, and the Andaman Islands are still commonly referred to in the anthropological literature as Negritos, a Spanish term meaning small negro, although use of this racial (or racist) label has also become controversial and appears to be declining. For a time, a link between the Southeast Asian Negritos and the inhabitants of the central African rain forest attracted considerable attention and agreement until a later study that sought to test the hypothesis found it wanting (Paul Schebesta, cited in Endicott 1979, 1). It also came to be supposed that the Negritos were one of the remnants of earlier Australoid populations. The ethnological significance of the physical differences between the Negritos and some other hunter-gatherers is that, while some present-day Southeast Asia hunter-gatherers have "always" been hunter-gatherers, others have become so as a secondary adaptation after being cultivators.

Such a hypothesis is also compatible with the possibility that Negrito populations were once more widespread throughout Southeast Asia. Here, language might offer evidence for further understanding, but this has been the case to only a very limited extent. The linguistic situation of the three main Negrito populations in Southeast Asia can be summarized in brief as follows: The languages of the Andaman Islanders were long considered to be an isolate (that is, with no established relationship to any other language), though recently an effort has been made to link them with Melanesian. The Negrito hunter-gatherers of the Philippines all speak versions of Austronesian, as do all of the other native peoples in these islands. If these Negrito groups do represent a different physical population from other inhabitants, their earlier languages were probably different, presumably having been replaced by Austronesian at some point.

The languages of the Semang (Negrito) groups of the Malay Peninsula form yet a third type. All of these Semang dialects are Mon-Khmer (Austroasiatic) rather than Austronesian.[1] Yet, most of the other non-hunter-gatherer, non-Negrito, shifting-cultivator groups of the interior of the peninsula also speak Mon-Khmer languages—although a few of them speak Malay dialects of Austronesian, like the Malays and other western Indo-Malayan peoples. Since all of the non-Muslim-Malay native groups of the Malay Peninsula are now referred to as Orang Asli ("original people" in Malay, the national language of Malaysia), the Mon-Khmer languages spoken by most of these groups have been named Aslian. Mon-Khmer is a widespread language family of mainland Southeast Asia, of which the Aslian languages are the southern extremity—and other mainland Mon-Khmer speakers are located well to the north. As has long been thought, was Mon-Khmer once more widespread—before it was partially replaced in the south by Austronesian and in north by Tai, Tibeto-Burmese, or Vietnamese? Was Mon-Khmer therefore the "original" language of the Negrito populations of Southeast Asia? Perhaps, but this is unlikely since it is not the language family of the Andamanese (the most isolated of the Negrito populations). Another possibility is that Mon-Khmer was preceded among the Semang Negritos by a different language, perhaps linked to Andamanese and also spoken among the Filipino Negritos. Here, there is at least a shred of evidence in the form of a few non-Mon-Khmer words found among the Negrito groups in different places that were retained from the earlier language. However, the proto-Negrito hypothesis, as it has been termed, will probably remain unproved for want of adequate information (Endicott 1979, 2).

TRANSITION TO FARMING AND
THE SPREAD OF LANGUAGES

The development of agriculture is one of the most important issues in the prehistory of Southeast Asia—partly because of the claim that this region was the first in the world where processes of domestication began and partly because of the possible association of the development and spread of agriculture with major languages. The first claim was made initially by the geographer Carl Sauer; the second, by the prehistorian Peter Bellwood.

Sauer's Theory of Domestication

Sauer's claim was made in 1952 in a small but very influential book about agricultural origins and dispersals throughout the world. By Southeast Asia, Sauer meant a somewhat broader region than the one usually so designated; specifically, he included the eastern and far southern coast of India as well. He included a map that shows lines of dispersal of plants and animals from the Southeast Asian hearth (or homeland) to other parts of the Old World, including Africa (Sauer [1952] 1969, 24–26). Southeastern Asia (perhaps a better label for his purposes than Southeast Asia) had the right combination of geographical conditions: a mild climate and year-round growing season; two monsoons a year; high physical and organic diversity; a great amount of water in the form of rainfall, vast river systems, and fresh and tidewater swamps; and a tremendous abundance of aquatic life in the form of fish and shellfish. Southeast Asia was also a hub of travel and communication between southern and eastern Asia and between Asia and the Pacific Islands. Southeast Asian domesticates Sauer mentions include yams, taro, rice, breadfruit, sugarcane, coconut, citrus fruits, durian, jackfruit, chickens, ducks, geese, dogs, and pigs.

Sauer was a theorist who went well beyond merely describing or generalizing from the known data. He was quite willing to fill in the gaps with guesses, and many of his statements are qualified with "seem," "probably," and "likely." And he sought to explain the bigger picture of what was behind what, stressing the complexity of domestication. As a part of his explanation, he subscribed to the theories of Wilhelm Schmidt that combined evolutionary stages with diffusion from points of origin, which by then had been abandoned in anthropology. For example, the first stage of agriculture was associated with matriarchy, for women, with their mysterious powers of reproduction, became linked with the fertility of plants and animals. As far as agricultural origins in Southeast Asia are concerned, his arguments and examples form a series of hypotheses:

1. The first plants to be domesticated were propagated by vegetative or asexual reproduction (or cloning). Humans learned first to plant cuttings of tubers, stems, and rhizomes and by dividing rootstocks. The first domesticated plants were roots and tubers, and others propagated in a similar way. As a result, many domesticated plants lost the ability they originally had to propagate sexually, bananas being perhaps the most famous example. Seeding only came later and was at first combined with asexual techniques of propagation. The coconut is a fertilized seed of a palm tree that falls from a tree and will in some instances take root and form a new tree. Humans help it along by planting it where they want it, but before they do this they hang it up and let it sprout. Wet rice planting also combines sexual and asexual methods. The fertilized seeds of rice are first planted in a seedbed (the sexual part) and then after clumps of shoots grow they are divided and replanted (the asexual part; Sauer 1969, 25–26).

2. The domestication of plants and animals in Southeast Asia took place under conditions of abundance rather than of scarcity and stress. Preagriculturalists tended to live in places where food was readily available, providing time for experimentation and various activities not dictated simply by a struggle to survive. There was time for ritual and for finding more effective or easier ways of doing things, for example, catching fish by stunning them by poisons, and by using traps and nets. People who must expend most or all of their energy on just getting enough to eat have a hard time making improvements in the ways things are done.

3. The preagriculturalists tended to live along rivers, swamps, and coasts. The adaptive culture in which domestication occurred was dominated by

fishing and aquatic collecting. The first food crops were therefore ones that grew best in damp soils, like yams, or in water and muck, like taro and, of course, rice.

4. The road to the domestication of food plants in Southeast Asia was indirect. People did not initially set out to improve the food supply by concentrating on increasing or otherwise developing some nice plant food as we know it today. Rather, people began to select plants because they were looking for things that fit into their existing lifeways—poisons with which to stun fish and fibers for cordage, nets, ritual materials, and medicines. Many domesticated plants in Southeast Asia have several very different uses (not to mention several edible parts), the importance of which may have changed over time, with the result that we cannot be certain of the original purpose. The jackfruit tree, for example, produces a very large, widely consumed, and (once you get used to it) delicious, calorie-rich fruit. But it is also a main source of bark cloth (used not only for clothing but also still widely used in Borneo for tying and carrying things) and edible yellow dye. The first step toward domestication of some plants could have been a complete accident. Rice may have originally begun as a weed in taro gardens, first transplanted by being pulled up and piled into what became a seedbed in which the plants proliferated (27–28).

5. The ritual importance of plants should also not be overlooked as a reason for their original attraction. This often has to do with the color of their fruit or foliage or the dyes the plant produce. Rice is again an interesting example. Westerners are mainly familiar with rice that is very white when cooked (or with a brownish color if unpolished). But Southeast Asians stain white rice—usually stained yellow, by Malays and others, with turmeric but also other colors including blue.[2] Southeast Asians also grow black and red varieties of rice. While these add color to a festive occasion, they also have ritual associations (27).

Animals

Minus the cloning, Sauer uses the same sort of argument to explain the domestication of animals that he applies to plants. In contrast to the herding animals domesticated in Southwest Asia and associated with fields and pastures, those first brought under human control in Southeast Asia were linked to the household. Here he subscribes to the theory that domestication began with capturing young animals and keeping them as pets (the term pet may be somewhat misleading if one of the motives for raising captured young animals was to eventually eat them). When the European explorers first reached the East and the West Indies, they found the villages overrun with pets. Sailors returned with parrots, monkeys, and other exotic creatures with which to amuse the folks back home (Sauer 1969, 30). And the capture and keeping of infant wild animals continues to be popular in Southeast Asia (fruit bats, monkeys, squirrels, and various birds and fish are all common sights in Malay and Dayak villages in Malaya and Borneo, but I have also seen gibbons, otters, and young bears; capturing and keeping orangutans in Borneo is now forbidden but continues).

Today, some animals are captured and raised for practical use. Short-tailed macaques, for example, are raised and taught to pick coconuts in northeastern Malaya and probably elsewhere. In Kelantan, a common sight on the back roads and lanes is a coconut picker riding a bicycle with his large macaque sitting up front on the handlebars. When someone wishes to have coconuts picked, the monkey is sent up the tree on a long line while the owner shouts instructions to the monkey, telling it to twist off and drop either green or ripe nuts. But most birds and animals are kept in or near the house purely for amusement. As he does plants, Sauer attributes the domestication of animals to the care and skills of women who managed the household. However, from the present perspective, there are exceptions or partial exceptions. Coconut-picking monkeys are trained by the men who use them, and the same is true of elephants, which are also captured when young and raised and trained in captivity.

The domestication of animals often took place in ways and for reasons that are not obvious from their later uses. The chicken is a prime example (32). The chicken was developed from the jungle fowl of Southeast Asia but not, according to Sauer, for reasons we are likely to suppose. We think of chickens as primarily in terms of meat and eggs. But he argues that such economic motives were not involved in the initial phase of domestication and only came later. The older use of chickens was for cockfighting, and they were bred for characteristics—big bodies and broad breasts—that were desirable for this practice. But there was more to it than this. Cockfighting was a ritual activity akin to sacrifice (as it still is among the Iban in Borneo, for example), so chickens were also selected for color. Black feathers, skin, and bones were preferred, for blackness had magical and medicinal value. Southeast Asians also fight a variety of wild and domesticated animals including fish, crickets, cattle, water buffalo, and elephants (elephants, strictly speaking, are not domesticated animals since they are normally captured in the wild and then tamed and trained to develop characteristics desirable to humans).

Dogs and pigs have a similar history of domestication and use in Southeast Asia, according to Sauer (31–32). Both began as captured infants kept as household pets and went on to be used for ritual sacrifice and as food. His claim that the dog was originally domesticated in Southeast Asia from a local wild dog is not supported by later genetic evidence showing clearly that all dogs are derived from wolves. But some of what he claims in terms of the varied uses to which dogs have been put over time in the region may be valid. He argues that dogs were not initially used for hunting in Southeast Asia or elsewhere—nor were they used for herding and other work until later. In Borneo, the Penan and Punan hunter-gatherers use dogs for hunting and, in some instances, gained a reputation for producing the best hunters, but this might be a recent development (Sellato 1994, 147). Once incorporated into the human household as a pet, the dog in Southeast Asia initially developed in the direction of ritual and symbolism rather than practical uses. Myths of the dog as a tribal ancestor are common in the region according to Sauer, who also cites an elaborate Chinese legend in which a princess marries an ever-faithful dog. And having become symbolically important, the dog became an object of sacrifice to be ritually consumed by the participants. Then it became and in some areas remained a more ordinary food item (dog meat can be bought in marketplaces in northern mainland Southeast Asia), especially at the time of feasts (Sauer 1969, 31). Eventually, the status of the dog declined, and it came to be kept mainly for its practical uses as an outside scavenger (dogs in rural Southeast Asia, like pigs, eat human feces), guardian, and hunter.

While the career of the domesticated pig may be similar in some ways to that of the dog in Southeast Asia, there are also obvious and important differences. Pigs and dogs are both scavengers, but the pig's utility for scavenging is offset by its inclination to root up gardens, which means that either pigs need to be kept penned up (in which case they cannot scavenge) or gardens have to be fenced well enough to keep them out. Both options are found, although the previous practice was to let them roam and scavenge, while the present trend is to pen them up or out. Pigs do not serve as guarding or hunting animals. Judging from present-day evidence, pigs are far more valuable than dogs as food, whether they are raised and sold or kept for household or village feasts. Sauer asserts that the ritual use of pigs was greatly reduced with the spread of Hinduism and Islam into Southeast Asia, although such use continued among the groups beyond the boundaries of these religions—for example, in Sarawak, Borneo, the domesticated pig is the main traditional animal for sacrifice among the Dayak groups, although in many other areas it is the water buffalo.

CULTIVATION AND THE ORIGIN AND
DISPERSAL OF LANGUAGE GROUPS

Much about the domestication of plants and animals and the transition to farming as a way of life in Southeast Asia remains only partially understood. For one thing, the beginning of domestication in the form of plant tending or the cultivation of plants for nonfood uses may have begun a very long time before true farming. Also, there is the issue of just where Southeast Asia begins, especially in regard to China. As noted already, limiting mainland Southeast Asia to the present-day countries, which is misleading in ethnological terms, may be even more so where archaeology and prehistory are concerned (Bellwood 2005, 223). But even using a broad definition of Southeast Asia, the first evidence of true farming lies to the north, in central China. According to Bellwood, there is not good evidence for any form of food production anywhere in Southeast Asia before 3,500 BCE, whereas domesticated rice was verifiably grown in the Yangzi River area three thousand years earlier (222–23).

The first stage of domestication of any animal or plant must have occurred within the natural geographical zone (and in or near the specific habitat) of its wild forebears, which may not be climatically the same now as when domestication first occurred. Once domestication occurs and humans develop the cultural capacity to select characteristics and develop new strains suited to different environments, the range can widen or, with climate change, expand or contract. If the natural range of a domesticated plant or animal is wide, the question of its specific origins is a matter of finding evidence of its earliest occurrence, which can also change over time with new archaeological discoveries. Also, of course, domestication may occur repeatedly in different places either more or less at the same time or at different times. Pigs, for example, were probably domesticated repeatedly both in Southeast Asia from various species or strains and in the Old World generally.

For rice, the zone of wild varieties is wide, centering on mainland Southeast Asia but ranging from central China in the north to southern Thailand and from western India to eastern China. But where within this large area did domestication first take place? Although the southern or Southeast Asian region has been proposed in the past, present-day archaeological evidence now indicates that it first occurred in the northern part of the natural range for rice, specifically, in the middle Yangzi River area. This area has been beyond the zone of wild rice since the Sung Dynasty (960–1279) but was within it before this time (Bellwood 2005, 130).

If the domestication and cultivation of rice began in central China, then how and when did it spread into Southeast Asia? As for how, there have been at least two major routes, one by land and one by sea. The main land routes were presumably along several great rivers that originate in the eastern Himalayas in China and flow roughly from north to south into and through mainland Southeast Asia. The valleys of these rivers, which include (from west to east) the Irrawaddy, Salween, and Mekong, have long served as corridors of population and culture southward from China. The sea route was that taken by the Austronesians from southeastern China through Taiwan and into the northern Philippines and then southward to central Vietnam, the Malay-Indonesian Archipelago, and the Malay Peninsula.

Once the expansion of rice cultivation reached the limits of the natural range of wild rice, several things happened. First, its further movement slowed, presumably as new varieties were developed to fit the newer environments. Most notably, while rice is originally tropical and subtropical, its natural home does not include the equatorial region, presumably because the light conditions there are not optimal. In the equatorial zone, the Austronesians who brought it emphasized instead the root and tree crops that had perhaps already begun the first stages of domestication and that may have preceded rice everywhere. Second, while rice was established throughout much of the Malay Peninsula and the western part of Indonesia, it faded in the eastern Indonesia islands and disappeared entirely before reaching Melanesia.

As important as rice has been in Southeast Asia, the presence of a separate zone of equatorial domestication and cultivation based on the vegetative propagation of root crops (especially yams and taro) and tree crops (including breadfruit, coconuts, and citrus fruits) appears to hold up. Whether this form of domestication and cultivation was developed by Neolithic peoples moving into Southeast Asia from the north or taken over by them from the earlier inhabitants is uncertain (139).

Bellwood's Theory and Its Limits

In his book *First Farmers: The Origins of Agricultural Societies*, Bellwood argues that domestication and the development of agriculture brought major changes to the linguistic maps of the world. The hypothesis is that the spread of the languages (or language families) that now predominate in various areas of the world reflect dispersals from early agricultural homelands. In other words, with the exception of regions where agriculture was difficult or impossible or simply never developed, you will tend to find a large or dominant family of languages and a prehistory of farming. Hunting and gathering had also enabled the dispersal of human populations and their languages over much of the world—into all or nearly all of the currently inhabited areas, with the exception of the Pacific Islands beyond Australia and Melanesia. But there were differences. Throughout much of hunter-gatherer prehistory, the spread of human populations was gradual, although there were also bursts of rapid movement and expansion—for example, from Asia into and throughout the New World. Domestication and the development of cultivation generally brought a much more rapid expansion of peoples, and therefore their languages. Further, the farmers were often moving into regions that were already occupied or at least partially occupied by hunter-gatherers (Bellwood 2005, 4–11).

The languages of the early farmers spread and became dominant for several possible reasons. Most importantly, they simply lived in greater population densities than hunter-gatherers and therefore outnumbered them. Cultivators also tended to have more developed and encompassing political, economic, and military institutions. What happened to hunter-gatherers and their languages when the farmers arrived is mainly a matter of inference. We know what has happened to them recently and what is still happening to what is left of them today, although present-day developments are not necessarily the same as those in prehistory. In Southeast Asia, the prevailing human physical types indicate massive but not complete genetic replacement. Languages probably changed as well. While the original hunter-gatherers survived in some places, often in encapsulated situations, and new groups of postcultivator hunter-gatherers formed, the old hunter-gatherer languages generally did not. The only hunter-gatherers in Southeast Asia who appear to have retained their ancestral indigenous languages (those spoken before the arrival of the farmers) were the remote Andaman Islanders, and this is presumably because the farmers never established themselves in the Andamans. Otherwise, all that seems to have endured of the prefarming hunter-gatherer languages are occasional isolated words.

Bellwood's thesis is meant to cover what happened in all of the areas of the world where prehistoric farming originated and spread. It seems generally convincing—even obvious—where Southeast Asia is concerned. But here not everything seems right or at least well explained, and this is somewhat puzzling. Bellwood is undoubtedly the leading prehistorian of Southeast Asia, and as he notes, it (along with Oceania) is his special area of interest and expertise, where he has been working on the big picture for a long time. But was Southeast Asia an independent region of domestication and agricultural origin? As discussed above, Sauer argued that Southeast Asia was the original center of domestication, which would also mean it was an independent one. Bellwood in contrast strikes Southeast Asia off the list entirely and deals with it as a derivative region into which cultivation spread from central China in the north. Or rather, he does this some of the time while also offering evidence of considerable or even very large-scale independent domestication in Southeast Asia. At the beginning of his book, Bellwood states, "We have clear signs of relatively independent agricultural origins in western Asia, central China, the New Guinea highlands, Mesoamerica, the central Andes, the Mississippi basin, and possibly western Africa and southern India. These developments occurred at many different times between about 12,000 and 4,000 years ago" (2). Southeast Asia is conspicuously absent. But elsewhere he writes of "a roster of native plants that includes yams, aroids (especially taro), coconuts, breadfruit, bananas, pandanus (a starchy fruit), canarium nuts, and many others, all originally domesticated in the tropical regions from Malaysia through to Melanesia" (139).

If this is not independent invention it would be difficult to know what is. Perhaps Bellwood means that, by the time these plants were domesticated, other cultivated plants had already arrived from elsewhere. But this possibility is not mentioned. He does suggest that Austronesians may have domesticated the tropical Southeast Asian plants and animals as they moved southward and into and through the equatorial zone. But he also states that the creation of the equatorial Southeast Asian cultigens could have been the work of native peoples before the arrival of the Austronesians. So here we have both conceptual ambiguity (what does "independent" mean as applied to zones of domestication and the development of agriculture?) and uncertainty (who did the domesticating, especially in equatorial Southeast Asia: the existing or pre-Austronesian people, or the southward-moving Austronesians?) Both of these issues could be further clarified if not resolved. The question of where rice was first domesticated is also very important. According to the latest edition of D. H. Grist's *Rice* ([1959] 1986), the standard authority on rice, "The weight of evidence points to the conclusion that the center of origin of *Oryza sativa* L is Southeast Asia, particularly India and Indo-China, where the richest diversity of cultivated forms has been recorded" (5).

Perhaps Bellwood prefers to emphasize the northern and derivative origins of Southeast Asian agriculture (while acknowledging the uncertainty of this) because he is seeking to correlate the prevailing language families of the region with the development and spread of agriculture—or of different forms or phases of it. But if the domestication and cultivation of a major set of the world's repertoire of cultivated plants took place in a region where the languages of the peoples who did the domesticating have disappeared rather than spread, then there would be a problem with his basic argument. In actuality, as Bellwood's discussion makes clear, the geographical origins of some of the major language families of Southeast Asia are also uncertain. Let us now look briefly at his interpretation of these families, their points of origin, and their relationship to the spread of farming.

According to Bellwood, current historical linguistic interpretation holds that there are five major language families in Southeast Asia. Four of these families are confined to the mainland, while one pervades the insular region and the southern mainland. Of these five families, three are associated with major agricultural dispersals. But of these three, two (Austroasiatic and Austronesian) are also found among hunter-gatherer groups, which leads to the inference that either the hunter-gatherer groups that now speak these languages acquired them from agriculturalist—or else some of the agriculturalists became hunter-gatherers.

The first dispersal involved Austroasiatic, the most widespread and fragmented of the mainland Southeast Asia families. Austroasiatic has two main branches, Munda in eastern India and Mon-Khmer in Southeast Asia, which extends from northern Laos and Vietnam to the Malay Peninsula. The Mon-Khmer languages encompass a wide range of peoples, including the wet rice–cultivating Vietnamese and Cambodian Khmer, many shifting-cultivating tribal peoples, and the hunting and gathering nomadic peoples of the Malay Peninsula, as well as those of northern Thailand. The distribution of the Austroasiatic languages suggests that in many places they were overlaid or displaced by those of later arriving peoples across much of Southeast Asia to the west of their stronghold in Laos, Vietnam, and Cambodia. In any case, the Austroasiatic languages pose two significant questions. The first concerns agriculture. Bellwood assumes that the early Austroasiatic peoples were agricultural on the basis of linguistic evidence that proto-Austroasiatic includes a word for rice cultivation—though whether this was of wet or dry rice does not appear to be known. The other question is that of the homeland or point of origin of the Austroasiatic languages. There is some reason to suppose that Austroasiatic languages were once spoken widely in southern China, but their homeland could have been in northern Southeast Asia, southern China, or even central China. Central China would fit best with Bellwood's early dispersal thesis (Bellwood 2005, 223–25; Goddard 2005, 32–33; Lebar, Hickey, and Musgrave 1964, 84–196).

The sequence of language dispersals in Southeast Asia after Austroasiatic seems somewhat vague, but at some point it had to involve Sino-Tibetan, the great language family that includes Chinese and Tibetan. The largest numbers of speakers of Sino-Tibetan are, of course, to the north of Southeast Asia. The main grouping of Sino-Tibetan in Southeast Asia is Tibeto-Burman, which includes Burmese, Karen, and a series of tribal languages in Burma, northern Thailand, and northern Laos, as well as in present-day southern China. In Southeast Asia, the Tibeto-Burman languages predominate in the western region of mainland Southeast Asia. Interpreted according to Bellwood's argument, this group of languages probably displaced or replaced Austroasiatic languages in the region. The assumption here is also that Tibeto-Burman peoples were also cultivators. Today, there are no known Tibeto-Burman hunter-gatherers in Southeast Asia, although there are many shifting-cultivator groups as well as wet rice agriculturalists. As would be expected, the reconstruction of proto-Sino-Tibetan includes a word for rice. But if the existing Mon-Khmer inhabitants were already rice growers, the significance of rice as a factor in the expansion of the Tibeto-Burman peoples is unclear. In addition, the point of origin for the Sino-Tibetan dispersal is not settled. In accord with his general thesis, Bellwood favors central China, but southern China, Sichuan Province, and even the Tibetan plateau have also been proposed (Bellwood 2005, 226).

The last of the great dispersals linked to cultivation is Austronesian. Since the Austronesian expansion took place mainly by water, it could have easily overlapped with those occurring by land. Austronesian is one of the most widely dispersed language families in the world. It includes nearly all of the languages of insular Southeast Asia, those of Polynesia, Micronesia, and some of Melanesia as well, not to mention those of Madagascar off the coast of east Africa. More seems to be known about the point of origin of proto-Austronesian than of any of the other language families of Southeast Asia. Unlike these other families, which spread by land routes, Austronesian moved mainly across water. The initial point of dispersal was the island of Taiwan. Here we find the proto-Austronesian antecedents of both the present-day Austronesian speakers on Taiwan and those of the Malayo-Polynesians, who include all of the Austronesian speakers outside of Taiwan. The proto-Austronesians themselves are assumed to have come from the mainland of southern China. But the initial point from which they moved southward was Taiwan, first into the northern Philippines and eventually into the central region of the Indonesian Archipelago including the island of Borneo. Here they divided, with one group moving eastward toward New Guinea and beyond to the farthest Pacific Islands and the other westward to Java Sumatra and the Malay Peninsula and eventually to Madagascar. Some Austronesians also became established in the central-southern region of present-day Vietnam. These include both the Chams and several the tribal groups of the central highlands and adjacent areas of Laos and Cambodia. The Austronesian expansion into Southeast Asia began perhaps five thousand years ago and reached the central part of the Indonesian Archipelago a thousand years later. Proto-Austronesian culture included the cultivation of rice and millet and the domestication of several animals including the dog, pig, and perhaps water buffalo. The Austronesians also took weaving with them and were of course highly skilled canoe builders and sailors (Bellwood 1997, 118; Bellwood 2005, 227–29; Goddard 2005, 30–32; Lebar, Hickey, and Musgrave 1964, 245–66; Lebar 1972, 1975).

In addition to the three major dispersals of Austroasiatics, Sino-Tibetans, and Austronesians, there were two others in Southeast Asia, both of which came later and involved less movement or expansion, and which Bellwood deemphasizes. The first was of Tai (or Dai); the second, far larger part, was of the greater Tai-Kadai family. Tai includes the language of the Thai of Thailand and Lao of Laos and the languages of many ethnic minority groups of Thailand, Burma, Laos, Vietnam, and southern China (the Black Tai, White Tai, Lue, and others). The divergence of these and other Tai languages may extend back about four thousand years. Bellwood suggests that the Tai dispersal was again basically from the north to the south. The correctness of this interpretation, however, depends on the place of origin of the Southeast Asian Tai. This may have been somewhere in southern China (the provinces of Guizhou, Guangxi, and Guangdong), which is today occupied mainly by speakers of Chinese. If so, the movement of the Tai into Laos and Thailand (and presumably into the other Southeast Asia countries where there are substantial Tai populations) took place within

the past one thousand years. An alternative interpretation places the homeland of the Tai within or closer to Southeast Asia, specifically northwestern
Vietnam (where there are a great many different Tai ethnic groups) during
the Neolithic period. Southern Yunnan (specifically Xishuangbanna, which
borders Burma and Laos) has also been considered a likely homeland of the
Tai. In any case, the link between Tai dispersal and farming remains unex-
plored. Bellwood suggests the Tai dispersal to the south may be attributable
to Chinese military and demographic pressure (Bellwood 2005, 226–27;
Goddard 2005, 35–36; Lebar, Hickey, and Musgrave 1964, 187–244). But
wherever exactly they came from and when and why, the Tai have become
one of the major ethnolanguage groups of mainland Southeast Asia.

The most recent dispersal has been that of the Hmong-Mien (also known
as the Meo-Yao). These groups are widely spread across southern China,
northern Vietnam, Laos, and Thailand. Presumably, the Hmong and the
Mien now occupying their present position in the Southeast Asia countries
have also been pushed southward by pressure from the Han Chinese, many
or most of them in the last several hundred years. Those in present-day
Southeast Asian countries are all upland groups who tend to occupy the
highest inhabited zones of hillsides and mountaintops, presumably because these areas were still open to settlement. They are also predominantly
shifting cultivators rather than wet rice farmers (Bellwood 2005, 226; Goddard 2005, 36; Lebar, Hickey, and Musgrave 1964, 63–93).[3]

In sum, of the five instances of language dispersal in Southeast Asia, only
the first three appear to be attributable to early farming. The possession of
agriculture may have something to do with the expansion and dominance
of the Tai, but the connection here seems at best unclear. Perhaps the Tai
expansion is more a matter of the practice of wet rice as opposed to dry
cultivation, which brought an increase in population and a displacement
of other groups that were limited to shifting cultivation. Although many Tai
groups are also shifting cultivators, some permanent and some temporary,
those that occupy the open plains and valleys of mainland Southeast Asia
are wet rice farmers with larger populations and therefore more powerful
political structures than the shifting-cultivating minorities. The Hmong and
Mien, who arrived long after wet rice cultivating had become established in
the lowlands, moved into or developed the highland niches where most of
them are still found today.

SOUTHEAST ASIA AT THE BEGINNING
OF THE COMMON ERA

By around two thousand years ago, the several forms of human adaptation known from present-day ethnography and ethnology were probably

in place—although archaeological confirmation is scarce (Bellwood and Glover 2004; Burling 1965, 64). These included nomadic hunting and gathering and coastal fishing, shifting cultivation in and around forests, and wet rice cultivation in the lowland plains. Both kinds of cultivators certainly had domesticated animals, including dogs, pigs, cattle, buffalo, and chickens. Metals including bronze and, to a more limited extent, iron were also in use in the lowlands. Boats and rafts were undoubtedly in wide use along the rivers and the coasts, and trade was surely extensive. Local warfare, including ritual headhunting, was probably widely practiced in both the insular and mainland regions and has been well documented, especially in Borneo and elsewhere in insular Southeast Asia, in historical and ethnological terms into the present century.

Houses may not have been very different than the traditional forms built of wood, bamboo, leaves, bark, and grass that can still be commonly seen today. Probably, hunter-gatherers then as more recently lived in simple temporary shelters made of bamboo and leaf thatch. Both the shifting cultivators and the wet rice farmers likely built a somewhat greater variety of houses, though most of them would have been raised above the ground on posts. Judging from their present distribution in both insular and mainland Southeast Asia, longhouses or other large multifamily dwellings were probably widespread, in part because of the sense of protection they provided.

Whether housed in separate houses or longhouses divided into separate family sections, the families in many societies were likely nuclear (based on a single married couple and their children), rather than extended—for this is also by far the most common family pattern known in Southeast Asia in ethnological terms. Both single and multiple dwellings would have usually been grouped together in compact villages rather than strung out along in single file along a river, stream, canal, or road, as can be widely seen today as a modern development. Beyond being clustered—in part at least for physical security—houses would have likely been commonly built and aligned in particular ways for ritual benefits. Such ritual practices were only one part of a great many supernaturally oriented beliefs and activities—involving spirits and aimed at healing, making the crops grow, gaining protection, and dealing with the dead—that we call religion and that will be discussed at length in later chapters. We do not yet have evidence of urbanization, the state, or most other features that we call civilization, though these were soon to develop.

3

Early States, Civilization, and Colonialism

As we have seen, it is assumed that, during the prehistoric period, the main source of outside influence on Southeast Asia was to the north. Just what or how much came from China in the way of crops, languages, pottery, metal-working and tools, and models or forms of social organization—in contrast to originating in South Asia—has not been settled. But few if any attempts have been made to trace prehistoric outside influences to regions other than China. But by around the beginning of the Common Era, the cultural alignment of Southeast Asia had shifted from the north to the west, first India, then the Middle East, and finally Europe. The new western alignment was based on trade, which ran from the ports of China to those of India and beyond. People from China never stopped coming to Southeast Asia. They continued to bring things to Southeast Asia to trade—especially ceramics— and they wrote important accounts of the places and peoples they visited. In more recent centuries, many millions of Chinese have migrated to live there and have contributed enormously to the economic development of modern Southeast Asia. Also in recent centuries, ethnic minority peoples including the Hmong, Yao, Akha, Lisu, and others have moved into the mountains of northern mainland Southeast Asian countries from present-day China (Hanks and Hanks 2001, 1–49). But the cultural influence of these groups has not penetrated much beyond them.

INDIC CIVILIZATION IN SOUTHEAST ASIA

The evidence that much of Southeast Asia was influenced by, and then became a part of, Indic civilization is overwhelming. It consists of scripts, inscriptions, statues, and monumental architecture found in many places. These reflect religion and philosophy that is not only Indic but also more specifically Hindu (involving Shiva, Vishnu, or other particular gods) and Buddhist (Theravada or Mahayana).[1]

The development of Indic civilization in Southeast Asia took place along two gradients. The first of these was directional. It was strongest in the western region that includes Sumatra, Java, Bali, the Malay Peninsula, and most of the remainder of the mainland. It was weaker in present-day eastern Indonesia and the Philippines. The second gradient is more complicated. It ran from the lowlands or coastal areas to the highlands or interior regions. The heavily Indicized areas of Southeast Asia therefore came to include the lowlands of Sumatra, Java, Bali, the Malay Peninsula, Burma, Thailand, Cambodia, Laos, and the central and southern regions of present-day Vietnam. Such influences among the highland and interior tribal peoples are more marginal or lacking.

EARLY STATES

Indic civilization in Southeast Asia had various dimensions, but scholarly anthropological and historical interest has focused especially on religion and the nature of the state. The early states that formed in Southeast Asia during the first century of the Common Era were based on a synthesis of indigenous developments and Indic influences. They were based on sea trade that by that time extended from India to China and therefore passed through peninsular and insular Southeast Asia. One of the earliest sites was on the Isthmus of Kra, where trade goods went across the Malay Peninsula from the Indian Ocean to the Gulf of Siam; another was on north Sumatra; and yet others on the northern and eastern coasts of Borneo. Larger centers developed on the east coast of southern Sumatra, the northern coast of Java, and the coast of (then) Cambodia near the mouth of the Mekong. Within a short time, however, inland states had formed, and by the eighth century these had become larger and more powerful. Such states developed in lowland areas where there was good rice land that would support dense populations—on the Mekong and around the Great Lake (Tonle Sap) in Cambodia, in central and eastern Java and Bali, in central Burma, and in the plains of Thailand. These became the great Indic states of Southeast Asia of which remain Angkor Wat, Pagan, Borobudur, and other monumental ruins. Besides Hindu-Buddhist architecture, these states had elaborate courts, massive armies, highly developed music and dance, and in some instances well-developed forms of water control (Jay 1963, 1–2).

While some were larger and some were smaller, most such states lasted a few centuries or less. Some scholars have tried with varied success to attach particular labels such as "galactic polity" or "theater state" (because of their emphasis on pomp and ceremony) to these states, but the larger and more powerful of them had much in common (Geertz 1980; Jay 1963, 3–5; Tambiah 1976, 102–31). The main cultural, ecological, and political features were as follows:

1. The king was a divine or semidivine being, usually believed to be the incarnation of an Indic god, especially Shiva, less often Vishnu or sometimes a future Buddha.
2. The fertility and well-being of the realm was a reflection of the spiritual power of the king and his regalia.
3. Social rank was based on proximity to the ruler. Most importantly, this was a matter of bilateral kinship, but it could also involve voluntary submission.
4. The king's domain spread outward in concentric circles, the area closest to the king being the center of spiritual and temporal power, which diminished as distance away increased.
5. While the power of the king weakened as it spread outward, it was potentially infinite. Therefore, no real boundaries to the state were recognized, and the ruler of a neighboring kingdom was, unless he had subordinated himself, necessarily an enemy.
6. In material terms, the strength of a ruler and his state was based on the number of subjects under control rather than size of the territory. Land without people was of little value, except as a place to settle more people. The subject population (a) created wealth for the ruler and state through the cultivation of rice and through other economic activities, (b) provided labor for royal and state building projects, and (c) provided military support.
7. Warfare between states usually had two main objectives: (a) to sack the capital and destroy the sacred center of the enemy and (b) to capture population and resettle it in the victor's territory and keep it there if possible.
8. State space was basically lowland space. The highlands and the tribal peoples that occupied them as shifting cultivators were generally a secondary or minor concern for the inland states. The highland peoples were a source of trade goods and slaves, but they were too few in numbers, too much trouble to get to, and too difficult to subjugate or keep subjugated to be of great concern. In some places, the uplanders had a limited role in state ceremonies, but their general inclination was—and for good reason—to be independent and to limit their relationship with lowlanders to trade. For the most part the highland minorities sought to remain ungoverned, and succeeded in doing so until the late colonial or modern period (Evans 1998, 141–52).[2]

Coastal States of Western Malaya on the Eve of Colonial Rule

As the inland states in some regions grew in power, they acquired control over the coastal states as well, and thus of the wealth of sea trade. In the long run, the most powerful and enduring states were those that combined the strengths of control over the interior and over coastal and foreign trade. For the most part, such indigenous development was prevented by the arrival of European colonial rule. But on the mainland, this happened in Thailand, the only country that had escaped colonial rule. Here, the still-ruling Chakri Dynasty succeeded Ayuthia, established its capital at Bangkok near the mouth of the Chao Praya River, and opened itself to international commerce and influence—developments that elsewhere in the mainland occurred under British and French rule.

But some coastal states remained independent because they were located too far from the inland states to be brought under control or because they were located in places (such as Borneo or Sulawesi) where there were no inland states. Some Malay coastal states lasted as independent polities until the late nineteenth or early twentieth centuries. Based on contemporary information by colonial scholars, those of the east coast of Sumatra and the Malay Peninsula have been described and analyzed in anthropological and historical terms by J. M. Gullick and others (Gullick 1958).[3] The separate Malay states on the eve of colonial rule in the late nineteenth century were at that time the largest political units in the peninsula. Each such state claimed a distinct territory that extended along the coast and then inland. The watershed of the main range of the peninsula formed a rough boundary between most of the eastern and western states, but most of the interior was sparsely inhabited.

The Malays lived mainly in the lower river areas and in coastal plains where they cultivated rice, fished, and traded. The interior regions (generally referred to as the *ulu* or "up river") were occupied by the Orang Asli (as they are now known)—indigenous shifting cultivators and nomadic hunter-gatherers, neither of which was recognized as having land rights or a place in the Malay state. Both were raided for slaves and therefore tended to live in remote areas, but both also engaged in trade with Malays, or those they could trust. The products of the forest were an important part of the state economy, as was tin, of which there were rich deposits in some regions of the west coast. Tin was originally mined by Malays but increasingly in the precolonial period by immigrant Chinese (5–6).

Traditional Malay society on the eve of colonial rule was stratified in several ways related to the nature of the state. To begin with, there was a general distinction between the ruling class (*raja*) and the subject class (*ra'ayat*). As Gullick and others have used the phrase, the ruling class consisted literally of those persons who were associated with either the sultanate or the district chiefdom of each state. Those of the first group were royal aristocrats, and those of the second were nonroyal nobles. Since there was only one ruler for a state and one chief for a district, most members of both sectors held lesser positions of authority. While the royal aristocracy sometimes controlled the district chieftainships, these were more commonly in the hands of nonroyal nobles. Of these, one served as chief (often known as *dato'*) and others held supporting or auxiliary positions. The headmen (*pengulu*) of villages were normally commoners who came from one of the prominent families in the village. Often the position of headman passed from father to son (65–94).

Slavery was another dimension of stratification. Slaves were owned by rulers and other members of the ruling class who could afford to acquire and maintain them as part of their households. The status of slaves varied in several ways, most importantly according to whether or not a person in bondage was a regular slave (*abdi, hamda*) or a debt slave. A regular slave was one who had been captured or purchased, or who was a descendent of such a person. Such slaves were used as household servants or, in the case of women, made available as mistresses or wives to the men of a leader's following. As Muslim Malays could not be enslaved, regular slaves were non-Muslim aborigines from the Malay Peninsula, from Sumatra, or elsewhere.

A Muslim, however, could become a debt slave (*orang berhutong*). Debt slavery came about when a person approached a ruler or a man of property, borrowed money, and placed himself in bondage until the debt was paid. Since the work a debt slave did while in bondage did not count toward the payment of the original debt, the status of a debt slave tended to be permanent—and it was also hereditary. One of the main motives behind debt slavery was to enable a chief or state ruler to acquire a personal following of fighting men. Such followers were provided with a home in their owner's household, with access to sexual partners or wives and economic support (97–98).

The traditional Malay states were shaped by geography, especially the rivers. Except around the local village or town, travel was by river rather than overland, for roads did not exist. The most important notions of direction were not the cardinal points of north, south, east, and west but rather upstream and downstream. A state generally consisted of the basin of a large river or, less often, of several smaller ones. The names of the various Malay states are often the same as the names of the main river around which the state is organized. In such a system, in which travel and trade are by river, and rivers and their tributaries form a tree shape, political control was in crucial part a matter of controlling the movement of river traffic—both in and out of the state itself and from the main branch in and out of the main tributaries. The capital of a state was located where the main river flowed into the sea (or where it broke up into a delta). The districts—the major subdivisions of the state—were in turn generally based upon the drainage basins of the major tributaries of the main river. And the district chiefs would have their strongholds at the points where the secondary rivers flowed into the main one. Monitoring traffic on the rivers was the basis of political power and the means of gaining revenue. The control of agricultural populations—the economic base of government of the inland states—was secondary (21–22).

The formal structure of a Malay state took the form of a pyramid, with the sultan or raja at the top, the district chiefs beneath him, and the village headmen at the bottom. The sultan was the head of state, and his position was bolstered by symbolism and ritual, some of it indigenous, some of it Hindu, and some of it Muslim. The sultan was thought to be endowed with majesty in the form of supernatural power, and it was supposed that anyone who infringed upon this would suffer magical retribution. The person of the sultan was sacred, and any touching of his body was forbidden. White blood was said to run in his veins. At ceremonies the sultan sat impassively, for immobility was a sign of divinity. On ceremonial occasions he was dressed in yellow clothing and surrounded by yellow trappings including umbrellas and hangings for this color was a royal monopoly. The sultan's majesty was also communicated in his regalia, including royal musical instruments (drums, pipes, flutes, and trumpets), insignia of office (scepter, betel box, secret formula, seal of state, and pillows), and hangings that were displayed on ritual occasions. The regalia also included weapons (swords, lances, and a dagger of execution), which were particularly important. The weapons were believed to be self-created and had supernatural power that could destroy any person who was not authorized to handle them. Along with the regalia there was a special vocabulary of terms used to refer to the sultan and his activities and surroundings. After his death he could no longer be referred to by the name he had carried in life. The supernatural influence of the sultan could bring or ward off disease and bad harvests (44–47).

Those beneath the sultan owed him complete loyalty, deference, and respect. The district chiefs formally displayed their submission to the sultan through the ritual of obeisance. This involved approaching him by sitting on the floor and scooting forward in a series of moves, between each of which they saluted him by putting their palms together and touching their foreheads. Such ceremonies of obeisance were required of all the chiefs upon the installation of a new sultan and periodically thereafter. They were also carried out when a district chief was installed, without which he could not be legitimate.

There was a contradiction between the symbolic importance of the sultan and his actual political power, as there was also between the formal ritual deference paid to him by his district chiefs and their attitudes and behavior in other respects. The real power in the traditional Malay state generally lay with the district chiefs, and what real power the sultan himself had was based on his position in his own district. The sultan was the head of state, the basis of all nobility, and the leader in the event of an external war. But while the British had not yet taken over, they did prevent war between the different Malay states, so the military role of the sultans was inoperative in the immediate precolonial period. There were internal or civil wars among the district chiefs. But unless a sultan was unusually powerful, there was little he could do about these, so that once the chiefs had been installed they tended to stay in their own districts and do as they pleased, though this was often counter to the interests of the sultan. The power of a chief in relation to other chiefs and to the sultan was based on the economic resources he controlled in his district (such as revenue from tin mining and duties from the import and export of goods to and from his district). Such resources were used to support the chief's own army of fighting men and other followers (95–97).

Spread of Islam, Christianity, and Buddhism

As did Hinduism and Buddhism, Islam came into Southeast Asia from the west. Before arriving in Southeast Asia (evidentially first in north Sumatra in the thirteenth century), Islam had already reached and become established in large parts of India. It was spread peacefully from here over the next several centuries. Brought to Southeast Asia by merchants, Islam moved especially along the routes of the spice trade and became established first and most heavily in the coastal centers of commerce. As with any instance of large-scale religious conversion, the decision to accept the new religion was of great importance. The egalitarian doctrines and ethos of Islam may have appealed as an alternative to the hierarchical social forms that had long prevailed. It brought political and economic solidarity among Muslims. The earliest arrival of Islam in Southeast Asia came before establishment of the first footholds of the European colonial empires. But there was much overlap between the spread of Islam and colonialism, with agents of the two religions competing for converts as well as control of trade. The Portuguese established Christianity in the Moluccas (the Spice Islands) in eastern present-day Indonesia in the sixteenth century, but Islam prevailed elsewhere in the coastal regions of the Indies and the Malay Peninsula as well as the interior of Java. In the Philippines, Islam was also established in the coastal areas of Mindanao and other southern islands against the bitter opposition of the Spanish, who were then vigorously and successfully spreading Christianity in the remainder of the Philippines to the north. The interior peoples of most of the islands of the southern Philippines, the Indonesian

Archipelago, and the interior of the Malay Peninsula remained outside of both religions, though most of these groups later (in the nineteenth and twentieth centuries) became Christian.

Islam did not spread widely in mainland Southeast Asia above the Malay Peninsula. The Chams of coastal present-day Vietnam, who speak an Austronesian language (close to Malay), are one exception. After their Hinduized states were defeated and incorporated into Vietnam, many Chams converted to Islam, moved into central Cambodia, and developed close ties to Malays and other Muslim groups to the south. There are also Muslim minorities in Burma mainly established from India and smaller ones in Thailand. But otherwise Islam made no headway against Theravada Buddhism in the mainland countries of Burma, Siam, Laos, and Cambodia or against Mahayana Buddhism and Vietnamese folk religion in Vietnam.

In the mainland, the main transition was therefore from "Hinduism" (a term that came into existence only much later) and Mahayana Buddhism to Theravada Buddhism. In the earlier Indic period (to about the fifteenth century) in the western insular region and the mainland, both Buddhist and Hindu cults were present, though the latter appear to have been more common and important than the former. After the fifteenth century, Theravada Buddhism became dominant and largely (but—down to the present—never entirely) replaced the Hindu cults as state religions in the mainland countries of Burma, Thailand, Cambodia, and Laos. Statues of Hindu deities continue to appear in popular shrines, including both the more elaborate popular spirit houses that appear outside of hotels and other larger businesses in Chiang Mai, Thailand. And the major shrine and pilgrimage center of Phnom Kulen (outside of Siem Reap, Cambodia) that dates to the Angkor period combines large numbers of Shivaic lingams with Buddhist relics, including a footprint of the Buddha (see photo 3.2).

Interpreting (as historians do) what took place mainly from the evidence of statues, inscriptions, and monumental architecture, the historical picture necessarily emphasizes a royal and elite perspective. This could also be called the religion of stone because that is the basis of most of what is known about it. Much of what ordinary village-dwelling people believed, cared about, or did regarding the supernatural has mainly fallen through the cracks of historical scholarship. This was a religion of wood, bamboo, cloth, and other perishable materials, little of which has survived over the centuries, and of oral tradition rather than writing. There is reason to suppose, however, that most of the inhabitants of the Southeast Asian countries did not make fine distinctions in religious doctrine. Their concerns were strongly pragmatic—ritually protecting themselves from physical harm, watching for omens, making the rice grow, curing the sick, placating the spirits, attracting and keeping a spouse, dealing with death and its

Photo 3.1. Venerated statue of Vishnu in Angkor Wat Temple, Siem Reap, Cambodia, 2008.

threats, and occasionally harming a rival or enemy. Shrines were importantly sacred less because they were theologically correct than because they were mystically powerful. We can suppose these things because this sort of religious orientation is still very evident today, as will be discussed in more detail in later chapters.

Nonetheless, Theravada Buddhism also probably spread and sunk deep roots into lowland-village society in the mainland countries for the same political reasons that Islam and to some extent Christianity did elsewhere. It deemphasized hierarchy and offered an identity of commonality, and it was organized around the veneration of monks who took vows of poverty and devoted themselves to service to others. Theravada Buddhism was willing to accept the practical, this-world beliefs and practices that were part of everyday village life, in part because this was the milieu from which the monks themselves came.

Photo 3.2.   Khmer women pouring water over the lingam of Shiva at the major Indic-Buddhist shrine at Phnom Kulen outside of Siem Reap, Cambodia, 2008. Along with this and many other carved lingams dating to the Angkor period, the shrine also has a relic of the Buddha (a footprint) and a large reclining Buddha carved into the nearby rock.

COLONIALISM

At the beginning of World War II, European colonial rule encompassed approximately one-third of the territory of the world. Of the world's then three billion people, seven hundred million (or almost one quarter) were subject peoples. Seven nations had the bulk of colonized territory. Great Britain held sway over the largest and most widespread empire in history, one "on which the sun never set." It ruled 500 million people, 350 million of whom were in "India," or South Asia, with the remainder in Africa, Southeast Asia, Hong Kong, the Pacific Islands, and a few other places. France and The Netherlands ranked next in colonial holdings, controlling about seventy million persons each. France's colonial holdings were concentrated in North and West Africa and in Southeast Asia, while nearly all of The Netherlands' empire consisted of the vast Indonesian Archipelago (or the East Indies) in Southeast Asia. Following these countries came the United States, with fifteen million subjects in the Philippines and a few other places. The remaining colonial powers had little or no role in Southeast Asia. Portugal, the first European colonizer of Southeast Asian territory, held only half of the small island of Timor in the eastern Indian Archipelago. Belgium and Japan had no colonial possessions in the region. With the exception of Thailand, which remained independent, Southeast Asia was thus divided among Great Britain, France, The Netherlands, and the United States.

European colonialism in Southeast Asia began early in the sixteenth century or about 450 years before it ended. Its development, particularly its early development, was much more gradual than its final phase and conclusion. It was built in part on existing political and economic structures and practices, especially those relating to trade. By the time the first Europeans established a presence in the region, some Southeast Asian peoples had a long history of trade involving China, on the one hand, and India and the Near East (and indirectly Europe), on the other. But with the exception of Vietnam (and at the time this included only the northern part of the present country), no region of Southeast Asia had been previously colonized by an external state. We consider here the nature and consequences of these developments.

Early Colonialism

European colonial empires in Southeast Asia were established in several stages, the first involving the Portuguese and the Spanish.[4] The most famous and world-altering consequence of the desire to find a direct sea route to China and the Indies were the westward voyages of Columbus. But European exploration was focused in the opposite direction as well. The Portuguese moved southward along the western coast of Africa and rounded the southern tip in 1487 and within a decade had sailed across the Indian Ocean and reached the west coast of India. What they found whetted their appetite for further movement to the east. In 1510, they took Goa on the east coast of far southern India. The Portuguese reached the Malay Peninsula in 1508 and conquered the port city of Malacca—then the main center of international trade in Southeast Asia—in 1511. From there they pushed on farther east into present-day eastern Indonesia and established control over what became known as the Spice Islands (the Moluccas) where nutmeg and cloves were grown. For the next century, the

Portuguese controlled both ends of the spice trade. During this period, the Spaniards had succeeded in sailing across the Pacific and begun the colonization of the Philippine Islands.

While the Spanish kept the Philippines for three and a half centuries, the Portuguese lost control of nearly all of their possessions in the East Indies to the Dutch at the beginning of the seventeenth century. The Dutch located the capital of their possessions in the Indies in Batavia (now Jakarta) on the island of Java and eventually extended their control from the northern tip of Sumatra in the west to the western half of New Guinea in the east.

For the first three hundred years or so, colonial intervention was limited mainly to external trade and political control of the sea-lanes, and hence to the southern or insular and peninsular realm of Southeast Asia (Burling 1965, 125–27). Apart from a few places, there was probably little direct effect on the lives of most of the inhabitants of the lands over which the several colonial powers claimed dominion. Other than in Java, the early centers of colonial power and economy were on the coasts rather than the interiors. Commerce flourished as it had for many centuries before the arrival of Europeans. The governing of settled agricultural populations in most areas was left to traditional rulers and chiefs. The indigenous inhabitants of the mountainous, mainly forest-covered interior regions, generally retained their previous autonomy. To the local peoples, the Europeans at first seemed not very different from the merchants and ambassadors that had previously come from China, India, and the Middle East. European technological superiority was not great, though sufficient to maintain power in the coastal zones, the lower reaches of major rivers, and over the international shipping routes on the seas. The numbers of Europeans present in the region were not large, and their interests were often in harmony with those of indigenous rulers and elites. According to circumstances, some local rulers remained autonomous; others aligned themselves with Europeans or accepted varying degrees of real or token subordination for shares in wealth and power.

Later Colonialism

The later development of colonialism in Southeast Asia had much to do with what was occurring elsewhere in the world. Put in general terms, the changes were a consequence of the Industrial Revolution and the continuing modernization of European culture. As had advantages in armaments, knowledge of geography and navigation, and shipbuilding several centuries earlier, the revolution in European manufacturing and in related changes in technology, public health, science, and other areas gave the colonial powers a renewed advantage in power and altered their motives for the further development of colonialism. A Marxist would say that the contradictions in the development of capitalism required the creation of new markets for European goods as well as new sources of raw materials. Colonies had the advantage of very favorable terms of export and import and the absence, at least for a time, of angry, exploited working classes, or at least ones in a position to cause trouble.

To be somewhat more inclusive, there were basic changes in ships, shipping, and trade. Steamships began to replace sailing vessels and had done so decisively by the latter part of the nineteenth century. Transportation between Europe and Asia thus became cheaper and faster, especially after the opening of the Suez Canal in 1869. The older trade had focused on silks, ceramics, spices, and other luxury goods. This was replaced by the European import of raw materials from Southeast Asian plantations, mines, and forests and the export of cloth and clothing, bicycles, pens and pencils, paper and books, and countless other finished industrial products. Improvements in communication as well as travel brought colonial administration under more direct control of metropolitan centers of government.

For whatever reasons, beginning around the middle of the nineteenth century a newer, and much more comprehensive and widely felt form, of Western imperialism began to develop in the Southeast Asia countries. During this later phase, colonialism was also extended to the mainland above the Malay Peninsula. Previously, the European presence and impact here had been minimal. In terms of geography, both the insular lands and the mainland consist of mountains, plains, and valleys naturally covered by forest and drained by many rivers. But the proportion of coast to interior is smaller in the mainland. Further, the deltas of great rivers dominate a larger portion of the coastal zone of the mainland than of the islands. And rich as they were in alluvial soils, these deltas were sparsely populated before the introduction of the modern technology of water control. Populations were therefore more concentrated in the open inland plains and valleys of the interior. Here, economies were based on peasant agriculture. Trade was of lesser importance, meaning there was also less to attract Europeans.

The traditional political systems were also different. In both the insular/peninsular and the mainland areas, traditional state political power involved a combination of symbolism, mysticism, military force, and economic control. But in the mainland states (and in Java and Bali), the economic basis of power laid more in the domination of interior rice-cultivating populations than of sea-lanes and commerce (Jay 1963, 2–3)—nor could the military advantages Europeans enjoyed at sea and in the coastal waters be as readily deployed in the interior. European armaments based on gunpowder were readily appreciated and adopted at an early point, although the traditional pattern of warfare among the Burmese, Thai, Khmer, and other states continued. Portuguese and other adventurers gained occasional employment as military advisors and mercenaries as early as the

first part of the sixteenth century, but otherwise Europeans had little to offer the rulers of the mainland states during the early period (Burling 1965,
123–24).

The cast of colonial characters also changed in nineteenth-century Southeast Asia. While the Dutch continued to be a major colonial power and the
Portuguese only a tiny one, the British and the French went from being
minor (in the case of the British) or nonexistent (in the case of the French)
players to major ones controlling large areas of Southeast Asia. Similarly,
the Spanish disappeared entirely as rulers in the Philippines at the end of
the century—the Americans arriving to take their place. Unlike the other colonial empires in Southeast Asia, the American one was thus established all
at once as a consequence of the Spanish-American War in 1898. The establishment of American control was fiercely resisted, especially in Mindanao
and other areas of the Muslim southern region. But the territorial boundaries of the Philippines remained as they were until independence in 1946.

The creation of the later European colonial empires in Southeast Asia
was accomplished through peaceful persuasion in some places and through
military force in others. In the insular countries and Malaya, the fuller development of colonial rule involved an extension from the older coastal
centers of commerce and administration to the more remote islands and
interior regions that had previously been minimally governed or (as in
much of the interior of Borneo, for example) left alone. In both the Malay
Peninsula and the Indies, consolidation and expansion began in the nineteenth century but was not completed until the early decades of the twentieth, and even then was often minimal. In the mainland, the acquisition
of colonial territories was largely a matter of starting from scratch. As in the
insular areas, it often involved the establishment of only limited control
in the more remote mountainous regions inhabited by tribally organized
upland peoples.

The British Empire in Southeast Asia came to include Burma, Malaya,
Singapore, and the northern part of the island of Borneo. The British had
established small trading stations in insular Southeast Asia early on and
took temporary control of the Dutch colonial possessions during the Na-
poleonic War. But their attention in the earlier period was focused mainly
on the development of the empire in India. The British move into Burma
therefore came from the west or India, rather than from Malaya to the
south, and involved three wars. The first of these gave the British control
over the disputed territories between British India and Burma; the second,
over southern Burma; and the third, the annexation of the remainder of
Burma in the north into the Indian Empire in 1886. The successful establishment of British colonial control has been attributed to the isolation of
Burma and the failure of its government to grasp the military power of the
British in India (Burling 1965, 125).

By the end of the eighteenth century, the British had gained a foothold in Malaya with the acquisition of Penang Island, followed in the early nineteenth by the founding of Singapore and the acquisition of Malacca from the Dutch (who had earlier taken it from the Portuguese). They eventually, if (as they claimed) somewhat reluctantly, took over the remainder of Malaya. As noted above, precolonial Malaya consisted of a series of independent states or sultanates, each often divided into semi-independent chiefdoms. These Malay states were brought under British authority in the latter part of the nineteenth century (the last, Trengganu, early in the twentieth). These states became protectorates and were ruled "indirectly," meaning they retained their sultans as formal heads of state and—up to a point—their traditional apparatus of government. Using language somewhat reminiscent of that used more recently to justify the American military intervention in Vietnam and the war in Iraq, the British generally professed reluctance, as well as noble motives, in the takeover of the Malay states. While the initial reluctance may have been genuine, with the development of its tin mines and vast rubber plantations, Malaya became a very lucrative corner of the empire (Tarling 1992, 23–24).

The extension of British rule to northern Borneo began slightly earlier when the English adventurer James Brooke arrived and created his own kingdom of Sarawak in 1842 out of the traditional Malay sultanate of Brunei. Sarawak eventually became a British protectorate, as did Brunei. The territory of Sabah, which consisted of the northernmost part of Borneo and which had not been an organized state, was first incorporated into the British Empire as a chartered private company (41–42).

The French Empire in Southeast Asia consisted of the modern countries of Vietnam, Laos, and Cambodia and was referred to collectively as Indochina. Of the three countries, Vietnam had by then expanded far beyond its earlier boundary to the south along the coast and into the Mekong Delta by destroying and absorbing the state of Champa and the eastern part of the Khmer empire—including the entire Mekong Delta. Precolonial Cambodia consisted of a small and weak remnant of its former self, having lost much of its territory to the Thai to the west as well as the Vietnamese to the east. For its part, Laos had no precolonial existence in anything like its present form. What became Laos consisted of several small Lao (or Tai-speaking) Theravada Buddhist kingdoms plus many different highland ethnic minorities amounting to probably half of the population (45–46).

Up until the early part of the nineteenth century, the countries and territories of Vietnam, Laos, and Cambodia, along with those of Siam (as Thailand was then known), had remained beyond European imperial rule. As with the British acquisition of Burma, the full French takeover of Vietnam and then of the remaining areas of what became Indochina involved a complex series of developments that extended over much of the nineteenth century and into the early twentieth. Although the French long had interests in the region, the issue that brought them into Vietnam and led to the creation of their empire in Southeast Asia developed in the first half of the nineteenth century with a dispute over Christian missionaries. French Catholic missionaries had been proselytizing in the area with some success for two hundred years. But by the 1830s, a reaction had developed against them and a number were arrested and executed. In 1843, the French demanded that five condemned missionaries be released and sought to obtain the guarantee of rights of French nationals in Vietnam, much as European countries were doing in China at the time. Misjudging the strength of the French (as the Burmese had the British in India), the Vietnamese continued to harass the resident French. After their demands were rejected, the French invaded Cochin China (present-day southern Vietnam) and took over by 1867. At the same time, they also turned their attention to Cambodia and forced the Thai, who then held it, to cede control to France. The French next addressed northern Vietnam and took Hanoi in 1882. The last piece of the French Empire in Southeast Asia was the territory of Laos, gained in the form of a protectorate in 1893, partly by getting Siam to cede control in the north. Together the three countries became the Colony of French Indochina (Cady 1964, 419–34).

THE NATURE OF COLONIALISM

With the American takeover of the Philippines at the end of the nineteenth century, the final contours of European colonial possessions in Southeast Asia were set. The consolidation of administrative control was far from complete, especially in the remote highland and interior areas. And there were important differences among British, French, Dutch, and American versions of rule. However, the colonial world as it existed in Southeast Asia on the eve of its dissolution following World War II had a number of general characteristics.

To begin with a negative but important observation, it was not settler colonialism. It did not involve efforts to find and develop new overseas territories for European family farming or ranching or the establishment of small businesses in towns and cities by Europeans, as occurred in North and South America, South Africa, Australia, New Zealand, and a few other places. Only relatively small numbers of Europeans ever moved to any of the colonies in Southeast Asia. And many of those who did move did so not as families but as single men, and for only limited periods in their lives. This sort of colonial demography was common in tropical or subtropical regions of the world, including the Caribbean, much of Africa, the Pacific Islands, and the Indian subcontinent as well as Southeast Asia. Unlike the temperate regions that attracted settler colonists, the tropical countries did not draw small-scale European farming. The humid tropics were economically well suited to large monocrop plantations. These were developed extensively in many regions, including parts of Vietnam, the west coast of the Malay Peninsula, the east coast of Sumatra, and Java. They were large capital operations that required extensive labor for forest clearing, planting, maintenance, and harvesting—not small-family enterprises. They provided opportunities for only small numbers of Europeans as managers and technical experts. Trade and commerce was also very lucrative in the tropical colonies but had the same general limits of opportunity as did farming. Europeans were needed only in small numbers in the higher levels of management—middle and lower levels being filled far more cheaply by Asians. If tropical colonial enterprises spent more on the local labor force they might have collectively gained it back in sales revenues, but this was not part of the business model. The same point can be made about mining, timber extraction, the military, and the various branches of governance. And if there were only small numbers of Europeans employed in these central colonial organizations, the opportunities for businesses and services for them were also limited.

Combined with such limits the tropical colonies in Southeast Asia had other drawbacks for Europeans. There was undoubtedly an appeal of romance and adventure, though this has probably been much advanced in retrospect by literature and Hollywood. There was also the belief that tropical climates posed serious hazards for the health of Europeans in general, and for women and children in particular. The concerns included the dangers of malaria, yellow fever, cholera, and other endemic and epidemic diseases, not to mention poisonous snakes, scorpions and spiders, and overexposure to the direct tropical sun. Tropical climates were also thought by Europeans to pose moral dangers for men, including an enhanced sexual desire and longing for alcohol. As Americans might put it today, tropical colonial settings did not seem to make for good family values. The children who were born there were best sent home for schooling.

CHARACTERISTICS OF COLONIAL RULE

Various scholars have described the characteristics of colonialism in Southeast Asia and elsewhere. In a survey of colonialism written during World War II, Raymond Kennedy, an American anthropologist and a specialist on the Netherlands Indies, referred to the colonial situation as a problem that had become a crisis (Kennedy 1945). "Crisis" turned out to be appropriate; the various colonial empires came to a rapid end in the years following the war. According to Kennedy, there was variation from one region and one colonial power to another. But all of the Western colonial empires from Africa, to India, Southeast Asia, or the Pacific Islands had by the beginning of the twentieth century developed a number of common characteristics.

The Color Line and White Authority

The first of these characteristics in Kennedy's view was the color line. This was the foundation of the entire colonial system. With the exception of Japan's control of Korea and Taiwan, colonial rule was the domination of Western white people over subjects with black or brown skins. In every colonial territory there was a caste system. The resident white population, a small minority of the total, was separated from the native masses by a social barrier that was virtually impassible. All of the relationships between the racial groups were ones of superiority and subordination. The color line cut across every colonial society in a way that left the natives on the bottom and the whites on the top. Although it was not the only thing involved, the heart of the colonial problem was the native problem, and the native problem was one of race or caste. As the British authority on colonialism John Furnival wrote in 1939 (1967),

> Although in British India the European caste is often overlooked, there are many economic functions from which the European, as European, is debarred. He cannot dig, to beg he is ashamed, and if he is reduced to begging, he is deported, as beggary is a prerequisite of the Indian castes. Moreover, as with Indian castes, the European caste has a quasi-religious sanction in the doctrine of racial superiority of Europeans. (450)

Other scholars have made similar points about related matters that were important in maintaining caste distinctions between Europeans and natives in colonial situations. The British historian Kenneth Ballhatchet has analyzed the sexual attitudes that were a fundamental part of British colonial rule and European-native caste principles in India and Burma. The British authorities officially sanctioned brothels staffed by native women for European troops, but white women were not permitted to engage in prostitution and were deported if found. And any sexual relation between a European woman and a native man was considered a serious breach of caste. The possibility of marriage, romantic or sexual encounters, or relationships with Indian princes (who in situations of indirect rule were accorded respect under colonial rule) were a continuing matter of concern to colonial authorities as a bad reflection on British prestige and authority—on which colonial rule was deemed to rest (Ballhatchet 1980, 57–59, 123–43; see also Stoler 2002).[5]

The color line was thus justified by racism, the doctrine generally accepted by Europeans and white Americans that the white race was innately superior to the darker races (Kennedy 1945, 312). The doctrine, Kennedy asserted, was disproved by all of the scientific evidence from anthropology, psychology, and sociology. But while false, it was believed. The doctrine came into existence some four hundred years ago with the power of Europeans to discover and capture or subjugate dark-skinned peoples as a result of Western achievements in armaments and navigation. The owners of guns and advanced sailing ships came to suppose they were also the owners of a superior racial heritage. They were white, and the conquered peoples were brown or black.

By the time—and to some extent as a result—of the Second World War, the notion of white racial superiority had begun to be undermined. The rise of small, able, and educated groups among colonial peoples was one factor, and the stunning military success of the Japanese in the first part of the war was another. And then the Nazi German espousal of Aryan racial superiority over all other peoples including other white ones tended to give explicit racism a bad name. But while such cracks had appeared in the doctrine of racism, it was still widely accepted among whites that they were destined to rule as a result of their racial endowment.

Government Control: Direct and Indirect

The second common characteristic of all colonial practice was political control by the colonial power. This left the natives little share in the government of their homelands, although this was more so under some forms and periods of colonial rule than others. The administration of the colonies was directed by the mother country whose local representatives held all of the important positions in the colony. This was not necessarily as it was supposed to have been according to the treaties by which colonial relationships were often established. The British made an important distinction between "direct" and "indirect" forms of rule, but other colonial governments had similar policies as well. In the former, the head of government of a colonized country was a representative of the colonial power—in the case of Great Britain, the King or Queen of England. The king or other traditional native head of state, if any, had been deposed; or the local king had ceded the territory in question to the colonial power in an agreement. In other words, the colonial power claimed ownership or sovereignty over the territory in question.

Under indirect rule, the local sovereign continued to be recognized as the formal head of state, and the government was supposed to be administered mainly by local officials. Under the British system, the highest colonial official in the state was often referred to as an advisor, whose advice was supposed to be given in political and administrative matters except those involving religion and custom. Here, traditional authority and customary practice were to be respected and preserved except perhaps where the most reprehensible activities such as warfare, headhunting, and human sacrifice were, among some groups, concerned. Even indigenous forms of human bondage were tolerated in some areas to the end of colonial rule. The one area in which the colonial powers claimed control was that of foreign or external relations, especially with agreements or relationships with competing colonial empires. The least intrusive or most indirect form of colonial government was often termed a "protectorate," whereby a local country accepted protection by a stronger colonial power so that its integrity and interests were secure.

Both direct and indirect rule was common in Southeast Asia and practiced by the British, French, and Dutch. The British abolished the monarchy in Burma and governed the country directly. They also governed the trade-based Straits Settlements of Penang, Malacca, and Singapore directly while preserving the sultanates of the Malay states of the peninsula and governing them indirectly. The French and the Dutch territories differed along similar lines. While ruling the northern (Tonkin) and southern most parts of Vietnam directly, the French kept the monarchies in Annam (central Vietnam), Cambodia, and Laos. Similarly, while again overthrowing some traditional regimes that were deemed unacceptable for one reason or another, the Dutch continued to recognize and support some three hundred indigenous regencies and sultanates throughout the vast Indonesian Archipelago (Kennedy 1945, 327).

Colonialists regarded indirect rule as the most suitable form of colonial government in many situations for several reasons. It fitted with the popular fiction that the colonial countries had not simply been seized, taken over, and exploited and that intervention had been necessary in the interest of peace, trade, and the welfare of the natives themselves. Further, since it involved relatively small numbers of European police, military, and civil officers and administrators, it was considered more efficient and less costly than direct administration. And since the traditional order had been preserved, indirect rule was thought to be less likely to inspire or justify native resistance to colonial control. The British in particular prided themselves in being able to keep order, provide decent government, and promote economic improvement with only small numbers of Europeans "on the ground." They liked to think this was because they had transformed or improved the oppressive, anarchic, or at least chaotic way things had been before their arrival, and because they had gained the trust and respect of the natives—or most of them, anyway.

For his part, Kennedy took the view that the differences in the practices of direct and indirect rule were in fact minimal. The native rulers were creatures of the central administration, and the whole system was a facade behind which the colonial authorities exercised real power. Except in matters of ceremony and prestige, the native rulers were figureheads. Also, the native colonial councils did not have authority except in limited areas of religion and customary law. Native aspiration and opinion had little if any influence. Democracy was not a part of the basis of government because, it was held, the natives were not ready for it. Whenever natives did try to organize their people for political action or to express opinions they were labeled as agitators and watched, and if they persisted, were imprisoned or exiled. In most colonies, the administration maintained a network of secret police, which with the regular police and the armed garrisons had the major purpose of finding and suppressing independent native political action. Remote penal institutions meant mainly for exiled native troublemakers were a common appendage of the colonies. Police and military garrisons were often composed of only a small number of European officers and a large number of non-European enlisted men. The latter were often from other colonies: Gurkhas, Sikhs, and other native regiments from India in the case of the British, and foreign legionnaires from North Africa and elsewhere in the case of the French. The British and the Dutch also relied on local ethnic minorities, including the Karen in Burma and the Ambonese in the Netherlands Indies, to help them govern. Such outsiders and local ethnic minorities were appreciated for their loyalty to the colonial government, their lack of local ties, and in some cases for their martial valor. The selection and command of military forces was thus dictated by the colonial regime. In most colonies, including those governed as native states under indirect rule, whites were governed according to special laws and procedures (309).

The political subordination of the natives under colonial rule was long justified by the doctrine that these people were incapable of governing themselves properly. This had also often been the justification for colonial intervention in the first place. Colonialists went further sometimes and advanced the view that the natives had no desire to govern themselves or even that they preferred to be dominated. The topic of independence was met with the claim that if this were granted the result would be reversion to the old precolonial forms of despotism, or a small clique would seize power. In their most extreme form, such doctrines included the opinion that the natives would never be able to govern themselves. And even if they were, there was the likelihood that after gaining their freedom from the Western colonial powers the former colonies would be subject to takeover by independent non-Western states such as Russia or China. As the decades of the twentieth century passed, and colonial control was increasingly challenged by nationalist movements, this older view was supplanted by the proposition that independence would eventually be possible or inevitable. This would require a long period of tutelage. However, no program of native education had been put in place by the beginning of the Second World War, except by the United States in the Philippines (312–13).

Economic Exploitation

The third general characteristic of colonialism was economic exploitation. The economic role of the colonies was twofold. On the one hand, they were sources of raw materials, including agricultural commodities, timber, and minerals imported for industrial use by the mother country and other industrialized nations. On the other, the colonies were markets for the sale of goods manufactured by the mother country and by other industrialized nations. The importance of various colonies as sources of raw materials or as markets for manufactured goods varied according to circumstances, including the availability of resources and the size of the populations. The Southeast Asian countries were generally very rich in resources but compared to China and India had relatively small populations, except for a few regions, including Java and parts of Vietnam. Little emphasis was placed on the development of manufacturing or industrialization in the colonies themselves. In some instances, local manufacturing was weakened or destroyed by competition from the cheaper goods produced by industrialized economies of the Western countries and Japan. If the colonial powers did not necessarily attempt to prevent the development of local manufacturing industries, neither did they do anything to promote them.

The economic consequences of such practices, in terms of wealth and poverty within the colonies and between the populations of the colonies and the controlling countries, were great. The colonial populations consisted mainly of peasants and fishermen. The peasants were small-scale cultivators who produced traditional crops mainly for subsistence, though increasingly for markets as well. Others were coolies (low-wage workers who labored on plantations, in mines, and for timber extraction) small traders and hawkers, and servants. The difference in the economic status of the native masses and the small numbers of resident whites was enormous. It greatly exceeded anything to be found in the Western countries themselves. A peasant farmer who left farming and became a coolie worker earned only very low wages. In some regions, landlessness and landlordism developed to a major extent. Occupational barriers were often set by race or caste. Resident whites held the higher and better-paid positions at the top of government.[6]

The economic arrangements of colonialism in Southeast Asia and elsewhere were justified by the colonial powers by several claims similar to those made regarding government. It was said that the native peoples were incapable of creating and operating the productive and distributive arrangements of their own countries beyond the level of local trade. Because of this they were incapable of developing the resources of their country to the full extent of their potential. This incapacity was in turn explained in various ways. These explanations ranged from racist doctrines that the natives were inherently incapable of the organizational and technical skills needed to the more reasonable admission that they simply lacked the necessary training and experience. Toward the end of colonial rule, the latter explanation had begun to displace the older one of racial inferiority. But in addition to training and experience, there was also the problem of obtaining capital for investment and development. The problems of obtaining training in commercial education, which was not available in the colonies, and of raising capital were made even worse by discrimination in favor of whites at the managerial level (Kennedy 1945, 315). The important economic role of immigrant Asian workers and businessmen (above all Chinese) was also explained by their special abilities.

Education

The final characteristic of colonialism was the low level of social services development, especially education, provided for the native population. The general absence of formal education (beyond the traditional forms offered by Buddhist and Muslim schools in Southeast Asia) has already been noted regarding native political participation and economic opportunity. In the case of the other social services, including medical care, colonialists attributed the poor level of development to the financial limitations under which colonial governments operated. In the case of education, there were other explanations as well, such as the natives lacked the capacity for learning or had no interest in formal education—or if they did it would not be a good thing. The commonly held view was that education for the masses of natives in colonial circumstances would be dysfunctional in that it would lead to frustration, discontent, and unhappiness by creating wants and ambitions that could not be satisfied. This was thought to be especially so where secondary and university education were concerned, for here graduates would find no positions available that were commensurate with their training and study. In British Malaya, it was recognized that the sons of the traditional royalty and aristocracy should be educated to some extent because of the special role they played in the system of indirect rule and because, in any move toward greater independence, they should provide the leadership needed—a development that did come to pass (Kennedy 1945, 317).

THE END OF COLONIAL RULE

Compared to its long period of development (or even its swift expansion from the last decades of the nineteenth century to the early decades of the twentieth), colonial rule in Southeast Asia came to a rapid end.[7] The real end began with the close of World War II as communist or nationalist anticolonial movements resisted the reestablishment of European imperial regimes, leading in some instances to armed struggles.[8] Sooner or later most colonialism would have ended anyway, for it contained the seeds of its own destruction: The local economies had been transformed from mainly subsistence-based, noncash operations to more market-based ones. Rice had become a commodity, and landlordism and landlessness developed especially in major rice-growing areas, including the great river deltas of the mainland. Rubber and other cash crops were developed both as smallholder and large plantation crops, the latter mainly in the hands of Europeans. Unfortunately, cash crops such as rubber, tea, or coco, especially for small farmers, cannot be or are not eaten and have no value except as commodities to be sold, and prices fluctuate—producing uncertainty and frustration when they are low. Great urban centers with large populations developed to replace the traditional royal capitals and small trading towns. Colonialism created ethnic pluralism where it had not existed or at least brought it to new levels of development.

However, the war and its consequences were decisive. The Western colonial countries were on the winning side of the war against Japan and were able to reestablish control of their colonies after it ended. But the rapid Japanese invasion and conquest of Southeast Asia and its defeat of colonial armies demonstrated the vulnerability of the westerners, the eventual defeat of the Japanese notwithstanding. In some places, indigenous anti-Japanese resistance movements and guerrilla forces became the core of nationalist anticolonialist forces after colonial rule was reestablished. The economies of the European countries had been devastated, and the will to rebuild colonialism as it had been was weakened or destroyed.

The various Western countries with empires in Southeast Asia gave them up with various degrees of willingness or resistance. The Americans and the British did so most willingly. The Americans had been committed to full Philippine independence before the war, and the United States became the first country to grant freedom to a Southeast Asian colony. The British gave up their Southeast Asian Empire more or less peacefully as well as willingly. The early independence of Burma in 1948 came a year following that of India to which Burma had been linked. The British had already seen the independence of settler colonies in other parts of the world and their transformation into an acceptable commonwealth status, though none in Southeast Asia followed suit. The British departure was not entirely without bloodshed. After the war, they fought a communist guerrilla insurrection in Malaya that had originated as an anti-Japanese resistance movement and that was limited almost entirely to immigrant Chinese (though most of the Chinese in Malaya did not support it). This delayed independence for several years.

Neither the Dutch nor the French colonies in Southeast Asia (except for Cambodia, which became independent in 1953) were granted independence willingly or peacefully. After the withdrawal of the Japanese in 1945, nationalists in the Netherlands Indies under the leadership of Sukarno unilaterally declared an independent republic. The Dutch refused to agree to this and attempted to reestablish control, thus unleashing a war of independence that lasted until 1949, when the Netherlands gave in and accepted the creation of Indonesia.

The end of Dutch colonial rule in Indonesia after three and a half centuries was mild in comparison to what happened in Vietnam, the far briefer history (about one hundred years) of colonialism there notwithstanding. In this case, the initial thrust for independence began with the emergence of the Viet Minh (short for Viet Nam Doc Lap Minh Hoi), the League for the Independence of Vietnam, in 1941 as a communist and nationalist movement opposing the Japanese as well as the French. Led by Ho Chi Minh, the Viet Minh declared a provisional independent government in Hanoi in 1945 after the withdrawal of the Japanese. The French attempted to suppress an independent state, and a war began in 1946 that lasted until 1954. This first Indochina war was fought mainly in the north. Here, the French held Hanoi and other cities while the Viet Minh controlled the surrounding villages of the Red River Delta. Over the years, a stalemate developed, with the French able to move beyond Hanoi and other bases only in strength. The Viet Minh engaged in classic hit-and-run guerrilla warfare and, as public support for the war declined back in France, were ready to move to the next and final stage of fixed battles. The end for the French came quickly in the spring of 1954 in the remote valley of Dien Bien Phu in northwestern Vietnam near the Laos border. Here they were decisively defeated in the most important single battle in the post–World War II period in Southeast Asia (and one of the greatest blunders in recent military history). The French had the military strength to continue to hold on, but they withdrew from Vietnam and Laos (the remainder of their empire in Indochina—they had given Cambodia independence in the previous year) and were out in a few months. At the international peace conference held later in the year, the French, the Viet Minh, and other signatories (not including the Americans) to the Geneva Peace Accords agreed to the temporary partition of Vietnam into north and south divisions, with a demilitarized zone at the seventeenth parallel, to be followed by elections in the south (never held in either division) by 1956. The reunification of Vietnam did not come until 1975. At this time, the American forces having withdrawn two years previously, the combined armies of the North Vietnamese and the Viet Cong defeated the government army of South Vietnam and took Saigon and control of the entire country (Osborne [1979] 2004, 190–95).

Economic Development

The consequences of colonial rule in Southeast Asia as elsewhere in the world include vast political, economic, social, and cultural changes. Some

Table 3.1.   Economic Development and Colonialism in Southeast Asia (gross domestic product [GDP] adjusted for buying power [PPP] of the larger Southeast Asian countries, from highest to lowest [of 180 countries]).

Country	Rank in World	Quartile	Colony of:
Malaysia	59	2	Great Britain
Thailand	83	2	none
Indonesia	120	3	Netherlands
Philippines	122	3	Spain/United States
Vietnam	129	3	France
Laos	136	4	France
Cambodia	143	4	France
Burma/Myanmar	161	4	Great Britain

Source: Wikipedia: The Free Encyclopedia, "List of Countries by GDP (PPP)," at http://en.wikipedia.org/w/index.php?title=List_of_countries_by_GDP_(PPP) (accessed August 1, 2010).

of these will be discussed in the next chapter and subsequently. Kennedy (1945) emphasized that none of the colonies had been adequately prepared for independence by their former colonial rulers—although postcolonial developments varied from one country or region to another to a greater extent than did colonialism itself. Some indication of how well the larger Southeast Asian countries (that is, excluding the geographically tiny states of Singapore, Brunei, and Timor) have fared in terms of overall economic development can be seen in the worldwide country rankings of buying-power-adjusted per capita income, as shown in table 3.1.

Such figures do not tell us how income is distributed in various important ways—among different ethnic groups or between urban and rural sectors, for example. For what they are worth they show that, among the 180 independent countries of the world (most of which are former colonies of one or another colonial power), the Southeast Asian nations range over the second, third, and fourth quartiles (or quarters). While the most prosperous of the larger Southeast Asia countries (Malaysia) is a former colony of Great Britain, the second (Thailand) was never colonized. At the other extreme, Laos, Cambodia (French colonies), and Burma (British) are among the poorest one-fourth of all nations. Of course, all of the poorer larger countries in Southeast Asia have been strongly affected in their postcolonial development by devastating postcolonial wars or repressive and violent governments (the extent to which these developments can be attributed to colonial policies and practices is a complicated matter). The latter include most notably the Khmer Rouge in Cambodia, and Burma, where military dictatorships have been in power since 1961, which has been involved with internal wars and endemic rebellions involving the Karen and other indigenous ethnic minorities since then.

4

Ethnic Complexity in Modern Southeast Asia

Southeast Asia is an ethnically very complex region, and it became more so as a result of colonialism. A good deal of anthropological, historical, and governmental thought and theorizing has been devoted to understanding this situation. One approach is to recognize two fundamental types of ethnic complexity: indigenous and pluralistic. Indigenous complexity is ancient. It is probably thousands or even tens of thousands of years old. It developed as various ethnolinguistic groups have formed or moved into and throughout Southeast Asia, subdividing, mixing, and adapting as they moved, peacefully or otherwise. Ethnologists and prehistorians have attempted to get a grip on this indigenous ethnic complexity in various ways—by referring to differing forms of adaptation, highland and lowland patterns, majorities and minorities, language groups, and so on. Begun under colonial rule, such efforts have continued under the postcolonial regimes. In the mainland, the favorite example is Laos. Here, where the very numerous indigenous minorities together are about as large as the lowland majority, they are classified according to the elevation at which they traditionally live—in the lowlands, uplands, and highlands. This threefold system is no longer official, but it is still pervasive. On the scale of ethnic prestige, the lowlanders are on top and the highlanders at the bottom.

Indigenous ethnic complexity is as great or greater in the island countries of Indonesia, the Philippines, and Malaysian Borneo as it is in the mainland. Indonesia, for example, is one of the most ethnically diverse nations in the world. It has proved difficult to characterize in ethnic terms. For a while it was popular to divide Indonesia into Inner Indonesia and Outer Indonesia on the basis of fundamental differences in geography, ecology, and history. Inner Indonesia consisted of the islands of Java and Bali. Here

· there were fertile volcanic soils, intensive wet rice cultivation, high population densities, and comparatively limited ethnic diversity (the Javanese, the Balinese, and a few other indigenous groups). Outer Indonesia in contrast was said to be marked by much less fertile soils, extensive swidden cultivation, light population densities, other rich natural resources, and far greater ethnic diversity. Though it helped to explain the economic and political fault lines of Indonesia, the division was a large oversimplification. We will continue to be concerned with indigenous ethnic complexity throughout the book.

PLURAL SOCIETY

Our concern in this chapter is with the other form of ethnic complexity: ethnic pluralism. This notion refers especially to the presence of (originally) immigrant or nonindigenous populations. But it also implies that the different groups play different roles in the economy and society. It is this form of ethnic complexity that increased most as a result of colonialism.

The British theorist of colonialism John Furnival gave us the notion of plural society. Furnival wrote about colonialism in Burma and Indonesia from an economic perspective and formulated the concept especially to fit these countries (Furnival [1939] 1967, 447). A plural society was one comprised of several or more ethnic groups but under the control of one. He noted also that plural social orders could develop in other places in other types of societies, such as the American South or parts of Canada, but most of these had a history of colonialism as well. The various groups in a plural society "mix but do not combine." The different groups interact, but this is limited mainly to the marketplace. Otherwise, the members of each group live separate lives in separate places. Each of the major ethnic sectors is mainly associated with a particular economic activity, or at most several. They would have been separate societies except that they were all part of one political regime. The separateness persisted over time. There was little assimilation or acculturation. Plural societies were stratified in the sense that one group dominated the others, and in colonial plural societies this was the ruling Europeans. Beyond this, there was no common pattern of stratification except that which could be put in the simplest economic terms. A common (if overly simplistic) generalization made about Malaysia, for example, is that Chinese have economic power while Malays have political power, and Indians have neither.

The concept of the plural society has been one of the two main, contrasting models of ethnicity bequeathed to us by social science. The other is that of the "melting pot," especially as applied to the United States and now part of the popular political vocabulary of Americans. The basic idea here is that people migrate to the United States and rapidly assimilate—or at least should. Ethnic identities may persist after a generation or so as a part of personal identity but lose their social significance, except where racial or, to a lesser extent, religious divisions are concerned. Powerful economic, political, and cultural currents push immigrants to become plain old Americans first and foremost. Doing so is a fundamental part of the American creed, although there are periodically (as at the present time) powerful anti-immigrant reactions that include the belief that some immigrants should not be here and the fear that they will not assimilate. Of course, as scholars have long been pointing out, the melting pot model is an oversimplification, more ideology perhaps than social reality. But clearly, Furnival was on to something when he formulated a way of talking about a very different pattern of ethnicity.

Scholars who have studied ethnic complexity more closely and more recently have also been critical of Furnival's notion of the plural society. One sort of criticism has been that he oversimplified the situation—both the extent to which the economy and social organization of colonial societies was organized along ethnic lines and the extent to which such divisions persisted with little or no change. Another line of criticism has been that the plural society model underemphasizes the significance of economic classes, which do not merely follow along or reflect ethnic differences. It directs attention away from the extent that ethnic groups are internally differentiated in social, economic, and political terms, and from the extent that there are commonalities of class among the different ethnic groups. Such arguments have often been stated in rather abstract theoretical terms, but they are best examined through more detailed case studies of the sort discussed below.

To a limited extent, ethnic complexity of the kind described by Furnival and others existed in Southeast Asia long before the arrival of European colonialism. Traders from China, India, and the Middle East had been coming to the Southeast Asian countries for centuries before the Europeans, and some of them established communities in the port towns and cities. Local Southeast Asia rulers generally welcomed them because of the economic (and sometimes military) services they provided. The foreigners lived in their own neighborhoods and regulated themselves according to their own customs so long as they did not become involved in conflicts that extended beyond their communities or otherwise cause problems. The early European regimes fitted into this pattern.

Nonetheless, ethnic complexity in Southeast Asia grew to an unprecedented extent as European colonial regimes developed into their final form in the late nineteenth and early twentieth centuries. Ethnic pluralism also developed in Thailand (Siam at that time), which shows that colonialism was not exactly a necessary condition (Skinner 1957; Wyatt 1984, 237, 417–18). But here it should be kept in mind that in Siam development from the mid-nineteenth century onward was strongly affected by colonialism in neighboring countries, that the government employed European advisors and administrators, and that the policies implemented were similar to those associated with colonialism. Ethnic pluralism therefore grew in Siam for the same basic economic reason it did elsewhere in the region: because it was useful for trade and economic development. Another problem is that in formulating the notion of the plural society Furnival was not much interested in indigenous ethnic diversity, which had always existed in a major way in Southeast Asia. He was rather concerned with situations involving groups that had come from the outside. The foreign ethnic populations that made the countries of Southeast Asia into plural societies were from many places. There were Europeans who under colonial rule dominated these regimes, but the largest numbers of outsiders were by far other Asians, above all those from India and China, especially the latter.[1] While it is perhaps not difficult to see why the notion of plural society appeared to fit the colonial regimes, it is less satisfactory as a way of viewing postcolonial ones.

PLURAL SOCIETY IN MALAYSIA

Ethnically complex societies of the sort described by Furnival developed to a greater or lesser extent in all of the Southeast Asian countries. The former British colonial territories in Malaya and northern Borneo, which became Malaysia in 1963, were the most fully developed or extreme instance. As imperialists, the British tolerated, encouraged, or actively engaged in the export and import of migrant populations from one place to another throughout the empire. Other colonial countries did this as well, though to a lesser extent. For one thing, of the various colonial powers in Southeast Asia, the British seemed to have favored pluralist policies to the greatest extent. This may have been because of their long experience in India with its great ethnic and social complexity and their confidence in managing it—at least after they got over the trauma of the great Indian Mutiny (insurrection) of 1857. Also, the British had ready access to the Indian populations that could serve their need for labor to promote development and commerce in their Southeast Asian colonies. But the British also recruited, encouraged, and facilitated the migration of large numbers of Chinese from the ports of southern China. In Malaya, the Chinese first settled in the coastal trading colonies and then moved into the Malay states of the peninsula. Some arrived before British rule, but most came after it began (Purcell [1951] 1966).

The British had several particular motives for the practices that led to the creation of a plural society in Malaya. The country had abundant land and natural resources, especially tin and timber. However, it did not have large or willing enough indigenous populations to provide the labor needed to support the developing colonial economy. And the British did not think the local Malays suitable for all of the labor tasks of the economy even if they had been numerous enough. The Malays were thought to be contented with their traditional village way of life based on rice cultivation, orchards, and fishing and therefore had little interest in becoming paid laborers. They were among "Nature's Gentlemen," as it was sometimes put. And even if they needed or wanted to exit their villages and work for wages, leaving them mainly to their customary way of life encouraged political stability. Some were employed in the colonial administration in various ways, depending on their status. And some Malays were involved in trade but were no match for the Chinese.

In Malaya, the number of both Indians and Chinese therefore grew very large. And while some Indians returned to India and some Chinese to China, the end of colonial rule saw the ethnic composition of the country transformed. In 1957, the year in which British Malaya gained independence, Malays formed 50 percent of the population, while Chinese amounted to 37 percent and Indians, 11 percent (in present-day Malaysia, these numbers are somewhat different, although Malays still form half of the total population). Both in terms of relative numbers and in some other respects (to be discussed later), Malaysia remains one of the more pluralistic nations in the world. Let us now look more closely at the Chinese and the Indians (Jain 1970, xv).[2]

INDIANS

While there are Indians in all of the countries of Southeast Asia, they went in the largest numbers to the former British colonies of Burma, Malaya, and Singapore, where their largest numbers are still found. Burma, which until 1937 was governed as a province of India, was open to immigration from the subcontinent. Indians who migrated throughout the colonial period became laborers but also worked as clerks and in various other occupations. In contrast, most of the immigrants who came to Malaya were deliberately recruited in organized arrangements involving colonial authorities in both countries. Before the practice was stopped, Indians who were recruited came mainly as indentured servants. This meant that, in return for passage, they were bound to serve a specific employer in a specific way at a specific wage for a specific number of years. After this, less coercive and exploitive forms of contract recruitment were developed.

South Indians on the Plantation Frontier

Plantations were early established as one of the principal means of making money in the colonies. As soon as the British established their first colonies on the periphery of Malaya they began to create plantations as they had done elsewhere in their tropical colonies. But the great development came after their move into the peninsula in the latter part of the nineteenth century. In creating plantations in Malaya, they initially tried different crops, including sugarcane, tea, and coffee, none of which proved as successful as they were in some other regions. By the turn of the twentieth century, the planters had settled on the new crop of rubber, for which demand was rapidly developing in relation to the auto industry. The hilly interior region that stretches all along the west coast of the peninsula was ideal rubber country—well watered by rainfall, well drained or drainable, and with adequate soils. Also, there was not much problem in obtaining land. Malay populations were concentrated in the flat plains of the far north and in lower river valleys and coastal zones. The Malayan aborigines, some hunter-gatherers and some shifting cultivators, occupied the hills and mountains of the interior. But the land rights of neither were recognized, and both were easily displaced. Western Malaya became one of the main centers of rubber cultivation in the world, and has remained so, though in recent decades rubber has been partly displaced by oil palm (see photo 4.1).

In addition to finding the best crop, the British also had to select the most suitable form of labor. Over time, workers from various ethnic groups, including Malays, Chinese, Indians, and Javanese, were tried and compared (Sandhu 1969, 55). The Malays were locally available but not, the British thought, willing to work hard, at least for the wages that planta-

Photo 4.1.   Oil palm section of a large plantation on Carry Island, Selangor, Malaysia, 1981.

tion owners wanted to pay or in the numbers needed. Opinion was mixed about the Javanese as workers, and the Dutch government placed restrictions on recruitment and migration. The Chinese were often considered to be in some ways the most capable, being hardworking, skillful, adaptable, able and willing to try to do whatever was called for—although such qualities were not necessarily the best combination of what was wanted in a plantation laborer doing highly repetitive tasks. When everything was considered, however, the natives of India were found to be ideal. But this still left the question of which Indians. Eventually, when all factors were weighed, Tamil and other ethnic groups from southern India were deemed to be the best—though even more specifically, according to the historian Kernial Singh Sandhu (1969, 56), the view was that, "of the people of the Subcontinent, the South Indian peasant, particularly the untouchable or low-caste Madrasi was considered the most satisfactory type of laborer, especially for light, simple repetitive tasks. He was malleable, worked well under supervision and was easily manageable."

Such South Indians were recruited not only to work on plantations but also to build and maintain roads, railroads, and other parts of the infrastructure of Malaya. But rubber plantations have a special and very strong connection with the immigration of large numbers of South Indians to Malaya in the twentieth century.

Often referred to as estates, plantations as a mode of production or an agricultural operation in Malaya and elsewhere have a number of common characteristics, some well known and some less so. Taken individually, these characteristics may be found in other forms of cultivation, production, or organization, but taken together they define the plantation. In brief, these include the following:

1. Plantations are devoted to the production of crops sold for cash rather than subsistence. Subsistence cultivating activities also commonly take place, but these are very secondary.
2. They are large scale in terms of land, in the size of the investment required to create and maintain them, and in the size of the labor force needed to operate them. In Malaysia, plantations are clearly differentiated from "smallholder" forms of cash crop cultivation.
3. They are usually highly specialized monocrop operations—that is, devoted to the production of a single crop (cotton, sugarcane, tea, and coffee being several of well-known older plantation crops; rubber and palm oil, the more recent ones in Southeast Asia). The activities of production usually include some processing or milling before the crop leaves the plantation for sale.
4. They usually rely on a permanent (rather than seasonal or migratory) and often resident labor force, very often one recruited or obtained

elsewhere through various means—slavery in the past, then indentured or free labor.

5. The organization of a plantation is hierarchical—when diagrammed
it takes the form of a pyramid. At the top is an owner or manager
often referred to as the planter; next, middle-level staff; and at the bottom, the workers or laborers who do the clearing, planting, weeding,
harvesting, and processing. This pattern of organization has various
corollaries including the well-known ones of status and architecture.

6. The hierarchy also often has a racial or ethnic dimension: those at the
top differ from those in the middle, and both of these from those at
the bottom.

7. Fully developed plantations also tend to be what have been called
total institutions. This means they are closed worlds that envelop
the lives of those who are a part of them, as do (to a more extreme
extent) prisons, concentration camps, and asylums. (Goffman 1961;
Jain 1970, xviii, 297)

Pal Melayu Estate

The Indian social anthropologist Ravindra Jain has provided the best and
most detailed account of the society and culture of a rubber plantation in
Malaya (Jain 1970). By the time Jain studied the large European-owned
estate he calls Pal Melayu in the west coast state of Malacca in the early
1960s, some things had changed since Malayan rubber plantations became
established in the late nineteenth and early twentieth centuries. The Indian
population of the estate sector no longer consisted almost entirely of single
men. The family household had become the basic social and economic
unit, and several generations had been locally born and raised on plantations. There had also been broader changes. Malaya had become independent of colonial rule, though only for a few years. Of the twelve plantations
in the region where Pal Melayu was located, all were owned by corporations. But while seven of these were in European hands, five had Chinese
owners. Labor unions and nationalist movements had been formed, and
Indians had begun to move from plantation work into other occupations
and into cities. Working conditions and benefits had improved somewhat,
but many of the basic characteristics of the plantation and plantation life
remained as they had been in earlier periods.

Jain found both similarities and differences between South Indian society in India and on a large plantation in Malaya. Caste had not been left
behind, but it was not and could not be the same in the two places. The
Indians who came to Malaya as labor recruits were from a much more
limited range of caste groups than existed where they had come from. Most
were from the lower castes, including many from the Adi-Dravida or "un-

touchable" groups, and this was also the case on Pal Melayu. The migrants themselves had known and lived as members of the caste system in India, with its ritual, social, and economic complexities and obligations. But those born and raised in Malaya had a much more limited and vague understanding of caste and its workings. Since no Brahmins had ever migrated to Pal Melayu or to other estates, one pole of the caste system, and the exemplification of purity, was missing. The Indians on Pal Melayu knew the specific caste groups to which they belonged by descent but they thought and talked mainly in terms of general caste categories. In such terms, there were the "non-Brahmin" grouping, on the one hand, and the Adi-Dravida, on the other. The non-Brahmins were Vanniar, a category of mainly cultivator castes in Madras. They formed just over half of the households of the laborers and were the "dominant caste." The Adi-Dravida category included four specific low-caste groups that together amounted to just under half of the households: the Pallan, Paraiyan, Ampatan, and Valluvan.

Some beliefs and practices of the traditional Indian caste system did prevail, though often in modified form. Since there were no Brahmin priests, a member of the highest caste would become a priest. But this priest would not serve members of the Adi-Dravida castes. Similarly, marriage could and did take place among the different Adi-Dravida groups but never between the higher caste group and those in the Adi-Dravida category. And finally, some members of the Adi-Dravida caste groups would perform their respective occupational activities in addition to their jobs as estate workers, but only for cash payment. The Ampatan were barbers and torchbearers, the Paraiyan were drummers and carrion removers, the Palla were gravediggers, and the Valluvan were funerary priests (Jain 1970, 350).

The Plantation as a Plural Society in Microcosm

While the Indians of Malaya formed an ethnic section of the larger society of Malaya, Pal Melayu and similar large plantations formed little plural societies in themselves. As did Furnival, Jain describes the different sectors and their relationships in terms of caste. So viewed, such an estate consisted of three castes based on ethnic differences. At the top were the Europeans who served as managers and medical officers. At the bottom were the Tamil laborers, who had their own internal caste hierarchy and arrangements, as described above. Between the Europeans and the laborers was an intermediate caste of the Asian staff or *kirani* (clerk in Malay) who served in various capacities in the plantation administrative bureaucracy. Like the workers, the Asian staff members were ethnically Indian, but they were generally different types of Indians. While the workers were Tamil laborers from the southeastern coast of India, the Asian staff had earlier been recruited from educated, often Christian Tamils from Ceylon (now

Sri Lanka). Later, Malayalee speakers from southwestern India who had earlier settled in Penang and Singapore were also hired as Asian staff. Also, smaller numbers of Telugu- and Tamil-speaking Indians and Sinhalese were from Ceylon. This general practice of hiring Asian staff from ethnic groups other than those from which the workers were recruited was deliberate and evidently due to the desire of European estate managers to avoid nepotism and corruption (Jain 1970, 211). But it also contributed to the creation of the plantation caste structure.

Each ethnic caste was closed, and the hierarchy was rigid. In addition to their traditional caste differences, workers were also ranked in terms of their labor assignments. Tappers ranked above weeders and general laborers, and foreman-recruiters or *kanganis* were far above both. There were various lines of authority among the Asian staff, and in the case of management there were sometimes assistant managers and a medical officer who served under the main manager or big boss. Within each caste sector mobility was possible. A weeder could become a tapper, and a tapper, a *kangani*; an assistant clerk could become a chief clerk, and an assistant manager, a manager. But mobility between ethnic castes was not possible. Asian staff or *kirani* could not rise to become managers, and workers could not rise to become *kirani* (296, 438–39).

There were also the other usual attributes of caste, those involving ritual, social interaction, marriage, and residence. Beyond the activities involved in directly doing the work of the plantation there was little or no open interaction between members of the different castes. Laborers did not publicly socialize with Asian staff, nor did either of these with managers. There was a certain amount of clandestine intercaste sexual interaction, but marriage was endogamous to each caste.

The differences in residential and other architectural embodiments of social hierarchy are probably the most obvious and spectacular characteristics of rubber (and probably most other) plantations. The main manager's or planter's residence is usually referred to as a bungalow. But to many readers this term may imply a more modest house—of one story and limited size—than is actually the case (15). Those on the rubber plantations of Malaya are among the most impressive forms of colonial architecture in the country (Jenkins and Jenkins 2007). Typically set apart from the other buildings and surrounded by extensive lawns and gardens, the planter's bungalow embodied the status of the head of the plantation hierarchy. The largest plantations, which have divisional or assistant managers, would have other bungalows as well (see photo 4.2).

Next came the houses of the Asian staff and then of the laborers. As would be expected, houses for the Asian staff are set separated from both the labor lines and the planter's bungalow and intermediate in size and quality. At the lower end of domestic rubber estate architecture are the houses of the

Photo 4.2. Plantation manager's bungalow, Carry Island, Selangor, Malaysia, 1981.

laborers. Because they are set in rows, these are commonly referred to as labor lines, a single house being called a line. Some are detached single structures, others are semidetached, and yet others are continuously joined. (see photo 4.3). In all cases, the houses are small, usually built uniformly on each estate or in each section, and cannot be expanded or otherwise modified. The houses are furnished by the estate and assigned to the occupants, in the past according to caste differences (Jain 1970, 13–20).

If there was little social or economic mobility on plantations like Pal Melayu, there was also little spatial mobility, at least for the laborers, among different plantations. From this perspective, the plantation was a largely closed world. Especially in the time prior to World War II, the laborer found it difficult to escape from the confines of the estate. "As long as he stayed in Malaya, serious limitations were placed upon an estate coolie's spatial movements and occupational mobility" (Jain 1970, 295). Laborers were shifted from one plantation to another, but one European-owned and managed estate was not much different from another. And aside from the difficulty of getting around because of the distances involved and the limits in transportation, there was not much reason to leave except to occasionally visit friends and relatives, to attend festivals on neighboring estates, or to have a periodic night out in the local town (for the men). The basic necessities of life and essential institutions were provided on all estates. Each had one or several Hindu temples and shrines devoted to one of the main

Photo 4.3.   Typical plantation labor-line housing, Kuala Lumpur, Malaysia, 1981.

South Indian deities, as well as clinics, schools, and shops selling provisions, snacks, toddy (palm wine), and the popular *Ekor* (three-digit lottery) tickets (113–17).

Later Developments

As mentioned above, at the time of Jain's study in the early 1960s, plantations had already changed from what they had been before the war. Malaya had become independent, and Malaysia was about to come into existence. The large European-managed estate remained a paternalistic and still partially closed community, but ethnically based political parties and a circumscribed version of trade unionism had arrived. Another study of a large European-owned and managed rubber estate that was carried out ten years later showed further change. The most striking characteristic of Ladang Getah Plantation, as studied and described by Paul Wiebe and S. Mariappen (who was born and raised on the estate), concerns the ethnic composition of the labor force. In the prewar period, the laborers had all been Indian, but afterward many Malays and a few Chinese began to displace them. By 1973, there were 218 Indians in contrast to 245 Malays and 12 Chinese working as laborers (Wiebe and Mariappen 1979, 25). The plantation was still a plural society in miniature, but a more general form of ethnic pluralism had displaced caste differences, which had been deemphasized. The labor lines that had formerly housed the low-status Adi-Dravida groups had been torn down, and households had been interspersed without regard to caste. However, the members of different ethnic sectors (Indian, Malay, and Chinese) were still separated in the labor lines and in most respects lived in isolation from one another—following different religions, speaking differ-ent languages, and reading different newspapers.

These and other such changes have continued in the postcolonial era. Because of educational policies, several generations of Malaysian Indians have now learned standard Malay, the national language, along with Tamil or another native South Asian language. Opportunities to attend middle school and higher levels have increased, as have employment opportunities apart from plantations and other laboring jobs. Because of these and other developments, plantations are no longer the isolated, closed societies they were in the colonial and, to some extent, postcolonial periods. Mobility has greatly increased. Indians who formerly walked, rode bicycles, or took local buses now have motorcycles, motor scooters, and in some instances automobiles. By the 1980s, the rubber industry had changed. Large areas of land formerly occupied by rubber estates had been converted into urban development, suburban housing tracts, and industrial zones filled with factories making calculators, electronic devices, and other high-tech gear. Rubber production had become more competitive and more highly refined, with marginal estates forced to close or to convert to oil palm in whole or part. As a result of such changes and their partial displacement as estate workers by members of other ethnic communities, one of the most strik-ing changes was the large-scale urbanization of South Indians, specifically involving the formation of huge squatter settlements built on abandoned tin mining lands in and around Kuala Lumpur and other cities of the west coast (Rajoo 1993).

CHINESE

The formation and development of Chinese communities in Southeast Asia is a more complicated and therefore less easily described matter than that of the Indians. There were and are far more Chinese throughout the region, living in a greater range of places and doing a wider range of jobs for a living. The range of cultural (and especially religious) differences among the peoples where the Chinese have settled has also been wide and has strongly affected their cultural development over time. Still, there are again commonalities that can be seen over broad areas of Southeast Asia, and both similarities and differences are considered for a good understanding of the Chinese and what has happened to them. In terms of numbers, the Chinese in Southeast Asia today are overwhelmingly an urban population associated especially with family businesses, but such an observation omits much variation. As we shall see shortly, there are or were large numbers of rural-dwelling Chinese in Malaysia.

According to current if inexact figures, some forty million persons of Chinese descent dwell in Southeast Asian countries today, making the region by far the largest center of Chinese overseas settlement in the world. The movement of Chinese into Southeast Asia has been seen as a further development of the longer expansion of China from the north to the south. As already noted, indigenous populations of the southern provinces of China that border Burma, Laos, and Vietnam include many of the same groups that dwell in these countries and in northern Thailand. Ethnic (or Han) Chinese have also moved overland from southwestern China by caravan routes into the northern Southeast Asia countries, some to trade and then return home, a few to stay. But the vast majority of immigrant Chinese in Southeast Asia came by sea rather than land. In this case, they have come mainly from the coastal provinces of southeastern China, specifically from Guangdong and Fujian, regions with a well-developed history of contact with the lands to the south. Chinese trade with Southeast Asian countries pre-dates the first European penetration into the region by several centuries or more, though the time of the first Chinese settlements is not known for certain. (Purcell [1951] 1966, 15–30). In Malacca, a Chinese trading community was present during the early Portuguese period of the early sixteenth century (238–41).

The link between the development of European colonialism and Chinese immigration is very strong. The Europeans recognized the economic value of the Chinese at an early point. The greatest movement of Chinese into the Southeast Asian countries came in the latter decades of the nineteenth and the early ones of the twentieth centuries, which was also the high period of colonial development. Like immigrants throughout the world, most arrived in cities and towns, and a great many of them remained in these places, forming ethnic enclaves. The largest populations of ethnic Chinese formed in the coastal regions and especially in the major commercial cities of these areas, including Singapore (which became a mainly ethnically Chinese city), Bangkok, Saigon, Jakarta, and Manila.

Chinese New Villages in Malaysia

In Malaysia, the fullest development of ethnic complexity has taken place on the west coast of the peninsula. Here are the largest urban centers, the tin mines, and most of the rubber plantations, all of which are associated with the immigration and settlement during the colonial period. Most Chinese in peninsular Malaysia therefore live in the west coast states, to which their forebears came in the late nineteenth and early twentieth centuries.[3]

Many began in cities or towns to pursue shopkeeping and trade. But many also sooner or later established themselves in rural areas, some as small farmers growing cash crops, some as tappers or laborers on rubber estates, and some as tin miners and loggers. By the middle of the twentieth century, Chinese villages were interspersed with those of Malays and with large rubber plantations and tin mines (Strauch 1981, 62).

Then, between 1948 and 1950, the nature of Chinese settlement changed drastically throughout the rural areas of the west coast, in response to the onset of the Emergency (as the postwar insurrection by the Malayan Communist Party [MCP] was called). The insurrection developed out of the anti-Japanese resistance during World War II that turned into an anticolonial movement. In 1948, the MCP became a terrorist movement based in the forested mountains of the interior and aimed especially at the assassination of Europeans living on remote plantations and attacks on other isolated outposts of the state. The colonial government mobilized a full military response against the insurrectionists, who were largely Chinese. How broad or deep the support was among the general Chinese community for the MCP was hard to establish. But one of the main aims of the counterterrorist effort was based on the assumption that the guerrilla groups in the forest were dependent upon rural villages for food and other support. The strategy therefore was to cut off supplies and other assistance. It was assumed that support would not come from Malay villages. This left isolated Orang Asli as well as Chinese communities, but the main targets were the Chinese living throughout the countryside (Strauch 1981, 60–62).

The Briggs Plan, as it was known, consisted of rounding up the dispersed villagers and moving them into fenced and guarded settlements (Strauch 1981, 63). Inhabitants were permitted to leave for work in the daytime but had to return by an evening curfew. The plan was implemented between 1948 and 1950 as a military operation rather than an effort at nation building or community development and was executed in that spirit. The Emergency was officially declared at an end in 1960, but the fences had been taken down in 1958. The Briggs Plan became a textbook case study of a successful counterinsurgency effort and helped inspire the strategic hamlet program in the Vietnam War. In *Seeing Like a State*, James Scott also argues that the military success of the "New Villages" as efforts at strategic and regimented resettlement also served as a model for the Malaysian Federal Land Development Authority (FELDA) schemes, which became a central pillar in the postcolonial effort to fight poverty and promote development among rural Malays—one difference being that the FELDA resettlements were not enclosed by fences (Scott 1998, 190–91).

The main point here is that the resettlement of most of the rural Chinese was a new phase in the development of the plural society in Malaysia. This is a central argument made by the anthropologist and Chinese specialist

Judith Strauch in her book-length account of the New Villages and the development of Chinese politics in the Malaysian state. Her study focused around lengthy ethnographic research in one of the New Villages (as the resettlements continued to be known) in the state of Perak that she calls Sanchum. She makes several central points, the first being that the demographic change involved was large both in numbers and in proportion. According to the 1952 official government annual report, 461,852 people had been relocated to 509 New Villages from 1948 to 1950. Later reliable studies raised these numbers to 780,000 persons and 574 villages (Strauch 1981, 63). This number may be compared to the approximately 100,000 Japanese Americans who were sent to internment camps during World War II. It also amounted to about 10 percent of the total population of the Federation of Malaya.

Second, the change was permanent. The fences were taken down in 1958, at which time the occupants were free to leave. But while some did, many remained for various reasons. The rural Chinese who were rounded up had been labeled as squatters—persons without any legal or acknowledged customary rights to the land they occupied and hence owed no compensation. Strauch states that the government's reason for the use of the term "squatter" was mainly ideological and that the assertions that the resettled Chinese were all squatters were false, though undoubtedly some were squatters (62–64). Nonetheless, many Chinese had no homes or land elsewhere to which they could return—a large problem for the many who were farmers.[4] In addition, the circumstances and nature of their origin notwithstanding, the New Villages had become real communities. People had built temporary shacks but then better, more permanent houses. They had established small businesses, had developed farms or other occupations, or were employed as rubber estate workers or loggers. There were shops and schools and transportation to other places. A few of the New Villages were abandoned, but most were still there in 1980 and probably are today, either as separate towns or as parts of larger ones (65).

The third point Strauch makes is that, while the establishment and development of the New Villages has had positive dimensions, it has also ghettoized a large portion of the rural Chinese. Before the New Villages, the rural Chinese communities had been interspersed with those of Malays and Indians on and around rubber estates. The purpose of the New Villages was to separate the Chinese villagers from the communist guerrilla insurgents, but the effect was to also separate them from their former non-Chinese neighbors. As of the late 1970s, the inhabitants of Sanchum had little relationship to the non-Chinese communities in surrounding regions, and with the exception of a few Malay government officials, the town itself remained entirely Chinese. A relevant question here is how typical Sanchum is of the nearly six hundred other villages and towns formed as New Villages. There can probably be no definitive answer. But Strauch did visit many New Villages and clearly did not think that Sanchum is unique (65).

Plural Society on the East Coast

In response to this observation, anyone familiar with Malaysia is likely to say that towns are always to some extent ethnically organized—that the business center of the town will be dominated by Chinese. This was the case with Pasir Mas in the Kelantan Plain, where I lived for several years, and in other towns in the region (see photo 4.4). Here the permanent shop-house sector of town is mainly Chinese—but not entirely so, for there are also Malay, Indian, and several Arab and Pakistani family business shops mixed in as well, and most of the customers of the businesses are Malays from the town and countryside (Winzeler 1985). The open market of small stalls is mainly made up of Malay hawkers and traders. Much the same arrangement can be seen in the market and administrative towns in Sarawak, such as Lundu and Dalat—small places set on the banks of rivers that do not seem to have changed much in a century or more and might have been in one of the Borneo novels of Joseph Conrad. Such towns are again ethnically mixed, but much of the surrounding population includes Dayak as well as Malay villages, and Dayak intermarriage with Chinese is not

Photo 4.4.   Malaysian Chinese shop-houses and Malay trishaws along the main street in the business center of Pasir Mas, Kelantan, (west) Malaysia, 1984.

uncommon. In far western Sarawak as well as in the Kelantan Plain, there are also many long-settled rural Chinese villages, for in neither place were the Chinese rounded up and placed in New Villages.

Of the two extreme models of ethnicity, such places, let alone the west coast of peninsular Malaysia, are closer to the plural society end of the spectrum than the melting pot one and seem likely to be so into the foreseeable future. But some melting has occurred and will continue to do so, and in the meantime people generally get along and cooperate.

5

Hunter-Gatherers, Real and Imagined

Southeast Asia is one of the few places in the world where hunting and gathering as a way of life has lasted to the present, or nearly so. When anthropologists use the phrase "hunting and gathering" they usually refer to a pattern of adaptation that does not include true cultivation, whether permanent or shifting, though here there are ambiguities. Hunter-gatherers may do a certain amount of plant tending, and specialists usually include those who have recently taken up limited farming in the category. Similarly, many peoples in Southeast Asia who practice cultivation, especially slash-and-burn cultivation, and live in or near forests, also do a certain amount (often a lot) of hunting and gathering, but such groups are usually considered agriculturalists or farmers. There are also sea-dwelling nomadic fishing communities of people who live on boats and have some of the characteristics of land-based hunter-gatherers (Sather 1995). However, our concern here is with land-based hunting and gathering as a way of life rather than with the supplementary or part-time foraging activities followed by many shifting cultivators. Southeast Asian hunter-gatherers are comparatively few in number and greatly outnumbered by peoples who practice shifting or permanent cultivation. An estimate of existing and former forest-dwelling hunter-gatherers placed the total at fifty thousand persons (Endicott 1999, 281; Sercombe and Sellato 2007, 3). Numbers aside, hunting and gathering ways of life are crucial to understanding the ethnological development of Southeast Asia.

Hunter-gatherers are found in both insular and mainland Southeast Asia, although unequally. In the mainland above the Malay Peninsula, there are relatively few groups; moreover, much less is known about these groups compared to those in the peninsular and insular region. The best known of the mainland groups above the peninsula are the Mlabri or Mrabri of northern

Thailand and Laos. Others that have been mentioned include the Saoch of Cambodia (Lebar, Hickey, and Musgrave 1964, 160). In the Malay Peninsula, hunter-gatherers are often lumped with swidden cultivators as Orang Asli. Of these, the hunting and gathering Negritos number about 2,500 of a total Orang Asli population of some 100,000. The number of hunter-gatherer groups throughout the Southeast Asian islands is much larger and found in a much wider range of places. From west to east, these include those of the Andaman Islands; the Kubu of Sumatra; the Penan, Punan, and others in Borneo; and the Toala of Sulawesi. Hunter-gatherers have also been reported from the Moluccas in eastern Indonesia (Lebar 1972, 119, 146). Large numbers of present-day or former hunter-gatherer peoples are also well known from a number of islands in the Philippines, totaling about thirty thousand (Sercombe and Sellato 2007, 2). Where hunter-gatherers have chosen to live is a matter of both the availability of resources and proximity to other types of people. In Borneo, for example, the availability or access to certain varieties of sago palm is a crucial consideration (Sellato 1994, 121).

The hunting and gathering peoples of Southeast Asia have attracted a degree of interest from anthropologists, prehistorians, and the wider public that far exceeds their number. Part of the interest has been because hunter-gatherers follow a way of life shared by all humans until ten or fifteen thousand years ago, although anthropologists have long stressed that present-day hunter-gatherers cannot be assumed to be exact models of those that existed before the beginning of cultivation and all of the other changes that sooner or later came with it. On a popular level, hunter-gatherers have often been taken to exemplify primitiveness, self-sufficient isolation, and vulnerability to extinction once contact with outsiders develops. Such themes have often been pursued by popular writers. The interest in hunter-gatherers has also frequently involved controversy, ranging from polite scholarly arguments over conflicting interpretations, to severe criticism and ridicule concerning accuracy and reliability, and to accusations of outright hoax.

This chapter is divided into four main parts. The first will provide an overview of the main features of hunting and gathering in Southeast Asia. The second and third will consider some of the main disputes, controversies, and popular causes involving Southeast Asian hunter-gatherers. The fourth will explore abandonment of full-time nomadic hunting and gathering, its consequences, and the state of hunter-gatherers at the present time.

AN OVERVIEW

Hunting and gathering is associated with a nomadic life. Only in very exceptional environmental conditions (none in Southeast Asia) have full-time hunter-gatherers been able to live in settlements as permanent as those occupied by cultivators. They move frequently because an area has been hunted and gathered out or because of seasonal movements of animals or variation in other resources. They may also move for other reasons, for example, to avoid contact with another group or, conversely, to be closer to one with which they have developed a useful relationship. Other characteristics to be discussed below are linked to a nomadic life.

Present-day or recent hunting and gathering in Southeast Asia shows adaptation to limited environmental variation. In some areas, hunting and gathering groups lived near the sea. But in Southeast Asia they usually live in interior, mountainous forests. Hunter-gatherers live where they do generally because of the presence of specific resources. Those in Borneo traditionally rely heavily on wild sago as a staple and always live in proximity to sago palm groves. Sago, the most common of which is *Eugeissonia utilis*, has a starchy pulp stored in the trunk. While some agricultural groups cultivate sago, the hunter-gatherers, who live where it is available, collect it wild. And with sago as a reliable staple, other subsistence provisioning involves hunting for wild pig and other forest animals and collecting fruits. Further, in addition to meeting their own subsistence needs, the hunter-gatherers of Borneo are able to forage various things to trade to surrounding groups. They are therefore also influenced in where they live by the presence of other, non-hunter-gatherer peoples, both those with whom they wish to trade and those they wish to avoid. In Southeast Asia as in most other places, hunting and gathering societies have lighter population densities than do those based upon farming, usually far lighter.

The technology and material culture of hunting and gathering is usually minimal, in part because gear and other permanent possessions must be carried each time a move is made, and in part because hunting and gathering adaptations in tropical environments do not require a wide range of tools or weapons. These include most pervasively and importantly an iron chopping knife that is used for many purposes. Weapons include spears and either the bow and arrow or a blowpipe. In Borneo, spears and sometimes blowpipes are tipped with long iron blades. None of the tools and weapons used by hunter-gatherers in Borneo are exclusive to them, and some are or were obtained from outsiders. The blowpipe, which was once widely used by cultivators as well as hunter-gatherers, is made in Borneo by drilling a shaft using an iron drill tip fixed to a long wooden handle. Before they took up ironworking themselves (now a specialty among some groups), the hunter-gatherers imported either the iron drills or the blowpipes. For use in hunting animals, blowpipe darts are tipped with small iron points and poison.[1] Hunter-gatherers as well as cultivators now also use shotguns (some homemade) for hunting.

Hunter-gatherers in Southeast Asia usually have simple forms of social organization that include bilateral kinship and little in the way of formal political authority, rank, or social strata. Hunting and gathering activities are generally reported to be gender based, whereby men hunt and women gather. This is generally so in Southeast Asia, but probably to a lesser extent than some other regions. In Borneo, both men and women hunt, using the spear for large game and the blowpipe for small game (Sellato 1994, 65). Here also, both produce the staple sago but do different parts of the work—men chopping down and splitting open the trees, women washing and straining the pulp and making the flour (122). In some communities, men as well as women gather forest products that are traded to agricultural groups.

As elsewhere, hunter-gatherers in Southeast Asia are organized as bands. A band is a small and not necessarily very permanent number of family groups that reside and move together, cooperate for some tasks, and recognize a leader usually referred to as a headman. The headman can lead, persuade, and influence but not command. Members engage in reciprocal sharing but are not really communal. They recognize members of other bands as friends, relatives, speakers of the same language, or allies but do not act in concert beyond the level of the band.

Hunter-gatherers in general are not very warlike. In Southeast Asia, they never seem to have been as warlike as cultivators, but there is a range from passivity and the avoidance of threatening contact to involvement in conflicts with other groups and an inclination to retaliate and defend territories. In the nineteenth century, the hunter-gatherers in Kalimantan (Dutch Indonesian Borneo) had a reputation for ferocity that was true of some groups in some situations but generally undeserved. Here, settled shifting cultivators traditionally followed the practice of headhunting while hunter-gatherers generally did not. But when headhunting was directed at hunting and gathering groups, some would retaliate; additionally, they were sometimes engaged by settled groups to take heads of enemies (136–39, 141–42).

Hunter-Gatherers and Cultivators

In Southeast Asia as elsewhere, the relationship of hunter-gatherers with cultivating groups has been a major topic of discussion. As known in ethnographic terms, all Southeast Asian hunter-gatherers (outside of the Andaman Islands, which are often not included in the literature on Southeast Asia) have dwelt in greater or lesser proximity to cultivating peoples, with whom they engage in economic exchange. Prehistorians have posed the question of whether hunter-gatherers could exist in deep tropical forest independently from cultivators. If they could not have done so, then their recent ecological niche is only as old as the presence of cultivation. For Southeast Asia, this is a matter of controversy to which we shall return. But certainly, while all hunting and gathering is an economic activity intended to provide food and other necessities, it also provides goods for barter and exchange. Some hunter-gatherers in Southeast Asia barter foods that they hunt and collect, such as wild game and honey, which they also consume themselves. Most or all collect forest products, such as rattan, for which they have only limited or no direct use, bird nests (those used in the famous Chinese soup), and Eagle Wood and other aromatic woods. Things that are acquired through barter include salt, iron or iron implements, tobacco, ceramic beads, and woven cloth that they cannot provide for themselves. Some, such as the Penan groups of Borneo, barter extensively with cultivating groups but only for things other than food, being self-sufficient in this regard. Today, the collection of goods for barter or sale is a very important part of the hunting and gathering economy. Contemporary or recent hunter-gatherers also work in the fields of cultivators in exchange for goods or pay.

While economic exchanges between hunter-gatherers and cultivating groups appear to be found in all areas where there are such outside groups, they do not involve all outsiders. Under traditional conditions, the foragers were very cautious about the groups with whom they established contact, and for good reason. In Borneo, "there is no lack of references in the literature to massacres of Punan by headhunters" (Sellato 1994, 137). In the Malay Peninsula, the Semang were raided and killed or captured as slaves by Malays (Endicott 1983). The Phi Tong Luang of northern Thailand have also been described as being highly suspicious of outsiders and cautious in approaching them (Bernatzik [1938] 1951). Yet, the hunter-gatherers did need or want things from the cultivators and sought them out. The initial exchanges in Borneo tended to take the form of the famous silent trade, whereby one group left what they wanted to exchange and then departed until the other had come, taken these goods, and left their own in return. As trust developed, face-to-face encounters took place, and groups of hunter-gatherers would visit the villages of the cultivators (Sellato 1994, 52, 59).

QUESTIONS AND CONTROVERSIES ABOUT SOUTHEAST ASIAN HUNTER-GATHERERS

Nomadic hunting and gathering in Southeast Asia, as elsewhere, has long generated argument and controversy. The issues involve evolution (or devolution), adaptation, identity, and authenticity. Most of these issues go beyond Southeast Asia. One already noted involves the question of whether hunter-gatherers could survive in deep tropical forests in the absence of groups of cultivators in the area with whom they could trade, and therefore of the degree and form of their separation from cultivators. Another is whether present-day hunter-gatherers are "pristine" in the sense of being the descendants of an unbroken line of foragers going back to when all people were hunter-gatherers, the alternative being that they descended from former cultivators—a situation referred to as "devolution." Finally, do the hunter-gatherers contacted by outsiders have the characteristics attributed to them or have they been exaggerated or even made up? Though they may involve broader comparisons, these issues have concerned three hunting and gathering groups in particular: the Punan of Borneo, the Phi Tong Luang of northern mainland Southeast Asia, and the Tasaday of the island of Mindanao in the Philippines.

The Punan of Borneo and the Issues of Devolution and Independence

The Punan are hunter-gatherers of Borneo, more specifically of Indonesian Borneo. "Punan" is used as a generic reference to all nomads (including now-settled ones) in Indonesian Borneo and sometimes to all those of Borneo. In Sarawak, the general term equivalent to Punan is "Penan" (although Punan is also used; Sellato 1994, 16).[2] Punan is also used in a narrow sense to identify a specific group, in which case Punan is usually combined with some other term, usually a toponym (a term for a place, in Borneo commonly a river or a mountain), for example, Punan Serata, or the Punan of the Serata River (Needham [1972] 2007; Sercombe and Sellato 2007, 11–12).[3]

The Punan have figured prominently in debates about hunting and gathering adaptation. One of these is whether some hunter-gatherers are secondary or "devolved." Groups deemed to be descendants of an uninterrupted line of hunter-gatherers have been referred to as "genuine" or "pristine" (Bellwood 1997, 134). For example, this is assumed to be the case with the Semang or Negritos of the Malay Peninsula and presumably the Negritos of the Philippines as well. There are no known Negritos or other Australoids, however, in Borneo or in Sumatra—all such populations, if they existed, have presumably been absorbed by Austronesians. All of the hunter-gatherers in Borneo speak Austronesian languages and have southern Mongoloid physical characteristics no different from those of the cultivators. The extent of cultural similarity of the hunter-gatherers to the cultivators is disputed, but it is apparent they are closer to them than are the Semang Negritos to the cultivators in the Malay Peninsula. Therefore, the Punan are just as Austronesian by descent as are the cultivators in Borneo.

But were the Austronesians at the time of their arrival several thousand years ago already cultivators? The answer here seems to be a firm yes. This would make the Punan as well as the Kubu of Sumatra the descendant of people who were once cultivators, that is, "devolved," or secondary hunter-gatherers. However, this may be an oversimplification. Did the shift from cultivation to hunting and gathering represent a drastic change or only a minor one? If the original Austronesians were heavily dependant on foraging as well as cultivation, then it would not be surprising that some became more fully specialized in hunting and gathering, while others placed greater emphasis on farming. And there is the question of whether the shift to full-time hunting and gathering took place only "once" in the past or whether it could have occurred repeatedly over the past several thousand years of Austronesian prehistory in Borneo. In the latter, "devolution" seems to be a somewhat misleading label for what took place.

Independence of Hunter-Gatherers

This brings us to the second question, which is whether hunter-gatherers could have gotten by independently of cultivators. As far as ethnological knowledge is concerned this is a hypothetical question, but it is important to Bernard Sellato (1994, 162–64), who argues that hunter-gatherers could and in the past did live completely independently of cultivators, that is, without iron or dogs or anything else the cultivators had first. Sellato's position is that, the possibility of devolution notwithstanding, the culture of hunting and gathering in Borneo has developed over a long period of time separately and very differently from that of cultivators, even though this is now coming to an end.

The general assumption about the settling down of nomadic hunter-gatherers in Southeast Asia is that it is a recent development, a process that began in the nineteenth century and has continued into the present. Sellato argues that the beginning of the shift from a nomadic hunting and gathering way of life to a settled one is much older—although the transition is continuing. He holds that what set the process in motion was the spread of iron into the interior of Borneo. Prior to this, the nomadic hunter-gatherers of Borneo lived lives of complete autonomy from the cultivators, generally far up the rivers and deep in the forest. They did not have iron, and they probably did not even have dogs, both of which later became very important parts of their adaptation. The got by with stone tools—quadrangular ground ones that could be mounted to be either axes or adzes. They could not have made the bored-through blowpipes (which require an iron bit), but there are hints of the use of the bow and arrow. With stone axes they could cut down and process the sago, which was and remains the staple in their diet. Much of their technology was bamboo and wood based, and they had an extensive knowledge of plant poisons, which are still used for fishing and dart points.

The technology of ironworking may have reached the coasts of Borneo between the fifth and the tenth century CE, after which it diffused slowly into the interior, reaching the most isolated groups only recently (Avé and King 1986, 15; Sellato 1994, 125). The iron axe or adze was a great improvement over the stone version for cutting and spitting sago palm. And iron brought the iron bit, which, attached to a wooden shaft, enabled the manufacture of the drilled-through hardwood blowpipe. The settled farmers got iron first, and once they had it they became attractive trading partners for the nomadic hunter-gatherers. For their part, the farmers welcomed trade with the nomads. However, this was not because they needed much from them for their own subsistence, which was based mainly on cultivation, especially of rice (though some researchers think the farmers also once relied more on sago). It was rather because the nomads could supply them with forest products: hornbill casque, bird nests from caves (for Chinese soup), bezoar stones, camphor and other aromatic woods, rattan, and wild honey. The farmers also gathered such things themselves for trade downriver in exchange for the imported goods they loved (especially brass gongs, Chinese ceramic jars, and trade beads). But getting the forest products from the hunter-gatherers was a profitable arrangement. Trade at first took the famous "silent" form (in which one side leaves its goods and then withdraws until the other has come, taken these, left its own, and departed). Such practices survived into the colonial period to be noted by government authorities, who sometimes intervened because they felt the hunter-gatherers were being taken advantage of. As trust developed, trade became face-to-face and the hunter-gatherers got to know the farmers and their way of life (Sellato 1994, 163–67).

The cycle went through several stages involving changes in diet, political organization, and ritual for the hunter-gatherers. With iron tools and the iron-bored blowpipe they could devote more time to foraging for things to trade to the farmers because they needed less time for just finding food to eat. It was also in the interest of the farmers to get the hunter-gatherers to do as much commercial collecting as possible. To achieve this end they tried various things, including the introduction of new "needs" among the hunter-gatherers, such as an appreciation for imported glass and ceramic beads, of which the farmers had long been connoisseurs. A crucial part of the farmers' strategy was to get the hunter-gatherers to shift their camps less frequently, to locate them closer to their own villages, and to spend even more time collecting valuable things from the forest. This meant teaching them to grow some of their own food, especially, at first, tubers. As cultivation took hold among the hunter-gatherers, the sexual division of labor changed further to one in which women did even more of the daily work of subsistence and men concentrated more on commercial collecting and trade. Such hunter-gatherers had become semisettled. Eventually, some of these partially domesticated hunter-gatherers acquired a taste for rice and began growing it as well (167–70).

Here there was an important fork in the evolutionary road. Some of the semisettled, part-time cultivating groups of hunter-gatherers continued as they were. Others, however, went on to become fully settled farmers (that is, as fully settled as shifting cultivators themselves were), building longhouses, becoming headhunters, and taking on the ritual complex of secondary mortuary practices (known as *nulang* and found over a wide arc in central Borneo) and other longhouse ceremonial activities. These former hunter-gatherers who became settled longhouse-dwelling farmers can still be recognized because, while they learned to eat rice, they never entirely lost their fondness for sago, as is the case with the various Kajang groups of Sarawak. As iron had been fundamental in getting the cycle started, rice became the key to the next stage in its development.

But from the perspective of the farmers, the full domestication of the former nomadic hunter-gatherers was a failure in strategy. This was because such groups lost their interest in commercial collecting, presumably because they were too busy growing rice, holding elaborate ceremonies, and doing the other things that go along with agriculture and settled village life. In some instances, the farmers (for example, the Kayan in the Apo Kayan Plateau in the deep interior of East Kalimantan) realized that rice cultivation and settled life for their client or partner hunter-gatherers was not a good idea as far as their own interests were concerned. They tried to dissuade their Punan collectors from eating and cultivating rice and resisted colonial government efforts to encourage them to settle. And in some cases, the Punan themselves saw rice eating and cultivation as an important symbol, a crucial line to be crossed, and resisted it. Also, the farming way of life was not always attractive to the independent Punan. Among the northern hunter-gatherers, the settled farming groups with whom they developed trading relationships were highly stratified into classes of nobles, commoners, and slaves. Not all Punan were necessarily willing to accept the low esteem in which they were held by their settled trading partners. When it came to assimilation, some chose the nonhierarchical groups such as the Iban rather than the stratified ones like the Kenyah and Kayan (171–75).

In addition, settling down was not always a one-way street. For one reason or another, some Punan groups began to settle into villages but then returned to a nomadic way of life in the forest. Sellato gives as an example the Punan Lusong who had begun to grow rice in 1941 but then returned to the forest after the Japanese invasion and did not settle again until 1961 (174). In the colonial and postcolonial periods, different groups of Punan continued to exist in varying states of nomadism and sedentism. Sellato stresses that hunting and gathering and cultivation are not polar opposites but activities that form points along a continuum on which a clear boundary between where one ends and the other begins cannot be found (162–64).

Moreover, evidence is limited regarding the prehistory of both hunting and gathering and farming ways of life in the interior of Borneo. Again, there is doubt about whether hunting and gathering in deep tropical forest was possible for hunter-gatherers before the arrival of the farmers, who could provide them with carbohydrates through trade. But the viability of swidden farming in the deep tropical forest before iron (especially swidden farming based on rice cultivation) is questionable, for rice and other cereal crops require extensive clearing. Iron tools made this much faster and simpler. Iron axes made it much easier for cultivators to cut down the great hardwood trees in the initial clearing of mature forest. And iron chopping knives would have greatly facilitated the clearing of brush, bamboo, and smaller trees in the second and later stages of swidden cultivation. In sum, this will probably not be the last word on cultural evolution in the interior of Borneo.

HUNTER-GATHERERS AS OBJECTS OF INTEREST, CONTROVERSY, AND CONCERN

Over the course of the twentieth century, various hunting and gathering peoples in Southeast Asia became the subjects of widespread public interest through popular accounts and journalistic attention. In this section, we shall consider three instances, beginning with the Phi Tong Luang of northern Thailand.

Spirits of the Yellow Leaves

Until early in the twentieth century, no hunting and gathering groups were known with much certainty to exist north of the Semang of the Malay Peninsula. However, there were rumors about a very primitive people living deep in the forests of far northern Thailand near the border with Laos. Or perhaps the rumors were not about people but rather spirits, for the Thai referred to them as Phi Tong Luang, which translates as "Spirits of the Yellow Leaves." The latter part of the name is supposedly a reference to their practice of building simple shelters covered with green leaves, abandoning them, and moving to a different place as soon as the leaves became yellow.[4]

Knowledge of the Phi Tong Luang came to outsiders mainly via Hmong, Khamu, and other upland cultivators who traded with them as well as with the lowlanders. Early in the twentieth century, written reports began to appear in the *Journal of the Siam Society*. Then in the 1930s, an Austrian ethnographer, Hugo Bernatzik, sought to contact and study the elusive and still mysterious Phi Tong Luang. By using Hmong guides in the region where Phi Tong Luang were supposed to live, he eventually succeeded. As a result, Bernatzik produced a lengthy account in *The Spirits of the Yellow Leaves* (first published in German in 1938 and in English in 1951). The account offered much in the way of reportedly factual information based on interviews and conversations conducted through Hmong interpreters with the Phi Tong Luang who were willing to visit Bernatzik's camp.

Especially after it was translated into English, Bernatzik's account became well known but also controversial. The most striking feature of his description of the Phi Tong Luang is his elaboration of what they lacked in the way of taken-for-granted human abilities: powers of reasoning and common knowledge. He writes that they were incapable of abstract thought and of drawing conclusions, and that they had no capacity for thinking ahead (Bernatzik [1938] 1951, 125, 140). While a few of the Phi Tong Luang had acquired spears from the Hmong, they did not know how to throw them, he wrote (138). They knew no fairytales, songs, or dances (141). They had no knowledge of either black or white magic, religious fraternities, religious dances, or cult centers (159). These and other claims Bernatzik makes about the extreme primitiveness of the Phi Tong Luang suggest a very cursory understanding involving especially inadequate communication, plus perhaps an inclination to exaggerate and to find what he was looking for.

Although the work is still cited today, not all anthropologists who read *Spirits of the Yellow Leaves* were convinced that the Phi Tong Luang were real or of the truth of Bernatzik's description of them. In his popular textbook *Hill Farms and Padi Fields* (1965), Robbins Burling suggests that Bernatzik had himself imaginatively named the Phi Tong Luang and that he had said such incredible things about them that his account could not be taken seriously. They were for Bernatzik the answer to his search for the ultimate primitive people. A linguistic anthropologist, Burling did not believe the Phi Tong Luang could lack personal names and first-person pronouns in their language, as he claimed Bernatzik had said. Bernatzik had perhaps let his own theories or the German racist doctrines then popular in his homeland get the better of him. This was too bad, Burling concluded, for if the Phi Tong Luang really did exist it would be interesting to know something about them (Burling 1965, 21–22). Burling himself may not have read any accounts of the Phi Tong Luang other than Bernatzik's, though they existed.

Actually, by the time that Burling's book was published, the Phi Tong Luang had in effect been certified as an authentic, if not well-known, ethnic group in no less an authoritative ethnological work than Frank Lebar, Gerald Hickey, and John Musgrave's *Ethnic Groups of Mainland Southeast Asia* (1964, 132–35). Burling was aware of this work, for Burling himself served as a contributing editor and had provided an entry of his own—though not on the Phi Tong Luang but rather on the Garo of Assam. The *Ethnic Groups of Mainland Southeast Asia* entry on the Phi Tong Luang listed them as Yumbri, which Bernatzik had reported as the name by which they referred to themselves. The book also provided a fairly lengthy description based on Bernatzik and several other sources. Information has continued to be published by Thai as well as European scholars. In the more recent accounts, Yumbri has been changed to Mlabri or "People of the Forest," while Phi Tong Luang was extended to include related or similar groups living elsewhere in both Thailand and Laos, and perhaps Burma as well. Although a geographical outlier (though not the only one), the Phi Tong Luang now appear to be similar to other, better-known, Southeast Asian hunter-gatherers. They speak a Mon-Khmer language with some loan words from Tai and Khmu (another Mon-Khmer language; Pookajorn 1992; Trier 1986, 7–9).[5]

Tasaday Controversy

By the time the reality of the Mlabri and related groups of Phi Tong Luang had been established and the ethnographic record about them had been filled out and corrected, yet another previously unknown Southeast Asia hunting and gathering group had been reported. Known as the Tasaday, this very small group had supposedly been contacted in the forested interior of Mindanao in the southern Philippines and also declared to be a primitive relic from former times. Compared to the questions raised by Bernatzik's account of the shy and elusive Phi Tong Luang, the controversy that eventually followed the claims made about the Tasaday was of a larger magnitude. As it later came to be phrased, the central issue was whether the initial introduction of the Tasaday to the outside world amounted to a hoax or whether they were, on the contrary, real—the exact meaning of "real" being part of the problem.

The possibility that the Tasaday were what they were first presented as being now, in the fullness of time, seems remote. Thus, the value of the Tasaday study as reliable information that contributes to our understanding of the ethnology of hunter-gatherers in Southeast Asia seems slight. This is perhaps why many specialists in hunting and gathering groups elsewhere in Southeast Asia did not become involved in the debates or otherwise seem to pay much attention to them, at least in publication. The Tasaday did become extremely important in terms of the interest that the broader public media took in the discovery of an alleged group of "Stone Age hunter-gatherers." The controversy that developed over the Tasaday was eventually officially taken up by the American Anthropological Association (AAA) to become one of the two principal disputes about indigenous peoples in the latter part of the twentieth century.[6] Hence, no discussion of Southeast Asian hunter-gatherers would be complete without some account of the Tasaday. Here in brief is what took place over a twenty-year period according to Thomas Headland, one of the anthropologists who did become involved:

In 1971 a band of cave-dwelling people called Tasaday were discovered living
in a remote area of rain forest in the Philippines. These twenty-six individuals
were reported to be following a Paleolithic lifestyle, surviving solely on wild
foods and wearing leaves for clothing. Throughout 1972 and 1973 there was
an almost continuous stream of outsiders flown in to visit the Tasaday people.
They included politicians, movie stars, journalists, filmmakers, and about a
dozen scientists. (Headland 1992, 3)

Somewhat reminiscent of Bernatzik's account of the Phi Tong Luang, but
going much further, the main emphasis in the early Tasaday accounts was
on their anachronistically primitive state. Reportedly, they only had crudely
made stone tools, simple digging implements, and sticks for making fire.
They lacked houses, art, weapons, dogs, and pottery. They had no knowledge of the outside world beyond their immediate forest surroundings,
although they were only three hour's walk from a village of farmers and
twenty miles from the sea. They were not even complete hunter-gatherers,
for they did not know how to hunt. They survived by foraging for roots,
wild bananas, grubs, berries, crabs, and frogs from streams.

The popular coverage of the Tasaday was extensive and accepting of
their authenticity and primitive uniqueness. There were two stories in the
National Geographic Magazine; a documentary film made for television, also
by the National Geographic Society; and another film made by NBC. The
journalist John Nance produced a long book in 1975, followed by a "photo
novel" and a photographic account for young readers. There was little published dissent to the story that was promulgated in the early 1970s. The
French-trained Filipino cultural anthropologist Zeus Salazar was alone in
writing scholarly articles in 1971 and 1973 questioning the basic claims
that had been made about the Tasaday (Salazar 1971, 1973). Cultural anthropologists or archaeologists who were familiar with hunter-gatherers in
Southeast Asia or elsewhere might well have been skeptical but, having no
firsthand knowledge of the group or the region, may have been reluctant
to weigh in.

In 1974, the government stopped all visits. After the international flurry
of articles and TV films by the news media in the early seventies, no further
word was heard about the Tasaday for thirteen years. Then in 1986, reports
appeared in the international press that the whole story had been a hoax.
In the following months, hundreds of articles appeared in newspapers all
over the world (Headland 1992, 3). The hoax phase of the Tasaday story
began when Oswald Iten, a Swiss anthropologist and journalist, visited
the Tasaday in March 1986 (Iten 1992). This was shortly after the fall of
Ferdinand Marcos, who had signed the decree in 1974 banning researchers
or other visitors from contacting the Tasaday without government permis-
sion. Having reviewed the earlier claims and finding the Tasaday wearing
regular clothes and living in houses, Iten pronounced the Tasaday of the

earlier accounts to be fraudulent. Other reporters and similar stories soon followed. Documentaries were again produced and shown on television, this time about the hoax. The *National Geographic* countered with the claim that the hoax story had been largely discredited. But the public story was that the researchers and others who had originally visited the Tasaday had been taken in, and the world had been deceived. Scholarly symposia soon followed. The first was held in 1986 in the Philippines where some scholars had long had doubts, though perhaps kept from publication by fear of retaliation by the Marcos government. The next symposium took place at an international anthropology meeting (of the International Congress of Anthropological and Ethnological Sciences) in Zagreb, Yugoslavia, in 1988. A third was held at the annual meeting of the AAA in Washington, D.C., in 1990 (Headland 1992, 10–11).

Headland, an applied American anthropologist and Philippines specialist, organized the AAA symposium. Not among the earlier scholars who visited and wrote about the Tasaday, he took an evenhanded approach. Headland invited both the earlier scholars who had produced the initial reports depicting the Tasaday as a genuine, isolated Stone Age relic and the critics of this position. He was then asked to prepare an edited volume based on the symposium papers plus additional comments by relevant specialists, to be published by the AAA in its scholarly series. This publication appeared in 1992 as *The Tasaday Controversy: Assessing the Evidence*. In addition, the AAA had also separately asked Fred Eggan, a well-known anthropologist and Philippines specialist, to also investigate the Tasaday controversy and prepare a report for the association. However, Eggan died in 1991 before the report was completed (1).

The Tasaday Controversy is the most important and complete scholarly document to be published on the controversy, but it does not fully answer the question of the authenticity of the Tasaday. The authors of the original "real Tasaday" accounts who contributed to the volume did a certain amount of retrenching and redefining but basically stuck to their original positions. Several of the most important early authors, including anthropologists Frank Lynch and Robert Fox, had died (3). So had Manuel Elizalde, the Filipino head of Panamin (Philippine government organization for the protection of indigenous peoples). It was Elizalde who had originally claimed to find the Tasaday living in the cave and (with Fox) wrote the first published account, introducing the various scientists and other visitors to them. Nance, who had written the widely read *The Gentle Tasaday*, did not contribute to the volume, although he did address the hoax charge elsewhere. The outside commentators had mixed views. The linguist Lawrence Reid concluded on the basis of linguistic evidence that there had probably not been a hoax. Another, the American anthropologist and archaeologist William Longacre, wrote that he could not make up his mind if a hoax had taken place but suggested excavating the cave (apparently never done) as a way of determining if it had really been occupied for very long, one of the crucial early claims. The skeptics included the cultural anthropologist Robert Carneiro from the American Museum of Natural History, a specialist in Amazon peoples who had a particular interest in stone tools. Carneiro left little doubt that the stone axes of the Tasaday were not plausibly made, hafted, or usable—and that they seemed to have been made by someone with no knowledge at all of how to make such tools. The disbelievers also included the cultural anthropologist Richard Lee, a well-known specialist in hunter-gatherers from the University of Toronto, and an expert on the !Kung hunter-gatherers of southern Africa. He listed six lines of important evidence that indicated some sort of hoax had to have been perpetrated (Headland 1992, 6; Lee 1992).

The hoax view was set out at the beginning of *The Tasaday Controversy* by Gerald Berreman, a cultural anthropologist at the University of California at Berkeley. Berreman was a specialist in India and in human inequality rather than in Southeast Asia or hunter-gatherers, but he had read the materials on the Tasaday and was convinced they could not be as they had been presented. He began by building upon the criticisms made by Salazar and presented a table of nineteen claims made in the 1970s about the Tasaday. These, he continued, had been or could readily be shown to be wrong—nor were they simply mistakes. They were the result of deliberate deceptions carried out by two individuals. One of these was a local indigenous man named Dafal who, it was said, was the first outsider to discover the Tasaday and who went on to introduce them to the ways and goods of the wider world. The other was Elizalde, who held a cabinet position in the Marcos government and was presumably the man behind it all. Elizalde had the assistance of several associates who among other things did the translating for the scientists and other visitors. Finally, the deception would not have worked without the participation of those local people who had dressed up in leaves and become the Tasaday (Berreman 1992).

Who then were the Tasaday? Some of those who accepted the genuineness of the Tasaday took them to be, as noted, cave-dwelling survivors of the Paleolithic. Another possibility was that they were "secondary" or devolved hunter-gatherers, the descendants of cultivator-foragers who, in the not very distant past, had for some reason (to escape an epidemic, enemies, or some other unknown threat) escaped into the forest, became full-time foragers, and lost the other cultural characteristics of their farmer ancestors. This explanation was a fallback position for those who accepted the implausibility of the original full caveman-survivor interpretation but did not want to abandon it entirely. It also has the virtue of accounting for both the troubling linguistic and physical similarity of the Tasaday to surrounding peoples. And it is compatible with the limited-hoax, partial-fabrication, or exaggeration (as you like) position. This is the position Headland seems to take in his conclusion to the book (Headland 1992, 215–24).

The Penan and Logging

As the Tasaday controversy was entering its hoax phase in the late 1980s, international public interest became increasingly focused on yet another Southeast Asia hunting and gathering people: the Penan of Malaysian Sarawak in Borneo. By this time, the scholarly dispute over the autonomy of hunting and gathering groups from cultivators in Borneo had been going on for several decades and was also reaching a peak. But the latter dispute did not become a public issue or have much bearing on the new development. The issue that attracted attention was rather an environmentalist one that concerned the consequences of logging or, more specifically, of greatly increased logging in Sarawak. Through the building of new roads in the forests and mountains in northern Sarawak, logging had been extended deep into the interior, thus both further depleting ancient equatorial forests and threatening the way of life of the previously remote and, to the outside world, little-known Penan hunters-gatherers. Although logging also affected the indigenous cultivating peoples, especially the Kenyah and Kayan, the very photogenic and appealing Penan became the poster children for the controversy (Bevis 1995; Brosius 2007).

The story of the Penan and the destruction of the rain forest had some things in common with that of the Tasaday. The assertion that the Penan were an incredible, previously unknown remnant of the Stone Age was never made. But in both instances, there was a story of the intrusion of the outside world on a simple people who lived close to nature. In both instances there was also a white outsider who had came to their assistance (though in the case of the Tasaday, a self-proclaimed one in the person of Elizalde)—a version that critics of Hollywood films, such as *Dances with Wolves* and *Avatar*, call the popular white-Messiah-who-tries-to-save-the-nonwhite-natives theme. For the Penan, this was Bruno Manser, a Swiss artist and traveler. Manser encountered the Penan in 1984 while exploring the Mulu Caves in northern Sarawak and lived with them for six years. According to his critics, Manser played a major role in organizing Penan resistance to the encroachment of loggers through blockades and in publicizing their struggle (Richie 1994). Manser went missing in Sarawak on a return trip in May 2000 and was declared dead by the Swiss government in 2005. Foul play was widely suspected but not proved. The story of the Penan and Manser has been told in newspaper articles, books (including one by Manser, based on diaries kept while he with living with the Penan), and several documentary films (Bevis 1995; Manser 1996; *Blowpipes and Bulldozers* [1988], *Tong Tana* [2001]). While some things remain in question, including what happened to Manser, the general outline of what took place is not a matter of dispute.

The story begins in the early 1980s following an expansion of logging based on a shift in how and where it was practiced: from mainly a river-based to an increasingly land-based system of transportation and to moving logging machinery in and logs out by road rather than river. This involved the use of trucks and dirt roads cut through forests and mountains, circumventing river rapids, waterfalls, and shallow water to get to previously unreachable forests. This shift resulted in the penetration of logging much farther into the interior of Sarawak. The change was especially significant for the watersheds of the Baram and Rajang rivers and their tributaries. These are the largest river systems in the state, among the largest in Borneo, and the home to the largest number of Penan as well as to large numbers of Kenyah and Kayan and other longhouse-dwelling shifting cultivators.

Put very briefly and simply, the public controversy that developed in the second half of the 1980s and 1990s pitted the loggers, the state government of Sarawak, and the national government of Malaysia against the Penan and other indigenous communities and against local and international environmentalists. Logging did not affect only the Penan, but it appears to have done so more adversely than in the case of the swidden cultivators. The latter groups had some control over what happened. The loggers were supposed to negotiate with the villagers if they wished to log on their customary lands or build roads across them. The villagers could and did ask the loggers for things like using their bulldozers to level land for the building of a new longhouse or a football field or to drag logs to the village for building materials. Many village men went to work in logging concessions, and the wealth generated is reflected in the new and elaborate longhouses that could be seen along the rivers of the interior of central and northern Sarawak, though the compensation paid by the loggers may have been paltry in comparison to the value of the timber taken out or destroyed and the game killed or driven away. Also, what would happen to employment once the forests had been logged out and the logging companies moved on? But commercial logging clearly had its attractions as well as its drawbacks for the swidden cultivators, who, further, were used to cutting the forest for their swiddens—though to a far more limited extent.

But for the Penan there were few benefits in comparison to the liabilities. Unlike the land rights of shifting cultivators, which are officially recognized under customary law in Sarawak, those of the Penan and other hunter-gatherers have been left out. However, according to J. Peter Brosius, an anthropologist and Penan specialist, of the two divisions of Penan in Sarawak (east and west), it has been the eastern Penan who have actively resisted logging, while the western Penan (although they do not like it either—to put it mildly) have accepted it and done what they can to benefit from it

(Brosius 2007, 290–92). The public controversy did not extend across the border to the Punan in Indonesian Borneo.

The environmentalist position was that the logging was destructive in both the long and short run, and that the rights of the Penan and their traditional way of life were also being destroyed. Such claims were countered by assertions by the pro-loggers that logging was legal, necessary to the development of the country—the usual justification for almost anything governments want to do in this part of the world—and practiced in a sound and sustainable manner (unlike, it was said, Western logging, which involved clear-cutting). The pro-loggers also asserted that the Penan and other local people would not have objected to logging at all if they had they not been stirred up and misled by outsiders, especially neocolonialist Western troublemakers who wanted to see Malaysia held back and the Penan kept in their impoverished primitive state. There were even hints of links between antilogging environmentalists and local communist terrorists. There were other complications, some with overtones of ethnic animosity. The logging companies were mainly ethnic Chinese-owned operations, though with substantial involvement of Malay and Dayak political leaders as well.

The controversy continued into the 1990s when most of the books and documentaries appeared, and was briefly revived with the news of the disappearance of Manser in 2000. The blockades of the logging roads ceased, and some accommodations with the Penan and other indigenous resisters were made, but the logging continued. In the meantime, attention came to be focused increasingly on a different (but not unrelated) environmental development involving the Penan and other indigenous groups on the upper Balui River, one of the principal tributaries of the Rajang. This was the construction of the Bakun Dam. Planning and preparations began in the late 1980s and have continued, on and off, until the present.

SOUTHEAST ASIAN HUNTER-GATHERERS TODAY

While Southeast Asia hunter-gatherers have undergone many and varied changes, the most important has been the abandonment of a totally nomadic existence based solely on foraging for a partially or entirely settled one usually based in part on cultivation and other income-generating activities. Foraging has also changed from being mainly or entirely subsistence oriented to involving, in part, collecting forest products for trade. The process of abandoning full nomadic hunting and gathering appears to have taken place all across Southeast Asia. How many hunter-gatherers continue to follow a fully nomadic way of life is not known, but the number in relationship to how many once did so must be very small—Peter Sercombe and Bernard Sellato suggest in a recent publication a few hundred in comparison to perhaps twenty thousand former hunter-gatherers for all of Borneo (Sercombe and Sellato 2007, 1, 7).

If we begin with the question of why nearly all former nomads now live in more permanent settlements, a simple but vague answer might be that the outside world has intruded on them to the extent that they no longer have much choice. Population increase, the expansion of permanent and shifting cultivation, the depletion of forests due to logging, the conversion of forests to oil palm estates, the construction of dams, and the development of national parks come readily to mind. For what it is worth, I asked the headman of a Mlabri settlement in Nan Province in northern Thailand in 2006 why his group had left the forest some years before. He replied that a Hmong village had been relocated nearby, and the animals on which they had depended for food had been killed or driven away. The village men are now working for the Hmong as agricultural laborers. As in this instance, governments in general want to see the nomads settle down, join the modern world, and become developed and, better yet, blend into the wider society. The hunter-gatherers are not unaware of what is happening around them or immune to the argument that they should become part of the national society—that their children will be better off if they go to school, have access to modern medical care, and can earn a cash income.

But while there appear to be commonalities, the processes that have led to the abandonment of nomadic hunter-gatherer lifeways have varied. The consequences of becoming sedentary and the current well-being of those who have done so have also varied somewhat. For the most part, the picture presented in the current literature seems bleak. This picture was drawn several decades ago by James Eder in his *On the Road to Tribal Extinction*, a study of the consequences of ecological and social change among the Batak of the island of Palawan in the Philippines. The title of the book seems somewhat exaggerated. While it suggests a process of physical annihilation, what had really happened was more a matter of cultural extinction, disorganization, dependency, and partial assimilation into the lowest ranks in Filipino society. But the title notwithstanding, what Eder discusses appears to be very similar to what researchers have described as having happened to the Semang and other Orang Asli in peninsular Malaysia, to which we now turn.

Settlement of Nomads in Peninsular Malaysia

The accounts of the settlement of the nomadic hunter-gatherers in peninsular Malaysia emphasize the role of government, though other developments are noted as well. Early plans to get the nomadic and other Orang Asli into sedentary villages began during the colonial period before World War II as a means of controlling contact and introducing agricultural modernization. These efforts were blocked by the onset of the war and the arrival of

the Japanese and put on hold until the 1950s. They were revived in a different form because of the development of the communist insurgency and the
government effort to resettle the Orang Asli out of concern they would be
used by insurgents as sources of food, shelter, and information. The goals
were limited to military counterinsurgency and did not include development. Conditions were crowded, food and housing were poor, malnutrition
and illness developed, and many Orang Asli died while others escaped and
returned to the forest. Eventually, the resettlement camps for the Orang Asli
were shut down and the inhabitants allowed to leave (Dentan et al. 1997,
61–66). While resettlement understandably gained a bad reputation among
the Orang Asli, government efforts to do so were revived a few years later.
This time, the settlements were located in or near the home areas of the
groups to be relocated and without the barbed-wire fences. The new efforts
had some success with those Orang Asli who were settled swidden cultivators but not with the nomadic groups.

One attempt involving the nomads was a settlement established on
the Lebir River in the deep interior of the state of Kelantan. Finding the
dispersed camps of the nomads and persuading them to be moved was
difficult, but the various bands in the area were found and resettled on the
promise that the government would be providing rice and other rations.
The plan was for the state government to supply rice while the nomads
cleared and cultivated land with the expectation that, by the end of a year,
they would be able to feed themselves. The scheme failed. After a year, it
was clear that the settlers had not been able to provide enough cultivated
food to support themselves. The government then decided to continue the
expensive rice rations for another six months, after which the settled nomads were told they were now on their own. The day they were so informed
they did what hunter-gatherers quite logically do when the local food supply runs out. Re-forming into their original small bands, they returned to
the forest and to full-time foraging (Carey 1976, 117–18).

Efforts at settling the Semang nomads, as well as resettling the other,
much more numerous Orang Asli groups who practiced shifting cultivating,
continued after Malaya became independent in 1957. Some of these were
more successful in that the settled groups did not simply abandon the area
and return to their traditional way of life in the forest. What happened initially was partial rather than full settlement. At a settlement established on
the other side of the main range in the state of Kedah, the settlers were given
a few acres of rubber as well as other land for cultivation. But they did not
really take to rubber tapping and tended to lease their trees out—nor did
they become good farmers, although they had not been given enough land
for cultivation in any case. The settlement became a base camp where they
would stay for a few weeks before returning to the forest for several weeks to
forage, leaving behind only the very old and the very young. However, the

partially settled villagers were drawn further away from subsistence hunting and gathering and into a cash economy. The main focus of foraging shifted from subsistence-oriented hunting and gathering to the collection of rattan and other forest products for sale to middleman dealers, who also tended to hook them on debt (119–21).

A partially settled life for the formerly fully nomadic Semang groups, based on a combination of limited cultivation and foraging concentrated on commercial collecting, might have continued if the wider world of peninsular Malaysia had not begun to change rapidly after the end of colonial rule. This, however, was what happened. More specifically, there were a number of interrelated developments. Most importantly, the forest, which had not long before covered most of the entire interior of the Malay Peninsula, began to disappear rapidly through logging. Moreover, logging was followed in many areas (especially in the western part of the peninsula) by the permanent conversion of the land to other uses, especially rubber and oil palm plantations. Therefore, except perhaps in a few protected areas, full-time foraging would not have remained an option for many hunter-gatherers. In addition to these changes in the environment, the Malaysian government became much more fully committed to the settlement of all Orang Asli groups, though without (except in rare instances) creating reserves or other recognition of their rights to land. The Malaysian anthropologist Alberto Gomes, who has been studying what has happened to the onetime nomadic foragers for several decades, has provided a recent account of resettlement and its consequences:

> In 1979 the government proposed to create twenty-five regroupment schemes to be implemented within ten to fifteen years. In these schemes large tracts of forest areas would be cleared and developed into cash crop plantations and settlements.
>
> By the late 1990s eighteen schemes were set up, involving roughly 10,700 people living in slightly more than 2,500 households. (Gomes 2007, 69)

The reasons given for the resettlement schemes by the government are to be able to provide education, medical care, and economic opportunities for the Orang Asli and to bring about their integration into national Malaysian society. However, "it is apparent that a large number of these resettlement schemes, if not all, have been implemented with other agendas in mind. . . . Many villages have been resettled to make way for commercial logging, land schemes for Malays, agribusiness plantations, golf courses, and the construction of roads and dams" (70; see also Dentan et al. 1997, 117–50).

More specifically, the model for the settlements created for both the former nomads and the other Orang Asli groups were the Federal Land Development Authority (FELDA) schemes created to relocate Malay villagers from regions where agricultural lands were deemed inadequate. The houses provided are similar in design and placement to those created for Malays in the Malay resettlement schemes, as are other aspects of the settlements and the economic base for the new life (Gomes 2007, 77–78). The Malay model also includes encouragement to convert to Islam, which in Malaysia is termed *masuk Melayu*, "to become Malay."

Hunter-Gatherers in Indonesian Borneo Today

We shall end this chapter on a more positive note, one of a sort that is hard to find in the literature on the present state of hunter-gatherers in Southeast Asia. In a recent account published in *Beyond the Green Myth*, Sellato takes up the question of the current position of the Punan, the now mostly former nomadic hunter-gatherers in Kalimantan. Here the main point is that in contrast to what has happened to the Penan in Malaysian Sarawak (especially as shown in the popular media that plays up their status as hapless victims of progress), the situation of the Punan has potentially improved considerably. As a result of several developments, the Punan have "come to occupy incredibly vast expanses of interior territories, to be recognized by the [Indonesian] Administration as the *de jure* holders of these territories and increasingly by the day, to be acknowledged as their rightful, exclusive managers and users" (Sellato 2007, 61). He goes on to say that the recent changes have not necessarily contributed much to improve the true social and economic welfare of the Punan. However, this is not as bad as often portrayed. The Punan today should not be regarded as poor, let alone helpless. Their economic circumstances are "in fact rather good, especially when compared to Indonesia's urban and peri-urban poor" (something that should probably not surprise anyone familiar with Indonesian cities; 86).

A number of developments have led to the present improvements, several of which are somewhat unique to Kalimantan. The interior of Kalimantan is vast, and much of it is still remote (more so probably than any other part of Indonesia outside of New Guinea). Roads are few, and river travel above rapids and shallows is difficult and expensive. The transmigration program of resettlement from Java and Bali has more or less ended. The population of the deep interior is very light in comparison to much of the rest of the country, including the coastal regions of Kalimantan. The tendency has been for some of the settled farming peoples (and some Penan) who have traditionally occupied the remote, mountainous, deep interior regions to migrate or be moved downriver to areas nearer to the coast where there are better economic opportunities, schools, and services. These somewhat unique (for Indonesia and Southeast Asia) geographic and demographic circumstances have worked in concert with changing political circumstances that have also favored Punan land rights. These include the governmental alterations that have taken place since the fall of the Suharto regime in 1998—toward decentralization, greater provincial autonomy, and a reduction in the power of the military. They also include the influence or pressure that environmental and other nongovernmental organizations (NGOs) and religious groups have brought to bear on the government in favor of Punan rights and welfare (82–86).

However, the Punan are not doing as well as they should be, given the favorable combination of circumstances that has emerged in recent years. Several other contributors to *Beyond the Green Myth* make similar points about both the Punan and the Penan of Sarawak.[7] According to Sellato, they are held back above all because they continue to be strongly influenced by attitudes and orientations that are part of what he calls the ideology of hunting and gathering. They are no longer living as nomadic foragers with only limited economic and social relationships with settled farmers. But they have not yet gotten beyond cultural ways that were appropriate to nomadic hunting and gathering but no longer suit present circumstances. They are individualistic and familial, and retain a short-term time orientation. Therefore, they have not yet been able to organize collectively or bargain as well as they should with government officials; logging, mining, or plantation companies; or coastal traders who now buy their forest products. And as a result, they remain dependent on NGOs and religious groups to represent their interests and will not act unless some form of immediate assistance is involved. Sellato concludes they will have to give up some of their "Punan-ness" in order to make further progress (86–89; see also Sercombe and Sellato 2007, 46–49).

6

Swidden Farmers

As elsewhere in the developing world, a vastly larger portion of the population in Southeast Asia lives by farming rather than hunting and gathering. Traditional farming includes two main types of cultivation. One of these is swidden or shifting cultivation, also referred to as slash and burn—though this phrase in particular seems to be losing favor. Here, the preparation of a field begins with cutting down trees, brush, bamboo, and grass and burning these after they have dried (see photo 6.1). The burned fields are not plowed and could not be without a great deal of additional work for they are strewn with stumps, partially burned logs, and large branches. The seeds are simply dropped into a hole made with a sharpened pole (usually referred to as a dibble stick) and covered (see photo 6.2). Swidden cultivation is commonly practiced as a pioneering phase in the development of permanent field farming. But sustained swidden farming occurs mainly among highland and interior peoples who are often referred to as tribal. Some scholars and development workers who feel that shifting cultivation has been unfairly maligned have begun to use the term rotation or rotational farming, because this phrase evokes more positive associations of modern farming practices.

The other form of farming is permanent field cultivation. Here, fields are prepared and planted every year and sometimes more often. Such farming is also termed agriculture, as opposed to horticulture. It is traditionally practiced by lowland or coastal peoples who are often referred to as peasants. In this chapter and the next, we shall look more closely at the two forms and then to the changing ways of life associated with each.

Photo 6.1.   Recently cleared and burned swidden field on a mountainside in Nan Province, northern Thailand, 2006.

RICE

In both types of farming, the main crop in Southeast Asia is usually rice. Permanent field cultivation usually involves wet rice, which means the plants stand in water throughout most of their growth cycle. Conditions of standing water can be contrived in several ways, including ones involving irrigation that enable a crop to be grown in the dry season. More specifically, wet rice is grown in fields that have been leveled and surrounded by low earthen walls or bunds that contain the water. The fields are plowed and harrowed after they have begun to fill with water. Wet rice fields are planted continuously from one year to the next without fallowing. If irrigation can provide water for more than one planting a year, double cropping may be practiced as well.

Dry rice by contrast is associated with swidden farming. Although called dry it also requires much moisture, but this must be in the form of rainfall—meaning that the growing season coincides with the rainiest part of the year, for the plants do not stand in water. This also means that fields can be made on slopes, and in fact are often made on very steep ones. Steep slopes have certain advantages. Trees felled in a downhill direction

Photo 6.2. Bidayuh villagers planting a swidden field, Kuching division, Sarawak, Malaysian Borneo, 1998.

make use of gravity and develop momentum, taking vines and smaller trees with them. And fire that is set at the lower end of a hillside field will burn better as it sweeps uphill. But there are also disadvantages to hillside farming, including the more rapid loss of topsoil due to the runoff of water. Therefore, such fields cannot be cultivated permanently but must be moved each year or so. If this is not done, especially on slopes, soils will become degraded through leaching and erosion. And as a result, dense grasslands may develop and the return of forest cover and the rejuvenation of soils delayed.

The amount of rice produced on a swidden field is usually substantially less than can be grown in a wet rice field of the same size. One of the reasons wet rice is more productive is that it is grown in two stages—first in a dense seedbed and then transplanted into rows in the mud beneath the standing water. Another reason is that the water helps to prevent weeds from growing. A further difference involves other crops. Rice is the only crop that is grown in a wet rice field. Vegetables and other useful plants are raised in separate gardens and orchards. In the case of swidden cultivation, vegetables and other crops are often grown along with rice in the same field, some from seeds or cuttings planted at the same time and harvested as they ripen. However, while varying from one place or group to another in terms of importance in comparison to other things, rice is the main crop throughout Southeast Asia.

If rice is grown in two fundamentally different ways, which came first? Assumedly, swidden is the more primitive and therefore the earlier form of cultivation—horticulture rather than agriculture, if agriculture is defined as the use of the plow and irrigation. The shifting cultivation of rice is simple though not necessarily easy to do successfully (this requires, among other things, that the burning goes well). The traditional tools are few and basic: an axe or heavy knife for chopping and slashing, a sharpened pole or hoe for planting, baskets for seeds and harvesting, and a harvesting knife. Iron axes and knives help a great deal, but wood, bamboo, stone, and shell suffice. Neither a plow nor a harrow is used, and all labor is human rather than animal. Some form of swidden cultivation centering on asexually reproduced tubers, bananas, and various tree crops almost certainly came before permanent field, grain-based agriculture in Southeast Asia.

The first steps in rice domestication have to have taken place in its natural environment. As discussed earlier, Carl Sauer suggested that the domestication of rice may have begun with its appearance as a weed in swampy taro gardens. Also, domesticated rice includes a form known as floating (or swamp) rice that can be planted in natural wetlands where the depth of the water or the levelness of the land are not artificially created and controlled. The differences between wet and dry varieties of domesticated rice are not as great as might be thought given the substantial differences between wet and dry forms of cultivation, and many varieties can be grown either way (Grist [1959] 1986, 196).[1] According to D. H. Grist, long the leading authority on rice, "There seems to be no agreement among experts as to whether rice was first a dry land crop which was then adapted to wet conditions or vice versa" (3). Once both wet and dry methods of rice cultivation had been developed, they became and remained stable and separate forms that have lasted for long periods of time—perhaps several thousand years.

Swidden cultivation may be practiced where it is because hill and mountainsides are all that are available, either because there are few or no lowland areas at all or because they have already been taken over by others. People in northern mainland Southeast Asia who are primarily swidden cultivators will plant wet rice if they have access to land where this is possible given the technology available to them. A common feature of the present-day upland landscape in this region is a steep-sided valley farmed by the same ethnic group—Hmong or Karen, for example. The higher sides of the valley will be covered with swidden fields in various phases of development, while the bottom or lower slopes will have been turned into wet rice fields.

Wet rice is found above all in lowland settings. But this has less to do with altitude than landforms, which include the bottoms and lower slopes of valleys where streams are easily dammed or diverted, fields leveled, and dikes or bunds built to contain the water. Lowland environments also include the broad open inland and coastal plains found along and between great rivers where rainfall can be captured and kept in the leveled and walled fields. However, the cultivation of wet rice has also expanded far beyond such "natural" or most easily cultivated lands. One direction has been into the great deltas of the major rivers such as the Mekong. Such regions pose difficult problems of drainage and appear to have been brought under rice cultivation mainly in the recent past through the application of modern machinery with which to drain and control water on a large scale.

Another way to expand wet rice cultivation has been to extend it up the sides of hills and mountains by the use of terracing. This is an ancient technique, spectacular examples of which can be seen today in Java, Bali, northern Luzon, and parts of northern Vietnam. Terracing is a more difficult and time-consuming process than the development of lowland wet rice agriculture. It is made worthwhile by the extraordinarily fertile soils found in some areas or by high population densities. Terracing involves both carving out flat fields from often steep mountainsides and ravines and developing often elaborate forms of hydraulic control that bring and distribute water to fields, take it away, and then stop it altogether, all at the right times and in coordination among different users. Such hydraulic devices include dams, weirs, canals, bamboo pipes, and tunnels; and even if rainfall provides enough water to fill the terraces, the necessity of drainage remains. Wet rice is more labor intensive than dry, at least if the initial construction of the fields and hydraulic devices are included.

TRIBAL FARMERS

The peoples of Southeast Asia who live primarily by shifting cultivation are often referred to as tribes, although this term is used more frequently in regard to some regions than others. It is very common in references to the highland peoples of northern mainland Southeast Asia—as in the phrase "the hill tribes of Thailand." It is less often used regarding the interior peoples of insular Southeast Asia who also live by shifting cultivation.[2]

The notion of tribal refers to certain forms of society. The meaning is evocative though not necessarily very specific. It may be approached positively or negatively—by the things tribal society has or what it lacks. For example, it is used to simply mean an ethnic group—one having an identity, a common language or a closely related set of languages, and common customs. As applied to Southeast Asia at least, the simplest anthropological meaning of tribe or tribal is negative—a society that is not traditionally part of a state, or at least not fully so. In this sense, the peoples of the interior of Borneo, for example, are or were tribal societies. In addition to this negative characteristic of not being a part of a state, or of being only a marginal part, tribal societies are sometimes assumed to have some features that tie different local groups together. Such features include forms of leadership, kinship and descent, alliance against outsiders, and forms of economic exchange. In Eric Wolf's (1982, 88–100) terms, tribal peoples have a "kin-ordered mode of production," by which he means that the exchange of goods and services within the society takes place primarily through kinship rather than other means. In Southeast Asia, this is more so of some regions than others. Patrilineal clan organization among the Hmong of northern mainland Southeast Asia would be a good example. But it is harder to find such features among the societies of the interior of Borneo. Here, for example, the exchange of labor in cultivation practices or in house building is very common and important but is done among neighbors and fellow villagers who may or may not be kin.

The Dayak of Borneo

Most of the Dayaks of interior Borneo are swidden cultivators of dry rice and other crops.[3] In the highlands of northern Sarawak, the Kelabit Dayaks grow wet rice in terraced fields on the plateau floor, though how long they have done so or how they got started does not seem to be known. Elsewhere, Dayak farmers who mainly plant dry rice on hillsides will sometimes also grow floating or swamp rice where conditions allow. And more recently and partly with government assistance, some have taken up wet rice cultivation in places with suitable ground. Then in the lowland, there are the Melanau and Kajang Dayaks who grow and process sago, as both a staple and a cash crop. With these exceptions, the farming peoples of the interior of Borneo are swidden cultivators who focus on rice but also plant other crops in their fields and in gardens around their houses.

All such Dayak farmers have much in common, though there are also important differences from one group or place to another. One such difference in northwestern Borneo involves where people live. Most Dayaks in Sarawak and elsewhere traditionally built their villages on the banks of rivers that are navigable with small boats for at least part of the year, and traveled by boat wherever they could. Some peoples, known in Sarawak in the past as Land Dayaks (and more recently as Bidayuh), build their villages away from navigable rivers on hilltops and mountainsides. Such locations were less vulnerable to headhunting raids. After headhunting had ended under colonial rule, most of the older higher-up villages were abandoned in favor of more accessible sites lower down—but some of them remained in the 1990s.[4] If you visit a Bidayuh village on a valley floor and ask where the old village was, the response will be to point to some surrounding mountain and say, "up there."

A second significant variation involves social organization. Some Dayak groups are egalitarian and some are stratified. In Sarawak, both the Bidayuh and the Iban are egalitarian in that they both lack hereditary class divisions. Status differences, especially among the Iban, are important, but these are achieved in various ways rather than inherited. Other groups recognize hereditary differences between aristocrats or nobles and commoners and, in the past, slaves. Such groups include especially the Kenyah and the Kayan who live in the deep interior of northern Sarawak and adjacent regions of East Kalimantan. Among these and other stratified groups, the nobles controlled the village; held most of the wealth, including the slaves; intermarried; had a monopoly on various artistic designs; and held the important religious offices. The differences between the egalitarian and the stratified groups are interesting in that they have no obvious economic or ecological basis. The stratified groups do not occupy richer or more diverse environments than do the egalitarian ones, nor are there differences in farming practices. Both types of society practice dry rice swidden cultivation, hunt, and gather. One difference was that the trading relationships in forest products with the nomadic hunter-gatherer groups involved the stratified farming groups, at least in the northern part of Borneo (Sellato 1994, 130–32).

Longhouses

The most striking feature of the Dayak way of life is the longhouse. In Borneo, a longhouse is a multifamily dwelling that is longer—actually much longer—than it is wide. The usual arrangement is for a series of single-family apartments to be built together side by side under a common roof, usually all raised to a common height above the ground on posts. Each individual apartment consists of an inner room and an open outer veranda all under the roof, plus often an outer platform. A longhouse is usually constructed at one time. Each apartment is owned by a particular family and built to its own dimensions. The anthropologists who first studied Dayak societies thus stressed that a longhouse was not a "communal" dwelling, at least in most respects. The inner part of each apartment is the private part with a single door so that the size of a longhouse (at least in Sarawak) is usually stated in terms of the number of doors—anything fewer than fifteen doors being small and over fifty being considered quite large. The open front section of the longhouse is the public part where people socialize and work and where ceremonies are often held (Winzeler 2004a, 64).

While these generally have the common features described above, longhouses in Borneo vary in a number of ways from one group or place to another. Some groups build larger or more massive ones, while others build smaller and flimsier ones. Some villages consist of only a single longhouse, while others consist of several. The Bidayuh, who traditionally located their villages high up on mountainsides or hilltops generally did not and could not erect a single longhouse and usually had several, along with some

Photo 6.3.   Bidayuh longhouse at Annah Rais, Kuching division, Sarawak, (east) Malaysia, 1997.

individual houses as well. The Iban traditionally built a single longhouse in each village. Yet, other groups have single longhouses in some villages and several in others, usually depending on the size of the village and the nature of the terrain. Longhouses are also built according to ritual and social values. Those located along rivers are placed parallel to the bank, not crosswise. In ritual terms, the upstream end is considered more auspicious than the downstream one. In terms of social values, however, the center of the longhouse is where the apartment of the chief and (if the group is stratified) other aristocrats will usually be located.

Longhouses are particularly characteristic of the interior farming peoples of Borneo, but they also occur elsewhere in Southeast Asia (see photo 6.3). This suggests they are an old form of residence in the region. They can be found today in highland areas of northeastern Cambodia, the central highlands of southern Vietnam, Laos, and in the past, other areas as well (see photos 6.4 and 6.5). Formerly, part of the appeal of longhouses was security. But while many former longhouse dwellers have shifted to single-family houses (generally regarded as more modern), some have retained longhouses long after the end of headhunting. In Indonesian Borneo, the government forced many Dayaks out of longhouses in the 1970s and 1980s as part of efforts to modernize its isolated peoples and because it regarded longhouses as communistic. The Malaysia government made no such effort, with the result that longhouses are far more common today in Sarawak than in Kalimantan (Indonesian Borneo).

Photo 6.4. Ka Chut longhouse village, Ratanakiri Province, northwestern Cambodia, 2008.

Photo 6.5. Small longhouse in Ban Don village, Dac Lac Province, central highlands, southern Vietnam, 2003.

The Iban

The outside world became aware of the Iban—though the name Iban did not come into use until much later—in the early decades of the nineteenth century. The circumstances under which they were initially encountered gave rise to a misunderstanding reflected in the name they were first given and long retained. They were initially encountered along the coast at sea and thus called Sea Dayaks. This served to distinguish them from their ethnic neighbors to the west who did not travel out to sea and who therefore were labeled Land Dayaks (now Bidayuh), a name also long retained (Pringle 1970, 19). In reality, the Iban lived in the interior and the vast majority of them had never seen the sea. And in fact the ones who had taken up coastal raiding were not the Iban who lived in lower river areas but rather those from the Saribas and Skrang rivers farther inland.

By the 1850s, the Iban had become known in England. This was because they figured prominently in a parliamentary inquiry into the doings of the adventurer James Brooke, founder of the kingdom (and later colony) of Sarawak and first of the three White Rajas. The Iban became known because some of them had begun to leave the rivers where they lived and engage in raids along the northern coasts of Borneo. Brooke, who had arrived on the Sarawak coast in 1839 looking for opportunity, took on some of them with his cannon-equipped ship and won. He later told parliament they were pirates. Sharp questions were asked about whether the raiders were really pirates or just ordinary Dayak headhunters going about their usual business (Pringle 1970, 67–96). But Brooke was exonerated, and Sarawak, Brooke, and the Iban all became famous—the Iban becoming among other things the prototype for the Wild Men of Borneo of circus renown.

As the Brooke regime expanded its authority over a larger and larger territory in northern Borneo, one of its main objectives was to pacify and bring the Iban and other headhunting groups under control. The basic strategy here was to begin in the lower areas and then extend control upriver, organizing and leading the Iban that had become loyal to the government to attack and punish those that refused to do so. The final subjugation of the Iban living in remote upriver areas took nearly a century to accomplish. Part of the problem with the Iban for the colonial government was that they would not stay put. They were strongly inclined to migrate to new areas, and they were quite willing to both attack other groups already there and defy the government in order to do so. The government attempted to contain the Iban and block "illegal" migrations by building a series of forts at the forks in the major rivers and forbidding the Iban to establish new villages beyond certain points. This generally did not work, although some of the forts still remain. The Iban circumvented the forts by crossing from one watershed to another and entering into the headwaters of the river of choice

(Pringle 1970, 177–282). As the Brooke regime expanded in Sarawak, so too did the Iban, often at the expense of other groups. The Iban are now the largest ethnic group in Sarawak (40 percent of the population of the state) and populate much of its territory.

Because of their prominence from the mid-nineteenth century onward, the Iban have also been the focus of more study than any other group in Borneo. Much has been written about them in colonial reports, travel accounts, ethnological works, and more recently, in ethnography and in travel brochures. Modern ethnographic research among the Iban did not begin until after World War II but has since then been very extensive. The war had brought an end to Brooke rule, and afterward Sarawak ceased to be a British protectorate and became a full colony. At that time, the new government consulted with the Colonial Research Council about socio-economic research concerning current conditions in the colony that would help guide its development and help prepare it for eventual independence (that came in 1963). The up-and-coming young social anthropologist Edmund Leach was engaged to do a survey of the country and prepare an official report on his findings. He was also to develop and oversee a series of specific prioritized research projects on the main ethnic groups. This he did, giving the highest priority to a study of the ecology and social organization of the upriver Iban (Leach 1950, 39–40).

Derek Freeman was recruited to carry out this study. Before the war, Freeman had lived and done research in Samoa—to which he later returned, becoming widely known in the 1980s for his assault on Margaret Mead's interpretation of Samoan adolescence. But beginning in 1948, Freeman spent more than two years studying the Iban of the lower Baleh River, a major tributary of the middle Rajang and one of the regions into which the Iban had originally expanded against the orders of the Brooke government.

Freeman's fieldwork was extensive, and his accounts of the Iban very detailed. In his primary account (*Report on the Iban*), he described and analyzed the Iban longhouse organization, household, family, kinship, and political structure (Freeman [1955] 1970, 1–151). He also included an ethnohistory of the lower Baleh River from the beginning of the nineteenth century. However, his main topic was an account of all phases and dimensions of dry rice shifting cultivation (152–305). In subsequent publications, he covered other matters, including bird augury, shamanism, the nature and basis of Iban egalitarianism and political leadership, and the motives for Iban headhunting. At the time of his original research, the Iban of the Baleh still lived a fairly traditional life. They had by then accepted the authority of the colonial government. Headhunting had ceased, but the skulls were still kept in the longhouses, and the headhunting ceremonies were still performed. Christianity had not yet reached the Baleh, though it was spreading downriver. The Iban had been supplementing subsistence cultivation, hunting and fishing, and forest foraging for several decades with cash crops, especially rubber. In place of headhunting forays, young men made journeys (*bejali*) of several years or longer to the coast or even foreign countries for adventure and employment.

Freeman described the cultivation of rice as being at the center of Iban culture. It was much more than a means to the end of getting enough food to eat and wine (made from rice) to drink. It was the end toward which much else was directed. The Iban were motivated to migrate to new places by the prospect of better harvests gained by bringing newly cleared mature forestland under cultivation but also from a sense of adventure. Families attained status by being successful migrants and farmers. He stressed the cultivation of rice was as much a ceremonial activity as a technical or physical one—the performance of the rituals, the gaining of the favor of the rice spirits, and the correct interpretation of the omens, especially those conveyed by birds. Headhunting was an activity aimed at pleasing the spirit of rice and hence enhancing its fertility, though it also served as an important tool in Iban expansion.

More than a half-century after Freeman's study, some things remain the same, but much has changed for the Iban and other Dayaks in Sarawak. The Iban now cut trees down and make lumber with chain saws and travel on rivers in boats powered by outboard motors. Most have electricity produced by generators in their longhouses and have televisions and various appliances. Except for the old, most have been to school. Many have gone

Photo 6.6. Rumah Engkara, a contemporary-style, two-story Iban longhouse built of cement block, concrete, and other modern manufactured materials, Lubok Antu area, Sarawak, (east) Malaysia, 1999.

to university, and some have graduate degrees—including PhDs in various fields, among them anthropology. Large numbers of Iban work away from their villages in logging camps or in towns and cities in stores and offices. Christianity is now widespread. At least a few Iban have become very rich through logging concessions. While some Iban, especially in downriver areas, have abandoned longhouses for single-family houses, many have continued to build multifamily dwellings, though these are usually now made from modern materials in modern designs (see photo 6.6). Over the last four decades or so, visits to Iban longhouses, especially ones on the tributaries of the upper Batang Lupar—once famous as a stronghold of rebellious headhunters—have become an important part of the Sarawak tourism industry, to which we shall return in chapter 11.[5]

7

Peasant Farmers and Their Transformations

Peasant farmers are the other main type of traditional cultivators in Southeast Asia. Like the term "tribal," that of peasant is less applicable than it was formerly and, for reasons we shall come to below, it is less used. The notion of peasant has been important in both anthropology and history as a way of characterizing the way of life of premodern farmers, one that falls between the tribal farmers we have been discussing and modern industrial farmers familiar in Western societies, for example (Wolf 1966). Like tribal cultivators, traditional peasant farmers in Southeast Asia have usually been discussed as fairly small-scale operators who earn their living from a few hectares of land or less, using mainly the labor of their household. But unlike swidden cultivators, peasant farmers also use animals—cattle or water buffalo—for plowing and some other farming activities that enlarge the amount of land they can farm. They also work with more equipment than do tribal farmers engaged in shifting cultivation.

Peasant farmers throughout Southeast Asia grow a variety of field crops including corn or maize, but rice is by far the main staple. While some phases in the production of rice for consumption or sale have been mechanized, much of it remains based on human and animal labor, and therefore small scale. Small tractors are now widely used for plowing but so are animals (usually water buffalo but also cattle; see photo 7.3). Animals are used because they have an intrinsic economic and cultural value (evident from the widespread keeping of water buffalo by swidden cultivators who do not use them for plowing or other work) that tractors do not. Water buffalo can also be used to plow steeply terraced fields not easily, if at all, accessible to tractors (see photo 7.3). At the other end of the production process, rice milling has been widely mechanized, but the activities in between, including transplanting,

Photo 7.1. Terraced wet rice fields, Ubud, Bali, 1971.

Photo 7.2.   Tilling a rice field with a bicycle tractor, Muang Sing, northern Laos, 2005.

harvesting, and threshing, are done mainly by hand. Traditional wet rice cultivation is basically a family-household operation, but labor pooling or sharing practices involving other households are also very widespread. This is especially so for activities such as harvesting and threshing that must be accomplished quickly.

The classic peasant is also basically a subsistence farmer, one who mainly produces food for household consumption rather than to sell in the market, though not entirely. Peasants also depend on the market to acquire some things. The peasant household needs to produce a surplus beyond what is needed for survival. According to Eric Wolf's (1982, 79–82) formulation of types of economy, traditional peasants are parts of a tributary mode of production. This means they are farmers who pay tribute to overlords in taxes, rents, corvée labor, or some combination of these—at least, this is what happens in general. Some peasants may have more than enough land, in which case they become landlords, or they do not have enough, in which case they become tenants—usually specifically sharecroppers. Southeast Asian peasants also have social and religious obligations, for example, in Burma, Thailand, Laos, and Cambodia to support Buddhist temples and monasteries.

Photo 7.3. Plowing a terraced rice field with a water buffalo, Ta Van village, Sapa, Vietnam, 2005.

Photo 7.4. Transplanting rice grown in a seedbed to an irrigated field, Ubud, Bali, 1971.

Photo 7.5. Shan (Tai) women harvesting rice in Mae La Na village, northern Thailand, 2004.

Photo 7.6. Shan villagers threshing harvested rice using cooperative labor sharing, Mae La Na village, northern Thailand, 2004.

As the reference to Buddhism suggests, the notion of peasantry also has a cultural dimension. Peasants are a part of what is usually referred to as the great tradition or civilization, which is usually taken to include literacy, cities, and some tradition of monumental architecture and an organized religion (Wolf 1982, 82–83). For Southeast Asia, the latter means they adhere to one of the world religions—Hinduism (mainly in the past), Buddhism, Islam, or Christianity. Tribal peoples today often also belong to one of the world religions, but this is a recent development. However, peasants have usually been described as being not outside the center of the great tradition but on the periphery of it. They do not live in cities and are partially, rather than fully, literate.

The connection between peasants and the economy and civilization is also political. As might already be clear, the peasant economic system with its inherent inequalities and obligations implies a form of political organization that goes beyond tribal organization—even the stratified tribal organizations found among some of the Dayak peoples in Borneo, for example. The religious obligations to support Buddhist temples and monks are met willingly and voluntarily, but other economic obligations are not necessarily so. The notion of peasantry therefore also implies the presence of the state. Put in ecological terms by the anthropologist and Thai specialist Lucian Hanks, the political development in the interior states that developed in present-day Thailand and surrounding areas of mainland Southeast Asia was limited:

> For at least the last 1,000 years Southeast Asia, excepting North Vietnam, has been a great forest with occasional savannah-like areas, a landscape lightly sprinkled with villages, with an occasional walled city. Yet the grass and jungle-covered ruins of past capitals are strewn up and down the Irrawaddy, Chao Praya and Mekong Rivers. . . . So capital cities like Pagan in Burma, Angkor in Cambodia, and Ayuthia in Thailand grew and fell into decay under the assault of some vigorous new leader. Few lasted more than a century or two. Ayuthia's three centuries was a remarkable exception. (Hanks 1972, 90)

At least until recently,

> government, as a centralized agency supported by the population at large for carrying out public services, does not occur in this part of the world [or at least has not until recently, he might have added]. . . . In Southeast Asia, as we have seen, the founder of a dynasty was a successful general who built or captured a walled town to sustain himself, his men, and their wives and children. . . . For example, in 1782, General Chakri raised a successful revolt against his aging and perhaps senile superior, the King of Thonburi, to become founder of the present dynasty of Thailand. . . . Government was (and is) the followers of a war-lord type, a brittle community, guarded and suspicious. . . . The nineteenth century European advisors to Thailand, who counseled with images in their

heads of hero kings ruling enraptured subjects, deemed the governing "ineffective and backward." (Hanks 1972, 110–11)

The Thai states that gained control in Thailand, Laos, and elsewhere were clearly not the first. The Tai were more like the Romans than the Greeks. They began as tribal peoples who conquered others, in the process became civilized, eventually created a large and enduring state that modernized, and escaped a colonial takeover (the only one in Southeast Asia). Historians and anthropologists have wondered what the early Thai states were like that enabled them to do this. According to Charles Keyes (also an anthropologist and Thai specialist),

> By the eleventh century, the Tai had established themselves on the peripheries of the Indianized states of Southeast Asia. These Tai were probably "barbarians," that is, they were neither "Indianized "nor "Sinified." The Tai introduced into the region a new type of social structure, which had similarities to that of the Mongols. The Tai were organized into territorial units, known as *muang*, which were ruled by chiefly families. (1977, 74–75)

DEVELOPMENT OF RICE CULTIVATION IN A THAI VILLAGE

According to Hanks, changes in rice cultivation have also been part of the process. For the most part, we have treated wet and dry forms of rice cultivation as separate and independent types practiced by different types of people in different types of places. Yet, many groups practice both wet and dry rice cultivation, depending on access to the appropriate types of land. Further, the development of wet rice cultivation, even in the most appropriate or easiest environments, probably did not begin as the first phase of cultivation after land has been opened. Hanks's study concerns the agrarian history of the Thai village of Bang Chan. The locus of a team study sponsored by Cornell University in the 1950s and 1960s, this village has been described in several books.

At the time of its founding around 1850, Bang Chan was located some twenty-two miles from the city of Bangkok, at the time a considerable distance, in an empty and forbidding region. Hanks describes the land as wild savannah covered by coarse grass and brush and inhabited by dangerous and destructive animals, including poisonous snakes, wild pigs, and elephants. Savannah may not have been the original sort of environment, for as he points out, the natural vegetation in this region as elsewhere in much of Southeast Asia is mainly tropical forest. But if savannah was the consequence of some earlier history of occupation and abandonment, he does not say what or when this may have been. In any case, the land was empty at the time of the founding, as was much of central Thailand except for regions along rivers. The establishment of the village was the result of the digging of a canal (the main means of transportation in the region then being water) through the trackless region. As was true of much of mainland Southeast Asia, land without people had little value to Southeast Asian rulers. The settling of the region therefore added value to it and so was encouraged. The canal provided a means of contact and, with Bangkok, a market where village produce (mainly dried fish—fish having moved rapidly into the canal and expanded after it was opened) could be sold.

Broadly speaking, what took place over the 120 years covered by the study was a change from dry to wet rice cultivation—combined with many other changes. Hanks describes the agricultural history of the village as consisting of three phases. The first was shifting cultivation, the second was what he calls broadcasting, and the third was full wet rice cultivation involving transplanting. Both shifting cultivation and broadcasting were used for limited periods of time before the adoption of the full practice of wet rice cultivation—although in the end, wet rice cultivation came to a halt entirely in the 1960s as the village was absorbed into the expanding city of Bangkok (Hanks 1972, 148–51).

The shifting cultivation of dry rice began with the opening of Bang Chan. It was not exactly the sort of shifting cultivation already described for Southeast Asia, that is, practiced on hills and mountainsides and involving cutting down trees. In this instance, the land was flat, and all there was to be cut was grass and brush, although it did involve the sequence of cutting, drying, and burning followed by the usual practice of planting seeds in holes punched in the ground with a dibble. In this case, the villagers also cleared, burned, and planted separate gardens for vegetables. All of this was mostly done separately by each household according to the number of mouths to be fed and the number of hands available for the work. Rice was produced for subsistence, and the villagers were lucky if they could produce enough to eat themselves. In addition to cultivating rice and vegetables, the villagers fished in the canal for their own consumption and, after drying, for sale in Bangkok (72–92).

The next phase of rice cultivation began around 1890. This involved the same initial steps of clearing and burning, but otherwise there were major changes, beginning with wet rice cultivation. The land chosen was low enough that it would flood during the rainy season and remained underwater for a sufficient period while the rice was growing. Next, the land was plowed using a pair of water buffaloes, this being done before the flooding began. And finally, the planting was done not by poking holes in the ground and dropping a few seeds but rather by broadcasting, that is, by throwing out handfuls of seed in broad arcs across the field and then pulling a harrow over the field to cover it up. Harvesting was done in the same older way, but instead of thrashing by hand, the buffalo were used to trample the rice. Whereas all of the labor in swidden cultivation had been done by humans, some of it was, therefore, now done by buffalo. At the same time, there was more social cooperation or labor pooling, especially during the harvesting. The practice here was for people from a group of households to go from one field to another and work together as each field was ready to be harvested. There were also more festivities and religious activities, for the village built its first Buddhist temple at about the same time that broadcasting began. The village had become more prosperous and also more economically complex and market oriented. The new method of rice farming actually produced lower yields per unit of land than had the old one. But since more land was brought under cultivation by each household, the size of the harvest increased. This in turn meant that there was sometimes rice to sell after the harvest, although the price was subject to much fluctuation over time. The buffalo had to be purchased at some point, but they could be bred and thus become a form of wealth themselves (93–118).

The final stage of rice cultivation in Bang Chan began around 1935 and lasted into or through the 1960s. Hanks labels this phase "transplanting," which means the wet rice cultivation had nearly fully developed. However, this was only one of several major changes. Before being plowed and harrowed, the land in each separate field had to be leveled and bunds built around it to contain the water to a uniform depth. The few areas where the land was very low continued to be planted with swamp (or floating) rice. At the same time, a system of canals and ditches with water gates had to be constructed that distributed water to each field and drained the excess. Since the main source of water was the canals, and the country was more or less flat, the water had to be lifted from the main canals into the ditches that carried it to the fields. This could be done in several ways; the most suitable was waterwheels powered by windmills and later by pumps run by gasoline engines. Plowing was still done by buffalo until some of these were replaced in the 1960s by small Japanese tractors. Harvesting continued to be done by hand and thrashing by buffalo, but machines replaced the older ways of milling, winnowing, and polishing rice (119–47).

Why did the villagers of Bang Chan switch—rapidly according to Hanks—from broadcasting to transplanting (the full wet rice regime) when they seemed to have had a good life as things were? While people had to work harder at first, Hanks reports that transplanting raised productivity, which means that a given amount of human effort produced a larger crop. This in turn meant that still more land could be brought under cultivation—that is, where more land was available. He suggests villagers may have been motivated to change because they had only been semiemployed in the earlier form of cultivation. The population of the village had increased naturally through procreation and by arrivals from elsewhere, and the expansion of rice cultivation provided additional employment. The standard of living was in general raised. People bought ready-made clothing and began to build larger and better houses of solid wood to replace their older, mainly bamboo, ones. The local Buddhist temple and monastery were enlarged and improved as various new buildings were added. The economy in general expanded and diversified. Until rice farming declined and was abandoned in the 1960s—as Bang Chan was absorbed in the expansion of Bangkok— it remained the center of the economy of the village, but it became ever more market oriented. The buying and selling of rice and commercial rice milling became a big, integrated, and internationally oriented industry dominated by ethnic Thai-Teochew Chinese. However, the cultivation of fruits and vegetables also became a major economic activity, some for local consumption but mainly for sale in the great markets of Bangkok. The villagers, who had first bought clothes, household goods, and other things from peddlers who came around in boats through the canals, began to open shops and sell those things themselves. More generally, labor became a commodity and traditional forms of cooperation and exchange between households declined. Thailand was approaching the full transition to industrialized agriculture of the sort that was (and still is) developing across Southeast Asia. This meant that farming was being mechanized. Small tractors were replacing human and animal labor in plowing fields and transporting materials, and power-driven rice mills were also coming into use, as were artificial fertilizers and pesticides, though the latter also got into the canals and streams and killed the fish and other aquatic creatures that had been an important part of the diet (148–63).

CHANGES IN PEASANT FARMING
ACROSS SOUTHEAST ASIA

Some of the changes that Hanks discusses in the final period of the development of agriculture in Bang Chan are ones that have occurred across larger regions of Thailand and Southeast Asia generally. Let us now turn to these broader changes, including those that have taken place in the socialist regimes.

The Green Revolution in Rice Cultivation

The changes that were occurring include the so-called Green Revolution. This phrase refers to both the development and introduction of new "miracle" rice strains and the implementation of other required changes. First applied to wheat production, the effort to raise rice production was launched in the Philippines in 1960 by the International Rice Research Institute (IRRI) with funding from the Rockefeller and Ford foundations, acting in concert with country governments that were supposed to enhance rural infrastructure (roads, communications, electricity, and irrigation). The implementation varied from one country to another. The wars and subsequent developments in Vietnam, Laos, and Cambodia, for example, delayed the implementation in these countries for up to several decades. The changes have been aimed mainly at wet rather than dry rice cultivation. The effects of the Green Revolution, positive or negative, on the swidden cultivation of rice are less well understood.

The Green Revolution and its side effects and consequences have been controversial. Proponents point to the great gains in productivity that have been achieved. Countries that had long been importers of rice became exporters. Grain production in Southeast Asia increased twofold between 1970 and 1995, and yields per hectare nearly doubled. Calories per person (or food availability) grew by about one–third, and rural incomes grew by nearly four times. Most of this increase in income involved urban industrial development and in rural nonfarming sectors (such as logging), but it was made possible through lowering the amount of labor that farming households needed to devote to food production. The cost of food has also declined, which most benefits the poor who spend a larger portion of their income on food than do the rich. The Green Revolution thus became the basis of broader economic growth. Markets expanded because farmers had more to spend. And the various mechanical changes (such as the spread of rice mills) decreased the drudgery in the lives of rural women who traditionally spent a lot of their daily time preparing rice for cooking after it had been harvested.

Critics of the Green Revolution point to various adverse effects (Brown 1970; Pearse 1980). Most of these are either environmental or social, though both sorts of effects derive from the same requirements or practices. High-yielding rice cultivation is linked to the use of fertilizer, insecticides, and herbicides, all of which are costly, and therefore more accessible to better off farming households (who can best afford the investment required) than to poorer ones (who cannot). This in turn means that the already more affluent farmers gain while the poorer ones do not. In areas where landlessness is a problem, poorer farmers are even more likely to become tenants or laborers of landowning farmers. Green Revolution improvements in rice production also have water requirements and therefore favor irrigation-based wet rice farming rather than dry rice or shifting cultivation (which depend on natural rainfall), and shifting cultivators already tend to be poorer than wet rice farmers. And finally, if women have been relieved of some of the burden of rice processing by mechanization (at least among wet rice cultivators), they have also become less central to the culture of rice farming, in which they embodied notions of fertility.

The environmental criticisms of the Green Revolution concern the polluting effects of fertilizers, pesticides, and herbicides that are washed from the fields into streams and rivers, reducing or eliminating fish and other aquatic life on which local people have long depended for food. A further consequence is that too much water has been pumped from rivers in order to satisfy the irrigation requirements of expanding cultivation. The heavy use of fertilizers may also be contributing to the depletion of minerals from soils, and all the more so if two crops a year are raised. The overuse of water and soil depletion in turn raise the prospect of calling into question the long-term viability of the Green Revolution or even the reversal of its trajectory of growth. And finally, there is the criticism that Green Revolution farming has brought a decrease in biodiversity. Traditional, localized varieties of rice that have been developed over long periods of time cease to be used as the new strains of high-yielding rice are adopted, though efforts are now under way to collect and preserve the older seeds.

AGRARIAN DEVELOPMENTS IN NONSOCIALIST AND SOCIALIST COUNTRIES

The spread of the Green Revolution in Southeast Asia was uneven. By the time it was taking effect in Thailand and in some other regions, other developments had or were altering peasant societies. The most wrenching changes occurred in Cambodia after the Khmer Rouge came to power. But there were also more general differences between what took place in the nonsocialist and the socialist regimes—though there were also differences among the countries within each of these categories. The general trend in the nonsocialist countries includes several developments, some of which had begun under colonial rule. One of these was the increasing capitalization and industrialization of agriculture, meaning the transition from peasant to a postpeasant way of life. At what point this transition occurs is hard to specify, but the changes involved seem clear. Land itself becomes a commodity that is bought, sold, and rented in open markets. Rice and other crops are also sold in markets rather than only consumed by the household, and fertilizers and insecticides are purchased, as is the equipment used to apply these. Another has been the effort to bring more land under cultivation through forest clearing and through drainage and irrigation projects. Increased reliance on nonfarm income has led to the migration of people from farms to cities.

Nonsocialist Countries

Nonsocialist countries have attempted to deal with rural poverty based on landlessness in various ways. For example, Malaysia has emphasized Federal Land Development Authority (FELDA) schemes. These schemes are designed to provide poor or landless (mainly Malay) farmers with the opportunities to resettle in planned communities on land cleared from the forest, first developed as cooperatively owned rubber and then increasingly oil palm estates—later collective ownership was changed to private holdings. Those who join and are resettled are provided with houses and land for individual gardens, plus shares or holdings of rubber or oil palm land, the costs of all to be repaid from the profits made once the scheme begins to produce. Malaysia has also encouraged and counted upon the development of large numbers of foreign-owned factories producing electronic goods to provide nonfarm employment for young Malays, especially women (Ong 1987).

The Indonesian government has attempted to help alleviate rural poverty and landlessness through *transmigrasi,* the transmigration program that was begun in the colonial period. To be considered more fully in chapter 12, *transmigrasi* involved moving impoverished peasant families from the crowded islands of Java and Bali to the much less densely settled outer islands, including Kalimantan (Borneo), Irian Jaya (western New Guinea), Sumatra, and the Moluccas in particular. Though this program was carried on for a long period, it did relatively little to reduce the scale of the problem of landlessness and poverty in Java and Bali. It generally failed to achieve the desired results for the families that were moved and sometimes brought conflicts between the settlers and the indigenous peoples whose lands were encroached upon (Duncan 2004; Hardjono 1977). For Bali, some of the slack has been taken up by the development of tourism—also to be discussed later.

To take a final example, one of the main means of dealing with landlessness and poverty in the Philippines has been to send people to other countries to work and remit a part of their wages to help support families back home. Large numbers of Filipinos (the Philippine's largest export is people, it is sometimes said) find employment in the more prosperous Southeast Asian countries (such as Singapore, Malaysia, and Thailand) and in other prosperous countries in the world that rely heavily on foreign labor, such as the Gulf states. Most of those who go abroad work as laborers in construction or as household servants. Large numbers of Filipino women trained as nurses also find foreign employment, including in the United States. The Philippines, like some other developing countries, including Thailand, also has a well-developed marriage market whereby foreign men acquire Filipino women as wives—though, as with the foreign employment of women as domestic servants, this can involve human trafficking.

Socialist Countries

The transformation of the peasantries in the Southeast Asian socialist countries (Vietnam, Laos, and for a time, Cambodia) include some of the same developments as in the nonsocialist ones, including resettlement. But these countries have also concentrated on other, more radical approaches. Here, there are also major differences in what has taken place in the different countries. Vietnam has one of the densest populations in the world, most of it concentrated in the Red River Delta in the north, the Mekong Delta in the south, and along the narrow coastal strip of lowland in between. Laos, in contrast, has a far smaller and less dense population. This suggests why efforts at land redistribution have been a more important part of the socialist agenda in Vietnam than in Laos. Also, the socialist land program in northern Vietnam was implemented earlier and over a longer period of time than in Laos. Socialism began in northern Vietnam in the years after the communist victory over the French in 1954 and, in some areas, where the communists had gained control before that. In Laos, as also in Cambodia and South Vietnam, this did not occur until after 1975.

Beyond overthrowing colonial rule and foreign domination, the communist movement in Vietnam had several main goals. Two of these reflect the agrarian nature of Vietnamese society. The first was land reform, implemented throughout North Vietnam shortly after the communist party came to power in 1954. The second was agricultural collectivization, which came next. Extended to the south after 1975, both programs involved or implied other changes, including the suppression or elimination of markets and the implementation of a command economy—one that was abandoned in 1986 in favor of reforms called Doi Moi or market socialism (Malarney 2002, 1).

Land reform refers essentially to the redistribution of agricultural land. It is deemed necessary in a society in which most of the population lives by farming but where land is distributed very unequally among those who depend on it. The general idea is that some households have little or no land, some have more or less what they need, and others have more than they require. Households that have too little must rent land from those who have more or work for wages. The main goal of land reform is therefore to acquire land from those who have too much and transfer it to those who have too little. The goal can be achieved in various ways, ranging from buying and selling to appropriation and reallocation. The existing inequalities can also be seen from a moral or political perspective—either they have developed over time and no one is guilty of trying to harm or exploit anyone else, or wrongs have been done. The Vietnamese socialists chose appropriation and reallocation and took a moral view, meaning those with excess land might be guilty of wrongdoing and deserve punishment beyond losing land.

Where party members created committees to deal with land reform, the basic approach was to divide villagers into categories ranging from landlords to the poor and landless. These general categories were ones previously developed by the Chinese and set out in a decree in 1953:

Landlords—those who own land but do not work it themselves, instead renting it out to others or hiring workers.

Rich peasants—those who own land and work it themselves but also exploit others as workers or tenants.

Middle peasants—the middle category of farmers who neither exploit nor are exploited by others.

Poor peasants—those who have little or no land and inadequate farming equipment, must rent land from others or work for them, and are therefore exploited, though not completely dependent on others.

Workers—those who have nothing and must sell their labor to gain a living. (Keyes 1977, 232–33; Malarney 2002, 27–28)

According to anthropologist Shaun Malarney (2002, 26–29), in the North Vietnamese commune (village grouping) of Thinh Liet, the classification system was more complicated than this, as were decisions about how to treat people who were put in each category. Landlords were subdivided into further categories in terms of reprehensibility. The worst were "cruel and exploitative landlords," who had committed other crimes such as murder, rape, or opposing or betraying the revolutionary struggles—and who therefore had a blood debt. Next were the "regular landlords," who had only exploited people as landowners, employers, and rentiers. After these were "administrative landlords," who did not own much land themselves but acted as agents for other landlords. And finally there were "resistance landlords," who were the good counterpart to the "cruel and exploitative" landlords in that they had supported the revolution.

The land reform effort was intended to overturn Vietnamese society by denigrating those who had previously been at the top (landlords) and valorizing those (poor peasants and workers) who had been at the bottom. More specifically, land was to be taken from those in the top two categories of landlords (depending further on the type of landlord) and rich peasants and reallocated to those in bottom categories of poor peasants and workers. In addition, other punishments—up to execution—and rewards, including honorable classifications that would be permanent and passed onto children, were dispensed. The whole process was extremely traumatic for the commune where Malarney studied, and a subsequent reclassification was done in which mistakes were acknowledged and some people reassigned to different, generally more favorable, categories.

Land reform evened out differences in the size of landholdings and there-fore in wealth. But it was only the first stage in the building of a socialist na-tion, for without further change, the old inequalities in wealth and position could return as differences in skill, effort, or luck enable some to rise and acquire land and others to fall and lose their holdings. The next stage was thus collectivization, which was intended to both perpetuate the equali-ties that had been created and make other improvements in the economy and society. This meant the formation of agricultural cooperatives. Here, groups of households would pool their resources, labor, and risks; work together; and share the rewards. Cooperatives could be developed in stages, the first being an organization for pooling or exchanging labor—an old and very widespread practice in Southeast Asia. The full development of a cooperative required that members contribute their land. Joining a co-operative was supposed to be voluntary, and those who joined were to be allowed to withdraw if they so wished. In fact, villagers in Thinh Liet felt pressured to join and to remain once they had (Malarney 2002, 49). By 1965, most farmers had joined. The operation of the cooperatives showed several interesting developments. One was that the middle peasants (those who had adequate land and did their own farming) were the most useful members in doing the work and in providing guidance and leadership. Another (which had also been noted throughout the country) was that the 5 percent of cropland that was allocated for private use and sale by house-hold produced more than the land that was worked communally. This was, of course, very troubling from the perspective of increasing productivity through collectivization.

Regardless of the difficulties and limits of socializing peasant agriculture in Vietnam, the prospects for doing so in Laos were much less promising. The population was far smaller both in total size and in relation to land size. Moreover, highland, shifting cultivators, in contrast to lowland peas-ants, comprised about 50 percent of the population. Highland swidden land throughout Southeast Asia is by tradition already based on communal tenure, with individual households gaining use rights through initial clear-ing and retaining them through continued use. Labor exchange is widely practiced. In the case of lowland peasant agriculture in Laos, poverty due to landlessness was a problem in some areas but not on the scale of Vietnam. Also, as Grant Evans (1990, 15) points out, it would not have been easy to control or suppress rural markets without resorting to the extreme and brutal tactics used by the Khmer Rouge in Cambodia. After the communists came to power in 1975, the economy in general declined steeply. But this was not because the new government made radical changes in agricultural policies or in other areas. Rather, it was because the foreign aid and military support that had been provided (mainly by Americans) was withdrawn, because of the devastation from the heavy bombing during the war, and because many owners of businesses and capital had fled to Thailand out of fear of what the communists might do—the total population of the country dropped by 10 percent (70). The communists who took over and formed the new government were full of socialist enthusiasm, but they moved slowly to make changes. And they were more interested in symbolism and cultural matters (getting people to abandon superstitious beliefs and practices and adopt attitudes of scientific rationality) than in initiating social and economic change. The people were simply urged to adopt "collective ways." Some land reform did take place, but this was more spontaneous than the result of specific government or communist party action. Seemingly, large landowners simply fled or sold or distributed some of the land because of concern about what might happen. In contrast to what occurred in Vietnam, landowners in Laos had little to fear, but they did not know that at the time (67).

The new government in Laos did become focused on building socialism through agricultural cooperatives among the Lao peasantry. By 1976, the government had decided to move the country toward collectivization but incrementally and with smaller rather than larger cooperatives. A national campaign was mounted, but progress was mixed. The government was enthusiastic and wanted to show results. "By the end of 1976 only a few thousand people had been drawn into low level cooperatives (low level meaning only labor exchange rather than collective ownership) in nine of thirteen provinces" (45). By the end of the 1970s, the government had accepted that the Lao peasantry and other circumstances in Laos prevented the implementation of full socialism, and that the only realistic option was market socialism—the socialist part of this phrase being somewhat vaguer than the market part (55). The campaign for collectivization continued. A table of numbers of cooperatives by province in 1986 shows a total of nearly four thousand for the country. Two years earlier, government figures revealed a total of 2,400 cooperatives to which some 38 percent of farm families (owning 35 percent of farmland) belonged (Evans 1990, 61). But Evans stresses that there is less to such figures than meets the eye. Most of the co-ops were of the "lower level" variety, or limited to the exchange of labor as opposed to common ownership of land, equipment, and other resources and the sharing of proceeds characteristic of the "higher level" ones. As a result, the co-ops brought little fundamental change to the social relations of production in the countryside, and eventually collectivization collapsed altogether (95, 151, 181).

Weaving

The changes that have taken place in weaving in Laos illustrate broader processes of economic change. Throughout Laos and Southeast Asia, the

**Photo 7.7.   Tai woman weaving on a fixed-frame loom, Natam village, Lai Chau, north-
ern Vietnam, 2005.**

production of cloth on handlooms has in the past been an important
activity among many highland and lowland peoples. There tends to be a
difference in that highland and interior peoples generally use the simple
back-strap loom, while lowland ones use a stationary handloom involving
a complex frame (see photo 7.7). There are also differences in the material
used. Highland weavers use cotton or occasionally other plant fibers, while
lowland weaving is based on silk as well as cotton. Cloth is also produced
for different purposes, which cut across the highland and lowland divide
and have more to do with regions. In insular Southeast Asian villages, much
of the weaving that has survived has been for ceremonial cloth. In Borneo,
the Iban *pua* or ritual blanket is a well-known example. Some fabric was
made into clothing—though some traditional clothing also had ritual uses
or was intended to provide supernatural protection. Today, ceremonial
cloths are widely sold in markets as artwork or handicraft for table and wall
decorations. But village weaving that has survived in Borneo has involved
ceremonial cloth, whereas cloth used for making clothing (some of which
in the past was not woven but made from beaten bark) has been entirely
replaced by either industrially produced cloth or manufactured clothing. In
some parts of northern mainland Southeast Asia, in contrast, handwoven

cloth continues to be produced and used for traditional homemade cloth-ing. This also means that people here wear such clothing on an everyday ba-sis rather than simply on ceremonial occasions or in dressing up for tourists.

The extent of household weaving, however, and the production and wearing of traditional clothing in northern mainland Southeast Asia differs strikingly by country. And here the comparison between what has occurred in Laos and Thailand is illustrative. Such a comparison is meaningful be-cause many of the ethnic groups in the northern part of these two countries are the same. In both countries, the highland peoples have retained weav-ing and traditional clothing to a greater extent than have the lowlanders. Native dress, especially for women, is a main ethnic marker among the highlanders. This is reflected in the widespread practice of identifying the various subsections of some of the main ethnolinguistic groups (Black and White Tai; Black, Red, and White Hmong, and so forth) by the predomi-nant color (or sometimes pattern, as with the Flower Hmong) of women's clothing.

Given such commonalities among the main ethnic groups, it is notable that household weaving and traditional dress are present to a much greater extent in Laos than in Thailand. Handloom (as opposed to industrial) weaving among the Thai in Thailand has mainly disappeared, and both men and, to a lesser extent, women wear Western-style clothing. Hand weaving and traditional clothing persist to some extent among the hill tribes in Thailand. Women wearing traditional clothing made of cloth from handlooms are a common sight in Karen villages, for example. The situa-tion among the Hmong, the Akha, and the Mien is more complicated. Tra-ditionally styled clothing is usually made from industrially produced cloth. Women sitting outside making clothing is a common sight in Hmong vil-lages around Chiang Mai and Chiang Rai in northern Thailand, but that of women working at looms is not. Moreover, the sewing seen in Thailand is being done on a foot-pedaled sewing machine rather than by hand, as is more commonly seen in northern Laos.

At first, the importance of weaving in Laos (and in northern Vietnam as well) would seem to be simply a matter of continuity from the past. But Evans argues that it is not quite so simple. In two of the three lowland Lao villages he studied, weaving was an important economic activity; in the third village, women had never learned weaving. Another published survey of weaving in Vientiane Province in 1980 showed that 75 percent of households did at least some weaving. But the frequency of weaving among the ethnic Lao (or Lao Lum) to be found in the 1980s did not reflect an unchanged cottage industry. Lowland Lao weaving had declined greatly in the 1950s and the 1960s as a result of competition from imported cloth. There was a resurgence of weaving in the later 1970s that was brought about by government restrictions placed on imports and the economic downturn that followed the takeover by the socialist government (Evans 1990, 83–86).

The revival was not strictly the result of economic forces, which were themselves the result of polices implemented by the socialist government after the war ended in 1975 (as well as by devastation caused by the war and the precipitous withdrawal of foreign aid). However, there was still a cottage industry to revive. The production of cloth by hand spinning, dying, and weaving, especially using the complicated fixed-frame looms, is a very complex activity learned by girls as they grow up—although the weaving revival had been based on the use of purchased, already dyed yarn. (Doing household weaving from scratch is much more difficult and less common, although some of this is still done.) But there was also a political consideration. The socialist government frowned on Western dress for women. They encouraged instead the traditional ankle-length sarong or *sin*, which, made of silk or cotton, is one of the main products of fixed handloom weaving today. Here, the contrast with developments in Thailand was very apparent, although the Lao government began to relax its opposition to Western dress in the late 1980s. The Thai government appears to have taken little if any interest in women's clothing. More recently, clothing styles in Laos have been influenced by the more Westernized practices of the Thai that have come with television, increased trade, and other cross-border interaction with Thailand and China. But handwoven *sin* continue to be common dress for women. Among the highland ethnic groups in northern Laos, weaving had never been displaced and continues to the present—as is also the case in northern Vietnam.

What has happened with weaving can also be seen in other areas of rural technology and material culture in Laos, including ones in which conservative or anti-Western government ideological attitudes do not appear to have played much of a role. One of the more striking things seen today on the roads and in the villages of rural Laos is homemade trucks and tractors ingeniously created from old parts salvaged from military machinery left over from the war. The motives behind the creation and use of these probably do not represent the perpetuation of traditional ways. The traditional way would have been a wagon pulled by water buffalo or oxen (which are still also seen). Homemade trucks and tractors that travel slowly down the road going "putt, putt, putt" and spewing black smoke reflect an effort to make do with whatever is available and affordable. This is also true of the use of other things seen occasionally that have been recycled into new uses—bomb shell casings used as planters, unexploded mortar rounds used as roof weights, and beer bottles used to make rodent guards on granary posts and glazing to let light into houses. The motives and values involved in all of these ingenious practices appear to be utilitarian.

8

Indigenous Religion

As applied to religion, the notion of indigenous can be used in two ways. One is simply in reference to the total religious traditions of the diminishing number of peoples who remain outside of any of the world religions that now dominate Southeast Asia—though this does not mean uninfluenced by them. Used in this way it refers to, for example, the religion of the diminishing number of non-Christian, non-Buddhist Hmong of northern mainland Southeast Asia or the non-Christian, non-Muslim Dayak peoples of Borneo. Such groups were formerly often referred to as "pagan" to distinguish them from those who had converted. The term "pagan" can probably be attributed mainly to missionaries, but it came to have an ethnological meaning as well. Although the word continues to be used in some regions (in the interior of Borneo, for example), anthropologists have generally gotten away from it because of its ethnocentric and negative implications. However, its abandonment has left some linguistic awkwardness in referring to the religious traditions of the nonadherents of the world religions.

The other way of using the notion of indigenous religion is much broader. This is to refer to religious traditions, beliefs, and practices that have been around a long time, that are widespread, and that are to be found among both the adherents and nonadherents of the world religions. The belief in many spirits; the recourse to shamans, spirit mediums, or other specialists to deal with them; notions of bad death, two-stage mortuary practices, agricultural fertility rituals; and many other things can be safely and usefully considered "indigenous."

ANIMISM

Animism is another widely used but problematic term. It refers simply to the belief in spirits and, as such, has also often been used as a label for religious traditions of those peoples in Southeast Asia who do not adhere to one of the world religions. This can be misleading in several ways. First, "belief" is only one dimension of religion; what people do in relation to beliefs is as important as the beliefs themselves. Anthropologists thus sometimes refer to "spirit cults" rather than simply spirit beliefs, for the notion of cult implies activity and organization as well.[1] The second is that referring to some peoples as "animists" makes it sound like such people are unique in believing in spirits. In actuality, Buddhists, Islamics, and Christians are just as likely to be animists as those who do not belong to these religions. Keeping these issues in mind, let us turn to some elementary beliefs and the practices through which animistic beliefs are manifest.

Souls

As elsewhere in the world, Southeast Asian peoples traditionally hold to the belief that all humans have "souls." In a nutshell, a soul is a spirit or spiritual essence that is connected with the human body, that lives in a person but survives death. As do many other peoples, the Southeast Asians also commonly suppose that souls have a degree of independence from the person. The body is regarded as permeable where spirits are concerned. External spirits can enter and take possession of a person, or alternatively, the soul may leave the body, for example, as a result of a person being startled or badly frightened. Illness may be seen as a consequence of soul loss, and one form of curing involves finding and restoring the soul to its proper place in the body. But it is better to keep the soul where it belongs in the first place. A woman among the Black Hmong of northern Vietnam, for example, sometimes wears a small chain and lock around her neck to keep her chest soul from getting away.

With death, the soul is believed to become a detached spirit. This is widely thought to be a time of peril for the living, for unprocessed souls of the dead may be dangerous, especially if the person who has died has done so in certain ways. One important purpose of funerals is therefore to secure the transformation of the spirits of the dead to another state or place of being, meaning one or more things. One is that the spirit finds its way to the land of the dead, where it will reside either temporarily or permanently, being unable to trouble the living. Another is that the soul will be reincarnated, that is, reborn into a new body. Yet another is that the ghost will be transformed into an ancestor spirit. In its most fully developed form (for example, among the Vietnamese), this will involve ancestor worship whereby the spirit will be prayed to and cared for with offerings by the living and will, in return, watch over and protect them. Regardless of what is thought to happen, the process may be accomplished simply and relatively quickly or it may require months or even years, as with two-stage mortuary practices. Also, however, the transformation may be hindered or blocked by the circumstances of death, in which case the soul becomes temporarily or permanently a malevolent and dangerous spirit.

All of this seems fairly straightforward. Given the several basic doctrinal premises about the soul, beliefs about what can or does happen to it seem to logically follow. However, there are complications. These involve a doctrine that has been widely noted in the literature on Southeast Asian peoples, that persons do not have only one soul. The number of souls that have been reported for different Southeast Asian ethnolinguistics groups range from the minimum of two to more than thirty. The various Tai groups, including both those who are Buddhist and those who are not, seem to be in the forefront of multisoul believers. The Shans of Burma and the Lao, both of whom are lowland Buddhist peoples, suppose there are thirty-two souls per person (Lebar, Hickey, and Musgrave 1964, 196, 219). One highland, non-Buddhist group of Tai believes there are thirty-six (236).

Of the multisoul believers, some refer to them all by the same term, while others use different terms. In either case, multiple souls tend to be differentiated in one way or another. The most common notion appears to be that the different souls are associated with different parts or organs of the body. For example, the head may be one place for a soul and the chest or stomach another. The Lamet, a highland, Mon-Khmer people of Laos, think they have one of their two souls in the head and the other in their knees (Lebar, Hickey, and Musgrave 1964, 119). Those Tai groups that recognize thirty-two souls simply see them as divided between the head and the body. A second form of differentiation involves purpose, moral character, or behavior. Here, the general idea is that different souls represent spiritual dimensions of personality. For example, the Katu, a Mon-Khmer group who dwells in the highland interior of central Vietnam, are reported to believe in two souls, one good and one bad—and that, fortunately, it is the good soul that survives after death (143). According to Carolyn Heinz (2004, 808), the Hmong of northern Thailand and Laos conceive of the soul as a loosely organized collection of seven different entities associated with the six sense organs (two eyes, two ears, a nose, and a mouth), each of which can escape the body either singly or together, a development that may occur in a serious illness or as a result of a bad fright. Escaped souls are thought of as being lost in the forest until they are found and returned home by a shaman or someone else who knows how to do this.

Some such notions of souls seem psychologically very complex. The Karen, a large and widespread indigenous Tibeto-Burmese highland minority living on both sides of the border in eastern Burma and western Thailand, identify a set of four souls with attributes that seem like they might have inspired Sigmund Freud. One is linked to consciousness and, a second, with the vital essence of the body. This latter soul is believed to sometimes leave the body, which results in illness. Then there is a third soul that seeks to cause death. This is the one the Karen fear after a death has occurred and attempt to prevent from returning. The last soul is associated with the personality, and it is this one that is supposed to be reincarnated (Lebar, Hickey, and Musgrave 1964, 62).

A final way of distinguishing among multiple souls concerns inheritance. The Lao, the dominant lowland Tai, and Buddhist people of Laos, who also suppose there are thirty-two souls, are reported to hold that twenty come from the father and twelve from the mother (Lebar, Hickey, and Musgrave 1964, 219). The Tho, a Tai highland people of northern Vietnam, have a model of multiple souls that seems like a complicated mystical version of *x* and *y* chromosomes. Here, some souls emanate from a male principle, called *hon*, associated with the sun and sky. Others manifest a female principle, known as *via*, linked to the moon. Both men and women are believed to have both *hon* and *via* souls, but not in equal proportions. There are only three *hon* souls compared to sixteen *via* ones of which, moreover, men have seven and women have nine—although how anyone manages to keep all of this straight seems hard to imagine and is not reported (235). While the forms and bases of multiple soul beliefs make for fascinating reading, it is pertinent to ask about their importance or about the extent they affect actual behavior. For example, the anthropologist Stanley Tambiah (1970, 58), who has written about Thai animism at length, states that the Thai of northeastern Thailand distinguish between two different kinds of soul, one labeled as *khwan* and the other as *winjan*. But while the *khwan* soul is believed to be fragmented into thirty-two parts, each associated with a different part of the body, no villager can actually list these locations. Moreover, the *khwan* soul is also conceived to be a single entity, and the rites performed to recall a lost *khwan* treat it as one thing, in which case the notion of multiple souls is, among these Thai at least, secondary and unimportant as a matter of ritual.

Gods and Spirits

The supernatural beings most frequently referred to in the literature as "spirits" form a broad category. The general Malay/Indonesian term for spirits is *hantu*, and the Thai term is *phi*, although these terms in both instances tend to mean malevolent beings in particular. Further, both Malays and Thais use the same term for the soul of a person who has died as for other types of spirit. In addition, some distinction is usually made among

Photo 8.1. White Tai man making an offering to the spirit of the forest and of the village at an annual festival, Bouammi village, Luang Prabang Province, northeastern Laos, 2010.

Southeast Asian peoples between spirits and gods, but this is not done consistently. The Malay term for gods is *dewa*, although this refers specifically to the Hindu divinities (and definitely does not include the Muslim god Allah). The Malays also recognize and refer to Muslim spirits as *jin* (genie) rather than as *hantu*. The Thai also make a very fundamental distinction between spirits (*phi*) and gods or divinities (*thewada*).

While the spirits live on earth and are generally capricious and harmful, the gods live in heaven and are benevolent. However, there are also helpful guardian or ancestor spirits, although they also punish immorality (Tambiah 1970, 60, 264). Spirits tend to be regarded more as a generic category of supernatural beings than gods or deities. Unless recognized as the spirit of some particular person who has died, spirits generally do not have personal names or individual identities. The famous Thirty-seven Nats of Burma, all of which are supposed to have individual names, though not known to ordinary peoples, are a partial exception (Lebar, Hickey, and Musgrave 1964, 43). Gods or divinities in contrast are more apt to be recognized as individual beings with personal names and personal characteristics. Gods are often known through both oral and written traditions and are associated with the mythology of the world religions. Spirits may have some association with written tradition but are primarily a matter of oral tradition. Or to put it another way, spirits tend be local while gods or divinities have a wider identity. Again, however, there are important complications and exceptions. While the rural Thai recognize a few gods (*thewada*) as individual beings, they see most of them as a general type (Tambiah 1970, 60).

Spirits often have an identity in terms of place. Sometimes referred to as nature spirits, these are commonly thought to occupy particular locations in the environment. Such places can include particular rocks or a rock formation; a bend or junction of a river; a fork in the road; a pool, lake, or spring; or a cave, to name only a few. Of all place spirits, those supposed to dwell in trees are probably the most common. While spirits may be thought to dwell in different types of trees (large trees seem to be favored), particular varieties stand out. The Banyan and strangler figs (all species of ficus), which begin by growing on an existing tree and eventually envelop and kill it, are widely, and not surprisingly, thought to be haunted. Driving along the roads of northern Thailand, you will see small platforms attached to trees or erected on posts nearby. The Thais thus often mark places where spirits are thought to reside either with such simple altars or with open or closed spirit houses designed as miniature palaces. These also appear at particular trees along the road.

Ancestor Spirits and Ancestor Worship

References to ancestor spirits and to cults of ancestor worship are common in the ethnographic and ethnological literature on Southeast Asia. The Human Relations Area Files (HRAF) ethnological atlases of mainland Southeast Asia and insular Southeast Asia contain a great many such references (Lebar 1972, 1975; Lebar, Hickey, and Musgrave 1964). For example, the entry for the Kachin of Upper Burma includes the following:

> The supernatural world is largely personal, two classes being prominent. First are the ancestral spirits. This class includes the major deities—those who have names and are common to all Kachins—remote ancestors of the chiefs and commoners in general. Minor deities like the household guardian spirits are the immediate ancestors of the living. All these are to some degree concerned with the welfare of their descendants in this world. Their attitude is generally benevolent or neutral. Their malevolent activities are provoked by their imagined neglect by the living, who must approach them as they would superiors

in this world, through gifts, sacrifices and the proper forms of speech. (Lebar, Hickey, and Musgrave 1964, 16)

Generally speaking, references to ancestors and ancestor worship need to be looked at closely and sometimes qualified regarding what is really involved. To begin with, ancestor sprits may take their place among many different types of supernatural beings that are recognized but not actively included in ritual activities; alternately, they may be (as apparently among the Kachin) the focus of organized cults of worship. Further, some groups seem concerned mainly or only with more ancient ancestors. Such ancestors are sometimes said to have been elevated to deities. In contrast, among some groups, important ancestors are "family ancestors." These are the immediate forbears of the living members of society. These will remain important or recognized for only a few generations or less. The Kachin, again, appear to have both types.

The fullest and most complex of beliefs and practices involving ancestor spirits probably occurs among the Vietnamese and the Chinese living throughout Southeast Asia. Beyond these peoples, such beliefs and practices are most common in the northern reaches of mainland Southeast Asia where, like the lowland Vietnamese, many of the highland peoples are known or assumed to have been influenced by the Chinese. Ancestors are also widely reported to be important in the religions of some insular Southeast Asian peoples as well. Throughout the Indonesian Archipelago, groups (outside those adhering to Islam) are often reported to hold beliefs in ancestors (Lebar 1972, 22, 35, 43, 57, 77, 86, 102, 105, 106, 121). Such beliefs also include both immediate family ancestors and more ancient "hero" ancestors who founded clans, established villages, led migrations, and so forth. Such ancestors are also sometimes said to have been elevated to gods (Lebar 1972, 40). Though widely reported, beliefs in ancestor spirits are not necessarily associated with full ancestor worship of the sort traditionally practiced by the Vietnamese or the Chinese.[2]

Whether or not a group practices ancestor worship is open to question. The Thai scholar Kingkeo Attagara (1968, 39–40) states that the Thai of northern Thailand believe in and make offerings to a house spirit (*phi ruan*) and that this is a form of ancestor worship. When a house is built, for example, an offering is made to a *phi ruan*, and when a family member dies and the funeral has been completed, a procession takes place in order to lead the spirit of the deceased back home. Tambiah (1970, 314–15) offers a more detailed discussion of beliefs and practices regarding ancestor spirits in northeastern Thailand in which he concludes they do not amount to ancestor worship. Ancestor spirits are supposed to be remembered and commemorated as a general category of the dead, not as named or individually recognized beings. Such spirits are believed in and propitiated—but propitiation is occasional rather than regular, as when an ancestor is thought to be causing illness in a living descendant. Ancestor spirits are believed to become troublesome when living descendents fail to make merit for the dead or when they quarrel over the inheritance of property. However, such situations are regarded as though the problem-causing ancestor is like any other malevolent spirit. Elsewhere, he summarizes:

> While it can be said that villagers commemorate the dead, it cannot be said that they practice "ancestor worship" in the sense of a systematized cult of propitiation of the dead and a formalized relationship by which the dead interact with the living. The possibility of occasional punitive acts by the "normally dead" is a far cry from a developed theory of morality of benevolence/punitiveness by which the dead live in the present and sanction the social order. (Tambiah 1970, 191)

Special Deities: The Rice Spirit and the Dragon

The rice spirit is one of the most important and widespread of the recognized and ritually propitiated supernatural beings in Southeast Asia. The rice spirit is female and usually referred to in English as the "rice goddess" or "rice mother," while local names vary from one group or language to another.

According to Attagara (1968, 42–43), in northern Thailand, the rice spirit is known as Mae Phosob, although sometimes other names are added as well. She is supposed to both protect the rice and embody its development, which is thought of in terms of becoming pregnant and bearing children. Rice planting therefore involves a set of rituals that are carried out parallel to the other activities of cultivation. Farmers first plant some stalks of rice grown in the seedbed in one corner of the field where Mae Phosob is supposed to stay. As the rice plants begin to form seeds, it is said that Mae Phosob has become pregnant. The farmers then make offerings to her of foods that are desired by a woman who is expecting—including sour fruits and desserts made of nuts and sesame seeds as well as cooked rice. They may also offer cosmetics and jewelry—for rice mothers, like mortal women, want to look beautiful. When the rice is harvested, Mae Phosob is formally invited into the farmer's house. Rice that has been grown in a special corner is cut and tied into a bundle, which is then fastened to a stick with a flag made of silk or other beautiful material and placed above the main stack of rice. The special bundle is then brought to the farmer's house in a small procession preceded by someone carrying the flag. This bundle is then kept in the house and is not eaten.

Details aside, activities of the sort described here are to be found over a wide area of both mainland and insular Southeast Asia. They are very similar to what is believed and done in the interior of Borneo, for example.

Here, Mae Phosob would feel right at home among the Kayan of central Borneo. The Kayan mother of the rice is called Hunyang Lahi. At the harvest festival, the women of the village households give her offerings and pray: "Now, I eat with you [plural], *padi*, you are mine, you who are the children of the mother [lit. women] of rice. From downriver, from upriver, from below, from above, from across the hillside, come to eat here. I eat with you, children of the mother of rice" (Rousseau 1998, 183). One difference is that the Kayan also make an offering to the *peliut* bird, which is said to copulate with the *padi* because it nests at the base of the *padi* stalks and is therefore also responsible for their fertility.

The Dragon

The dragon is also an important supernatural being throughout much of Southeast Asia. It is associated with the underworld and with water, including rainfall. It is also important in India and, especially, China and may have come from either or both of these places to Southeast Asia, though local Southeast Asian origins probably cannot be ruled out. There are differences in the characteristics of dragons from one place to another. But there are also enough widespread commonalities for it to be appropriate to use the same English term for all such creatures.

In Southeast Asia, the dragon is widely known by the Indic term *naga* or derivatives such as *nag* in Thai. The dragon is a basically a reptilian creature and is, therefore, generally depicted with scales. They are usually but not always shown with small legs and wings. The legs tend to associate them more with lizards or crocodiles, but dragons are also usually shown with an undulating form characteristic of serpents.

In Thailand, Laos, and elsewhere, the dragon has been incorporated into Buddhism. Dragons therefore often form the tops of balustrades on each side of the steps leading up to temples, the head at the bottom and the mouth open. In northern Laos, the mouths of such dragons usually contain balls of sticky rice, put there as offerings by those who visit the temples or pass by (see photo 8.2). And one of the common statue forms of the Buddha shows him sitting on the coils of a *naga* with its seven cobralike heads forming a protective hood over him.

The dragon in northern Thailand also has a role in rice cultivation. As a creature of the underworld, the dragon is implicated in preparation of the soil. According to Attagara (1968, 41), the time of the initiation of plowing is a matter of ritual concern. People prefer to begin on Wednesday although this is not normally an auspicious day. But because on this day the dragon is supposed to have a dirty bottom, it is a good day to turn the soil. It is also important to "follow the scales of the dragon." The dragon moves around under the ground in accord with the time of year. In the sixth lunar month

Photo 8.2.   Dragon balustrade at the entrance to Wat Nam Kaew, Luang Buddhist Temple, Muang Sing, Luang Namtha Province, northern Laos, 2005. The dragons' mouths contain balls of sticky rice given as offerings.

when the plowing is done, the dragon's head is in the west. Therefore, plowing should begin in an easterly direction, for the dragon's scales point backward from its head—that is, at this time, to the west. Beginning to plow in the wrong direction—against the scales of the dragon—will often result in a broken plow.

Throughout the interior of Borneo, the dragon is the most important of the lower world divinities and is associated especially with water. Though known here by a variety of local names, it is usually depicted in similar ways as a motif in painting and carving. As the main lord of the underworld, the dragon oversees the transition from life to death and beyond, and is therefore a prominent design in traditional Dayak mortuary images painted on coffins or carved onto tombs (see photo 8.3). The dragon in Borneo is also a powerful protector against other sprits and, as such, appears frequently in Dayak tattoos, on baby carriers, and on carved longhouse doors and funeral monuments and containers (Sellato 1989, 44–45).

But while protective, dragons can make serious trouble if crossed. In the late 1990s, a dragon was said to be causing difficulties in the small town of Bau in western Sarawak. A popular recreational lake outside of town was

Photo 8.3. Image of a dragon swallowing a soul painted on the lid of a Taman coffin, Melapi, upper Kapuas River, West Kalimantan (Borneo), Indonesia, 1994.

drained so that gold could be mined in the area. A dragon long known to be living under the lake was angered, and rightly so many people thought. As a result, the surrounding land began to subside, destroying or damaging houses and other buildings in the area. The situation only improved when the mining was completed and the lake was refilled.

MALEVOLENT SPIRITS AND BAD DEATH

Discussions of spirit beliefs in Southeast Asia often distinguish between benevolent and malevolent types. As we have seen, the rice spirit is an extremely important benevolent spirit who provides the food on which most people depend and regard as sacrosanct. Ancestor spirits are also held to be benevolently disposed to their living descendants, at least as long as they are properly remembered with worship and offerings and otherwise not offended by breaches of morality. The *naga* dragon in Theravada Buddhist Southeast Asia is also benevolent as a protector of the Buddha. The Bornean Dayak version of the dragon is extremely fierce, but it is also the most important protector of all. The omen birds of Borneo are supposed to be benevolently inclined toward humans, their purpose being to warn of danger or signal an auspicious opportunity to proceed with an activity or a journey. Yet other helpful spirits or divinities include those invoked by spirit mediums or shamans to help them in their curing activities.

Many other spirits are regarded as malevolently disposed toward people. Generally, they bring trouble, for example, by invading a person's body and causing illness, in which case they are dealt with by engaging an expert who will attempt to drive them out or persuade them to leave. In this regard, they can provide an explanation of the illnesses and other misfortune that befall human beings. Some spirits are thought to be dangerous mainly if their space is intruded upon or they are offended in one or another way. Others that cause trouble move around. Finally, just as most benevolently disposed spirits are not beyond causing harm for either vain or moral reasons, some basically malevolent ones can be tamed or gotten to provide assistance, for example, by becoming household or village guardian spirits (Tambiah 1970).

Although Southeast Asian beliefs about spirits do not seem to form a coherent integrated theology, there are certain widespread ideas. Some spirits are believed to have always been there in the sense that people do not have any idea where they came from. But many spirits are supposed to have originated as the ghosts of persons who have died in certain ways and have not made the proper transition to the afterlife. Such forms of death are most commonly referred to as bad or unnatural. References to beliefs and ritual practices involving such death are common in the ethnological and ethnographic literature on Southeast Asia. In Frank Lebar, Gerald Hickey, and John Musgrave's (1964) ethnological handbook, the entries for many groups make reference in one way or another to notions of bad death, its consequences, and its special ritual treatment. Such entries include those for the Akha, Burmese, Garo, Hmong, Jarai, Katu, Khmer, Lamet, Lao, Mon, Paluang, Shan, and Tai Lu. The entries of the Lebar handbooks (1972, 1975) for insular Southeast Asia include references to the Nicobar Islanders, the people of Roti, Kai, the Idahan Murut of Borneo, and the Tagbauua and Hanunoo in the Philippines. Such lists are certainly far from complete. There are also more detailed ethnographic discussions of bad death notions and ritual activities for groups including Malays, Thais, Burmese, Vietnamese, and Dayaks in Borneo, some of which we shall discuss. While some anthropologists who have described bad death for a particular group may be aware of other accounts of it elsewhere, many appear to be unaware of its scope.

To begin at one of the geographical extremes of Southeast Asia, we have James Fox's (1973, 351–56) account for Roti, a small island in eastern Indonesia, which mentions most of the same features noted in the northern mainland. Here, as elsewhere, people make an explicit distinction between good and bad death. To die a good death is to "die in one's house" (*mati nai uma-low*). Such death is also referred to as "an ancestral death" or "death of the good spirits." There are also several ways of referring to bad death, although Fox finds these somewhat difficult to translate. One has the implication of murder, although literal murder ("to be killed by a man") is only one of many forms of bad death. Others include death in childbirth, falling from a Lontar Palm (not uncommon since these palms are tapped very frequently for food), being gored by a water buffalo, being struck by lightning, being carried away by a flood, drowning at sea, or being bitten by a crocodile. As for consequences of these deaths, perhaps the most important consideration is that bad death is dangerous to others. This is usually above all because the person who has died a bad death will become a malevolent spirit. For example, a woman who dies in childbirth becomes a *buntianak*, a particularly dreaded spirit that will attack other women in childbirth. A bad death entails special ritual procedures aimed at thwarting such a spirit. Though things are now changing, these procedures, mainly in negative terms, include not burying such a person in a coffin, not bringing the body into the house, or, if the death has occurred in the house, getting it out right away—and headfirst rather than feetfirst (so the spirit will have to wander around upside down). On Roti, the bad dead are also buried away from the good dead, without the normal ritual.

The most extreme practices in dealing with bad death seem to be found among those peoples who follow only indigenous traditions. Peter Metcalf (1982, 254–56), for example, vividly describes what traditionally happened in a pre-Christian Berawan Dayak longhouse in northern Sarawak, Borneo, when a woman dies in childbirth. In such an event, there is no hope the soul will achieve the desired afterlife, and therefore no point in performing the death chants or other normal mortuary procedures. The main concern is to get rid of the body as quickly as possible and in a way that the spirit poses the least threat to the living. It falls to the husband alone to remove the body as quickly as possible. He does this by moving the floorboards of the longhouse, removing the body through this hole, taking it into the forest, and burying away from the graveyard. This is done in the hope that the woman's spirit will not find its way back to the longhouse and cause trouble.

As this summary should make clear, bad death is bad in several senses. One is obvious: it refers to death that would be regarded anywhere as premature, unnatural, frightening, bloody, or painful, and that involve in some instances the disfiguration or mutilation of the body. Although the list of types of bad death varies somewhat, there is remarkable similarity over a very wide area. These include suicide, drowning, being killed by an animal, death in childbirth, death by violence, or sometimes death by dreaded disease. Note that with the possible exception of suicide, these ways of dying do not imply a moral lapse on the part of the person who has died.

The other and perhaps more important sense in which bad death is bad concerns its supernatural consequences and the danger these pose to living people. It results in a malevolent ghost, which must be handled in special ways. One local explanation for this development is that the spirit of the person who has died badly is angered because his or her life has been cut short, unfulfilled, and ended in a violent rather than a natural and peaceful way. Although this varies, the denial of full or regular mortuary procedures is a consequence of what has happened to such a soul.

Bad Death among the Burmese, Thai, and Malays

For Muslims, Buddhists, or Christians, the normal ways of handling the dead are fundamental provisions of religious doctrine and practice that could not be easily or completely ignored. Such peoples are less likely to go to the extreme of simply abandoning or hastily disposing of bodies without any ritual whatsoever. Nonetheless, bad death notions and special ritual procedures have been discussed for both Buddhist peoples, including the Burmese and the Thai, and for Muslim Malays. And a somewhat particular bad death pattern has been recently described in detail concerning Vietnamese who died in the war with the United States.

In the case of the Burmese, the general pattern is similar to that already noted. Bad death here is known as "green death." It includes the death of women in childbirth and of anyone who succumbs to a dreaded disease, has died in an accident, or has been murdered. Such individuals are supposed to not undergo reincarnation but instead remain on earth as malignant ghosts. The bodies of those who have died a green death are buried with little ceremony (Lebar, Hickey, and Musgrave 1964, 43). Such death is best known in relation to the famous Thirty-seven Nats, all supposedly spirits of persons who died violently, mainly by execution.

Bad death beliefs and ritual procedures among the Thai, as described by both Tambiah (1970, 189–90, 315) and Attagara (1968, 117–18), are somewhat milder than those noted for the Burmese, but still present. Both state that bad or abnormal death is feared because of the dangerous ghost that results and that the body is buried hastily, without the usual involvement of Buddhist monks and cremation. But both scholars also report that such ritual treatment eventually takes place. In her study of the folk religion of a Thai village in central Thailand, Attagara notes "people do not seem to mind the return of the spirits [of the dead], so long as they are benevolent. Thus the spirits of the older members of the family who die a natural death are very much respected and prayed to." The implication here is that those who die an unnatural death are not prayed to. There is also a difference in the handling of cremation.[3]

For Malays of peninsular Malaysia and present-day south Thailand, the literature on bad death is extensive but comes mainly from colonial accounts produced a hundred years ago. Kirk Endicott includes an extensive discussion of these accounts in his *Analysis of Malay Magic* (1970). Here he presents a complex description and analysis of Malay notions of bad death and related notions and proclivities.

The common Malay term for bad death is *mati di bunoh*, which literally refers to murder but could, Endicott suggests, mean simply "death by being killed." This would include being killed by a malevolent spirit, but would also include other sorts of violent or unusual death (Endicott 1970, 66). It is again the usual notion, and the special concerns raised in dealing with the bodies resulting from bad death are also familiar. In 1903, the colonial scholars Nelson Annandale and Edwin Robinson reported that "the corpse of a murdered man was formerly 'cast forth to be eaten by vultures and dogs,' now, most commonly, it would be buried in the jungle or some waste place, or, it in the cemetery, in the part furthest from human habitation" (quoted in Endicott 1970, 71). *Mati di bunoh* also includes death in childbirth, again, the most dreaded form. And here, if the death is double, it results in two infamous demon spirits. The mother's spirit becomes a *langsuir*, a kind of vampire who will drink the blood of children and can take the form of an owl or a beautiful woman who also attacks and preys upon men. The stillborn child becomes a *pontianak* (literally dead child), also a vampire that attacks and kills both mother and child at birth (71, 62).

The vampire demons are among the best known of Malay spirits. Another example of a result of bad death is the *penangallan*, an immodest woman who one day was sitting naked in front of a vat of palm wine in order to strengthen her body and attain magical power. A man came along and startled her badly. As a result, she kicks her chin so hard that her head flew off with her intestines attached. The woman immediately became a demon ghost that takes the form of head and intestines and is bent on revenge (Laderman 1983, 126–27).

Tales of the *langsuir*, the *pontianak*, and the *penangallan* are classic Malay vampire ghost stories first collected and published in English a century or more ago. But do they have any presence or meaning for Malays in more recent times? Today, older Malays probably know these stories well. And new versions continue to emerge in urban (and rural) folklore. When I was in Kelantan in the mid 1980s, the *langsuir* had been turned into a version of the well-known vanishing hitchhiker. In one version of the tale, a man driving along a rural road sees a good-looking woman who is waving at him to stop. He pulls over, she gets in, and they drive away. Then, at a lonely place in the road, the woman asks to be let out in front of a cemetery. As she turns to open the door, the man notices that beneath her long hair she has a gaping hole in her back at the base of her neck. As everyone will know at this point, the man had picked up a *langsuir*. This was the family version. There was also an adult version in which, after getting in the car, the woman offers the man sex. Just as they begin, however, the woman turns into a dried-up coconut, the man's penis inserted into a hole eaten through the shell by a squirrel.

But do Malays still (that is, more recently) show concern about attacks by demons when women are giving birth? In a study of Malay midwives, pregnancy, and childbearing (published in 1983), medical anthropologist Carol Laderman dealt with this issue in a limited way. Her research involved villagers in the rural Malaysian east coast state of Trengganu. Here, the activities of traditional midwives (*bidan kampung*) include matters of magic and ritual, and traditional ritual specialists/curers (*bomoh*) are brought in whenever supernatural danger threatens. She describes in detail one instance of a difficult birth in which the child was stillborn though the mother lived. In this instance, Muslim rather than the customary magical rituals were used by the *bomoh*. But after the birth was complete, the midwife blamed a spirit for the death of the child. She recounted that she could feel the spirit (*hantu*, presumably a vampire) pushing the baby back inside as she tried to get it out. She explained that the spirit had been able to suck the blood out of the child because it had been weakened by the umbilical cord being wrapped around its neck (Laderman 1983, 164).

Bad Death and the War in Vietnam

The lengthiest discussion of bad death in Southeast Asia in the contemporary period concerns Vietnam, specifically in relation to what the Vietnamese call the American War. This war produced bad death on a massive scale. One discussion is in Shaun Malarney's (2002) study of social, political, and religious change in postwar Vietnam. Heonik Kwon (2006) provides a longer account, devoted entirely to the trauma of war. Kwon's special concern is the consequences of the massacre of civilians at My Lai and Ha My, but all battlefield death is bad according to traditional Vietnamese views, especially those instances in which the remains are not recovered, identified, and returned to their families. Because of the scale of death among both combatants and civilians, the number of bad dead has been very large. It has probably touched a very large proportion of families in Vietnam. Kwon's detailed and highly contextualized discussion focuses on how the Vietnamese in the postwar period have attempted to cope with bad death from war. He also notes the conflicts that have arisen between traditional Vietnamese beliefs (that death in war is ritually bad) and the efforts of the government to create a cult of heroism of those who died in the war as a means mobilizing and perpetuating political loyalty and solidarity.

Kwon uses the English words "good death" and "bad death" throughout the book. He also provides both the Vietnamese terms for good and bad death and literal translations of them. The Vietnamese terms refer specifically to where the death occurs. Good death is *chet na* or "death at home," which interestingly is the same as the meaning given by Fox for good death in Roti. The Vietnamese term for bad death is *chet duong* or "death in the street." Kwon states that the Vietnamese phrases should not be taken literally; rather, death in the street implies a violent or accidental demise, and death at home means a peaceful and normal one. A violent death at home would be considered *chet duong* or bad. Vietnamese notions of good and bad death, as reflected in the terms used, overlap to a significant degree with those of other Southeast Asian peoples (Kwon 2006, 7, 12–16, 89).

Kwon stresses that the grief family members feel is greatly complicated when the remains of the war dead are often never identified, recovered, and returned for a proper funeral. A proper funeral is necessary for the spirits of dead to be installed as ancestors. There can also be a major problem if a man or a woman dies without leaving offspring (as a great many did in Vietnam); there will be no one to properly perform ancestor worship. The death of children, who will also have no proper place in the ancestral scheme, is also a complication that worsens the grief (Kwon 2006, 70–71). A further complication arises from massacres where bodies were buried in mass graves (120). Here, the recovered bones may not be correctly sorted and identified. Malarney (2002, 180) adds to this the observation that, for the northern Vietnamese, a body must be whole: "A corpse that is missing body parts or is otherwise incomplete is doomed to roam the earth and never cross to the other world."

In one respect, Vietnamese concerns about bad death seem to be almost the complete opposite of those of other peoples in Southeast Asia. Kwon stresses that, in Vietnam, a major source of suffering and anxiety for the family members of those who die a bad death is that the bodies cannot be obtained, given proper funeral rites, and incorporated into the family tomb where they will rest in peace and provide support as ancestors. Elsewhere in Southeast Asia, the common inclination is to have as little to do with the bodies of the bad dead as possible, and to be rid of them as quickly as possible, either permanently or at least until they have lost their malign nature. The general tendency ranges from the complete abandonment of the body to its rapid disposal with minimum ritual treatment. The predominant emotion other than grief seems to be fear of the supernatural consequences of bad death.

The Vietnamese pattern is based on principles of Confucianism and ancestor worship that it shares with China and other East Asian countries rather than with most of the remainder of Southeast Asia. These principles require that those who have died and who qualify on the basis of kinship and descent be ritually transformed from ghosts into ancestral spirits. At least, this is to be done if the death has been a good one and the body is available to be given the proper funeral. The Vietnamese, also like the Chinese, order their family and kinship in terms of patrilineal descent (through the male line) and preferably virilocal residence (whereby a couple after marriage goes to reside with or near the family of the husband). This also determines who becomes an ancestor of whom, and in which household an ancestor will reside and be worshipped. Apart from the Vietnamese, most of the surrounding peoples of Southeast Asia (the Thai, Khmer, Burmese, Malays, and most Indonesians and Filipinos, among others) do not follow patrilineal descent or reside according to patrilocal rules. References to beliefs in ancestor spirits and their powers to affect their living descendants are common elsewhere in Southeast Asia, but the practices involved are much less organized than those of the Vietnamese or Chinese.

TWO-STAGE MORTUARY PRACTICES

The notions of what can happen to the soul are related to the complex mortuary practices that are widespread in Southeast Asia. Many groups throughout both insular and mainland Southeast Asia practice "secondary burial." Of all mortuary practices known, these are perhaps the most difficult to understand in terms of what we are apt to think about funerals: that is, the ritual disposal of the remains of the deceased, the separation of the soul from the living, and its conveyance to the land of the dead or rebirth into a new person. The use of the phrase secondary burial is somewhat inappropriate to what often happens in Southeast Asia. Here, the second stage does not necessarily involve "reburial" in the literal sense. Indeed, reburial in the ground is not common. What usually occurs is therefore more accurately termed "secondary treatment," and this could include cremating or placing what remains of the bones in an aboveground receptacle. The term "secondary" is also misleading insofar as it implies "lesser," for the second ceremony is usually the larger and more elaborate one. An even broader and more appropriate phrase would be "two-stage mortuary practices."

Described in the simplest of terms, two-stage mortuary practices involve two funerals rather than one or a funeral cycle divided into two very distinct stages. These include an initial ceremony of disposal that is usually modest and often hurried, and a later and often far larger one that usually includes the reburial or other reprocessing of the remains.[4] Why should some people follow such two-stage mortuary practices? What is the logic involved? One possibility is that, when a death has occured, something must quickly be done with the body, but there is also a desire to hold a large ceremony that requires time to accumulate resources and for people to gather from far and near. In actuality, while such considerations are involved, they are not necessarily the main ones, at least in Southeast Asia. The real or most crucial part of the explanation was formulated a century ago by the French anthropologist Robert Hertz ([1907] 1960) on the basis of ethnographic evidence from Southeast Asia, especially Borneo, where two-stage mortuary practices are, or until recently were, especially common.

A crucial part of Hertz's explanation of two-stage mortuary practices was the belief held about the nature of death, specifically, that it is a drawn-out process rather than an instant transformation. In the modern Western view, life and death form a simple dichotomy: a person is either alive or dead; a person is alive until breathing has stopped and other vital signs have ceased. Of course, advanced medical technology has complicated this, and we are fascinated and troubled by states that are between life and death, such as coma (consider the highly politicized national controversy over stopping life support for the long-comatose Terry Schiavo). But none of this alters our fundamentally dichotomous, black-and-white view of life and death.

Hertz realized that, in the case of two-stage mortuary practices, the belief is that death as we would define it is only the beginning of a transformation. Even in the absence of two-stage mortuary practices, there is abundant evidence from Southeast Asia that the dead are thought to continue to be animated in some sense. For example, a common ritual practice in Borneo and elsewhere in insular Southeast Asia was to set the body of the "deceased" up in a chair to be addressed and offered cigarettes and drink. While the rapid disposal of bodies in an tropical climate would seem to be the natural and sensible thing, and was and is usually done, the practice was in some instances to keep them around in a coffin or jar for a long time—the idea being the more respected the deceased person, the longer the delay of the funeral. In Thailand, the cremation of highly regarded monks is often delayed for a lengthy period.

The transformation of the soul, as Hertz came to understand it, was a process that would continue for a period of months or more and not be completed until the second ceremony was held. Before this time, the soul of the dead person lingers about the grave or in the vicinity of the group where it is a danger to the living. The final ceremony will also be delayed until the resources for what Hertz called a "great feast" can be accumulated. In Southeast Asia, this will involve animals to be sacrificed, rice and other food for feasting, and often rice wine for drinking. But the most important consideration is that the second ceremony must wait until the flesh of the body has disintegrated, leaving only the bones. In other words, Hertz concluded that the process of death involving the spirit was believed to mirror the physical transformation of the body. It is with the disappearance of everything but the bones that death is complete and the soul can be released for its journey to the land of the dead or to be reincarnated.

Two-stage mortuary practices of the classic Hertzian sort appear to be most common in insular Southeast Asia. They were formerly common among Dayak groups in the interior of Borneo, where both their ethnological contours and distribution have been studied and described in various accounts (e.g., Rousseau 1990, 17, 28, 213). There have also been several longer ethnographic treatments, including one for the Berawan of northern central Borneo and several for the Ngaju and other southern peoples (Metcalf 1982; Schiller 1997; Weinstock 1987). Most Dayak two-stage funeral rites have been discontinued, often as a result of conversion to Christianity or Islam, but some have continued in southern Borneo. Outside of Borneo, the famous, often spectacular, tourist-attracting cremations of the Balinese are second-stage mortuary ceremonies.

Two-stage mortuary practices in mainland Southeast Asia have been described for several peoples, including the Thai, the Vietnamese, and some of the other indigenous groups of the central highlands of southern Vietnam, including the Bahnar and several related peoples of northern Cambodia. For the Thai, the usual practice is a single funeral involving cremation held within a few days of death, although this may be delayed for a long period for esteemed monks believed endowed with miraculous powers.

Among the Thai, two-stage practices are reserved for special circumstances, which include bad death. According to Attagara (1968, 118), among the central Thai, an immediate cremation will not take place following an unnatural death. Instead, the body will be first buried in the ground for a period of time. If death has been unnatural, it is also necessary to remove the body from the house as quickly as possible so the house spirit will not be offended. Until it has been put in the ground for a period of time, the body is in a state of pollution. This does not entirely rule out Buddhist rites, for which the body is taken to the temple before it is buried. The length of time in the ground required to decontaminate the body should be at least one hundred days, but a shorter period of seven days or even a token burial may be substituted if the relatives are anxious to have the cremation completed. A proper longer period will make the body easier to handle, however. In this case, the undertaker will exhume the body and then separate the flesh from the bones, reburying the flesh in the grave and taking the bones for cremation.

The secondary practices of the northern Vietnamese have been recently described by Malarney in his larger account of ritual change in postrevolutionary Vietnam (2002, 142–44).[5] The activities he describes are those that took place in the commune of Thinh Liet near Hanoi in the 1990s. Here, about three years after the initial funeral, a series of commemorative rites are held with the reburial as the final act. The essential and distinctive activity is the exhumation of the remains that have been temporarily buried in a casket in one part of the cemetery and their reinterment in another part. The reburial of the bones rather than their placement in some aboveground chamber, or their cremation, differs from the more common practice elsewhere in Southeast Asia. However, two other common customs are followed. One is cleaning the bones and placing them in an urn (as done also in the interior of Borneo). In Vietnam, the excavated bones are ideally free of other matter and black in color—the blacker the better—though whether this is a matter of ritual importance or simply of aesthetic preference is unsaid.

The exhumation and reburial are, however, carefully carried out according to ritual considerations. One is that the casket must be excavated and opened and the bones cleaned early in the morning. This is because it is imperative that the light of the sun should not fall on the bones. Another is that great care must be taken to recover every bone, even if the casket is filled with mud. The incomplete transfer of the bones is regarded as bad form, and it could complicate the process of the soul finding peace. And finally, the bones are placed in the urn in careful order, with the skull on top.

Following the physical transfer and reburial of the remains, the family returns to their house. Here, they have a small feast for friends, relatives, and neighbors, from ten to twenty in all. The size of the gathering is far smaller than that of the first funeral for which the turnout is a major indicator of family status. This is the opposite of the case elsewhere in Southeast Asia, where it is the latter funeral that is the greater event. In Vietnam, however, the secondary ceremony has actually increased in size over what it had been several decades earlier. The increase seems due to government efforts to eliminate or deemphasize the size and cost of the initial funeral. But, large or small, the secondary ceremony accomplishes the same religious ends as elsewhere. With its conclusion the family members have discharged all of their mortuary obligations to the deceased. If done correctly, the soul has left its dangerous liminal state in which it could have become a malevolent ghost and has become a benevolent family ancestor (Malarney 2002, 144).

Tomb Abandonment in the Central Highlands of Vietnam

The practices followed by a series of non-Vietnamese ethnic groups in the northern central highlands of southern Vietnam constitute yet another form of two-stage mortuary practices.[6] These ceremonies do not involve exhumation and reburial. But the second ceremony, which is referred to as "tomb abandonment," again completes the ritual obligations of the living to the dead, to ensure the soul's transformation, and celebrates this development. Some of the peoples who follow such traditions include the Giarai and Ede (Rhade) who are speakers of Austronesian languages, which links them to the Indonesian peoples to the south; others, such as the Bahnar and the Mnong, speak variants of Mon-Khmer. The tomb abandonment ceremonies held in the central highlands have attracted the attention of

Vietnamese ethnologists in part because they are the largest and most important of the ritual activities followed by most of these groups.

Although what takes place in the central highlands varies somewhat from one group to another, the general ritual sequence is similar. After death, the body is placed in a coffin and buried in the village cemetery. (Or more accurately, this is the procedure with normal death, for again, bad death—said to include drowning, dying in childbirth, being killed by a tiger or in battle, or dying by suicide—complicates matters. Persons dying in bad ways are not buried in village cemeteries or accorded the two-stage treatment.) Single burials are the norm, but some groups will inter several members of a family together. In either case, a roof is erected over the grave and a stockade of logs or a fence is built around it (Nguyen and Luu 2003, 50).

This is also the occasion for the creation and erection of often elaborate and spectacular mortuary architecture and statues. The statues are diverse. They include carvings of birds, animals, and people, and those of people are clothed in modern as well as traditional dress, including military uniforms and Western attire. Many are of people doing ordinary things, such as women pounding rice and men playing gongs. Some statues are intended to be amusing or trendy, including ones of young people dressed in jeans and playing guitars; others are serious. Several traditional kinds of figures are particularly common and striking. One involves the so-called Hokker motif that is common Southeast Asia. This is a carving of a squatting man or woman with elbows resting on knees and head resting on hands, in this case, said to be showing a grieving mourner at the tomb. Others are of pregnant women and of men and women preparing to copulate or engaged in doing so. The traditional meaning also includes fertility, for the female figures are usually carved with swollen stomachs, and fertility is in keeping with the belief that the souls of the dead will eventually return into one of their descendants.

The burial begins the liminal phase, during which time it is assumed the soul of the deceased remains in or near the grave. Family members are in mourning and visit the grave regularly with offerings of food and drink for the soul. All of this continues for a year or more until the tomb abandonment ceremony is held. These ceremonies commonly take place in the dry season and require large-scale, villagewide preparations of food and drink, ritual materials, work on the tomb, and the carving of statues. The wealthier, more prominent, or important deceased get bigger ceremonies. Guests come from the surrounding area and much farther in the case of an important funeral. Over a period of three days, people eat and drink, animals are sacrificed, rituals are performed, and drums and gongs are played. The activities include a dance of farewell in which everyone forms a circle and dances in single file slowly around the tomb to say good-bye to the

Photo 8.4.   An abandoned Bahnar tomb, Rolay village, Kontum Province (central highlands), southern Vietnam, 2004.

soul of the deceased. Although the bones of the dead are not excavated, the ceremony is nonetheless a decisive point of transition. At this point, the soul is believed to leave the grave for good, the mourning period has ended, and the tomb is abandoned forever, the wooden roof, fence, and statues to decay and collapse (see photo 8.4).

SPIRIT POSSESSION, SPIRIT MEDIUMS, AND SHAMANISM

Several traditions of belief and ritual practice that form an important part of indigenous religion in Southeast Asia are based on the assumption that human bodies or personalities are supernaturally permeable—both to the exodus of a person's own soul and to the intrusion of spirits from without. These include spirit possession, spirit medium activities, and shamanism. The term spirit possession is used for what occurs when someone's personality has been entered and taken over by an alien spirit. Anthropologists recognize two basic forms of spirit possession, each involving its own ritual procedure. In one type, those involved suppose that possession is involuntary and may take place without conscious awareness of the person affected, and in the other, possession is voluntary or deliberate.

Involuntary Possession

In Southeast Asia, involuntary possession by external spirits is viewed negatively, that is, as a dangerous affliction. The symptoms of a person attacked may be mental, physical, or both, but in each case, the person possessed is in need of help or curing, that is, the invading or possessing spirit must be persuaded or forced to leave the afflicted person. The process by which such a spirit is driven out or persuaded to depart is, as most people are already aware, exorcism. The spirits thought to possess people are of various types. They may be ghosts—spirits of dead persons, especially, as we have seen, of those who have died bad deaths. Such spirits lurk around the places where they died or were buried and may possess people who come to such places. They may be nature spirits associated with certain trees, rivers, or swamps that attack and possess persons who have disturbed them. A further, and in some places very common, possibility is that possessing spirits have been sent by another person, in which case spirit possession is a form of sorcery—to be discussed below. It is also commonly assumed by those who accept possession as reality that the person possessed is unconscious, or at least powerless to resist, and therefore cannot be held responsible for whatever she or he may do. Spirit possession can have a sexual dimension. In Malaysia, unmarried women have sometimes offered this as an explanation for inappropriate pregnancy and childbirth.

Beyond description, those who study spirit possession have offered two kinds of explanations. This first is psychological: what is experienced and locally interpreted as possession is really emotional trauma. The person who manifests symptoms of involuntary possession is experiencing internal conflict, depression, anxiety, or other negative emotional states and expressing these in a traditional way that is readily understood by everyone and that is likely to gain help. A person who is suffering from some organic physical ailment will also experience fear or anxiety, especially if it involves severe pain, does not respond to organic medical treatment, or does not proceed through an expected cycle of improvement. Having an exorcist séance for a person experiencing psychological or physical illness will do several things that are likely to help, if not necessarily cure in a biomedical sense. It will demonstrate that others are concerned and provide an explanation for suffering and a means of dealing with it. Further, such an explanation can be a bridge between modern and traditional views of illness and other affliction. Rather than regarding beliefs and practices involving spirit possession as backward superstition to be put aside in favor of modern biomedical diagnosis and treatment, such a psychological interpretation offers respect for customary interpretations and procedures without requiring that anyone accept the literal truth of spirit possession, mediumship, and exorcism.[7]

The other sort of explanation, which is by no means incompatible with the first, is sociological. Here, spirit possession is interpreted as an expression of social conflict and an indirect form of protest. Anthropologists who have studied involuntary spirit possession have often found a pattern. According to the British anthropologist I. M. Lewis ([1971] 1989), who has made a broad study of this pattern and has developed the fullest and most single-minded explanation of it along this line, those who are attacked and become possessed and often those who attempt to cure them tend to represent the poorer or more marginal members of a society. In many instances, this means women. The general assumption is that women and others in such positions are particularly likely to experience emotional distress, and the most effective way of expressing this and to be taken seriously is through the "idiom of possession."

Involuntary Possession among Malays

In places where people accept the reality of malevolent spirits and their capability of entering into and taking over the personalities of humans, possession is treated seriously. However, this does not mean that some people are not skeptical of incidents of possession and of the motives of those who are afflicted. This was the case among Malays in rural west Malaysia, for example. Here, the traditional interpretations were often challenged by modern Western psychiatric ones that label what takes place as "hysteria." In the 1970s and 1980s, incidents of possession were considered in both ways, depending in part on the type of people engaged in the interpretation. In this period, episodes of spirit possession hysteria were very common in some areas. In the more traditional and rural part of peninsular Malaysia with which I was familiar at this time, "spirit possession hysteria" was well known among adolescent schoolgirls. This should not be taken to mean that the context was exactly traditional. Mass schooling in Malaysia was at that time relatively recent, and even more so for women than men. Moreover, one way to interpret what took place is to see the incidents as reflecting stresses derived from putting young women in a situation they have not been in before: in close and sustained proximity to, and in competition (for very limited opportunities to continue on to higher levels of schooling) with, large numbers of young men.

In the incidents of possession that took place, more than one person was affected at a time. At some point during the school day and for no apparent reason, a girl would begin to scream, laugh, or cry and not respond to efforts to help or inquiries about what was wrong. Soon, others would begin to behave in a similar way. The school might then be closed and the girls sent home. When the girls regained normal consciousness, they would sometimes report they had seen or felt spirits. If the school was located near a place where Japanese soldiers were thought to have died during World War II, the disturbance was apt to be locally attributed to their ghosts.

Another cause considered likely was that a boy had used love magic on the girl and it had a more powerful effect than anticipated. School authorities might interpret the incidents, which often continued or recurred over some period of time, as "hysteria" rather than as spirit possession and try to deal with them accordingly. Regardless of the real cause, the best way to proceed was as though these were episodes of possession, by bringing in a traditional curer (referred to as a *bomoh*) or a Muslim curer (a *bomoh Islam*), either of whom would engage in rituals of exorcism and cleansing.

This type of spirit possession was not limited to the relatively traditional areas of the country such as the east coast state Kelantan. Episodes also began to take place in the most modern areas of the country, in and around the rapidly developing urban centers of the west coast. These were occurring among the young Malay female factory workers employed in the plants set up by Western corporations to produce calculators, computer parts, and other gear associated with the rapidly growing field of consumer electronics.

These occurrences were studied, described, and analyzed by the anthropologist Aihwa Ong (1987). She interpreted them from various perspectives but in line with Lewis's sociological theory of spirit possession. She noted the seeming paradox of traditional spirit possession occurring in the ultramodern context of multinational, west coast (by far the most modern and developed geographic region of peninsular Malaysia), high-tech factories (141). But as with adolescent female school spirit possession, the context was less modern than a mixture of traditional and modern elements. The women were from fairly traditional backgrounds and subject to fairly traditional social controls and stereotypes, even if these were less traditional than in the east coast. Traditional attitudes toward women depend on their sexual status. Virgin daughters and married women were highly regarded, but divorced (not uncommon) and younger widowed women were something of a problem in traditional rural society. Such women are sexually experienced and are thought to be on the lookout for a husband, not necessarily excluding one already married, and inclined to trap men with love magic. The women themselves are raised with beliefs in malevolent spirits and familiar with spirit possession.

Ong's argument is that spirit possession episodes represented a form of protest against exploitation (low wages, low status, long hours, and generally unpleasant working conditions) in a situation in which other and more positive means of objection (such as unionizing or seeking more favorable government regulation) were precluded. She did not say that the women were consciously using spirit possession as a strategy of resistance or protest but suggests that such motives were present. But while episodes of possession could be highly disruptive, they did not necessarily lead to real improvements. Village elders blamed the spirits. Factory managers tended to blame the women who become possessed, seeing them as hysterical, as vic-

tims of their own superstitions and poor eating habits, rather than acknowledging the strains and difficulties of factory work, let alone the conflicts
the women faced because of the situation they were in (as sexually mature
but not under the control of a husband or family), looked down upon as
pleasure seeking and perhaps promiscuous. Management went through the
process of engaging a traditional Malay *bomoh* (curer, exorcist) and sponsor-
ing rituals of cleansing and exorcism but also adopted the policy of firing
women who had been possessed on more than one occasion.

Voluntary Possession and Curing

Incidents of spirit affliction are usually dealt with by specialists. A person
who seeks to summon external spirit beings into his or her personality and
thereby give them a voice is generally known in the literature on such matters as a spirit medium or a shaman. Here, there are certain real differences.
One is that shamans are believed to be summoned by spirits (often in
dreams) and that the consequence of rejection is physical or mental illness
or even death. Another is that shamans are supposed to possess the ability

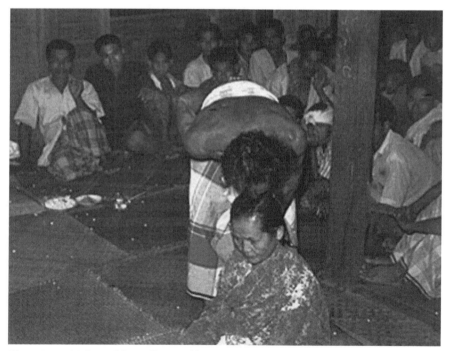

**Photo 8.5.   Malay spirit medium seeking to cure a woman using *main peteri*, Pasir Mas,
Kelantan, Malaysia, 1971.**

Photo 8.6.   Bidayuh Dayak shaman engaged in a curing séance, Lundu, Kuching division, Sarawak, (east) Malaysia, 1989.

to project their souls beyond their bodies to other realms of the universe, to retrieve souls that have been lost, or in some instances, to escort the souls of the dead to the land of the dead. In Southeast Asia, true shamanism appears to be limited to tribal societies such as the Iban and other Dayak peoples of Borneo or the Hmong, Yao, Akha, and other highland groups on northern mainland Southeast Asia. However, both Malay and Burmese spirit mediums are also referred to in the literature as "shamans."

The ability to summon spirits is generally assumed to be learned. Both spirit mediums and shamans normally practice at the request of others, usually for a fee of some sort. The specific purposes for which spirits are summoned and given voice vary, but several are especially common: one is to consult them about why a person is ill or otherwise afflicted, or about what may or will occur in the future; a second is to seek their help in curing or some other activity; and a third is to enable the living to communicate with the dead, which also may be done for many of the same reasons that living persons communicate with one another. As elsewhere, in Southeast Asian societies with cultural traditions of ancestor worship, communication through a spirit medium with deceased relatives is very common and important. Whether for curing or for some other purpose, a ritual event in which a spirit medium is involved is commonly referred to as a séance. In Southeast Asia, séances often involve music (especially powerful drumming and gong playing) and dancing, and often have the character of a play or performance in which mediums—often wearing a costume—act out the characters of the different spirits who possess them.

SORCERY AND WITCHCRAFT

There is no unanimity regarding the exact scholarly meaning of witchcraft and sorcery in Southeast Asia or elsewhere. However, these terms are widely taken to involve beliefs that some persons are capable of destroying, harming, or manipulating others through mystical means. Anthropologists also reasonably conclude that witchcraft and sorcery are practices attributed to people who will seldom freely admit to them. Some scholars have gone further and assumed that witchcraft or sorcery involve beliefs that are impossible to verify. In this case, all that can ever be studied are rumors, gossip, and accusation, and the things done to discover and deal with suspected witches or sorcerers. Also, when anthropologists speak of witches, they have in mind real persons who are believed to have a malevolent supernatural dimension to their nature. Otherwise, what you have are beliefs about spirits or demons such as the Malay/Indonesian *pontianak* and *langsuir*, which, though witchlike, are not usually considered to be witches.

Sorcery and Ethnicity

In Southeast Asia and probably elsewhere in the world, there can be a relationship between sorcery or magical curing and ethnicity. The relationship between ethnicity and economic specialization is a characteristic of ethnic pluralism. The belief that some groups in polyethnic areas are knowledgeable about, skilled in, and willing to engage in occult activities for hire falls into the same general category. Gypsy fortune-tellers, to the extent that they are taken seriously, are a familiar example in the West. The anthropologist Louis Golomb (1985), a specialist in Thais and Thailand, makes the argument that sorcery and countersorcery are often ethnically organized in ethnically complex regions in Southeast Asia. He has studied sorcery and ethnicity in central Thailand where there are Malay minorities and in northern peninsular Malaysia where there are Thai minorities. In the latter region, there are small Thai Buddhist minorities living in separate villages among Malay Muslim majorities. In the state of Kelantan, which borders on Thailand, the Thai curers have a reputation as the most potent sorcerers around. As such, they attract many Malay clients, especially ones looking for love magic or counterlove magic. Many of these are women seeking relief from problems with husbands and other women. Husbands can and do divorce wives and remarry, as it is frequently pointed out, younger women. Men are also permitted to marry additional wives. Since plural marriages are costly and limited mainly to well-off men, it is much less frequent than divorce and remarriage. Sorcery is considered immoral and is therefore more a matter of speculation and gossip than of direct accusation or open knowledge. Countersorcery by a woman whose husband is believed to have strayed and may divorce her to take a second wife is much more acceptable and therefore more openly acknowledged.

But why were Malays drawn to Thai ritual specialists rather than their own, some of whom are also thought to deal in sorcery? The Thais in Kelantan have a particular reputation for mystical powers. Buddhist temples and monks impress Malays, and Thai festivals and folk theater attract Malay audiences, or at least did so in the 1980s and earlier periods. The local Thais are polite people and fluent in the Kelantanese dialect of Malay.

Based on his first research in Kelantan, Golomb concluded that the situation involving Malay reliance on Thai mystical curing and sorcery was distinctive. Then he did fieldwork around Bangkok in Malay communities that had been formed when the Thai government moved Malay political prisoners from the south to central Thailand as a source of labor. He also did fieldwork in the southernmost provinces of Thailand where there are large Malay populations.

His results led him to conclude that there was a more general or cross-cultural tendency for people in ethnically complex settings to turn to members of external communities for mystical help with personal problems. In central Thailand, the situation was thus the reverse of the one in Kelantan. Here, it was the Malays who had developed the reputation as potent sorcerers and who were sought out by Thai clients for magical help in coping with problems in love and marriage. In central Thailand, the Malay communities were very small in relation to those of the surrounding Thai, just as were the Thai communities in Kelantan in relation to the Malay ones. In the Pattani region of far south Thailand, the size of the Thai and Malay communities is more balanced. Here, the pattern of out-group sorcery was one of mutuality—Malays went to Thai sorcerers, and Thais went to Malay ones (Golomb 1985, 5–8).

Golomb's explanation for the preference for ethnic others as sorcerers or countersorcerers is simple: a combination of social distance and geographical proximity. It has been noted in anthropological studies that people tend to prefer distant curers, spirit mediums, and shamans to local ones. This is partly a matter of reputation and prestige, for both the specialist and the client. The greater distance and expense incurred by bringing in an outsider to deal with a medical or magical problem is better, assuming this is affordable. There can also be advantages in the form of confidentiality if there is a desire to keep what has happened from becoming general knowledge in the local community. Although, poorer people who want discreet help with personal problems involving love and marriage are not in a good position to acquire it. This is more so, as Golomb points out, since the person in need of help is often a woman—because women, for both economic and social reasons, are generally less mobile than men. Here, therefore, the ethnic outside specialist nicely fills an available (and lucrative) niche—geographically close but socially distant (194–229).

This is a neat explanation. There is more to understanding the pattern than this, however. The role of the exotic itself (the Gypsy fortune-teller principle) must be of some significance. The traveling hawkers who sit on the sidewalk of the cities and towns of Malaysia and Thailand and sell charms and curios come from distant places—Nepal especially. But not all ethnic outsiders who follow exotic religious practices develop an ethnic specialization in providing occult services. In Kelantan, both the Chinese and the Hindu Indians are adherents of exotic religions. But neither has developed a reputation for magical powers. So we are left with several questions. How prevalent is the pattern of ethnic specialization in sorcery and countersorcery in Southeast Asia? If the prevalent pattern is widespread, is this because of the out-group explanation that Golomb favors, or is it because some groups simply develop a reputation for exotic mystical powers, or (as seems likely) some combination of both?

Witchcraft

Anthropologists make a conventional (although not uniform) distinction between sorcery and witchcraft. This goes as follows: sorcery is simply black magic—manipulative ritual activity aimed at harming, controlling, or influencing other persons in mystical ways. Sorcery can be practiced by anyone who has the knowledge and the inclination of doing it. It can be done by someone himself or herself or it can be performed by a specialist who is engaged for the purpose. It is real insofar as people attempt to practice or counteract it. However, whether people really practice sorcery or simply believe that others do so is again not easy to establish. In contrast, witchcraft involves the belief that some persons are inherently evil in a way that can cause harm to others through psychic means. Witches may be believed to be evil as a result of inheriting this quality from a parent or as a result of having become so, as for example, with the European Christian notion of becoming a witch by making a pact with the devil. While the notion of witchcraft implies deliberate activity, the harm done others can also be passive.

In Southeast Asia, beliefs about the practice of magic and sorcery are certainly well developed, though how much real practice takes place is something else. Less note has been taken of witchcraft (Ellen 1993). One way of explaining this is that most Southeast Asian peoples are simply less inclined than those in some other regions of the world to suppose that some people are or become inherently evil.

Certainly, beliefs in witches and witchcraft exist. However, when we look at the places where this is so, we tend to find particular circumstances or other ambiguities.[8] For example, one place where witch beliefs are well known is the island of Bali in Indonesia. Here, witches or *leyak* are well-known figures in mythology and ritual drama (Bateson and Mead 1942, 28–34, 164–71; Covarrubias 1937, 321–57). The most famous such witch is Rangda. The Balinese also believe that real humans can be and are witches, but less can be easily said about these than about the distinctly mythical and theatrical versions. According to Leo Howe (1984), who has studied and written on the topic, Balinese witchcraft is vast and confusing. It is not open to explicit investigation for people are very reticent to talk about it. Even to mention the name of a suspected witch is likely to bring disaster on one's head. Therefore, witchcraft accusations are rarely made and mostly confined to indirect and hushed gossip (212). Such restrictions limit the investigator to the general conclusion that witches are widely feared, especially by women, and to a cultural summary of how people become witches (a very esoteric process of self-transformation) and what they are like. Not surprisingly, *leyak* are supposed to be bad people, chronically disposed to be greedy, jealous, angry, and prone to erupt in violent emotion (216–17).

Sorcery and Witchcraft in the Philippines

The lowland Philippines are another region where witchcraft as well as sorcery has been reliably described. In his account of a study of the Cebuano people of the Bisayan Islands in the late 1950s and early 1960s, the anthropologist Richard Lieban (1967) leaves little doubt that these peoples recognize witchcraft and witches as well as sorcery and sorcerers. Sorcerers are people who are believed to have learned their craft and who manipulate objects and recite spells in order to achieve their ends. Their motive is believed to be simply economic, as when they are hired to cause harm to or manipulate someone else, or to counter or cure sorcery done by someone else. Cebuano witches may also manipulate external objects, but this is not the usual way in which they cause harm. Rather, they mainly operate by using inherent mystical powers. One of the most important of these is the capacity to turn themselves into demons or an animal such as a crow or a dog and then attack someone. Some witches can cause harm simply by looking at a person—in other words the evil eye. Witches become witches in some instances because they have inherited their power from a parent or parents. In some instances, witchcraft is transmitted to another person as a result of being attacked by a witch.

A question that needs to be raised about Cebuano and other notions of witchcraft in the lowland Philippines is this: how much have they to do with Spanish influence? (the same question that has been raised about Native American witchcraft in the Southwestern United States). Lieban does not ask this question, but he does bring Spanish influence and Christianity into his discussion at several points. He begins by comparing a form of sorcery he recorded from an interview with a Filipino informant in Negros in 1958 with the same form described in a Spanish manuscript concerning the same place thought to date to 1578, or nearly four hundred years earlier. His point is that the particular type of sorcery described has a long history. It also shows that the Spanish took an interest in the vernacular occult at an early point in the colonial period in the Philippines. Lieban goes on to say that the early manuscript describes an impressive example of cultural persistence in spite of extensive social and cultural change brought first by the Spanish and then by the Americans (1967, 2). Also, how much did the Spanish contribute to the development of lowland Filipino culture of sorcery and witchcraft? Here we need to keep in mind that the early period of Spanish colonialism and Christianization in the Philippines (as also in the Spanish New World) took place while the European witch craze was still going strong.

Later on we learn more of links between Christianity and Cebuano sorcery. The spirits used by Cebuano sorcerers "are frequently conceived by the Cebuanos as followers of Satan, and sorcery is often referred to as 'the work of the devil'" (21). "Early Spanish missionaries and colonists defined the spirits of the pagan religious world as representations of the devil in a universe where God was supreme. The effort to convert the Filipinos to Christianity was seen in terms of the struggle between God and the Devil" (32).

A Witch Craze in Java

Anthropologists have often suggested a relationship between beliefs about supernatural malevolence and social change. While sorcery and witchcraft may be traditional or long-standing notions in a society, witch crazes (periods of mass, hyperfear of sorcery and witchcraft, including deadly attacks on persons suspected of such practices) frequently recur or increase during or following periods of change and trauma. Again, little along this line has been noted as occurring in Southeast Asia.[9] In Indonesia, however, we have a classic witch craze described by the anthropologist James Siegel for the immediate post-Suharto period in Java. In his recent book *Naming the Witch* (2006), Siegel describes and analyses a series of incidents in which persons accused of being witches or sorcerers were brutally lynched by neighbors or fellow villagers. In Banyuwangi, east Java, Indonesia, about 120 persons were so killed during a three-month period between

December 1998 and February 1999. In the region of East Malang, another ten persons were murdered as witches at this time, as presumably some others were elsewhere as well. This series of attacks came just after the dictator President Suharto, who had come to rule in 1967 following a military coup, finally lost power and resigned in 1998. While there may have been other such incidents both before and after this series of killings, what happened clearly amounted to a localized witch craze within a specific historical context. Those who died were killed by mobs, so the killings were not simply a matter of individuals settling scores or acting out of personal malice. The bodies of those killed were generally mutilated. Few if any of those who led or took part were arrested, tried, and convicted (113).

The central point that Siegel (2006) makes is that both the Javanese post-Suharto witch and the witch craze are new. As he puts it,

> The sorcerer in the period after the fall of Suharto was, and at the moment I write this, continues to be, one's ordinary neighbor. Some accused of sorcery, such as Muki, were curers. But most were not. The post-Suharto witch is just like everyone else. . . . As an intermediary between the spirit world and the human world the sorcerer should be a figure. But unlike the case in the West, there is no image of the witch, at least the witch of this period of mass accusations. (116)

Some of the accused witches were traditional curers, but most were not. The witch's powers were believed to be greater than those attributed to earlier sorcerers or practitioners of witchcraft. Siegel was often told during his fieldwork that there had long been witches in east Java and that they were sometimes killed. But the evidence of this is slim. This is because there were no real ethnographic studies of Javanese witchcraft, and, he thinks, there had been few previous attacks on people believed to cause supernatural harm. Assuming that attitudes and practices concerning witchcraft or sorcery changed, why did the changes occur? Siegel's explanation of the origin of the recent pattern is complex and cannot be easily summarized in brief. It was not that the Javanese never engaged in mass or mob assaults on people who they thought had harmed them. Such attacks on the Chinese had been made in the past over a long period. But the Chinese were ethnic others who mainly lived in their own neighborhoods in towns where they ran businesses. They were attacked because they were resented for being economically better off and because they were thought to exploit others. Siegel himself asks the question, "Where does the violent aggression inherent in suspecting that one might be a witch originate?" He suggests beginning with the social killings that occurred in Java on a large scale (hundreds of thousands of deaths) with the massacre of alleged communists. These took place as a prelude to the establishment of the New Order under Suharto in 1965–1966. The attitude toward the alleged communists at that time was, "If we didn't kill them they would kill us" (162). This view was then transferred from communists to witches. Siegel also suggests elsewhere that Javanese who engaged in mob violence against accused witches were not acting rationally but rather out of an obsession (135). The Javanese witch craze was thus a legacy of the political developments and conflicts of Suharto's New Order regime (161).

9

Religion, Society, and the State

Southeast Asia has sometimes been referred to as a "crossroad of religions," the subtitle of an early book on the main religions of the region (Landon 1949). When such terms are used, the reference is to the long-standing presence of most of the so-called world religions. Of course, Southeast Asia is not the only region of the world marked by such ancient religious diversity. But unlike India or the Middle East, which most readily come to mind as other regions of great variation, Southeast Asia has not been the original home to any of its world religions—hence, the crossroad reference. But insofar as the crossroad metaphor is meant to signify traffic in religion that moves in both directions, it is somewhat inappropriate. Except for Mahayana Buddhism and other religious influences transmitted to Vietnam from China, the movement of religion into Southeast Asia has been from the West: Buddhism and Hinduism from India, Islam from India and the Middle East, and Christianity from Europe.

WORLD RELIGIONS AND THEIR CHARACTERISTICS IN SOUTHEAST ASIA

As we have seen in the preceding chapter, many beliefs and ritual practices (relating to the growing of rice, for example) are common to both practitioners of indigenous and world religions in Southeast Asia. Nonetheless, there are various important differences in the two types of religion, though these are blurred in some instances (in Balinese Hinduism, as we shall see). Let us begin with some general consideration of the differences:

1. *A Name and Identity.* To begin with, the named identity that western-ers and most other adherents of the world religions take for granted is lacking in the indigenous ones—unless such a named identity has been created as a result of outside influence. Therefore, indigenous traditions of religious belief and practice do not form a separate sphere of interaction or activity. For example, rituals for planting rice are simply part of the whole apparatus of planting rice. Insofar as we know, until recently, most of the nonadherents of the world religions would have been puzzled by questions about their "religion," unless these were put in terms of specific examples of belief and ritual practice. And in such a case they might well point out that "everything we do involves religion." However, it did not take long to learn from the adherents of the world religions that not having an explicit religious identity was regarded as primitive or backward. This is turn served as an incentive to either create a named religion of their own (as was done in several instances in Indonesia) or to convert to one of the world religions that were available.

2. *Organization.* The world religions are often referred to as being "orga-nized." Such a notion seems to refer to two things. One is a coherent and integrated set of core beliefs and ritual practices, based on or helped greatly by written texts. The other is organization involving a social, political, and economic set of offices, committees, hierarchies, and power structures. World religions are, by definition, "universal," or they at least extend be-yond the boundaries of particular local communities or ethnic groups in terms of identity, doctrine, and institutionalization—the fragmentation, localization, and diversity that are also an inevitable part of the develop-ment and spread of the world religions notwithstanding.

3. *Religious Ends.* All "religions" can be said to have practical or mundane as well as transcendental or cosmic concerns. Westerners tend to think of re-ligion mainly in terms of transcendental concerns and to leave out practical ones. Practical religious concerns include all those things that involve get-ting through, coping with, or prospering in life in this world. These include obtaining magical or spiritual protection from harm (traditionally from spirits, sorcery or witchcraft, sickness, blows, knives, arrows, bullets, and more recently, from bombs or automobile and motorcycle accidents). Prac-tical religion also involves efforts to cure the sick or afflicted, make the crops grow and the game animals accessible, cause enemies to become weak or harmed, attract a spouse or sexual partner, and now passing school exams, winning the lottery, and finding a job. While death may seem to epitomize transcendental concerns, it can also pose serious practical problems—at least where, as is often the case in Southeast Asia, the spirits of the dead are believed to pose threats to the living until they can be gotten to the land of the dead, transformed into benevolent ancestors, or reincarnated. But while

all religions include such practical concerns, they loom somewhat larger in the indigenous than in the world religions as known in the West.

4. *Ritual Versus Belief.* The relative importance of practical versus transcendental concerns is closely related to the significance of ritual versus belief or myth. This is an old issue in anthropology and religious studies. William Robertson Smith set it out in his *Lectures on the Religion of the Semites* at the end of the nineteenth century. Here, Smith argued that the importance of belief or myth in the ancient religions was much overrated. He explained that the adherents of modern religions tend to assume that belief is the core of religion. But this, he said, will lead you astray if you assume it is also true of the ancient religions. These religions consisted mainly of rituals. Of course, there were also beliefs or myths, but these varied endlessly from one place to another, and no one seemed to worry much about which was the correct version. In other words, there was no such thing as organized or official doctrine (Smith 1901, 16–17). We find the same point made today by anthropologist Leo Howe (2005, 57) about Balinese Hinduism. Or more specifically, about the traditional version of it that he refers to simply as *adat* (custom or customary) religion or *adat* Bali. Howe writes that, at the turn of the twentieth century, "it would have been very difficult to isolate and identify something in Bali called 'Balinese religion' as a separate, distinct and organized sphere of life." Instead, religion was everywhere in Bali. But what really mattered in religion was ritual rather than specific belief. And what mattered about ritual was that everyone participated who should be participating and that the procedures were followed correctly. The extent to which the village Balinese at this time even referred to their religious activities as "Hinduism" is not noted. Later, Balinese reformers had to work hard to have their religion recognized by the government as Hinduism (Geertz 1964; Howe 2005, 92–95).

5. *Permanent Religious Buildings.* The sort of *adat* religion traditionally practiced by the Balinese seems very similar to the indigenous religious traditions of the highland and interior peoples of Borneo and of many other places in Southeast Asia—seamless, unidentified, and connected to everything else, and with an emphasis on ritual rather than belief. There are differences, however. One is that the priesthood in Balinese religion is a more formalized or institutionalized set of specialists than is usually found in the indigenous religions of Southeast Asia. Another is that traditional Balinese religious architecture is highly developed and "permanent," in the sense of the famous Hindu-Buddhist ruins of Angkor, Pagan, Java, and elsewhere, that is, it consists of many different kinds of temples made of stone and other materials meant to last.

Such buildings generally have no real parallel among practitioners of indigenous religious traditions in Southeast Asia. Among these peoples, religious activities are mainly carried out either in ordinary dwellings or in communal buildings used for both ritual celebrations and other activities. Among the longhouse-dwelling Dayak peoples of Borneo, for example, much of the festive and ritual activity takes place on the open or closed verandas of the often very large multifamily buildings. Among some groups, ritual celebrations are also held in separate communal buildings such as the men's houses of the Bidayuh (often referred to as "head houses" because they held the skull trophies of the village from the period when the Bidayuh still engaged in headhunting). But these structures were not dedicated religious buildings. They were also the sleeping quarters of the older boys and unmarried mature males of the villages and meeting halls for nonritual communal activities. The alternative to using dwellings and multipurpose communal buildings for ritual purposes is to build temporary ritual structures. These are usually constructed from bamboo and thatch for a particular ceremony, and then abandoned when it is over and rebuilt when the ceremony is to be held again (Winzeler 2004a).

The general absence of dedicated, permanent religious buildings among the indigenous interior and highland people of Southeast Asia is a striking contrast to the architectural traditions of the adherents of world religions. The ancient Hindu and Buddhist shrines, monuments, and temples of Southeast Asia, especially of Java, Burma, and Cambodia, are well known among the architectural treasures of the world. But all of the world religions in Southeast Asia, as elsewhere, are marked by the presence of enduring buildings—some grand and lavish, some small and drab, but all devoted principally to religion in one way or another. In the case of Hinduism and Buddhism, this is the temple (or temple and monastery complex). In Islam, the mosque is used for collective Friday prayer as well as individual daily prayers; the *surau* in Malaysia and the *langgar* in Indonesia are used for daily individual prayers, for evening chanting sessions, and often for teaching the Koran to children. And in Christianity, it is the church or cathedral. There are also other permanent religious structures, especially shrines, often involving the graves of local or regional holy men or saints, or relics such as footprints of the Buddha.

6. *Religion and Ethnic Boundaries.* Many of the indigenous religious beliefs and practices described in the previous chapter are similar across ethnic boundaries. But indigenous religious traditions as totalities are essentially local. They vary from one ethnic group to another and sometimes within a group from one locale or region to another. In contrast, though the world religions become localized, they exist far beyond the boundaries of particular ethnic or linguistic communities. They have spread far beyond their points of origin. The characteristic of being shared rather than limited to a single ethnic group is one of the criteria used by the postcolonial Indo-

nesian government to identify and legitimate a "monotheistic religion" in contrast to the primitive and isolated "not-yet-religions" religions.

ANTHROPOLOGICAL STUDY OF WORLD RELIGIONS

In Southeast Asia as elsewhere in much of the world, anthropological studies of religion formerly concentrated on indigenous beliefs and practices rather than the world religions. The latter were left mainly to historians and Orientalists, many of whom in the earlier periods were colonial scholars. By the 1950s, anthropological interest in religion had begun to change to include the world religions as well. Southeast Asia became one of the regions where pioneering studies of these religions took place.

When anthropologists turned to the world religions, they attempted to study them in much the same way they had indigenous ones. The focus therefore remained on villages or other local settings, and the main concern was with the religious beliefs and practices of ordinary people. Yet, there were clearly new issues that had to be addressed. For one thing, the societies involved were complex, and ordinary people were far from homogenous. Even villages were apt to be stratified in terms of poverty, wealth, and power. For another, the world religions, including their local versions, are based on written traditions and have long histories, even if they are mainly orally transmitted at the village level. And finally, the relationship of the state to religion became very important.

The specific theoretical or conceptual ideas that were developed to interpret the world religions in local places included a theory of civilization, in particular, the notion of the great tradition and little tradition, especially as formulated by the American anthropologist Robert Redfield (1957). The great tradition was that of the overarching civilization, cities, national or sacred languages, and educated religious elites, scholars, or literati, including the Brahmins of India and the Mandarins of China. The little tradition was the village or folk tradition whose religious and broader cultural traditions varied endlessly from one region to another. Here, the transmission of religion and culture was primarily oral rather than through reading and writing. Religious syncretism (or hybrid characteristics) flourished, that is, local beliefs and practices involved a mixture of indigenous and imported elements. New traditions were added without abandoning old ones.

Between the great and the little tradition were cultural mediators, those local people or outsiders who had gained at least a rudimentary ability to read and write. Such persons also included those who had traveled and gained a wider knowledge of religion and civilization through visits to pilgrimage sites and study in monasteries or religious schools. Such mediators stood for orthodoxy and made some effort to spread or support it. But they were also tolerant or accepting of local customs and practices—because they had been first socialized into these, and because local acceptance and approval required some degree of tolerance of local ways.

Jack Goody (1968) and others developed the notion of restricted or partial literacy. The main idea is that, where few local persons are literate, writing becomes a basis of social power or symbolic domination. The use of writing and numbers serves in such situations not only to convey learning and knowledge but also to enhance the practice of magic through the production of charms and amulets.[1] Books also tend to acquire magical and messianic qualities. As discussed in the following chapter, a common myth among the highland peoples of northern mainland Southeast Asia explains their domination by the Chinese or other lowland groups by the loss of a book. The myth describes the group in question that once had a book but foolishly lost it and became powerless and poor as a result. This myth played a role in the early spread of Christianity (Keyes 1977; Tapp 1989a).

DISPUTES AND DISAGREEMENTS
ABOUT ISLAM AND BUDDHISM

Given the complexities of the world religions, it has sometimes been difficult to provide completely convincing interpretations. Both Islam and Theravada Buddhism, the two largest of the world religions in Southeast Asia, have been variously interpreted and argued over by anthropologists. Here we consider two important instances, the first concerning Islam in Java; the second, Buddhism in Burma and Thailand.

Religions of Java?

In Southeast Asia, the best known and most important of the controversies has concerned the nature of Islam in the Indonesian island of Java. Of special concern has been its relationship to older religious traditions, specifically Hinduism, Buddhism, and indigenous beliefs and practices. By the time anthropological studies of Javanese religious traditions began in the early 1950s, the prevailing position among Dutch colonial scholars was that Javanese religion was syncretic. The Javanese professed themselves to be Muslims, but in actuality they had never given up their pre-Islamic beliefs and practices. Similar assertions were also made about Islam and pre-Islamic traditions among the Malays and other Muslim peoples of Southeast Asia (and in Burma about the Buddhism of the Burmese). Richard Winstedt ([1925] 1961) said the real religion of the Malays was magic, which included indigenous spirit beliefs, Hindu divinities, sorcery, and rituals to make the rice grow and the sick well. It was common to express such views in terms of elaborate tropes such as the one published by R. J. Wilkinson in 1906:

> The average Malay may be said to look on God as a great King or Governor— mighty, of course, and just, but too remote a power to trouble himself about a villager's affairs—whereas the spirits of the district are comparable to the local police, who may be corrupt and prone to error but who take a most absorbing interest in their radius of influence and whose ill-will has to be avoided at all costs. ([1906] 1957, 1)

With its many Hindu and Buddhist ruins spread over the landscape, Java epitomized religious syncretism more than anywhere else. But such an interpretation also raised the question of why the Javanese had converted to Islam in the first place if they were going to remain much as they had before. One answer was that, while they had not been forced to convert, they had been influenced to do so by the example of their kings and chiefs and that the latter had been led to do so by the changing alignments of political power. These changing alignments included the arrival of European colonists seeking to control trade and spread Christianity. Another possible part of the answer was that Islam both in parts of Java and elsewhere in the Malay/Indonesian world fit with the interests of the trading classes. The centers of Islamic strength in Southeast Asia were established in the coastal centers of international commerce that grew with the spice trade. While Hinduism fit the interests of kings and courts, the egalitarian ethos and universalism of Islam better served the emerging middle class of ethnically mixed merchants and traders. But trade and commerce did not remain confined to coastal urban centers. At least as colonial control expanded into the interior of Java and other islands of Indonesia, so also did trade and with it a commitment to Islam that was more than superficial syncretism.

This was the situation as understood in historical terms that Clifford Geertz (1960), Robert Jay (1963), and other members of a research team found when they began a study of the town of "Modjokuto" (a pseudonym) in east central Java in the early 1950s. It was shortly after the end of colonial rule and a period of intense political activity involving both religion and nationalism. Geertz and Jay found the religious diversity and complexity that were to be expected, perhaps even more. Modjokuto was clearly no tribal or isolated village where a single description of religious beliefs and practices would cover most everyone. Some people were devout Muslims, and of these some were traditional or orthodox while others were modernist or reformist. Yet others were not devout Muslims at all but rather syncretists whose religious orientation owed much to Hindu-Buddhist traditions and was dominated by animist ritual practices rather than Islamic doctrine. Of the nonorthodox Muslims, some were oriented to simple, pragmatic religious values and activities, the most important of which was a small neighborhood ritual feast. Yet other nonorthodox Javanese were oriented to Hindu-Buddhist-oriented mysticism, high art, and meditation.

The problem that presented itself was how to sort out, name, and explain all this rich religious diversity. It was apparent that it could not all be called Javanese Islam, for example—nor, however, could the religious complexity be separated into several entirely different religions or sects analogous to Protestant and Catholic forms of Christianity. Instead, Geertz called it all the "religion of Java," which he then divided into three variations, each labeled according to the local names—though just what these names referred to was to become a matter of some dispute. The first name was *abangan*, for the simple nominal Muslims or animist-syncretists. The second name was *santri*, for the devout Muslims who adhered to the core rituals and doctrines of Islam, especially the five daily prayers. The third and last name was *prijaji*, for the other group of nominal Muslims whose religion consisted mainly of mysticism and meditation.

In formulating his interpretation of Javanese religion, Geertz drew on several theoretical orientations, including Redfield's ideas on the great and little traditions of civilization. But his overall formulation is based on class and above all on Max Weber's generalizations about religious orientations (Weber [1922] 1963, esp. chap. 1 on "Castes, Estates, Classes, and Religion"). The class basis of Javanese religion is set explicitly and succinctly in the following statements:

> There are, it seems to me, three main social structural nuclei in Java today: the village, the market, and the governmental bureaucracy—each of them taken in a somewhat more extended sense than is common. . . . The *abangan* religious tradition, made up of the ritual feast called the *selamatan*, of an extensive and intricate complex of spirit beliefs, and of a whole set of theories and practices of curing, sorcery and magic . . . is associated in a broad and general way with the Javanese village. . . . The purer Islam is the sub-tradition I have called *santri*. Although in a broad and general way the *santri* sub variant is associated with the Javanese trading element, it is not confined to it. There is a very strong *santri* element in the villages, often finding its leadership in the richer peasants. . . . The market is, on the other hand . . . clogged with swarms of small *abangan* traders attempting to make a marginal living, although the largest and more vigorous traders are still *santris* . . . the third [variant] is the *prijaji*. . . . This white-collar elite, its ultimate roots in Hindu-Javanese courts of pre-colonial times . . . stressed neither the animistic element in the overall Javanese syncretism as did the *abangan*, nor the Islamic as did the *santri*, but the Hinduistic. (Geertz 1960, 5–6)

The Religion of Java, published in 1960, has probably been the most influential of all modern ethnographic works on Java, perhaps of all Indonesia. However, it has also been in some ways controversial. The disagreements expressed over the years since its publication have not mainly concerned the factual descriptions Geertz provided in great detail. The criticism has focused instead on his overall parsing of Javanese religious traditions into three parts or traditions, each linked to a status group or class. Some critics appear to agree that Javanese religion is complex and cannot be adequately described as simply "Javanese Islam." On the basis of research in different places in the Javanese culture area (central and eastern Java) at different times, other scholars tend to favor a twofold division between orthodox Muslims (Geertz's *santri*) and syncretistic, nominal Muslims (including both Geertz's *abangan* and *prijaji*). Further, some have agreed that, while Javanese may use the term *abangan*, it is not common, and that most prefer *kejawen*, meaning "Javanese," as a term for nominal, syncretistic adherents. The term *prijaji* is also used widely but only to refer to class or status group and not to both this and a religious orientation. The *prijaji*, it is held, tend to be *kejawen*, although they favor different types of religious activities within this tradition than do poorer townsmen and villagers (Beatty 1999, 29).[2] In one of the most recent book-length ethnographic accounts, *Varieties of Javanese Religion* (a neutral title it may be noted), Andrew Beatty suggests the game of "find the real religion of Java" may not have been played on a level field. His point is that Western scholars have tended to prefer a negative view of Islam. They have a liberal bias against Islam and therefore have been inclined to diminish or discredit it by downgrading its authenticity and importance in Java and elsewhere in Southeast Asia (29).

Theravada Buddhism and Spirit Cults in Burma and Thailand

The study of Buddhism in Southeast Asia has also had its share of controversies. The anthropological study of Buddhism and other beliefs and practices of Theravada Buddhist peoples of mainland Southeast Asia also began in the 1950s and has concerned mainly Burma and Thailand. Burma was initially the most important focus of interest, but the opportunity for sustained fieldwork closed quickly there after the military takeover in 1962 and has remained more or less closed to the present (Brac de la Perrière 2009). While initially of less apparent interest, Thailand subsequently became the main focus of research and has remained so. Interest in Buddhism in Laos and Cambodia, though also Theravada countries, never developed to the extent that it did in Burma and Thailand. This is partly because field research in both countries was closed or discouraged for a long period in the second part of the twentieth century by war and subsequent political instability. Vietnam is also to some extent a Buddhist country. Here, however, Buddhism is Mahayana (and derived from China) and less important or dominant as a part of the totality of religious belief and practice than is the case in any of the Theravada countries of Southeast Asia. Vietnam was also closed to Western research for a long period of time.

Though Islam and Buddhism are very different religions with different histories in Southeast Asia, anthropologists have approached them in somewhat similar ways. As with Islam, the central issue with Buddhism has been how to understand the "official" or great tradition religion in comparison to local understandings and practices, and to various non-Buddhist beliefs and practices. Can Buddhism any more than Islam be separated from earlier Indic and indigenous beliefs and practices? Are there important contradictions? And if so, how can these be explained? Again, there are differences between the place of Islam in Java and Buddhism in mainland Southeast Asia. Buddhism appears to be revered and universally identified with (at least by the Buddhist-majority populations) in the Theravada countries in a way that Islam is not in Java. And social and political disagreements about who is a real or correct Muslim appear to have no counterpart in the Theravada countries regarding Buddhism.

The argument began with Melford Spiro's *Burmese Supernaturalism* (1967). In this work, Spiro begins by asserting that wherever Buddhism is found it is accompanied by "some other religious system." In Southeast Asia, the other religious system is a folk religion that includes beliefs in supernatural beings and practices for dealing with them. Which of the two religions is the more dominant, real, or important is an "empirical question." But they are in fact separate and in conflict, even though the same people believe in and practice both. Explaining how and why this should be the case is the main purpose of his study.

As with Islam in Java, Buddhism in Burma is a sophisticated, text-based (in a "restricted literacy" sense) religion focused on the worship or veneration of the Buddha—his image, his relics, and his teachings—and in the earning of merit. Buddha showed the way to enlightenment and therefore to salvation. Buddhist doctrine includes the law of karma (the sum of good and evil done in past lives and in the present one that determines one's well-being in this and in future lives). Religious practices include the support of monks and monasteries, other good deeds, and the avoidance of various undesirable or forbidden deeds and practices. Buddhism also stresses suffering, the cause of which is desire.

But while the Burmese are Buddhists, their "other religion" consists of elaborate spirit cults and various other animistic, mystical, and magical beliefs and practices. The general term for spirit is *nat*, the most important of which are the Thirty-seven Nats, each of which is supposed to have a name and to be the spirit of a real person who in all instances died a bad death, usually by execution—although few people know the names or identities of most of them. Religious practices involving any of the *nats* include making offerings to them, avoiding actions that offend them, and employing spirit mediums to either get them to stop causing trouble or to obtain their help. The latter practices are highly developed and include various festivals where the spirit mediums offer their services. The spirit mediums are nearly always women who have developed relationships with (male) *nats* that are thought of as a form of marriage. People approach the spirit mediums for healing and other types of assistance. The mediums in turn go into a trance and invoke their *nats* to cure or provide other forms of help for clients.

Up to a point, the situation described by Spiro for Burma seems similar to the one described by Geertz for Java. In both instances, a world religion exists along with a presumably earlier tradition consisting of indigenous and Indic as well as Buddhist or Muslim (as the case may be) elements. Beyond this, however, there are important differences. Geertz took the position that religious differences in Java are variants in one "religion," while Spiro holds that those in Burma are "different religions." This may be a matter of wording or emphasis, with Spiro making the stronger assertion. However, Geertz made an important claim about the Javanese that Spiro did not about the Burmese—that the Javanese explicitly recognize and label their religious differences—specifically with the terms *abangan, santri,* and *prijaji.* Moreover, he claimed that the differences have social (and political) reality in being associated with different social classes in Javanese society. Later critics have disputed Geertz's formulation, including his effort to correlate religious differences with class or status. But most seem to agree that the Javanese recognize their religious differences and apply some sort of labels to them. Spiro made no such claims about the Burmese. The terms he uses are "Buddhism" and "supernaturalism," and while the former is undoubtedly recognized and used by the Burmese, the latter is simply his own etic label. The Burmese in general do not appear to recognize and name a contrast between those who are said to be more purely Buddhist than others, as the Javanese do regarding Islam. It is true that some intellectuals and rulers have (like counterparts elsewhere in Southeast Asia) attempted to get rid of "superstition."

Both Spiro and Geertz say that religious differences are a source of conflict, but in different ways. Spiro's interpretation of the conflict between Buddhism and supernaturalism is that it is a matter of doctrine (that the principles and values of Buddhism are incompatible with the beliefs and practices of supernaturalism) and that the conflict is experienced in psychological terms. Geertz's interpretation of the differences between the adherents of the different religious variants in Java (especially between the *abangan* and the *santri*) is sociological or interpersonal. Spiro attempted to show how the doctrines and values of Buddhism are incompatible with the cult of *nats* and other aspects of supernaturalism. He lists five ways in which this is so, including *morality* (Buddhism is a religion of morality, whereas the *nat* cults manifest amorality), *sensuality* (Buddhism teaches that desire is the cause of all suffering and advocates the subjugation of all passions, while the *nat* cults express the indulgence of passion), *personality* (Buddhism idealizes serenity as an emotional state, whereas the *nat* cults manifest turbulence and even violence), and *society* (Buddhism is otherworldly and world rejecting, while the *nat* cults are concerned with worldly or practical problems). While there seems to be considerable overlap among the various conflicts in value Spiro discusses, the general point seems clear (1967, 258–63).

But while the Burmese in general may see (or be induced to see) the conflicts that Spiro finds between Buddhism and supernaturalism, the question is how much they generally seem to care. According to Geertz (1960, 355–70) and others, the Javanese both recognize the differences among their religious variations and appear to be concerned about them a lot. Religious differences were recognized and formed part of the basis of differing social identities and political parties. Buddhism and the spirit cults may be in conflict from the perspective of Buddhist doctrine and values, but such conflicts do not appear to have been expressed in social and political terms. Spiro himself suggested why the conflicts involving Buddhism and supernaturalism do not concern the Burmese as much as they might. For one thing, all Burmese not only regard themselves as Buddhists but also revere Buddhism and regard it as their most important tradition. Even those who rely heavily on the advice and assistance of spirit mediums, or who are spirit mediums themselves, consider themselves devout Buddhists and consider Buddhism to be, theoretically at least, superior to anything else. Conversely, Buddhist authorities (the monks), at least at the village level, do not reject beliefs in spirits or their propitiation as forbidden or wrong. Spirit shrines are to be found in Buddhist temple monasteries, and monks as well as others make offerings at them.

By the time Spiro's book was published in 1967, Burma was closed to fieldwork by Western scholars. Had this not been the case, it seems likely that research on Buddhism, spirit cults, and other dimensions of Burmese folk religion would have continued. And if so, sooner or later, challenges along the lines of those directed at Geertz's interpretation of Javanese Islam would probably have appeared. Spiro's interpretation of Buddhism and supernaturalism as being "two different religions" was subsequently challenged and rejected. But his chief critic was Stanley Tambiah, who studied Buddhism, spirit cults, magic, and mysticism in Thailand. Possible cultural differences between Burma and Thailand might have served as a restraint on criticisms and conclusions, but this does not appear to have been the case. For one thing, Spiro (1967, 271) had acknowledged an alternate interpretation to his own. This was Michael Mendelson's conclusion that Burmese animism and Buddhism were opposite points on a continuum, between which there were quasi-Buddhist sects he termed Messianic Buddhism. This was the position endorsed by Tambiah. He concedes that there may be inconsistencies between Buddhist *doctrine* and animism. The belief that spirits can cause or relieve suffering is a contradiction of the doctrine of *karma*, which explains suffering as entirely a consequence of previous acts. Tambiah acknowledges that there is some awareness of this conflict among Thai Buddhists in Thailand, but he does not think it is a very significant problem, and it hardly justifies the conclusion that Buddhism and animism are two different religions. The conclusion that Buddhism and the spirit cults are different religions is a result of comparing apples and oranges, the animist beliefs and behavior of villagers with the written historical doctrines of Buddhism. Spirit cults and other syncretist and animist beliefs and practices are better examined in relation to Buddhism as understood and practiced at the village level (Tambiah 1970, 41–42; 1984, 315). Most other scholars who have addressed the issue of Buddhism and supernaturalism, the spirit cults, or superstition (you may choose whichever you like) appear to agree with Tambiah.

RELIGION AND THE STATE

In all of the countries of Southeast Asia, the state has been actively involved in religion in one way or another for a long period of time. And in a variety of ways, postcolonial governments have tried to shape and control religious beliefs and practices for one ideological reason or another. This is so in the contemporary Buddhist countries of Thailand, Cambodia, Laos, Vietnam, Burma, and the Muslim countries of Malaysia and Indonesia. Developments in Cambodia, Laos, and Vietnam have been strongly affected by political change in the postcolonial period. In Cambodia, Buddhism was attacked by the Khmer Rouge in the late 1970s. Temples and monasteries were destroyed or closed, and monks were targeted for extermination. In the decades since the overthrow of the Khmer Rouge by the Vietnamese, temples have been reopened or rebuilt and monastic life resumed, thought not to their previous extent. Conversely, Thailand had a policy of seeking to convert the hill tribes to Buddhism as a means of furthering their integration into national Thai society, and the government in Burma was reported to be coercing non-Buddhist minorities to convert to Buddhism, at least until monks turned against the Myanmar regime.

Of the larger predominantly Muslim countries of Southeast Asia, Malaysia is officially Islamic but asserts the freedom to practice other religions. But such freedom does not include permitting Muslims to convert to another religion or to renounce Islam. The place of Islam in Malaysia is complicated by the plural makeup of the country. The demographically and politically dominant Malays are entirely (and by definition) Muslim. All Muslims are subject to special state religious courts established under British colonial rule and to certain religious laws enforced by special religious police. At the same time, British colonialism left Malaya with a very large and economically vital non-Muslim Chinese minority as well as a smaller, non-Muslim Indian minority associated with rubber and other plantation-grown industries, and an even smaller minority of Thai Theravada Buddhists. The Chinese, Indians, and Thai have been relatively free to practice their own religious traditions as long as these do not impinge upon Islam. Furthermore, there are the Orang Asli and the large non-Muslim Dayak populations in Malaysian Borneo whose loyalty is important for the stability and development of the country. Most members of all the ethnic communities acknowledge that the continuing prosperity and development of Malaysia requires ethnic cooperation and religious compromise.

The historical development of Islam in Indonesia has been somewhat similar to that of Malaysia, but the state here has developed very different policies. While claiming the largest (if not necessarily the purest) Muslim population of any nation in the world, Indonesia has never been an officially Muslim country (unlike Malaysia). Rather, Islam is one of six religions that are recognized and designated as legitimate—the others being Buddhism, Hinduism, Confucianism, and both Catholic and Protestant Christianity. All of these recognized world religions are defined as "monotheistic" and therefore privileged, in contrast to indigenous animistic traditions of belief and practice that are not. Here, the state definition of religion as one of the monotheistic world religions has been both crucial and stringent, although its application has been flexible, especially in permitting several indigenous or tribal religious traditions to be accepted as "Hinduism."

Of the Christian communities in Southeast Asia, all are mainly limited to ethnic minorities except those of the Philippines, the only Christian-majority country in Asia, in fact. Beginning in the sixteenth century, Christianity was established throughout most of the Philippines under Spanish colonial rule. Islam spread into the coastal regions of Mindanao and other islands in the far south as an extension of the same historical circumstances that brought it to Borneo, Sulawesi, and the smaller islands of the eastern Indonesian Archipelago. In addition, many of the highland and interior peoples in the Philippines as elsewhere remained beyond Christianization throughout the Spanish period, or from the mid-sixteenth century to the end of the nineteenth. As in Latin America, the spread of Roman Catholicism was a major part of Spanish conquest and colonial policy. As a result, the closest parallels between the development and nature of Christianity in the Philippines appear to be found in Latin America rather than elsewhere in Southeast Asia. After the Americans took control in 1898 as a consequence of the Spanish-American War, Christianity in the Philippines became more diverse, especially as a consequence of Protestant missionary activity, local religious movements, and the formation of independent Filipino sects

(Goh 2005; Wiegele 2005). Efforts at conversion have been aimed at the unconverted highland and interior groups (as elsewhere in Southeast Asia) as well as at the conversion of Roman Catholics to Protestant denominations, especially evangelical or fundamentalist ones.

Roman Catholicism was also established at an early point elsewhere in Southeast Asia, including Vietnam by the French and in parts of eastern Indonesia by the Portuguese. In these places, however, the Catholics remained small minorities. The Portuguese lasted for only a century, to be replaced by the Dutch in what became the Dutch East Indies and then Indonesia; the Dutch were less inclined to pursue conversion and sought to block Roman Catholicism. Meanwhile, in Vietnam, the French established colonial control over the entire country, and missionaries had some success in creating a Catholic minority. Overall, the vast majority of lowland populations in French Indochina, as elsewhere in Southeast Asia, showed little interest in Christianity (see chapter 10).

Gaining Recognition as an Official Religion in Postcolonial Indonesia

The religious laws and policies of Indonesia are unique in Southeast Asia. At first, these policies seemed open and tolerant, and in a way they are. Although the great majority of Indonesians declare themselves to be adherents of Islam, Indonesia never became a Muslim state, nor did it become a secular one. Instead, it officially recognized a series of world religions as acceptable forms of worship. This was done in accord with the founding principles (*panacila*) of the constitution, one of which was that citizens should belong to one of the acceptable monotheistic religions. The decision to approve a religion as acceptable was up to the Ministry of Religion, which was mainly in the hands of Muslims, who added several other requirements: An acceptable religion (*agama*) had to have a "book," as well as a prophet. A religion had to exist among more than one ethnic group. To qualify, some of the world religions required a flexible interpretation of one or more of such provisions.

The initial set of approved religions included Islam, of course, the religion of most Indonesians, as well as Christianity, the religion of many minorities that had developed under colonial rule in Sumatra, Borneo, Sulawesi, and eastern Indonesia. The government also included Buddhism. There were few Buddhists (and no Buddhist ethnic groups) in Indonesia at the time, although Indonesia's most famous monument, the great ninth-century Borobudur in Java, was a Mahayana Buddhist shrine and a testament to the historical significance of Buddhism in Indonesia's past. As Catholicism and Protestantism were recognized as separate religions, this made a total of four. Hinduism was not among the original officially recognized religions, though, with Buddhism, it had been part of the pre-Muslim civilization of western Indonesia, as the many Indic ruins throughout Java indicated. Until Hinduism was eventually recognized, the Balinese were left without a recognized *agama*. Confucianism, which covered many or most of the Chinese, was originally omitted as well, but it was eventually added. These additions brought the approved religions to six.

The officially recognized monotheistic religions were afforded state protection and support. This meant among other things that their members could proselytize among and convert nonbelievers whereas others could not. Those Indonesian peoples who did not belong to the recognized religions were declared to not yet have a religion (*belum bergama*) or to have only "beliefs" (*percayaan*). Such people without religion were regarded as primitive or backward. Their conversion to one of the recognized universal religions was a step toward modernity, which was strongly desired by the Indonesian state. Those who were categorized as not yet having a religion included several different kinds of peoples including the hunter-gatherers of Borneo and Sumatra and the many highland-interior shifting cultivators of Sumatra, Borneo, Sulawesi, and eastern Indonesia. These peoples were all classified as being isolated and backward communities.

The category of "not yet having a religion" initially included the Balinese as well, who were, like the Javanese, heirs to an ancient Indic civilization. However, they were labeled polytheistic—people who indiscriminately worshipped stones, trees, and a vast array of local spirits, and who possessed neither a holy book nor a high god. To many Muslims, Balinese religion was hardly a religion at all, especially compared to Islam (Howe 2005, 63; see also Geertz 1964). The Balinese became aware of such views, which, along with the state designation of lacking a religion, hurt their ethnic status in modern Indonesia. It also made them vulnerable to conversion to an official religion. Some Western-educated and intellectual Balinese had in fact already been rethinking their religion and culture since the early twentieth century. But the official postcolonial classification gave this task a much greater urgency. The general goal among Balinese reformers was to create a unified, coherent, and organized body of doctrine and ritual that could be called a religion and that was more comparable to Islam, Buddhism, and Christianity. The specific objective became having Balinese religious beliefs and practices recognized as Hinduism. To this end, the modernist Balinese leaders intensified efforts to simplify ritual procedures, especially for cremation, and emphasized that their religion included sacred books—the Hindu epics. They also began to use the term *agama* to refer to their religion. Balinese supernatural beliefs and practices naturally included Hindu traditions dating back to the Indic period. It is unclear how many Balinese thought of themselves as "Hindus," or for how long. And remember, "Hindu" and

"Hinduism" as terms applied to the religious traditions of the Indian sub-continent, let alone Bali, only developed in the nineteenth century.

The Balinese religious reformers and modernists achieved their goal in 1958 when Balinese Hinduism was officially recognized as a legitimate monotheistic religion. Indonesia's newest old religion was named *agama Hindu Bali*, later changed to simply *agama Hindu* to show that it was not the religion of only one ethnic community (Howe 2005, 65). Such recognition in turn opened several new doors. One was that, since Hinduism had become an official religion, non-Balinese could convert to it, and some Javanese did so. And for these Javanese, the Balinese became the recognized authorities on proper Hinduism (Beatty 1999, 219–25).

State efforts to guide and transform the development of the religions of Indonesia began before the military coup in 1965. However, religious change became more urgent and more politicized after the coup. Having an approved religion became not merely a matter of religious reform, ethnic prestige, or political correctness but also a matter of survival. The official government version of the 1965 military coup was that it was provoked by an attempted communist takeover. The coup was followed by massive killings, above all in Java and Bali. Anticommunism became one of the main ideologies of the Suharto regime. Real and alleged communists were widely perceived as very dangerous. Here, there was a chain of assumptions. Communists were known to be atheists, and to lack a religion was to be an atheist. To be seen as an atheist came to be seen as placing oneself on the side of communism and the wrong side of government. To be an official member of one of the recognized religions provided cover, if nothing else. The onset of the Suharto years thus brought large-scale conversion of people who had previously not belonged to a recognized religion to Islam or Christianity (Kipp and Rodgers 1987b, 19).

The other door that was opened was for several indigenous "not yet religions" to become officially Hindu—not by "converting" to Hinduism, as some Javanese had but rather by having their own religious beliefs and practices governmentally recognized as Hinduism. This would lift the stigma of having a primitive nonreligion and bring the other benefits of official sanctions. But could it be done?

With the right strategy, yes it could be and was, by the Toraja in the central highlands of the island of Sulawesi and the Ngaju and other Dayak groups in southern Borneo. In both instances, there had been a preceding history of conversion to Christianity, or in the case of the Ngaju, to both Christianity (for some people) and Islam (for others). The Toraja, who had by then gained recognition and prestige as a tourist attraction (through their architecture and their spectacular death ceremonies), were granted recognition as official Hindus in 1969 (Volkman 1987, 166).

Next came the Ngaju, the Luangan, and other Dayak adherents of a reformed religion named Kaharingan in southern Borneo. This effort succeeded in 1980 (Atkinson 1987; Schiller 1997, 118–20; Weinstock 1987, 71–73). Like the Balinese, the Ngaju and other southern Dayak religious reformers had for a long period been attempting to modernize and rationalize their religion by eliminating or deemphasizing the more unacceptable beliefs, including those involving "unclean" lower world spirits, and by reforming rituals, especially the lengthy and costly two-stage mortuary practices. Conversely, the main upper-world male god was promoted to new importance.

The initial strategy for gaining state recognition was to have Kaharingan added to the official list as a separate religion. But not surprisingly, this approach did not meet with success. The government had already made clear that it was not inclined to add further religions to the existing list. And Kaharingan was more or less ethnically exclusive, thus failing to meet one of the government's criteria. A better strategy was therefore to try to do what the Toraja had done and have Kaharingan declared a version of one of the existing official religions, and here the obvious choice was Hinduism. This worked right away. Although the southern Dayaks were not a major tourist attraction, several other things favored the acceptance of Kaharingan. There were known Hindu relics from Kutei in East Kalimantan; in fact, these were thought to be the oldest anywhere in Indonesia. The Balinese Hindu community (which included many *transmigrasi*—or government-resettled—Balinese communities in the Ngaju region of Borneo as elsewhere in Kalimantan) welcomed the religious reinforcements. And Kaharingan political strength had already been building in the New Order regime. The proposal was developed, presented, and accepted, and Kaharingan was officially declared to be Hinduism—although much work remained to further develop the correct standards of Indonesian Hinduism. Government identity cards were ordered to show Kaharingan members were now Hindus (Schiller 1997, 116–21).

Religion and the State in Postwar Vietnam

There are perhaps parallels between developments involving religion and the state in postwar Vietnam and those in postcolonial (especially New Order) Indonesia: the forceful or coercive role assumed by the state and, therefore, the importance of religious political correctness. There also seem to have even been limited areas of substantial agreement—that superstition and wasting money on needless ritual celebrations is to be discouraged. However, the main thrust of government interest in the two places (neither fully succeeding) was very different, indeed diametrically opposed. In Indonesia, the goal was to get all citizens into a proper monotheistic religion.

But in Vietnam, it was to get everyone out of religion altogether—though out of some things more than others, and eventually official antireligious policies toward some beliefs and practices changed to very positive acceptance.

Policies toward religion by the communist government have been developing over a long period of time, and there have been differences from one region of the country to another. In addition to the older differences between the northern and southern areas of Vietnam, the north has been governed by the communist regime since the French withdrawal in 1954, while the south only since the unification of Vietnam in 1975. This means that the communist regime began to implement its policies concerning religion and other cultural matters twenty years earlier in the north. In addition, many Christian Vietnamese moved south after the partition in 1954. There have also been changes in official policies and popular practices over time.[3]

In his book *Culture, Ritual and Revolution in Vietnam*, Shaun Malarney discusses policies and changes based upon his study of a commune (an administrative grouping, usually of several or more village hamlets) of Thinh Liet in northern Vietnam, not far from Hanoi. He points out that, regardless of possible preference, the revolutionary government of Vietnam never attempted to eliminate all religion per se. But it did attempt to redefine legitimate religion, to eliminate or diminish various practices, and to introduce new ones in their place. At the base of the communist party's objections to traditional religion was the Marxist notion that religion served to support and perpetuate the ancien régime. More specifically, the revolutionary government objected to all beliefs in supernatural agency. This included the doctrine of fate, luck, and fortune as opposed to human effort and rationality. And it objected to superstition and superstitious practices, such as the propitiation of spirits, exorcism, and the use of spirit doctors and spirit mediums. Such practices were deemed wrong both because they involved beliefs in "false causation" and because they were a waste of effort and resources; in the case of spirit mediumship, these included chicanery and exploitation as well. Next, the party objected to religious ritual activities that involved conspicuous consumption whereby the rich demonstrated their superior position over the poor and used it (as in marriage) to perpetuate or create alliances among themselves. And finally, some practices were objectionable for reasons involving public health, most notably, the exhumation and reburial of the dead in secondary mortuary rituals. The latter were not banned but over time were subjected to increasing restrictions (Malarney 2002, 52–76, 80–83).

Reactions to party and government efforts varied along lines of gender and background. Women, especially mature women, were mainly responsible for the well-being of their families, including their spiritual well-being. Women were therefore less willing to give up traditional beliefs and practices than were men. Among men, there were also differences. Those who had been extensively exposed to party education and doctrine, such as soldiers and party members, were more apt to agree with government efforts to eliminate, diminish, or alter religion than were other men (102–5).

The government and party efforts to diminish and alter religious beliefs and practices did bring many changes. For example, funerals were simplified, made more egalitarian, and purged of some "superstitious" practices. But efforts at secularization were only partially successful. Some people never accepted the revolutionary religious changes, and some people who had once accepted the changes reverted to prerevolutionary practices. What happened to Ho Chi Minh is a telling example. After his death, a great official effort was made to commemorate Ho's standing as the central revolutionary hero of Vietnam. But in some places, this led to full deification. In Thinh Liet, a bust of Ho was placed in the central position on a refurbished altar devoted to memorializing the souls of the dead. The initial claim by those supporting the placement (older men with party backgrounds) was that it was strictly a matter of memorialization and that no superstition was involved. But then, in 1991, their position changed to advocating that Ho be recognized as the guardian spirit of the village and treated accordingly. The argument in favor was that the existing guardian spirit had not been doing a very good job and that no spirit was more deserving of the position than Ho. The deification of Ho was in keeping with a well-developed tradition in Vietnamese history whereby cults form around deceased military heroes (both male and female), especially ones who have defended the country against foreign control. Some villagers went even further and took the position that Ho had actually been a living god in his lifetime, sent to free the Vietnamese from French colonial and American oppression (201).

Malarney gives other examples of the reversion to traditional religious sentiments and practices by aging party members and former military men. A full colonel and veteran of the American War took up his family's traditional occupation of making ritual papier-mâché objects for sale, to be burned as offerings in ancestor worship, and came to be regarded as the most skillful such artisan in the community. Another party official became a spirit doctor—for which, however, he was expelled from the party, though how this affected his new profession or his life in general is not discussed (221).

Over the years, the state in Vietnam has continued to relax restrictions on religious activities. The government has continued to promulgate enactments, including a lengthy one in 2004. These guarantee freedom to practice any religion—or none—although such freedom is qualified by various restrictions included in other laws. As in Indonesia, the state in Vietnam has created a list of officially recognized religions, though unlike in Indonesia, this includes local as well as world religions. State recognition in this instance means that these religions are permitted to operate as organizations within the country. The world religions on the list include Buddhism, Catholicism, Protestantism, and Islam. The Vietnamese ones are Cao Dai and Hoa Hao, both of which began as syncretic religious movements under colonial rule (Wells-Dang 2007, 401). Neither Hinduism nor Confucianism, both among the state-approved religions in Indonesia, is on the Vietnamese roster. There are probably few Hindus in Vietnam, but the absence of Confucianism left the Chinese community without an official religion, except for Buddhism. Likewise, the religious traditions of the highland ethnic minorities are not recognized except where people have converted to Catholicism, Protestantism, or Buddhism. The successful tack taken by several Indonesian societies of having a reformed and named version of their own indigenous religious traditions recognized as one of the state-approved religions has apparently not been tried. The distinction at one time emphasized by the communist party and government between lawful religion and improper superstition appears to have waned.

Here, the practice of ancestor worship is significant. The apparently superstitious nature of practices of ancestor worship (at least that go beyond expressions of devout respect) notwithstanding, ancestor worship has come to be officially regarded as at the center of Vietnamese national religious traditions and practiced by adherents of all religions and ethnic communities in Vietnam (Jellema 2007, 69–72). In an earlier period, ritual practices that involved lavish spending or that served to display inequality in economic resources were one of the main objections to superstition. Such objections appear therefore to have greatly diminished as well. According to a recent account by the Vietnamese anthropologist Do Thien, a three-year study of several villages in northern and southern Vietnamese shows a very large expenditure (from 30 to 60 percent of all household spending) went for the costs of life-crisis rituals, including those of birth, marriage, death, and death anniversaries (Thien 2007, 173). These are presumably the kinds of expenditures the communist party and government had previously sought to discourage.

In another recent account, the American anthropologist Kate Jellema attributes the increase in ritual expenditures to the opening of Vietnam to international capitalism and its penetration throughout rural society. Her specific concern is with ancestor worship. She notes the living standards of the dead have risen along with those of the living. Ancestor worship includes the ritual transferring of paper offerings of money and goods from the living to the dead, and paper votive models have come to include name-brand mopeds, home entertainment centers, and even Mercedes-Benz automobiles (Jellema 2007, 60). In Vietnam, "ghost money" (also offered in votive form by burning) is available in American dollars as well as Vietnamese dong. Paper votive credit cards cannot be far behind.

The State, Superstition, and Buddhism in Laos

Postwar religious policies were introduced into the Lao People's Democratic Republic (PDR) with the establishment of the communist government in 1975. These were largely inspired by and modeled upon those previously put in place in North Vietnam after 1954. The situation in the two countries was not the same, however, and neither were the changes in religion that were sought or implemented. Although many indigenous beliefs and practices are similar in the two countries among the dominant, lowland Lao in Laos and the Vietnamese in Vietnam (and even more so among the highland ethnic minorities in the two countries), there are also major differences. To begin with, Buddhism is the major world religion in both places. But Buddhism is both different and comparatively more important in Laos than in Vietnam. Buddhism in Laos is Theravada and dominates the religious life of the ethnic Lao, whereas Buddhism in Vietnam is Mahayana and is but one dimension of religious traditions. The matter of how to deal with Buddhism in Laos was therefore a much larger issue than it was in Vietnam. Another major religious difference is ancestor worship. As with the Thai in Thailand (as discussed in the previous chapter), whether or not the Lao engage at all in ancestor worship, they do not do so in a similar way to the Vietnamese, among whom the practice is a central dimension of religious life.

After the communist party came to power, it was faced with what to do with spirit mediums and other forms of animism and magic, and about Buddhism. It treated each in a different way, though in both instances the initial strategy was eventually relaxed or abandoned. The party and the government objected to the practices of spirit mediums both as superstition contradicted by science and as a relic of the feudal order. However, the party also had practical political concerns, including the fear that troublesome spirits might make an appearance at a séance and say embarrassing things about the new regime. Such spirits might include the ghosts of past kings—traditionally popular characters at séances—or of recently deceased politicians of the previous regime. Such spirits might even speak through the medium and say that the present communist regime would soon fall (Evans 1998, 71). Worse still, the risk was that ordinary people might believe such things if spoken through the mouth of a reliable medium.

According to Grant Evans (1998, 72), the broader and more basic problem was that, while party leaders and intellectuals might be convinced of the falsity of spirits and the powers of mediums to give them voice, ordinary people (including ordinary party members) accepted such things. Additionally, the government had little to offer in the way of practical help as an alternative to the information and advice offered by spirit mediums as well as monks. The well-publicized early campaign against superstition made Buddhist monks less willing to provide their customary forms of practical advice and ritual assistance to people with personal problems. This reluctance, based on the fear of being attacked by the government for engaging in superstitious activities, promoted greater use of the less public services of the mediums.

The problem of persuading ordinary people to give up superstitious beliefs and practices sometimes led to more creative solutions of a fighting-fire-with-fire type—that is, of *exorcizing* spirits in place of simply trying to debunk them in rational terms. Evans (73–74) recounts an amusing story told to him in the 1990s by an old party member: Two decades earlier, the party member attempted to get rid of the spirits then occupying Luang Pra-bang (the old royal capital, now a World Heritage Site) in northern Laos. The party member announced in 1977 that all of the spirits of the place belonged to the deposed feudal regime and would therefore have to go as well. He organized a ceremony at his own temple at which he summoned the spirits and informed them that the king was now gone. Then he offered them a choice of several alternatives: they could become monks; they could follow the king to where he had been sent (his death, it turned out); or they could leave the country altogether and become refugees. The spirits were then told to go off and think it over, and that night all the people dreamed they heard a great commotion among the spirits. Next, the party cadre organized several ceremonies. One of these was a Buddhist ceremony to ordain the spirits that had decided to become monks. Another ceremony was held to send off the spirits that had chosen to join the deposed king. For the spirits that chose the last alternative of leaving the country to become refugees, no ceremony was held. However, people heard these spirits riding away on elephants.

Buddhism for the new communist regime presented a different set of problems and opportunities than did popular recourse to spirit mediums and other activities deemed to be blatant superstition. It is true that Buddhist monks engaged in the exorcism of spirits and engaged in magical activities that party elites and intellectuals were inclined to regard as superstition. But the general population did not make a distinction between orthodox or legitimate Buddhist beliefs and practices (focused on the central causal doctrine of karma) and superstitious ones. Buddhism had a name, an identity, organized institutions, and great meaning and prestige among its adherents. Therefore, the communist party and the government never attempted an assault on Buddhism in the way the Khmer Rouge did at the same time in Cambodia (Evans 1998, 57; Stuart-Fox 1996, 65). Yet, the party and government did seek to transform Buddhism in a number of ways. The general idea was to associate itself with the prestige of the religion while attempting to change its emphasis from its traditionally otherworldly orientation to worldly practical political concerns. More specifically, the party and government wanted to place the *sangha* (monks) under their control, and to turn Buddhism into something closer to socialism. Monasteries were to become cooperatives, and monks were to plant their own food or receive rations of rice for teaching rather than be dependent on gifts from the faithful. Such efforts were in accord with the party's desire to legitimize the new regime in the eyes of the population. But socializing Buddhism was not well received by the Buddhist Lao, for whom supporting monks with daily gifts of rice and other contributions were the fundamental means of earning merit.

As were other efforts to build Marxism in Laos, the attempt to socialize Buddhism in a radical way was deemphasized (though not entirely abandoned). The other goal of using it to strengthen the legitimacy of the government therefore prevailed (which should not be taken to mean the Buddhist sentiments and loyalties of Lao government and party officials were not genuine). This of course also had its problems. A large part of the population of the country was comprised of non-Buddhist highland peoples who were well represented in the party and in the revolutionary struggle against the monarchy. And for these people, Buddhism—which had been the state religion under the monarchy and which was associated with the assumed cultural superiority of the Lao Lum (or lowlanders)—had little positive appeal (Stewart-Fox 1996, 73). Nonetheless, the link of Buddhism with the new Lao state grew and became more formalized. In 1991, That Luang, the Grand Stupa of Vientiane, replaced the Hammer and Sickle as the national symbol of Laos, becoming the central feature of its currency (see photo 12.3) and the seal of all government ministries and official documents. And Buddhism had a prominent role in the elaborate state funeral held in November 1992 for Kaysone Phomvihane, the leader of the Lao communist party since its founding in 1955, and of the Lao People's Democratic Republic since 1975 (Evans 1998, 24, 41).

10

Religious Conversion on the Ethnic Margins

As elsewhere in much of the developing world, conversion to one of the world (or universal) religions is a fundamental part of the changes now taking place among many of the indigenous minority groups of Southeast Asia. Although information is uneven, the pattern of religious change seems fairly clear.[1] Before their conversion, most of the interior and highland minority peoples adhered to their own indigenous religious traditions. In contrast, the dominant lowland and coastal peoples had for centuries followed one of the world religions: mainly Buddhism throughout most of mainland Southeast Asia except for the far south of Thailand and Malaysia; Islam in Malaysia and Indonesia; and Christianity in the Philippines. Some of the indigenous minorities throughout mainland Southeast Asia have converted to the religion that prevails among the dominant lowland or coastal population of the country in question. For example, some Karen and members of other highland minorities in Thailand have become Buddhists. However, the general direction of change among the indigenous minorities of mainland Southeast Asia has been conversion to Christianity. In contrast, the loyalties of the lowland peoples to the religious traditions to which they have long adhered have changed relatively little.

The same is true of much of insular Southeast Asia where the dominant religion is Islam. In both Malaysian and Indonesian Borneo, for example, some Dayaks and members of other indigenous groups of the interior have converted to Islam. However, most have become Christians. Although few specific numbers are available, the same appears to be the case for much of the rest of Indonesia outside of Java and Bali. In Indonesia, the government requires that all inhabitants of the country adhere to a "monotheistic" religion, which includes Islam, Christianity (Protestant or Roman Catholic),

Photo 10.1.   Karen village church in Ban Nam Hoo, Mae Hong Son Province, northern Thailand, 2004.

Hinduism, Buddhism, or Confucianism. While members of several indigenous minority peoples in Indonesia have succeeded in having their own reformed religious traditions officially recognized as a version of "Hinduism," the majority have accepted either Christianity or Islam, and for the most part it has been the former.

In Southeast Asia, it is therefore overwhelmingly the indigenous minority peoples who are converting, and they are mainly converting to a religion other than that followed by the dominant people in the countries concerned. The Philippines appears to be the only major country in Southeast Asia that forms an exception to the general pattern. Because of early Spanish colonization, most of the peoples of the Philippines north of Mindanao and other far southern islands have long been Christian. Here, therefore, indigenous minority converts to Christianity have entered the world religion that prevails among the national majority, though differences between conversion to Protestant denominations as opposed to the prevailing Roman Catholicism may be of some significance.

The general pattern of conversion may seem somewhat paradoxical. The separation between the indigenous minority groups and the dominant lowland/coastal national populations has been declining through acculturation and political and economic integration. Roads are being pushed into the forests and mountains of the interior, national schools are being built, and the highland and interior peoples are learning national languages. Many are living, working, or trading in lowland and coastal regions, while lowlanders and coastal peoples are moving into the interior and highlands in search of land or for other, mainly economic, reasons.

THE EXTENT OF CONVERSION

Though to a varying extent and at different rates in different countries, conversion is occurring in most regions unless it has been halted or inhibited by governmental restrictions or other developments. The conversion of indigenous peoples to Christianity began in the nineteenth century, or earlier in some places, but increased considerably throughout the twentieth. In a large area of mainland Southeast Asia, including Vietnam, Laos, and Cambodia, the proselytizing of Christianity in much of the second half of the twentieth century has been limited by the Indochina wars and government prohibitions on missionary efforts. But in some areas of these countries, extensive conversion had already occurred. And where such impediments have not existed, the spread of Christianity has been extensive enough to suppose it may eventually prevail among most of the indigenous minority peoples in much of Southeast Asia, as already appears to be the case throughout the insular countries. Accurate figures or estimates are difficult to find, but those that exist illustrate these points. A recent estimate regarding Laos, where the spread of Christianity from the 1960s to the present has been very restricted, suggests the number of Christians among the Hmong to between 12 to 15 percent of the Hmong population (Ovesen 2004, 460). In contrast, for Thailand, where Christian proselytization in recent decades has probably been less impeded than in any other country in mainland Southeast Asia, it has been more extensive. Here, an estimate made in the early 1990s by Charles Keyes (1993, 272) places the number of Christians at between one-third and one-half of the population of the hill tribes. This portion has probably increased a great deal since then. In the case of the Karen of Burma and Thailand, a recent estimate suggests that the majority of Karen in Burma are Buddhists and that 20 percent are Christians, while in Thailand, where Christianity and Buddhism are both widely received, Christians form approximately 10 percent of the population (Hayami and Darlington 2000, 141).

COLONIALISM AND OTHER
INTERPRETATIONS OF CONVERSION

Why has this pattern of religious change developed? One answer is that it is rooted in Western colonialism. The links between colonialism and efforts to spread Christianity are undeniable. Colonial takeovers and pacification often preceded efforts at proselytization and provided the opportunity to do it more safely. It would be impossible to explain the pervasive nature of Christianity in the Philippines except in the context of Spanish colonial rule. Throughout Southeast Asia, colonial policy did not require that Christian proselytization efforts be directed specifically at the indigenous minorities rather than Muslims and Buddhists, and in the early phases of colonization, it probably was not. But except among some Vietnamese, such efforts had little success. The result was that missionaries became aware that their best or only chance for spreading Christianity was among the minority groups (see Keyes 1993, on Thailand).

Yet, colonialism only explains so much. Missionary efforts did sometimes precede colonial control. At least outside of the Philippines during the Spanish period, once established colonial governments in Southeast Asia were not necessarily interested in missionary activities. Sometimes, colonial regimes saw mission efforts as a source of trouble. And since colonialism ended decades ago in Southeast Asia, it no longer has the relevance it once had as an explanation for the continued expansion of Christianity. Except in those countries noted above where its further spread has been limited or blocked by war and government policy, the growth of Christianity has been greatest in the postcolonial period, although rooted in the developments that occurred under colonial rule. In Indonesia, the greatest increase in conversion among adherents of indigenous religions appears to have come in the mid- to late 1960s when the acceptance of a world religion was coerced by governmental and military threats against those who did not follow an approved monotheistic religion (Kipp and Rodgers 1987b, 19). Moreover, Thailand, where conversion to Christianity among the hill tribes has been particularly extensive, was never colonized, which is not to say colonization elsewhere or westernization had no effect.

Rice Christians

The link of conversion to colonialism is also associated with the notion that many of those who have converted to Christianity have done so for economic or other material reasons—to take advantages of resources or services provided by missionaries in order to escape poverty or to achieve upward mobility through education. Sometimes persons who convert for such reasons are referred to as "Rice (or Rice Bowl) Christians," literally referring to people who are poor and hungry and therefore convert in order to obtain food. Both Western missionaries and critics or opponents of Christianity have used this term as a derogatory label for what is deemed to be inauthentic or nonspiritually based conversion. More broadly, it has been applied to people who convert in order to gain material benefit or to improve their life chances. Rice Christians are associated with India and China more than Southeast Asia, which lacks a comparable history of sometimes massive famine and starvation.

However, the possibility that people convert for support or other material reasons has some applicability to Southeast Asia as well. The provision of relief for refugees and survivors following natural disasters or in the aftermath of war has provided opportunities for religiously linked assistance in Southeast Asia as well as in other places. In Thailand, the string of refugee camps along the Burmese border, which contain 170,000 or more of mainly Karen refugees from Burma, are supported by a consortium of Western-based nongovernmental organizations (NGOs), most of which are religious organizations. These camps also have Christian churches supported by mission efforts, often several or more. In Mae Ra Ma Camp in southern Mae Hong Son Province, there was (in 2006, when I was there for a few days) a Baptist church and a Roman Catholic church, as well as a Buddhist temple and a mosque. I do not know if any of the refugees in Mae Ra Ma had become Christian in order to help their chances for leaving the camp or otherwise improving their lives, but it would not be surprising, for their prospects for doing either are generally bleak.

Elsewhere in Thailand—in Chiang Rai (northern Thailand)—in 2006, I met a group of American Baptist volunteers who were there to build churches in Akha Christian villages. I also visited an Akha Christian village whose inhabitants told me they had received or were expecting such assistance. In such cases, however, the conversion had already occurred, and it would be difficult to know if the anticipation of material support was a factor or, if so, how important it was. In the past, Christian missionaries throughout Southeast Asia often established schools and hospitals to which people were attracted and for which they were grateful. In the case of mission schools, there is the opportunity of influencing students.

The role of missions in providing medical services and education may have been greater in the past than it has been in the recent period. Previously, Christian mission schools and hospitals were all that existed in some regions. This is no longer the case in most places, but it probably continues to be so in some. In Borneo, some Dayaks who had been politically or economically successful told me their success was due to mission schools. And in West Kalimantan, Baptists run the reputedly best hospital in the province. There is a strong mission presence in some areas such as northern Thailand, but here and throughout many regions, government hospitals, clinics, and especially schools are now also widespread.

While I have never heard the phrase "Rice Buddhists" or "Rice Muslims," the notion that people may be attracted to material benefits that organized religions can provide is not limited to Christianity. Individuals in both Borneo and mainland Southeast Asia have sometimes told me they were drawn to Christian missions in order to learn English or to gain an education. However, I heard the same thing about entering Buddhist monasteries by both Buddhist and non-Buddhist men in Laos. Here, I was told of even more elementary motives for entering a monastery. In southern Laos, one man from an indigenous non-Buddhist ethnic minority group said that he and a friend were able to survive the civil war (and get an education) only because they were taken into a monastery and put under its protection.

As might be expected, others often view conversion critically or cynically. In the interior of Borneo, the occasional individual or village conversion to Islam is sometimes seen by non-Muslims in this way, that is, becoming a Muslim in Malaysian or Borneo or Brunei is interpreted as a strategy for obtaining development assistance for a village or for improving an individual's prospects for getting a desirable government job (or improving the chances for advancement)—also the case in Kalimantan or Indonesian Borneo.

Scholars who have written about conversion among the Hmong of northern Thailand have stressed the importance of economic motives, though not to the exclusion of others. Nicholas Tapp (1989b) notes the primary motivation for Hmong to become Christian was to achieve some form of social or economic advantage (100). This was shown by the many cases in which impoverished families or individuals adopted Christianity in order to be sponsored educationally by missionaries. Similarly, in his account of several Hmong villages, Robert Cooper (1984) states that Christianity appealed to the poor and that the six families who converted to Christianity in the village of Khun Sa were the poorest in the community (79, 82, 169, 179). Both of these scholars also found that the attraction of conversion to Christianity was not only a matter of gaining the support and resources that missions and missionaries could provide. It was also a means of escaping costly traditional ritual obligations. Cooper suggests the poor Hmong of Khun Sa were led to convert because it spared them from paying bridewealth and having to provide animals they could not afford for sacrifice in traditional ceremonies.

Cornelia Kammerer (1990) has offered the same argument in greater detail regarding the conversion of the Akha of northern Thailand. She writes that for many years Western Christian missionaries sought to spread Christianity among these Akha with little or no success. However, when she

returned some years after her first period of study, many Akha were converting. She does not think it was because the Christian message had finally
gotten through in a way that it had not earlier. She argues that the Akha
remained indifferent to Christian theology. What had changed therefore
were the economic circumstances of the Akha. Because of the policies of
the Thai government, especially in restricting shifting cultivation, the Akha
had become poorer. They were forced to become more integrated into the
lowland cash-based Thai economy. So, they could no longer afford their
customary ceremonies, and Christianity provided a way out.

Religious conversion in Borneo has sometimes been interpreted along
similar lines, although with certain differences (Metcalf 1989, 214–15;
Rousseau 1998, 26). Here also the appeal of Christianity has been attributed in part to its liberation from burdensome traditional religious practices, in this case ones involving taboos and other ritual restrictions. These
were burdensome not so much in terms of materials but in time. Seeing
or hearing an omen bird from a wrong direction would bring a journey or
even a trip to work in the fields to a halt and a return to the villages, with
the loss of a day or more of work. Similarly, a death would also close a village to either entry or exit, again with a loss of work for a number of days.
As missionaries began to work among the Dayaks, they became aware of
the role of the omens and taboos of the traditional religion and used this as
an argument in favor of conversion to Christianity. Some Dayaks or whole
villages did convert, and others watched to see if disaster struck, and when
it did not, others followed suit.

The appeal of shedding the burden of the omens and taboos of customary religious traditions took another form in the northern part of central
Borneo. While many Dayaks here converted directly to Christianity, some
took a roundabout route via a religious movement known as Bungan
(named after Bungan Malam, who was a lesser goddess among the Kenyah
until she was elevated to the main deity of the movement). The movement
was almost certainly provoked by Christian missionary activity and formed
an alternative to it. It was a reform movement rather than a messianic or
millennial one, for it mainly got rid of most of the taboos and much of
the ritual of the old religion without requiring conversion to Christianity.
While Bungan practices lasted a number of decades (and still survive in a
few places), it has generally been replaced by Christianity.

Mystical Appeals

In addition to such diverse materialistic attractions, the appeal of Christianity among some groups has also been linked to indigenous mythical
themes. In northern mainland Southeast Asia, the Hmong, the Karen, and
evidently other highland indigenous minorities have similar myths that

explain their status regarding their more powerful lowland neighbors in terms of literacy, scripts, or books—the idea being that these were the key to wealth and power. In some sense, such notions are undoubtedly true, but in any case the myths tell how the scripts and books were lost and how one day a mystical hero or heroes would return. In the Karen version, the creator deity Y'wa gives books to his children, each of whom is the ancestor of a different ethnic group. The Karen foolishly let their books be eaten by animals or destroyed by fire from their practice of shifting cultivation, hence their inferiority to the Thai, Shan, or Burmans who had kept their books. But someday, foreign brothers will come and bring back their magical books. When the early Christian missionaries to the Karen learned all this, they bought into it themselves. Here was the hand of the Lord at work. They supposed that Y'wa was none other than Yahweh of the Old Testament and the Karen were one of the lost tribes of Israel, and they associated themselves with the mystical brothers who would return the Golden Book (Keyes 1977; Tapp 1989a, 76). Tapp similarly attributes the messianic fervor that followed the arrival of the first Christian missionary among the Hmong in southern China to the rumor that the missionary had a powerful book meant for them and that he was in the process of translating it into Hmong.

Although myths about the return of lost scripts and books were not involved, Jennifer Connolly (2003) argues in her study of conversion to Christianity in East Kalimantan that many Dayaks attracted to Christianity were seeking new forms of supernatural power (205–11). For these Dayaks at least, the great theological claims were of less interest than pragmatic applications. While the missionaries stressed salvation as the ultimate and central purpose of conversion, they also offered prayer as a means of gaining divine help in their earthly concerns. Dayaks were thus especially interested in stories about miracles and the possibilities of faith healing—one of the few specific forms of material help modern Christians were prepared to offer. As stated before, for people in Southeast Asia and many other places, religion has an important practical side. Sometimes Bidayuh in Sarawak (Malaysian Borneo) erect small wooden crosses in their swidden fields before planting rice to help ensure a successful crop. And a Dayak villager in West Kalimantan, Indonesia, once told me he had made the right decision in becoming a Baptist rather than a Catholic because the Baptist part of the village was getting better rice harvests than the Catholic one.

CONVERSION, ETHNICITY, AND DEVELOPMENT

Whatever the various possible motives or attractions may be, patterns of conversion in Southeast Asia are also ethnic in nature. As noted, the adoption of Christianity does not occur equally among all ethnic sectors: common across ethnic lines of the highland and interior groups but rarely among the dominant lowland and coastal populations. The latter groups are generally reluctant to convert because they are already adherents of a world or universalistic religion. These named religions have great prestige and authority and are a fundamental part of the identity of their adherents. In Malaysia, for example, both the official and the popular definition of being Malay include being Muslim—and to become a Muslim in Malaysia is popularly referred to as becoming a Malay (*masuk Melayu*). In Thailand, the situation appears to be more complicated. Here the government has sought to make "Thai" a nationality rather than a specific ethnic or religious one, that is, equivalent to "Malaysian" rather than "Malay."

None of this really explains why the indigenous ethnic minorities are converting mainly to Christianity rather than to religions of the dominant lowland and coastal peoples. One possibility is that the ethnic minorities have been approached by the Christians rather than by the Buddhists or the Muslims, as the case may be. In the past, the dominant lowland and coastal peoples or their rulers may have had little interest in spreading their religions to the highlanders, and in some places it may still be true. However, in other instances, serious efforts have been made to convert indigenous peoples to the dominant national religion, and such efforts appear to have had only limited or little success. For example, in the case of the Orang Asli (or "original people") in the interior of the Malaysian Peninsula, according to Kirk Endicott and Robert Dentan, Muslim Malays were permitted to proselytize among them but were not encouraged to do so. By 1968, only about 3 percent of the Orang Asli had converted to Islam. After this time, the government began an effort to convert the Orang Asli, but after thirty years of heavy proselytization, only about 16 percent had become Muslim (Endicott and Dentan 2004, 44–45; see also Dentan 2000, 222–23, on the Semai in particular).

In the case of Thailand, several researchers have commented on government efforts to promote conversion to Buddhism among the hill tribes (Gillogly 2004, 122; Keyes 1993, 261; Tapp 1989b, 5). Such efforts began in the 1960s, in part as a result of a shift in policy toward integrating the highland minorities into the national state. Encouraging the indigenous minorities to become Buddhist was seen as a way of strengthening ties with them and increasing their loyalty to the nation. By this time, the Thai *sangha* had also become interested in spreading Buddhism to the hill tribes and began to do so under the government-sponsored Thammacarik program. Although no figures are given, these accounts suggest the effort had only limited success overall—though it did have some effect among the Karen (Hayami 1996, 345–46). Possible reasons for the limited success of converting hill-tribe peoples are that it was "culturally inappropriate" or that the tribal peoples were too poor to build temples or support monks. Tapp (1989a, 88) writes, "It is because the type of Buddhism presented to the Hmong and other ethnic minorities is so closely associated with the fundamental values and orientations of Thai Society that it has largely failed to be adopted by them in any widespread or meaningful sense."

The same sort of government effort to promote Buddhism among non-Buddhist minorities is reported to have been made in Burma, although in a much more heavy-handed manner. Here, according to a recent account, the government has been attempting to disrupt the practice of Christianity among some groups and of Islam among others by closing religious schools operated by the adherents of these religions, and by preventing people from attending religious services or from proselytizing, while promoting the construction of Buddhist monastic schools in minority areas. Also, reports of forced conversion to Buddhism by the army have been noted (Lambrecht 2004, 163). Of course, these governmental efforts to promote Buddhism among non-Buddhist minorities took place before Burmese Buddhist monks began to openly oppose and confront the government on a massive scale in 2007.

Throughout Southeast Asia, the indigenous peoples of the mountains and forests of the mainland borderlands and of the interior of the insular countries have become "national minorities" in a way that they previously were not (Duncan 2004). Though never completely isolated, they have also become much more involved with and knowledgeable about the countries in which they live and of the wider world. Traditionally looked down upon as backward and primitive, if also sometimes fierce, by the dominant society, as reflected by the widespread use of terms like "savage" and "slave" to refer to them, their status in the national societies is still often not high. For various reasons, the indigenous minorities do not want to give up their identity or their "culture." But they do want to raise the respect they get, improve their economic fortunes, and gain the other benefits of development. Conversion to Christianity is therefore attractive in several ways apart from the material benefits and support discussed earlier. First, it gives them a real, named religion, since their traditional religion of "animism" is often not regarded as a religion (in Indonesia, it is officially not). Second, it gives them a religion that does not lead to assimilation, as the adoption of Buddhism is assumed to do in Thailand or as Islam is assumed to do in Malaysia. And third, Christianity gives them a prestigious religion, one at least on the same level as Buddhism or Islam, in the sense that Christianity is the religion of the rich, powerful, and developed Western world.

That Christianity is linked to colonialism is probably not of much concern to the indigenous minorities in Southeast Asia to the extent they are even aware of such a thing. According to Tapp (1989a, 77), Hmong Christians now believe they have always been Christian, their old myth of the loss of their books having been forgotten or disregarded. But even if they are aware, it does not matter. Many westerners and Southeast Asians view colonialism as a form of oppression from which liberation was a great national achievement. It does not seem to be widely known that the indigenous minorities do not always view things this way. A friend of mine who was a Christian Dayak schoolteacher in Sarawak once told me he had said to some Malay schoolteachers when they were critical of British colonial rule that Sarawak was now "a colony of Malaysia." Some Dayaks have a cultural view of the colonial period in Sarawak as a sort of golden age, even though some of them had fought against the colonial takeover and had remained rebels throughout much of the colonial period. The Orang Asli of peninsular Malaysia appear to regard the colonial period as one in which the British were their friends and protectors, who reduced or ended Malay slave raiding among them; in contrast, they see the postcolonial period of independence and development as one in which they are treated badly in regard to land rights and pressured by the government to become Muslims and assimilate into Malay society (Dentan et al. 1997). Farther to the north in mainland Southeast Asia, some indigenous minorities formed close relations with colonial rulers—the Karen in Burma being a well-known example.

CONSEQUENCES OF CONVERSION

The consequences of conversion in Southeast Asia are both national and local. At the national level, the fact that many among the various ethnic minority communities have converted to a recognized world religion that is different from the one followed by the lowland or coastal population means that ethnic diversity is strengthened and sharpened by religious diversity. Therefore, efforts to absorb ethnic minorities into the dominant majorities are prevented or hampered in spite of other tendencies to acculturation and assimilation. Most countries in Southeast Asia officially proclaim themselves to be multicultural and multireligious and to guarantee the rights of ethnic minorities and religious freedom, though how much they do so in fact is sometimes a different matter. Indonesia perhaps goes the furthest in defining itself as a multicultural nation and in specifying Islam, Christianity, Buddhism, Confucianism, and Hinduism as legitimate and acceptable religions for its citizens.

At the local level, conversion may have various consequences. In some instances, entire communities may convert at once or within a short period of time, but if only part of a community converts, the village may split. Missionaries who proselytize may urge converts to disassociate from nonconverts or at least to withdraw from participation in traditional ceremonies, which is a problem when everyone in the community is supposed to be involved. Sometimes the differences are reconciled, but sometimes the village physically divides into separate sections or one group leaves entirely and forms a new community elsewhere. All of these developments have been common in the interior of Borneo in relation to conversion. How frequently they also occur in mainland Southeast Asia is a matter with which I am much less familiar. However, several years ago, I visited an Akha village in northern Thailand where, I was told, anyone who became a Christian had to leave the community. Such divisions do not only develop when a part of a village converts while another part does not. Sometimes, in Borneo at least, everyone converts but to two or more different religions. Bidayuh villages in Sarawak very often consist of several different denominations of Christians living in separate areas.

Messianic religious movements can be another consequence of proselytization and conversion, though here other developments and stresses are probably involved as well. In northern mainland Southeast Asia, such movements have been frequently noted among the Hmong, where they were often linked to political turbulence (Tapp 1989a). Writing during the civil war in Laos, Joel Halpern and Peter Kunstadter (1967, 242) observed, "The Meo [Hmong] messianic myth foresees Jesus Christ as the messiah, appearing among them in a jeep, giving them arms and summoning them to action. According to this myth, the Meo will dispose of the local Lao officials, and will then take over the national capital."

While not necessarily or usually leading to messianic religious movements, conversion can bring new political alignments. Robbins Burling (1967, 220–22) reported several decades ago that, among the Nagas of far eastern India, all political leaders, including ones in the rebel movement, were Christian. This suggests that conversion was seen among these people as a prerequisite or a means to achieving political influence, though it may have partly been that Christianity provided access to an education that had become necessary to modern political leadership. In either case, the same pattern can be seen in the interior of Sarawak in Malaysian Borneo. Here also, modern Dayak political leaders tend to be Christian. Once everyone has become Christian, such a distinction ceases to be relevant.

The more distinctly religious consequences of conversion may vary significantly according to whether Buddhism or Christianity is involved. Yoko Hayami (1996, 346, 348–49), who studied conversion to both Christianity and Buddhism in Karen villages in Thailand, reports a difference between those who converted to Christianity and those who became Buddhists in terms of the perpetuation of traditional Karen ritual practices. The Karen Christian converts were required to immediately give up the traditional practices, but the Buddhist converts were not and did not, or at least only gradually, even after a Buddhist substitute had been provided. Karen Christians include both Baptist Protestants and Roman Catholics, although those Hayami studied were Baptists. In any case, she notes no differences between Baptist and Catholic converts regarding the abandonment of traditional ritual practices or other consequences of conversion. In contrast, Tapp (1989b, 99) asserts there are major differences in the consequences of conversion to different versions of Christianity among the Hmong of northern Thailand, regarding, in part, the perpetuation of traditional rituals. The Hmong have also become both Protestants (again mainly Baptists) and Catholics, and the missionaries for each have taken different approaches to traditional Hmong beliefs and ritual practices. The Catholics were more tolerant and took a more gradual approach in leading the Hmong converts toward orthodoxy than the Protestants. Such differences were based on different views of Hmong beliefs in spirits. The Catholic missionaries were skeptical of these beliefs but also sympathetic to them. The Baptist Protestants, in contrast, tended to believe that the Hmong spirits were real in the sense they took them to be manifestations of the devil, who they believe is real; therefore, they regarded traditional Hmong rituals as devil worship, to which they strongly objected. The Catholics permitted the Hmong to continue many of their customary ceremonies as well as the use of alcohol, which the Protestants did not. As a consequence of these differences, conversion to Protestantism has been more stressful. And this in turn, Tapp argues, is linked to a greater likelihood of messianic religious movements among the Hmong who have been proselytized by Protestants rather than by Catholics.

Such differences in the nature and consequences of Protestant versus Catholic mission efforts among the Hmong seem similar to what has taken place in Borneo. Here also, Roman Catholicism is widely associated with a greater tolerance of traditional religious beliefs and practices and with a positive encouragement for Dayaks to continue perpetuating or reviving much of their rituals and culture. This can be seen in various places in the interior, especially in the elaborate artwork to be found in some Kenyah and Kayan longhouses, mortuary structures, and churches in Sarawak and Kalimantan (which I have described in Winzeler 2004a). The interior of the old Catholic church at Long San on the upper Baram River in central Sarawak was covered with spectacular Kenyah-painted spirals and whorls, and the main crucifix showed Christ in a Dayak loincloth and ceremonial helmet (see photo 10.2). You can (or could) also find upriver Kenyah and Kayan longhouse murals showing Christ on the cross flanked by dragons making offerings of flowers. And on the middle Mahakam River in East Kalimantan (Indonesian Borneo), I once witnessed a traditional funeral for a Dayak Catholic teacher that culminated in a water buffalo sacrifice and the daubing of blood on a post carved as an idol. Afterward, I talked to the French priest who was present and asked him what he thought of the funeral; he said he did not approve of all the drinking and gambling

Photo 10.2.   Christian Kenyah Dayak crucifix, St. Pious Catholic Church, Long San, upper Baram River, Borneo (since demolished and rebuilt).

that was going on but that otherwise the ceremony was interesting and he hoped to write about it. On another occasion, I talked to a Catholic priest in Kuching, Sarawak, who had recently transferred downriver after many years on the upper Baram where he had been much loved by his Dayak parishioners. He told me being a Christian was all that was really important and that what the Dayaks continued to believe and practice from their old religion was secondary.

However, there are also differences from one area to another that seem to be associated with conversions. The Catholic Bidayuh in far western

Sarawak retained much less of their old religion and culture than had some Dayak groups in central Borneo, apparently in part because they had been Catholic for so long and had succumbed to other modernizing influences. However, my Bidayuh Catholic friends also said that, when they had been converted, the missionaries had been too strict about getting rid of their old practices. They now regarded themselves as devout Catholics but expressed some bitterness about having to give up things like playing drums and gongs that were not necessarily wrong from a religious perspective. Now they were free to play drums and gongs and were making an effort to use these and other traditional things in religious ceremonies, but the young people were not interested, and much of the old culture was gone beyond recovery.

CONVERSION AND MARGINALIZATION

Most importantly, does Christianity serve the interests of interior, highland, and minority peoples? Most of those who have studied and written about conversion to Christianity in Southeast Asia make similar statements about its ethnic dimensions and consequences: it is a way for these groups to gain greater respect from other groups including the dominant majorities; it contributes to the development of broader ethnic awareness and solidarity with others who have also converted; and it keeps those who convert from disappearing into the dominant majority. But is conversion entirely a good thing, or are there costs as well as benefits to remaining apart?

To begin with, in many areas, pressures on the indigenous ethnic minorities to convert to a world religion will probably continue to increase. The sort of post-Christian movement now occurring in parts of the developed world (especially Western Europe) will probably not arrive in Southeast Asia anytime soon. Hence, the real question in most places will be which world religion to embrace rather than whether to do so at all.

While the accounts of conversion in Southeast Asia seem to agree on the ethnic consequences noted above, they do not answer the question of whether these are necessarily good for the group in question. In her account of conversion among the Karen of Thailand, Hayami seems to have a positive view. She describes the Karen as having some understanding of the effects of conversion to either Buddhism or Christianity. Conversion to Christianity furthers the development of broader Karen identity, creates wider networks and contacts with the greater world of an international religion, and removes some of the stigma of being regarded by the Thai as primitive animists. Conversion to Buddhism strengthens their relationship to the Thais and their status as citizens in Thailand (where, though she does not say so, they are unquestionably far better off than the Karen in Burma). Also, conversion to Buddhism does not necessarily mean they cannot keep some of their customs and thus protect their identity. At the same time, the younger Karen who move beyond their own villages and experience the Thai world realize they are looked down upon and will still be even if they become Buddhists. So there are things for and against conversion to either religion. The question of why some Karen have chosen Buddhism and others Christianity (and Hayami does not offer estimates of how many have done each) is a matter of local history and circumstances: close geographical links and good relations with local Thais, the influence of charismatic Thai Buddhist monks in some places but not others, and so forth (Hayami 1996).

Tapp (1989a) is more positive about the effects of conversion to Catholicism than to Protestantism among the Hmong, but he is ambivalent about the eventual consequences of either. He notes that, early in the twentieth century in southeastern China, conversion to Christianity helped raise the status of the Hmong and to end the abuse of the Hmong by the more powerful Yee and Han Chinese landlords, but eventually this led to a backlash and repression by the Chinese government, which presumably left them even worse off and led to millenarian movements. More generally, he argues that conversion has led to the further marginalization of the Hmong in Southeast Asia.

In China, Tapp (1989a, 78) points out, the minorities are among the poorest peoples in a poor country, and the Hmong are among the poorest of the minorities. Thus, enhancing ethnic identity and marginalization from the dominant majority may not necessarily be a good thing for a people living close to the economic margins and lacking food security. This interpretation seems more questionable when applied to the Hmong in the Southeast Asian countries. For one thing, it is difficult to separate the effect of conversion from other changes that have affected the Hmong. In Thailand, these include the reduction of their isolation from the Thai, the end of large-scale opium growing, and the efforts of governments to reduce or end slash-and-burn cultivation, all of which appear to have affected the status of the Hmong in the view of the Thais. Further, in Thailand, the issue of conversion involves the question of whether to convert at all and, if so, to Christianity or Buddhism. In Laos, many Hmong fought with the Americans against the communists who won and now control the government.

The question of whether the conversion to Christianity is a positive development has also been raised regarding the Dayaks of Indonesian Borneo, specifically those of East Kalimantan, by Jennifer Connolly. It is also relevant to other regions of Borneo and, for that matter, to other indigenous minorities of Indonesia and Malaysia. Throughout these regions, the indigenous minorities of the interior face or have faced the same range of choices as have the highlanders of Thailand and other predominantly Buddhist countries of the mainland, that is, whether to convert at all and, if so, to which religion. Again, the pressure to convert (or in Indonesia to have their own religion officially declared a form of Hinduism) is such that remaining outside of a world religion will not be an option for much longer. However, the question of whether to convert to Islam or to some version of Christianity remains and is important. After reviewing the choices facing the Dayaks, Connolly (2003, 304) concludes that, while Christianity is risky, given their circumstances, it may be the only real option.

In Malaysia, the situation is different from both the national perspective as well as that of local regions. Here, there are no official national requirements that all citizens must adhere to a recognized monotheistic religion. The national government is controlled by Malays, has Islam as the official religion, and would like to further Islamize the country. Yet, the government is also committed to economic development and political stability, especially ethnic and religious stability, and has never had the degree or severity of religious strife that has taken place in Indonesia in recent decades. And while the Malays form one half of the population, the Chinese, Indians, indigenous minorities, and other minorities—most of whom are non-Muslim—form the other half. The Malays continue to be officially favored not only because they are Muslim but also because they are Bumiputera (native sons). Thus, their favored status is based on birth. The indigenous minorities are also supposed to have the same special rights as the Malays whether or not they are Muslim, all of which lessens governmental pressures to convert. While the government has brought pressure on the indigenous Orang Asli groups in peninsular Malaysia to convert, it has not been very successful (Dentan et al. 1997, 147–50). In Malaysian Borneo, the national government has less leverage over the indigenous minority populations than it does over the Orang Asli (or that the Indonesian government perhaps has over its Dayak populations). In Sarawak, Dayaks outnumber Malays. And if their numbers are added to those of the Chinese, who are also numerically very large (not to mention very economically powerful), non-Muslims considerably outnumber Muslims. The national Malaysian government is dominated by Malays who would like to promote the further spread of Islam in Sarawak and who make efforts to do so. But since migration from peninsular Malaysia to Sarawak is restricted by the original terms of federation, and since the ruling national party's political control of the state depends upon the inclusion of both Dayak and Chinese parties, there is not a great deal they can do. Here also, however, the main choice for those Dayaks wishing to be modern or receive the benefits of development seems not be whether or not to convert but whether to become Muslim or Christian. Most of them choose Christianity.

11

Tourism and Local Peoples

Southeast Asia has some of the most popular tourist destinations in the developing world, including Thailand, Bali, and Cambodia. The governments of the countries of Southeast Asia want tourists and include them in plans for development and the alleviation of poverty. Tourists visit Southeast Asia in search of beaches, tropical forests, exotic foods, indigenous peoples, monumental ruins, and, in Bangkok and a few other places, sex and nightlife. Tourism has thus become an important part of the process of change involving some local peoples of Southeast Asia. Travel for recreation is primarily Western in origin. However, tourism as an activity and as an industry has also spread widely among Asians, including Southeast Asians who travel both to other parts of their own country and to foreign destinations. The economic and other effects of tourism are therefore broad. Villagers as well as urban peoples are strongly influenced for better or worse. They work as guides, taxi drivers, bearers, cooks, hawkers, stall operators, and artisans making weavings, stone carvings and woodcarvings, and other souvenirs.

This chapter is mainly about ethnic tourism—also referred to as ecotourism or cultural tourism—which focuses on local peoples and their cultural lifeways, especially in their villages. Sometimes ethnic tourism is the main focus of travel or some phase of it, but often it is combined with other tourist activities, such as visits to archaeological sites, national parks, nature preserves, temples, shrines, and waterfalls, or river trips. In Sulawesi, Indonesia ethnic tourism most famously focuses on visits to Toraja villages for the purpose of viewing funeral feasts. In Sarawak, ethnic tourism often takes the form of travel by river to Dayak longhouses. In northern Thailand, it includes mountain trekking to hill tribe villages. For Cambodia, the tourist industry (and much of the entire economy of the country) centers on the

221

ruins at Angkor, but guidebooks suggest visits to local villages as interludes to temple viewing.

Tourism as we know it today in Southeast Asia and elsewhere in the developing world is mainly a twentieth-century development, and one that began as an elite rather than a mass form of travel. Travel for the purposes of exploration or for seeing places and meeting people is old. But it was also limited in earlier periods to very small numbers of travelers whose impact was generally negligible. With the establishment of European empires in Southeast Asia, tourism doubtless increased, although much of late nineteenth- and early twentieth-century European travel and sightseeing was linked to local colonial life, as for example, when Europeans began to establish hill stations in India and Southeast Asia in order to escape the heat of the lowlands. Beyond this, discretionary travel or mass tourism continued to be held back by several factors. Travel, especially when involving women and children, was often limited until many regions were considered to be sufficiently pacified. Fear of malaria, cholera, and other diseases, especially in interior areas, worked against mass travel for relaxation and pleasure until well into the twentieth century. And while colonial governments may have aided or encouraged tourism in some instances, it was not a priority. Tourists on the loose outside of larger cities could be problematic in various ways. There was the matter of what could happen to the traveler and, if something unfortunate occurred, who might be blamed.

In contrast to colonial regimes, postcolonial governments have generally been very interested in tourism, both as a source of national income and foreign currency and as a means of promoting development at the local level. The arrival of jet-plane transportation, and then of jumbo-jet flights, has also been very important, as has the decrease in risks to health from infectious diseases. Tourism, including ethnic and cultural tourism, came to be heavily advertised by tourist associations and airlines stressing a combination of spectacular sights, exotic foods and accommodations, and unique experiences. News of the availability of other, more distinctly adult substances and experiences also spread. Low-budget or backpacker travel came into vogue.

While all of the large countries of Southeast Asia have tourist attractions, not all of them have been in a position to receive many tourists throughout the post–World War II period. In Cambodia, tourist travel slowed with the spread of the war in Indochina, came to a halt with the takeover of the Khmer Rouge, and was inhibited for a long time after they were driven from power but remained a threat in some areas, including Angkor. Today, Cambodian tourism is in full swing but remains focused on the archaeological zone around Siem Reap, in the capital of Phnom Penh, and at several beach resorts. Ethnic and nature tourism involving the highland minorities of the eastern provinces of Mondulkiri and Ratanakiri is less developed. Buddhist

Photo 11.1. Tour group being photographed at Angkor, Siem Reap, Cambodia, 2008.

Photo 11.2. Tourists photographing monks on their early morning begging round, Luang Prabang town, Laos, 2010.

temples, shrines, and ceremonies attract both Asian devotees and Western tourists.

The wars in Vietnam and Laos also discouraged or prevented tourism for a long period of time after the withdrawal of the French in 1954. Mass tourism is now promoted in both countries, though in Vietnam ethnic tourism among the indigenous peoples in the central highlands of southern Vietnam has continued to be restricted. Burma has generally remained open but only to limited tourism. Here, the military government has usually favored tourism in cities, historic sites, temples, and resort areas both for the usual economic reasons and because they regard the presence of tourists as legitimizing the regime. But ethnic tourism among indigenous minorities has been largely precluded because many of the regions where such groups are located are closed to outsiders. The Philippines has long been open to ethnic tourism in most areas. However, travel to the far southern islands has been discouraged for several decades because of ongoing conflict between Muslim political groups and the government.

Other countries have been more open. Thailand is one of the most developed mass tourist destinations in Southeast Asia and has multiple tourist attractions. Ethnic tourism is highly developed, and has been for a longer period of time than elsewhere in mainland Southeast Asia. Ethnic tourism in Thailand is focused largely on the northern hill tribes (as they are known there) that are easily reached from the cities of Chiang Mai and Chiang Rai. Malaysia seeks tourists, but ethnic tourism varies considerably between the developed and industrialized peninsula or west Malaysia and the Borneo states in east Malaysia. In the peninsula, tourism mainly takes the form of general sightseeing and nature and recreational tourism. The government does not encourage ethnic tourism among indigenous Orang Asli, in part because it is sensitive to criticism regarding the harmful effects of resettlement, development, and efforts at assimilation. The situation is much different in the Malaysian states of Sarawak and Sabah in Borneo. Both environmental (or nature) tourism and ethnic tourism are well developed in both of these very large states. The nature of tourism in Indonesia is more complex than in much of the rest of Southeast Asia. In addition to the spectacular scenery (volcanoes, intensively cultivated mountain slopes, small islands, and vast forests), Indonesian arts, architecture, and ceremonies are also often stunning. Like Thailand, Indonesia has long been open to tourism. Political instability or ethnic and religious conflict have occurred at times throughout the postcolonial period, but this has generally prevented or disrupted tourism in particular regions rather than throughout the entire country. Over a long period, Bali has been the main center of ethnic and cultural tourism in Indonesia. Among the interior indigenous ethnic groups, the Toraja of the central Sulawesi (the island just east of

Borneo) have also received considerable attention, both from tourists and anthropologists studying tourism.[1]

THE IMPACT OF TOURISM ON LOCAL PEOPLES

As elsewhere, the anthropological study of tourism in Southeast Asia has lagged behind the development of tourism. The first ethnographic studies and accounts go back only to the 1970s and became common only later. Previous to that time, anthropologists tended to avoid tourists. They preferred to conduct research in more remote places than tourists visited, they were generally negative about the effects of tourism on local peoples, and they did not want to be confused with tourists. But as tourism increased, and as more tourists became interested in the kinds of peoples and places anthropologists studied, it became harder to ignore tourism and tourists. By now ethnographic studies have been done of tourism among many of the peoples of Southeast Asia, although particular attention has focused on a limited number of instances.

Scholars and researchers have written about many dimensions of tourism in Southeast Asia. The main anthropological interest has been on how it is organized and practiced, how it has affected local communities, and how local people have reacted to it. In some ways, the impact of tourism is very wide in that it often provides a major source of national income. Other effects may be more localized, depending on where tourists visit and spend their time and money—in archaeological zones, in and around national parks, in villages visited by trekkers or tour vans and buses, and at World Heritage Sites, to name a few. These places, along with the cities where tourists arrive and depart and which contain resort hotels, hostels, restaurants, travel services, museums, and so on, are part of what is often referred to in the travel literature as the tourist circuit or "bubble."

The amount of research done notwithstanding, the anthropological study of tourism has not been well developed in theoretical terms. Is tourism to be regarded as primarily an economic activity or something with other important dimensions as well? And in either case, what terms should be used to describe or interpret it? An early book of anthropological studies of tourism is titled *Hosts and Guests* (Smith [1977] 1989). These terms—which are still sometimes used—have a nice anthropological ring that implies tourist interaction is more than a simple economic exchange (which it certainly is). But the notion of ethnic tourism as organized interaction between "hosts" and "guests" can distort or leave out some important things. For example, it may imply that, as hosts, the local people have more control over what takes place than they do, and it omits the role of tour guides, agencies, and others who organize what takes place and mediate between tourists and local people. These and other complexities can be seen in several examples to which we now turn.

BALI

The small but densely populated island of Bali is one of the main tourist destinations of Southeast Asia and the central one for Indonesia. Its attractions are multiple and easily accessible at a range of prices. With its steep volcanic mountains, Bali is a place of great natural as well as man-made beauty. Here, culture includes not just artistry, ceremonies, dances, and music but also material culture, including temples and the landscape of terraced fields and waterworks that cover much of the volcanic mountains of the island. Its visual and performing arts are highly developed, in part because they are linked to court traditions that survived intact longer than those in Java. The Dutch did not fully impose colonial rule on Bali until early in the twentieth century, and then sought to protect and preserve its culture.

Because of its culture and history, Bali has long attracted anthropologists (Boon 1977). The prewar Bali written about by Dutch colonial scholars and then by Margaret Mead, Gregory Bateson, Jane Belo, Miguel Covarubias, and others was mainly presented as a traditional if not timeless or ahistorical place. European residents and travelers or tourists were sometimes mentioned in their accounts, though they were mainly avoided as a topic in favor of Balinese personality, ceremonies, art, trance performances, village organization, traditional states, calendars, and cockfighting.

Around 1970, tourism became a topic of anthropological interest, and Bali was an obvious choice for study. Tourism in Bali had a history extending to the early decades of the twentieth century. It developed at first as an elite form of travel, as Bali became widely known as one of the most beautiful and exotic places in the world. Between the world wars, a community of expatriate artists and intellectuals flourished. In the post–World War II period elite tourism turned into mass tourism. With the arrival of jet travel, vacations in Bali, including airfare, were said to be cheaper for Australians than a vacation in Australia. Depending on their budgets, their intellectual interests, and their other appetites, there were a range of options. Tourists could choose Kuta Beach or other resort areas of the south coast, which offered both expensive hotels and cheap lodging along with good beaches and endless bars, eateries, and souvenir shops. Or they could seek Balinese culture and head by bicycle, motorbike, van, or bus for Ubud or other towns in the mountainous interior to stay in smaller hotels and guesthouses tastefully designed in a Balinese style, visit temples, view the spectacular scenery, watch Balinese dances staged for their benefit, and if the time were right, see a real festival or cremation.

It was time for anthropologists and other social scientists to study tourism, and where could there be a better place to do so? In an early study, the anthropologist Philip McKean evaluated the effects of mass tourism on the Balinese and on Balinese culture (McKean [1977] 1989). By then there were conflicting views of the effects of tourism on the Balinese and other traditional but rapidly changing societies. The view championed by both the local and the international tourist industries was that tourism was good for the Balinese, both economically and culturally. Economically, the Balinese were poor. The land was carefully and intensively cultivated, but there was not enough of it, and the population had continued to grow. Large numbers of Balinese and landless Javanese were being moved in the government's transmigration program (see chapter 12) to Kalimantan (Indonesian Borneo), Sumatra, New Guinea, and Halmahera, where population densities were much lower. The diverse economic activities of tourism brought relief from poverty and opportunities for betterment. Tourism was good for Balinese culture because it provided a reason to preserve it; that is, tourists wanted to see the ceremonies and costumes and purchase handicrafts. Other forms of economic modernization, such as high-tech factories, simply brought westernization and abandonment of traditional cultural values and practices. With cultural tourism, the Balinese were able to continue to perform their culture for both traditional religious reasons and for tourists as well. This was one view.

The other view, which prevailed outside of the tourist industry among educated westerners and modern educated urban Balinese and other Indonesians, was that "touristification" of Balinese culture would, regardless of its short-term economic benefits, turn it into a commodity. This was also the view of some sophisticated tourists themselves who valued the still unspoiled, or better yet even undiscovered, haven of traditional, interesting, and beautiful cultural lifeways—the same attitude, of course, held by the tourists who today speak of Laos as similar to what Thailand used to be like. For his part, McKean acknowledged that mass tourism in Bali was not all good—the undesirable effects of Western introduction of the culture of sex, drugs, and rock and roll music were obvious in Kuta Beach. But he argued that, on balance and with various qualifications, the Balinese had managed to control tourism as a reasonable exchange of their culture, which they had in abundance and did not lose by sharing it with tourists in return for income, which they lacked in sufficient quantity (cited in Howe 2005, 135).

Other scholars, including Michel Picard (1996, 1997) and Leo Howe (2005), who have both done long-term research among the Balinese, take the more critical and darker view of the nature and effects of tourism. They point out that the successful management of the exchange of Balinese culture for tourist wealth requires understanding which aspects of culture are suitable for tourists to acquire (to see, hear, or buy) and which are not. As mass tourism developed, the Indonesian government attempted to encourage the Balinese to evaluate their culture in order to make such discrimination. In Western terms, this was clear in the distinction between the "secular" or "profane" and the "sacred." But the Balinese traditionally make no such distinction. Most dances and performances (except ones made up for tourists) had a religious context, especially those performed at temple festivals. The result was confusion and conflict about where and how to draw a line that had not before been drawn. Beyond that, it was necessary to alter the performances to shorten and simplify what are traditionally long and complex enactments and therefore beyond tourist comprehension and patience. From the outside perspective, the Balinese appear to have made such adaptation creatively and very well; the costs and concerns for the Balinese were not as apparent.

There were unquestionable benefits in infrastructure. When I revisited Bali in 1994, after several decades of mass tourism, Bali seemed prosperous and developed, especially in comparison to Java and, even more so, West Kalimantan, where I spent much more time. In Kalimantan, the cities, towns, and villages seemed more relentlessly "third world." I had traveled for a longer time in Bali in 1971, and the differences in 1994 were striking. Outside of the rural landscapes of rice fields, irrigation ditches, and temples, little that I had seen was as it had been. The roads were much better; the towns were neater, cleaner, and less rustic; and the Balinese seemed more Westernized and more adapted to tourism. Balinese handicrafts were still creative but were mass produced and standardized. The older styles of carving and painting that had been influenced by colonial-era Western artists were gone except in museums.

Tourism, including mass tourism, is commonly justified by both the tourist industry and governments as an essential route to economic development that generates revenues and provides work and income for otherwise poor people. This can be true, but scholars and critics point out that, in Bali, large investments in hotels and resorts have tended to come from other parts of Indonesia and foreign countries, and much of the wealth leaves Bali. Another problem is that the economic opportunities for employment, small-scale trade, and other low-income or entry-level activities related to tourism have also attracted many non-Balinese Indonesians to the island. And this development has led to ethnic resentment and antagonisms—all the more so in that most of the immigrants are Muslims, in contrast to the Balinese, who are overwhelmingly Hindu.

The political consequences of Balinese tourist development appear to have been mixed. In the past, traditional Balinese religion and culture were considered to be inferior by the neighboring and far more numerous Javanese (Howe 2005, 64–65). More recently, as some Javanese have become Hindu, the Balinese have become authorities on the religion (Beatty 1999, 222–23). The economic success of Balinese tourism, which has brought a measure of prosperity—however uneven—to Bali, appears to have considerably raised the status of the Balinese (as has the success of tourism for the Toraja) in the eyes of the broader Indonesian public and the national government. But it has also evidently incurred resentment in a country that is overwhelmingly, if also uniquely and comparatively moderately, Muslim. In 2002, there were two suicide bombings in the south coast tourist village of Kuta that targeted clubs frequented by tourists. More than two hundred people, most of them foreign tourists, especially Australians, were killed. The attacks made instant headlines across Indonesia and around the world. The Indonesian government attributed the attacks to Jemaah Islamiyah, a violent Muslim group, and arrested, tried, and convicted a number of members, including three who were executed.

The bombings struck a number of blows at once, including the most obvious one against Western, non-Muslim tourists. Additionally, it was likely aimed at hurting Indonesian tourism in general and the government, and was also an effort to extend the communal violence that had occurred in the preceding years between Christians and Muslims in Ambon and elsewhere. For the Balinese, the bombings added to other problems brought by tourism and its unfortunate consequences, including increased theft of sacred relics from temples, previously a rare occurrence. While tourism-dependent Balinese worried about the practical consequences of keeping away tourists, some Balinese interpreted matters in spiritual terms—as punishment for having sold their culture and religion. Even the "ecumenical" efforts the Balinese made by inviting many foreigners to the ceremonies for atonement and commemoration sometimes had a mixed effect. The ceremonies often involved the sacrifice of live animals, including dogs and water buffaloes (Howe 2005, 1–5, 144). Many tourists who go to visit interior highland peoples in northern Southeast Asia, the interior of Borneo, or the Toraja on the island of Sulawesi are prepared to see blood sacrifice. But some of those invited for the special ceremonies were apparently unprepared and revolted.

LONGHOUSE TOURISM IN SARAWAK, MALAYSIA

From Bali, which is small, compact, densely populated, and where tourists can see the sights in a few days, let us now turn to ethnic tourism in Borneo, specifically Sarawak. Borneo is huge—the third largest island in the world. The Malaysian state of Sarawak, which comprises the northwestern region of the island, is as large in area as the whole of peninsular Malaysia.

Borneo in general is lightly populated, especially in the interior, and tourist attractions are spread across great distances and require considerable travel time to reach. With few roads, travel in the interior is either by river or small plane. The Malaysian states of Sarawak and Sabah and the Indonesian province of East Kalimantan have developed tourism as nature and ethnic adventure tourism. Sarawak has some of the largest caves in the world, and these (Niah and Mulu, the latter a World Heritage Site) are frequently visited, as are other national parks. Ethnic tourism in Sarawak centers on river trips to Iban longhouses on the Skrang, Lemanak, Engkari, and Ai rivers, all tributaries of the upper Batang Lupar. Here, I draw especially on an anthropological account by William Kruse, an Australian anthropologist whose research was done in the mid- to late 1990s (Kruse 1998, 138–69; see also Kedit and Sabang 1992; Zeppel 1992). Kruse paid attention to all three groups involved: the tourists, the tour operators, and the Iban themselves.

By the early twentieth century, a visit to Sarawak by an elite tourist (such as the writer Somerset Maugham) was not complete without a river trip to an Iban longhouse, there to be entertained by a night of music, dancing, and rice wine drinking. By the 1960s, ordinary tourist visits to Iban longhouses had begun and are ongoing. Iban longhouse tourism developed at the initiative of tourist agents and companies rather than by the Iban themselves. Tourism in Sarawak is based mainly in Kuching (the state capital, the largest town in Sarawak, and the main gateway into the state). Successful tourist longhouses need to be neither too close nor too far from Kuching. The farther a longhouse is from Kuching, the more costly the trip to reach it becomes. Tourists begin a trip to a tourist longhouse by road in a van and complete it by river in a longboat powered by an outboard motor. It is more or less essential to reach the destination within a single day; that is, by late afternoon. The only alternative would be a longer and therefore more expensive trip with overnight stays at two or more longhouses. Being too near to Kuching or to another town is also a drawback for several reasons. The trip itself is part of the experience, especially the latter part of the journey on a narrow, fast-moving river through overhanging forest. Further, the trip by river is symbolically important. It contributes to the impression of traveling back in time to see a primitive, jungle-dwelling people as they once were. Longhouses passed on the road closer to town may be surrounded by cars, pickup trucks, and motorcycles and are often built out of modern materials, such as cement block (see photo 6.6).

Additionally, in longhouses located too close to town, the inhabitants are apt to lack motivation to be involved in tourism. Here, the families are likely to have one or more members working for wages as an alternative to traditional farming, fishing, and gathering. Wage earners have less use for tourism, which, while interesting for a while, can become undesirable for various reasons. In addition to this, visits to longhouses close to town do not require a stay overnight, and this means there is much less money to be made for tourist agencies and almost none for villagers. In addition to the Iban longhouses, there are also a few Bidayuh villages with longhouses to which tourists are taken. But these are day visits involving only a few hours and without a river trip. The tourists arrive by van, walk around, look at the longhouse or longhouses for an hour or so, take a few pictures, and then leave. The village will be paid an admission fee, perhaps some villagers will be paid to put on a dance or sell a souvenir or two, and the local store may sell some snacks or soft drinks. Since many of these villagers will be working for wages, there is little reason to be interested in tourism.

A few Bidayuh villages have obtained government grants and built special longhouses for tourists to stay in or traditional men's houses for tourists to see but that have no other use. Such built-for-tourists buildings are constructed in customary styles with hardwood posts, wood and bamboo framing, and thatch roofs (sometimes put over a metal roof). These unused buildings appear to have little interest for tourists. Tourists want to see "real" buildings with people engaged in ordinary daily activities, preferably traditional ones like women pounding rice in mortars or weaving on a back-strap loom.

Becoming a Tourist Longhouse

An Iban longhouse usually becomes a tourist destination by entering into a written agreement with one of the travel agencies based in Kuching. Such agreements commonly specify what the longhouse will provide in the way of food, services, and entertainment, and the prices the tour company will pay. The arrangement usually includes a guesthouse where the tourists will stay for one or more nights and where their meals will be eaten. The tour company will also provide instructions regarding appearance and behavior of longhouse residents when tourists are around. The people of a longhouse may desire to attract tourists without the help of a tourist agent, but they cannot really initiate or carry through with the enterprise because they do not have the knowledge of how to do so or the contacts that are necessary. It is the agents in Kuching who are in control in selecting a longhouse as a tourist destination, and this is entirely a business decision. Kruse (1998, 159–60) reproduces an interesting letter written in English from a tourist agent to the headman of an Iban tourist longhouse. It suggests the extent to which some agencies attempt to micromanage the tourist experience at a longhouse:

Dear Tui Rumah [headman]

I would like to say a big thank you to you and all the people of [name omitted] longhouse for your co-operation with us to make the tourists welcome in your longhouse. For [next year] I would very much [like] to look to all your support to make it even better for the benefit of all of us. Please take note of some of the matters we need to improve with the helping hand from all of you as stated below.

1. For individual dancing please advise them to dance longer and the warrior dancers must be with shield.
2. For group dancing please advise them to make three rounds.
3. For special welcoming ceremonies please advise them to pre-arrange offerings at the *tanju* [outside veranda].
4. For the blowpipe demonstrator please advise him to bring along knife for tapping rubber trees.
5. Posters and TV aerials are not to be displayed openly at the *ruai* [inside veranda] and *tanju*.
6. Bridge and jungle path are to make the jungle walk more safe and interesting.
7. More people are needed to be presented at the *ruai* to make tourists feel welcome.
8. Please take note that for the kitchen helpers we will pay M$5.00 per person in the evening and M$5.00 per person in the morning but helpers must bring along firewood for cooking.
9. We will bring along our own rice or buy directly from the helpers.

We look forward to your strong support.
Thank you

Kruse does not comment on the Iban view of the letter, though sarcasm does not seem implausible—nor does he say anything about the extent to which the agent's suggestions were implemented.

The relationship that develops between tourist agencies and longhouse tourist villages also has an ethnic dimension that is common in Southeast Asia. The agents in this instance are nearly all Chinese at the level of ownership and management, though they usually have Iban or other non-Chinese as boatmen, drivers, guides, and workers. The Chinese, who are an old ethnic community in Sarawak, have a good relationship with the Iban, but they are culturally very different. For their part, the Iban are well suited to tourism, perhaps more so than some other indigenous ethnic groups in Sarawak.

In "adopting" (the favored terms used by the tour companies for establishing a business relationship) a longhouse, there are several important considerations. There are a great many longhouses throughout Sarawak, only a small portion of which have the potential to become tourist operations. As noted, the first consideration is location—a successful tourist longhouse needs to be neither too far nor too close to Kuching.

The second consideration is the desire of the longhouse residents to become and remain a tourist village. This again is related to location. The Iban on the upper tributaries of the Batang Lupar live by shifting cultivation and forest collecting, supplemented by cash crops of pepper, rubber, or cacao. Unless there is a logging concession or commercial plantation in the vicinity, there are few opportunities for wage earning that do not involve long-distance travel or migration to the cities on the coast or areas elsewhere in the interior. For some, earning money by staying in the longhouse and continuing the usual activities is attractive.

The third consideration is the appearance and circumstances of the longhouse. To the practiced eye of the tourist agent, an attractive longhouse should or must have certain features and lack others. A scenic location, one that provides a panoramic view of the river and surrounding hills, is ideal, though not always present since the Iban have their own criteria for placing a longhouse. The appearance of the longhouse, especially from the vantage point of the river—the tourists' crucial first impression of what they have paid so much for and traveled so far—is important. The longhouse and its setting should therefore have the right "jungle look," as it is sometimes put in discussions within the business. It should be made of natural materials from the forest and built in a traditional style as illustrated on postcards, tourist brochures, and websites.

Tourists are not given much background information on the Iban or on how they have changed as a result of colonial and postcolonial developments. Some of what they learn from the tourist brochures and are told by the guides may be misleading. The trip by van provides abundant views of development and change, including very modern longhouses. But the river safari is supposed to be a journey back in time to see a still primitive people living close to nature. Tourists are not experts on longhouse materials and design; they are willing to accept or even want architectural modification, such as safe wooden steps rather than the traditional notched log ladder up to the entrance. But the overall look and the major features should seem authentically primitive. An obviously inauthentic characteristic can bring disappointment and the anxiety of having been misled. Metal roofs are a particular problem. Corrugated metal sheets have long been in use in the interior of Borneo as elsewhere in Southeast Asia as a substitute for traditional thatch or wooden shingles. There is little that can be done about a metal roof except, as is sometimes done, cover it over with thatch, which does not last. However, metal roofs are not all the same in terms of their visual effect. Those that are well rusted into a rich brown color blend in and look better than shiny new ones. A postcard sold in Kuching shows a very dilapidated Iban longhouse with a rusted tin roof. Nonetheless, metal roofs can be a problem for tourist longhouses, as Kruse (1998, 144–45) stresses:

In the field I was presented with one scenario time and time again. It involved tourists standing by the riverbank, having just stepped from their longboats, and gazing at the sight of four hundred foot long, wooden longhouse built on stilts, only to say, "This is not a real longhouse, it has a tin roof." This exclamation was so common that many tour guides would pre-empt it by explaining that the longhouse would have a tin roof, but often it made little difference. For the Iban in the longhouse, it was a common joke but also a matter of some bitterness.

Other signs of modernity in and around a longhouse are also discouraged by tourist agencies. The agency may cut back or entirely halt tours to a longhouse that adds discordant visible signs of contemporary technology. Kruse gives several examples that tend to show the paradox of longhouse tourism. Tourism increases the income of a longhouse. This enables residents to buy modern goods, but these can cause trouble. In one longhouse with a well-developed tourist business, the headman used some of the profits to buy and install a large satellite dish. As a result, the large agency owned by a leading international tour company pulled out of the village and reestablished its business with a different longhouse farther up the river. However, it turned out that this new longhouse had acquired a diesel-powered rice-husking machine. The company asked that the machine not be used when the tourists were present and that the women go back to the traditional practice of pounding rice with a mortar and pestle on the longhouse veranda when tourists were around.

As these examples suggest, visible or audible characteristics of a tourist longhouse are important. Longhouse residents can have otherwise unacceptable modern goods if they are out of sight and hearing. While in a longhouse, the tourists remain in the veranda area and do not enter the private inner household apartments. Television sets, VCRs, sewing machines, and Western-style furniture, which a prosperous family will acquire, remain out of view behind closed doors. These items are okay if kept inside, invisible, and quiet when tourists are about.

Some modern architectural features can be disguised. New Iban longhouses are built with manufactured, louvered windows, and in older longhouses these are sometimes retrofitted into the wall separating the inner apartment from the inside veranda. Such windows are a problem from the perspective of tourist agents, both because they look modern and because they can reveal modern furnishings inside the apartments. The solution of one aspiring tourist longhouse was to replace the windows with wooden planks. But Rumah Nangaukum, a longhouse on the Engkari River that I visited in 1999, had found a less drastic solution (see photo 11.3). This longhouse was not architecturally perfect. It had a tin roof and some tin siding, but the metal had aged and mellowed, and the longhouse had an old, rustic look. Its assets included a picturesquely dilapidated outer veranda (*tanju*) and a magnificent, long inner veranda (*ruai*) with fighting

Photo 11.3. Outer veranda of Rumah Nangaukum, Engkari River, Sarawak, (east) Malaysia, 1999.

cocks tethered to thick supporting log posts, and other chickens and dogs wandering around loose. Overall, from a tourist company's perspective, the longhouse would probably have been a six or seven on a ten-point scale. The longhouse had hopes for tourism after a nearby longhouse had been torn down the year before for rebuilding. Other than the metal roofing and siding, the only problem was that modern windows had been added all along the wall. However, this wall had been covered with military camou- flage netting and decorated with small baskets and other souvenirs made for sale to tourists. The camouflage netting did give the wall a jungle look.

What had been done was also in keeping with what Kruse stresses: while longhouse tourists seek authenticity, they really want the illusion of it rather than the real thing—and this is what has to be provided, archi- tecturally and otherwise. Pigs traditionally roam free and scavenge under the longhouse. They are picturesque as well as a part of the local ecology, but they can be a problem. One longhouse was asked to pen up their pigs (as many longhouses are now doing anyway) away from the longhouse because they made bad smells that bothered the tourists. The barking and fighting of the dogs, which is part of the normal background noise of a longhouse, can also disturb tourists, and one longhouse was asked to get rid of its dogs. Tourists can also interfere with the observance of *adat*, or customary law. For example, deaths cannot be timed to take place only when tourists are not around, and tourists cannot be sent away so that the customary closing of the village to outsiders for six days or more can be followed. One tourist village went ahead with the usual evening program of dances and celebration after a funeral that afternoon—an inconceivable practice according to *adat*.

The gap between what tourists want to see and experience (or what they are willing to put up with in order to do so) and the realities of longhouse life is where the tourist guesthouse comes in. It does not solve all the problems, but it helps. A tourist guesthouse is a practical solution, but it is also a symbolic one. It mediates or provides a bridge between what tourists are used to in terms of physical comforts and cultural understanding and the realities of longhouse life. The guesthouse is typically a rustic structure raised on posts, with split bamboo or bark walls and a thatch roof with a jungle look. It will generally include at least some private rooms and have running water, Western-style toilets, raised beds, chairs and tables, and a common room for eating. There may be an outside veranda overlooking the longhouse or the river. The guesthouse is often built between the longhouse and the river or across the river. It provides cold drinks and basic food—something between that of a decent hotel in town in terms of comfort and what would be available in the longhouse. The guests are removed from the annoying smells and sounds of the longhouse, the latter further muffled by the sound of the river. The tourist can gaze on the primitive surroundings without being entirely in them.

Tourist longhouses are therefore sites of cultural exchange and architectural struggle (Kruse 1998, 144–46). As the forgoing examples suggest, elements are removed, disguised, rebuilt, or added to suit the needs of an industry seeking to reflect the tourist mythology of a timeless "jungle people" living in authentic jungle sites that can be experienced, however, with reasonable comfort. The most acute problem develops in relation to the physical deterioration of a successful tourist longhouse and the desire of its inhabitants to build a new one. The central problem of longhouse tourism from the perspective of the tourist industry in the 1990s was a classic issue of supply and demand. The number of tourists seeking longhouse trips had increased, as had the number of agencies seeking to provide them. But the number of longhouses suitable for visitors remained constant or decreased as older ones were torn down and rebuilt. In the mid-1990s, the Hilton Batang Ai Resort was completed and opened. This is a luxury resort built on the shore of the Batang Ai Reservoir in the form of a series of natural wood Iban longhouses with views of the lake and carefully designed natural landscaping. This provides much closer access to previously distant longhouses in the upper reaches of the Engkari and Ai rivers, both of which flow into the lake. But the general problem remained.

The increasing volume of tourists and the limited number of suitable longhouses can provoke a crisis when a tourist longhouse community decides their old and dilapidated but picturesque longhouse needs to be rebuilt. Such a decision can itself have an ironic, "killing the goose that lays the golden eggs" dimension. The profits made by tourist visits to the old longhouse have made building a nice new one possible, but the new one will probably be unsuitable for tourism. For example, in 1996, one longhouse community on the Engkari decided that the existing longhouse should be rebuilt because it was beginning to collapse in places. Moreover, thanks to tourism, they now had the money to cover the costs, and a new, nearby logging road meant that construction equipment and materials could easily be brought in. The longhouse had a profitable contract with a major tourist company, though one that did not prevent rebuilding. The community decided to proceed. The company learned to its great dismay that the small jungle-covered hill behind the longhouse had been obliterated in a day's work by a logging company bulldozer. This left a highly visible, bright red swath of level bulldozed land where a new longhouse would be erected. Negotiations aimed at saving the company's investment and the tourist business of the village ensued (Kruse 1998, 162–64). When I was there briefly in 1999, the old longhouse was gone, and the inhabitants were living in a small temporary longhouse built partly of materials salvaged from the old one. There were several tables set up in the inner veranda with souvenirs for sale to tourists, but none were there. The guesthouse by the river remained, but it was empty, dusty, and beginning to be overgrown by grass.

ETHNIC TOURISM IN NORTHERN MAINLAND SOUTHEAST ASIA

In northern mainland Southeast Asia, trekking is the most famous form of tourism involving visits to highland peoples in rural areas, although it is not the only form—and the highland peoples visited are not necessarily very remote. The appeal of trekking, as the term itself suggests, involves hiking as well as visits to ethnic villages. Like longhouse tourism in Borneo, it combines nature or environmental tourism with ethnic tourism. Trekking tourism is most fully developed in northern Thailand. Here its ethnic object are the "hill tribes," especially those of the romantic-sounding Golden Triangle region where Thailand intersects with Burma and Laos, and which was formerly known for opium production. The ethnic groups of this region include the Hmong, Mien or Yao, Akha, and others. These groups are spread across the northern massif of mainland Southeast Asia and are found in Laos and Vietnam as well.

Trekking Tourism to Hmong Villages in Thailand

Ethnic tourism in Thailand has similarities to longhouse tourism in Borneo, although there are differences. River travel is often a part of the trip but a considerably lesser one. Treks also often include an elephant ride, which does not occur in Borneo. In both Borneo and northern mainland Southeast Asia, the village and its visible activities are themselves of interest. The indigenous houses are often *National Geographic* picturesque but less striking than the longhouses of Sarawak, and their arrangement provides much less opportunity for organized visiting and entertaining tourists. The replacement of thatch or wood shingle roofs with metal is also common, but trekkers have not been reported to be upset with these, as have Iban longhouse tourists. Native costume and body decoration are an important part of the tourist experience in both places, but probably more so in mainland Southeast Asia. Here, natives in full costume, jewelry, and headgear are a central symbol in tourist publicity.

The anthropologist Jean Michaud has provided a detailed and insightful analysis of the impact of trekking tourism on a Hmong village in Chiang Mai Province in northern Thailand (Michaud 1997; see also Cohen 2001). He makes the central point that tourism is among the major sources of change affecting the highland peoples of the region. But tourism came to be economically and socially more marginal than the number of trekkers involved would indicate.

Photo 11.4. Thai tourists being photographed with Hmong women and children in fancy dress in Doi Pui village on Doi Suthep outside of Chiang Mai Province, northern Thailand, 2005.

Trekking tourism in northern Thailand began with the Thai government's extension of dirt roads into the highland villages. This was done as a means of gaining control over the hill tribe peoples and integrating them into the national society. Hill tribe tourism was not the purpose, and initially the government took little interest in what went on, but it became an interest to the Tourist Authority of Thailand as an additional tourist draw to Chiang Mai. Before the network of mountain roads opened, the highland villages were connected by trails used by traders with pack trains of mules or small horses. Trekking to such villages would have been real adventure tourism for several reasons. While some trekkers may have found their way to remote highland villages, their numbers would not have been large.

Trekking began in the Hmong village of Ban Suay (which Michaud studied in the early 1990s) around 1980 as tour guides began to bring a few tourists (Michaud 1997, 133–35). Friendly villagers initially provided places to stay as an expression of traditional hospitality. The tourists liked the experience, and the guides and agencies were quick to recognize the potential of trekking tourism. For the villagers, the development came at a time when other ecological and economic restrictions had begun to take effect. The opportunities for highland migration to new village sites with mature forest or well-fallowed land (needed for productive swidden cultivation) were closing—both because of restrictions imposed by the government and, in some areas, rising population densities. The latter came as a result of highland refugees from the east, north, and west who crossed into Thailand to escape ethnic conflict and repression in Burma and the war and its aftermath in Laos. This was also the time the Thai government had begun to clamp down on poppy cultivation, on which the Hmong and some other highland peoples had long relied as a cash crop. New economic opportunities at home had thus become attractive. Some villagers took the opportunity offered by trekking.

A trek to Ban Suay began with a trip in the back of a pickup truck to a drop-off point at a trail a few kilometers from the village—the truck continuing to the village with food and other supplies. Trekkers were recruited primarily among travelers staying at the less expensive guesthouses in Chiang Mai and offered low-budget treks. After a hike of several hours with the guides, the trekkers arrived in the village and were usually taken directly to the guesthouse where they would stay. After this, they would buy drinks, wander around the center of the village, and take photos. Their local interaction was mainly with the village children who wanted to play or have their photos taken for a few baht (Thai currency). The guides then provided supper made from food purchased at lowland markets. Adult villagers were not interested in interaction with the trekkers but would gossip later about what they wore, how they looked, and what they did. After dinner, the trekkers socialized among themselves or with the guides, sang songs, or smoked opium. The next day, the trekkers would travel to another village. This trip would include several hours of hiking plus an elephant ride. The routine in this village was the same. The return journey back to Chiang Mai the following day included a river raft trip (Michaud 1997, 135–38).

According to Michaud's (1997, 138–39) account, what the tourists learned about Hmong villages and the Hmong way of life was primarily visual and focused on the center of the village, plus what they were told by Thai guides—from a Thai perspective. The sort of organized activities that were part of Iban longhouse tours in Sarawak (dances, blowpipe shooting, blessing rituals, or walks to see fields and forest) appear to have been lacking in trekking tourism in north Thailand, or at least lacking in the low-budget form involving Ban Suay and other Hmong villages at the time. From the Hmong perspective, the rewards of tourism were almost entirely economic, and here the range of opportunities was more limited than in longhouse tourism (where residents could also earn money participating in ceremonies and performances and in guiding local walks and selling handicrafts). With tourism in Hmong villages, the main opportunity appears to be income from the night's lodging in a family house or guesthouse, followed by sales of snacks and drinks by the village store and, perhaps, locally made handicrafts.

Despite the number of years it persisted, the Hmong in Ban Suay did not really take to tourism, nor was economic success from tourism a source of prestige. It is difficult to know how much this was a consequence of Hmong cultural dispositions or the circumstances of tourism in Hmong villages, mediated as it was by Thai guides with apparently limited knowledge of or sympathy for the Hmong and their problems (Michaud 1997, 140–43). The Iban are critical of longhouse tourists and tourism, but they took to tourism. Apparently, this was partly because they tend to be outgoing and like to interact with strangers, emphasize hospitality and festivity, and somewhat like the Balinese, know how to put on a good show. Also, the Iban have not been passive about their role in longhouse tourism. They have limited control over whether tourist guides bring guests, but the tourist longhouses have tourism committees that discuss and negotiate terms and fees and are sometimes willing to go against the desires of the tourist agencies.

Judging from Michaud's account, the Hmong have reacted differently to tourism than have the Iban. In part, this is for cultural reasons, though Michaud also stresses broader circumstances, including the attitudes of the Thai authorities toward the Hmong—as recent, non-Thai, troublesome arrivals in Thailand. He refers to the Hmong reaction to trekking tourism as "cultural resistance" and as limiting their participation in it. Despite the number of trekkers in Ban Suay, tourism did not become a collective enterprise for the village. It appears that negotiations and decisions to get into the tourist business were household matters. After initially renting space in their own houses, households that wanted to be involved in tourism were urged by guides to build a guesthouse, and they did. Several larger guesthouses were also built, but these appear to have not been collective enterprises either. When tourist households stopped taking trekkers, their guesthouses were converted to storage space.

While the first households to take in tourists were better off and respected members of the village, these villagers eventually got out of the business. It required too much time away from their work in the fields, it diminished their privacy, and therefore became, on balance, undesirable. Other households that needed the money took their place. These were households that were poor because they either had lost their land or had a male head who was an opium addict and thus lacked the strength and stamina to work in the fields. Tourism was desirable to these households and probably helped alleviate their poverty. The men of these families who were opium addicts had been so before they had gotten into tourism and not as a consequence of it. They were willing to follow the wishes of tour guides to provide opium to those trekkers who wanted to smoke it, although this eventually caused problems as the government moved to suppress poppy growing and the opium trade. The households that became associated with tourism were also, as might be supposed, socially marginal. The men had often not been wanted as husbands by other Hmong families and had married non-Hmong women who had come to the region as refugees from Burma (Michaud 1997, 141).

Green Tourism

The picture presented so far of cultural and ethnic tourism in Southeast Asia does not seem entirely positive either from the perspective of the tourists or the local communities involved. From the tourist point of view, the studies discussed suggest that most tourists neither arrive nor depart with much knowledge of how the peoples they see have changed throughout the twentieth century or what they are like today. For example, from Kruse's account, we have seen that Iban longhouse tourism involves a lot of theater. The intrusion of modernization in the form of diesel generators, rice mills, satellite dishes, TV antennas, manufactured louvered windows, and tin roofs are generally unacceptable, at least as far as the tourist industry was concerned in the late 1990s. The problem here may be in part the consequence of the promotional literature put out by the longhouse tourism agencies, creating the image that a trip to a longhouse is a journey back in time to see an authentic primitive people living in the jungle. Perhaps theater is all that some tourists want. But others might value a more balanced, realistic picture of how Iban life is changing, even in the remote upriver places. The same can probably be said of hill tribe tourists among the Hmong or other highland peoples of Thailand.

From the perspective of the local people who are, as it is put, the hosts, there are unquestionably economic benefits from tourism. Without such benefits, there is no reason to suppose that ethnic tourism would have been accepted or at least that it would endure. But tourism usually seems to bring at least some dissatisfaction, annoyance, or frustration if not social conflict over perceived inequities over the division of economic returns. Let us therefore turn to some attempts at improvement. These involve efforts by local peoples to take greater control of tourism. The goals are to increase the share of tourist revenue that goes to the village rather than to tourist agencies, to inform tourists about themselves rather than simply entertain them. They want to emphasize what they are proud of, such as spinning, dying, weaving, and the use of natural dyes, and in general to tell their story and the value of the way they live. My information in this section comes mainly from my own experiences in Thailand, Laos, and Vietnam in recent years.

To begin with a simple example, in 2006, I visited the Lahu village of Jalae on a well-trod hill-tribe tourist path outside of Chiang Rai in the heart of the former Golden Triangle in far northern Thailand. On the edge of the village was a tourist operation consisting of a small shop with snacks and souvenirs, a basic noodle restaurant, rustic cabins for trekkers, and elephant rides. Judging from the houses, little tourist wealth had spread broadly into the village itself. But there were several things to be seen along the entrance-way into the village. On the one side was a small museum with displays of local tools and other artifacts. The building was covered with brown stucco that would have fit right in in Arizona or New Mexico but contrasted strongly with the unpainted wood, bamboo, and thatch construction of the highland village houses. On the other side was a matching building with a sign in front indicating that it was the temple for their traditional, non-Christian religion—the only such building I had ever seen in any of the many highland villages I have visited in mainland Southeast Asia.

The third feature, and the main point of this example, was five well-built and roofed-over permanent signs. On these were printed texts that told something about the village and some of the main dimensions of Lahu culture (see photo 11.5). Lettered neatly in English, the story on the first sign is titled "Lahu Life in Transition" and goes as follows:

> Like each of the hill tribes in Thailand, the Lahu have a unique language and culture—and like all the other hill tribes, that culture is undergoing tremendous change. Five years ago, before we were forced to move down to this location, we grew, hunted, or gathered all our own food, purchasing only salt. Today, due to limitations on land, we purchase 80% of our diet. Integration into Thai society brings many benefits, such as health care and education, but it comes at the high cost of losing a traditional lifestyle. March 2002

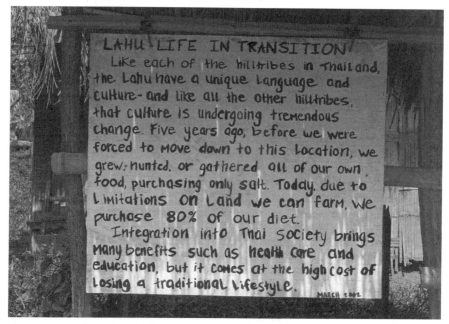

Photo 11.5. The Lahu of Jalee village outside of Chiang Rai tell tourists what it wants them to know about themselves and what has happened to them on a neatly lettered sign, Chiang Mai Province, northern Thailand, 2006.

The next sign tells of the village's determination to resist complete absorption into Thai society and to keep their identity alive, followed by a sign that summarizes their non-Buddhist, non-Christian religious beliefs, and another that concerns Lahu traditional dress. The last sign is on the pervasive use and importance of bamboo. It notes the use of over ten species, for everything from building houses to baskets, irrigation systems, mousetraps, and musical instruments.

Community-Based Tourism

Community-based tourism has begun to spread in northern Thailand and in other countries in Southeast Asia. "CBT," as it is commonly known, is a movement to reform ethnic tourism. The efforts have been promoted and supported by international nongovernmental organizations (NGOs) but requires local organization at the village level. There is variation from one place to another, but there are several general purposes. One is to shift the balance of economic benefits of tourism from tourist agencies to the local ethnic communities visited and to promote the use of local ethnic guides. Another is to control tourism at the local level by promoting responsible tourist behavior in villages and by exposing tourists to what villagers think they should see and learn, including both the traditional way of life and the changes taking place. Friendship and exchange between tourists and villagers is emphasized, especially through homestay arrangements. The local control also means that tourists and the money they spend on homestay accommodations are allocated between participating households by the villagers rather than by outside guides or agents. Finally, there is an emphasis on ecotourism, or environmentalism expressed in the usual buzzwords of "sustainable," "renewable," "natural," and "local." CBT is relatively new, and its scale of success and endurance remain to be seen. For one thing, CBT tourism in any village requires tourists in the first place, and CBT-style ethnic tourism is probably not what every tourist is looking for. My own exposure to CBT tourism was limited to two Karen villages and one Shan village in Mae Hong Son Province, Thailand. The Karen villagers were Christian and were therefore familiar with Christian missionary notions of doing good and fellowship.

In both the Karen villages, groups of visiting tourists are taken to open visitors' centers located near the village entrance for a welcome and introduction to the village. In both villages there are signs posted that list rules for guests. Each village individually created the content of the signs, and therefore the rules were somewhat different. Together, however, they illustrate some of the policies of CBT (see photo 11.6). In Ban Huay Hee, the first of the villages, visitors were asked to observe the following rules:

Pay the rates set by the group
Use local guide from CBT group
Do not pick up plants
No littering!
Respect Karen culture
Dress properly
No alcohol and no drugs

The rules for Ban Nam Hoo, the second of the Karen villages, were written on a professional blue and white sign, and are more detailed:

Don't play cards or gamble
No alcohol allowed
Please don't pick anything—flowers, plants, etc.
Please bathe in a *passin* (women) /*pakomao* (men) or bathing suit—no
    nudity!
Tourists must be polite, respectful, and appropriate at all times
Please follow traditional Karen customs

Photo 11.6. **Rules for visitors posted at the information center in a Karen community-based tourism village of Ban Huay Hee, Mae Hong Son Province, northern Thailand, 2004.**

The same sign also posted prices for accommodations and guides. It informed the visitors about how the payments made by the guests are distributed (90 percent to the host household or the guide and 10 percent to the village), and how this is allocated to further develop and spread CBT practices.

In the brief visit to Ban Huay Hee, the main emphasis was ecological. There was a trip to see a fallow swidden field where the group was shown many plants that were still gathered some years after the main crop of rice had been harvested. Part of the purpose here was political: to refute the government position that swidden cultivation is destructive and wasteful.

In Ban Nam Hoo, where our group spent the afternoon and night, the program was more extensive. In the late afternoon, there was a demonstration of spinning cotton thread, dying the yarn with indigo leaves and other local plants, and weaving with a back-strap loom. In the evening, villagers who could speak English gave talks in the village community building about why the village had gone into CBT, how it worked, and problems that existed—mainly getting tourist agencies in town to cooperate since there were lower profits.

Ethnic Tourism in Northern Vietnam

The final example shows yet other differences in both the circumstances of ethnic tourism in northern mainland Southeast Asia—most notably what it is like in a polyethnic setting—and how it is managed where a socialist government plays a larger role than in laissez-faire Thailand. Ethnic tourism in Vietnam involving what are referred to as "national minorities" occurs elsewhere in Vietnam but is highly developed around the town of Sapa. Located in Lao Cai Province in the far northern part of the country near the China border, Sapa was first developed early in the twentieth century as a French colonial hill station. It provided escape from the heat and humidity of the lowlands to the high, cool mountains and the spectacular scenery of the area. As international tourism was revived in Vietnam in the last decades of the twentieth century, Sapa became a leading destination for ethnic tourists and ecotourists. The population of the region is made up, for the most part, of nonethnic Vietnamese: mainly Black Hmong, Dao, or Dzao (Yao), and a variety of Tai-speaking groups, including the Giay.

Ethnic tourism and ecotourism, including trekking, is concentrated in the great valley that extends a long distance below Sapa. The sides and bottom of this valley are covered mainly with spectacular wet rice terraces. Above the irrigated terraces are dry fields used for rotational farming, especially corn, the government having attempted to phase out shifting cultivation in the valley. The ethnic composition of the region is important for understanding the impact of tourism, for different groups have become involved in tourism in different ways. The common human ecological pattern throughout the northern massif of mainland Southeast Asia is that Tai groups are concentrated in the lowland regions. Here, the Buddhist Tai (including the Thai of Thailand, Lao of Laos, and Shans of Burma) occupy the main open plains and the largest river valleys. The Tai minority groups, some of which are Buddhist and some of which are not, are mountain dwellers but tend to occupy lower slopes and the valley floors where wet rice can be grown. The non-Tai ethnic minorities tend to be distributed over higher elevations, according to how long (by one common ethnological interpretation) they have been present—the later the arrival, the higher the elevation of the villages. This pattern also holds for the Sapa region. Here, the Tai groups occupy the lowest levels of the valley where wet rice cultivation is most concentrated. The Hmong and the Dao are higher up, though some of both are located far enough down the mountainside that they cultivate wet rice in terraces as well. Finally, most if not all of the ethnic Vietnamese (Kinh) in this region are town dwellers who do not farm.

Tourism figures prominently in the development plans and efforts of the government of Vietnam. Poverty is acknowledged to be a problem in the Sapa region, with about 10 percent of the population said to lack food security, that is, enough to eat throughout the year. The Muong Hoa River Valley below the town is a crowded place, in part because the government has moved and consolidated villages into larger administrative communes. Tourism is taken very seriously as a means of raising the living standards of the ethnic minorities and is regulated. Most tourist guides must be licensed after undergoing a course of study in tourism, usually at the university or college level, and this includes ethnological information on ethnic minorities. Households that provide homestay accommodations for trekkers or other tourists must be certified, and in order to be so must meet certain standards. The economic and cultural differences within and among the various ethnic groups influence their opportunities to participate in tourism, as we shall see below.

Ta Van, one of the major tourist communes in the valley, is located fifteen kilometers from the town of Sapa. For those who are taken there by motor vehicle (vintage Russian jeeps in 2005), there is a spectacular but harrowing drive on a narrow, unguarded road cut along a steep mountainside. The population of the commune is ethnically mixed and includes Black Hmong, Yao (here called Dao), and a Tai group known as Giay. The households of these groups are not interspersed throughout the commune but rather grouped into different hamlets separated by distances of up to several kilometers or more. The road extends only into the center of the commune by the river. Access to the villages beyond this is by foot or motorbike over trails or paths. The center of the commune surrounding the government buildings and the school is ethnically Giay. The Dao hamlets are farther out and the Hmong ones farther still. The commune is partially electrified—the part, not surprisingly, being the central region.

Tourism provides various economic opportunities, but these are not evenly distributed. In Sapa, there are hotels, guesthouses, restaurants, coffee shops, stores, tourist agencies, and other businesses. These businesses, which are at the top of the tourist food chain, are run primarily by Kinh, though members of the minority groups may be employed by them. In Ta Van in 2005, participation in tourism includes homestays, on the one hand, and hawking and a few other activities, on the other. Though not by deliberate design, these are organized along ethnic lines. Homestay is in the hands of the Tai Giay. Their houses are located around the center of the commune where the road comes in and electricity is available, whereas those of the Dao and the Hmong are much farther out. But, according to our Vietnamese guide, even if the Dao and Hmong houses were close in they would not be used for homestay. The Dao and Hmong houses look more exotic and picturesque but are otherwise unsuitable. Government approval for homestay requires certain features, including proper toilets, bathing facilities, and sleeping arrangements, which only the Giay houses had. Also, the Dao and Hmong houses were deemed not clean enough. Our Kinh guide stressed that he was very concerned that a homestay house be clean and comfortable, with a decent kitchen area, a refrigerator, and modern chairs for guests.

But even among the Giay community, not all houses qualified for homestay. Some of the factors that excluded the Dao and the Hmong also worked against a part of the Giay households. Some of these houses were not large enough or lacked the proper facilities. The families in them either did not want to have tourists at all or could not afford the improvements that were required. Of these families, some were apt to think that the benefits of tourism were not fairly allocated in the village—that the rewards went disproportionately to the richer households that had better houses and could afford the upgrades. For those households not involved in providing homestay, tourism provides several other opportunities, though these are of lower economic value. Young men with motorcycles use them to transport people around the village or farther out. This is not strictly or even perhaps mainly for tourists, for local people also use motorcycles as taxis. The selling of handwoven and embroidered cloth around Ta Van and in Sapa is a very important economic activity, and one that is focused entirely on tourists. Here, it is possible to easily discern the ethnicity of the sellers by their dress, which clearly differs both in color and design among the three groups. The Hmong and Dao women are exceptional weavers and embroiderers, and the cloth trade for new and old fabric is in their hands. In the villages where tourists are to be found, Hmong women walk around with a bundle of cloth over one shoulder and, often, an infant in a sling on their side. Both Hmong and Dao women hawk cloth in the streets of Sapa and in the cloth market in the center of town. Most of the cloth sellers in Ta Van were Hmong who had learned to speak enough English to sell, and

Photo 11.7.   Hmong and Yao women chatting with tourists and selling cloth and souvenirs in Sapa town, northern Vietnam, 2010.

some knew enough to engage in boarder conversation and to banter with tourists. Some of them had become very good at this. One endeared herself to my wife by joking that she had become the "husband" in the family because she was out earning money while her husband stayed home to take care of the children (Judy eventually gave in and bought a large weaving).

Five years later, in early 2010, Sapa was in the midst of a building boom and there were more tourists than ever. The shops, restaurants, hotels, and tour businesses continued to be in Vietnamese hands. Hmong and Yao women still had a monopoly on selling pieces of cloth and souvenirs where the tourists were accessible in the streets in town, on the roads to the villages, and in the tourist villages (see photo 11.7). Some things had changed. Hmong women who had formerly been porters and had learned to speak English had become trekking guides. In Ta Van, commune homestay continued to be limited to the Giay households, but a major change had occurred. About three years previously, lowland Vietnamese had begun to move into Ta Van and buy land near the center of the commune from the minority inhabitants to open shops, either by themselves or in partnership with Giay occupants. Most significantly, the Vietnamese had begun to take over the lodging trade from the local households. They built guesthouses that offered private rooms, common areas with simple restaurants, and even pool tables, against which the older form of household homestay had difficulty competing.

12

Development for Better or Worse

With the exception of the very modern city-state of Singapore and perhaps the very small oil-rich Malay sultanate of Brunei, the countries of Southeast Asia fall into the category of developing nations. The United Nations Human Development Index is based upon the four criteria of Life Expectancy, Literacy, Education, and Standard of Living. "Development" as used within and regarding developing countries includes deliberate efforts to make changes in the adaptation, economy, culture, political structure, religion, tourism, ideology, environment—or just about anything else—of a country, region, or specific people. Development as meant in this way is initiated and pursued by governments, though often with the assistance or urging of foreign governments or nongovernmental organizations (NGOs). Development is usually thought of as positive attempts to make improvements. It can also include efforts to reduce or eliminate practices deemed to be harmful. Efforts to eradicate opium poppy growing in the northern countries of mainland Southeast Asia are an important example (United Nations Office on Drugs and Crime 2008). The object here has been to reduce the supply of opium (especially as refined into heroin) on the world market rather than to improve the living standard of the highland peoples who have relied on it as a cash crop. The assumption has been that since some of these people become debilitated addicts themselves they are also better off, but this has not been the main consideration. In order to eliminate commercial opium poppy growing (now mainly accomplished in the Southeast Asia countries outside of Burma), it is necessary to provide substitutes—without which the standard of living is reduced or people are forced out of their homeland. Many efforts to promote development have mixed outcomes for local peoples.

Table 12.1.   Human Development in Southeast Asia (larger countries in Southeast Asia as ranked in the United Nations Human Development Index [based on literacy, education, standard of living, and life expectancy], from highest to lowest [of 182 countries])

Country	Rank in World	Quartile
Malaysia	59	2
Thailand	87	2
Philippines	105	3
Indonesia	111	3
Vietnam	116	3
Laos	133	3
Cambodia	137	4
Burma	138	4

Source: Wikipedia: The Free Encyclopedia, "List of Countries by Human Development Index," at http://en.wikipedia.org/wiki/List_of_countries_by_Human_Development_Index (accessed August 9, 2010).

Development means various things but, above all, the attainment of a higher standard of living for the population in question. In the developing world of Southeast Asia, development means the reduction of poverty (sometimes defined internationally as having income of less than some number, such as the equivalent of one U.S. dollar per day). The concept of development is often qualified with the adjective "sustainable," meaning the resources on which it is based are renewable and the environmental and other negative consequences can be controlled. Development also implies simple things such as the creation of infrastructure—including roads, bridges, systems of water control, and airports. It also means improvements in standards of health, including declining infant mortality rates, increasing life expectancy, and the reduction of infectious diseases, including malaria, dengue fever, and cholera—all based on advances in public health, such as water-seal toilets, sewage disposal, and clean drinking water. Development also implies improvements in literacy, years of schooling, and the learning of national languages. Increasingly, development has also come to mean the protection and restoration of the environment through the establishment of national parks and game and nature preserves, the protection of watersheds, the control of erosion, and the reduction of pollution. And, of course, development means improvements in transportation. The model here being a transition from walking and the use of animal-powered vehicles to bicycles, motorcycles, tractors, and automobiles and trucks—different places in Southeast Asia can be seen to reflect these in different stages.

And who can be against any or at least most of these things? Development in Southeast Asia is greatly emphasized by governments and therefore

Photo 12.1. Development effort at the local level. Khamu villagers in Buan Xing in Luang Prabang Province, Laos, taking a break from cooperative work on a new school built of modern materials donated by an NGO, 2005. Such schools symbolize progress for villagers.

in and of itself is a form of patriotism. People who live in backward ways are seen to be letting the country down. The models of development for Southeast Asian countries were once limited mainly to the Western industrial nations, but they now include the Asian Tigers, including Hong Kong, Taiwan, and Singapore. These places were once underdeveloped but have now made the transition. The goals and general strategies of development therefore seem simple, if not necessarily easily carried out or achieved. There is not a great deal of disagreement among the Southeast Asian countries on these things. I have heard westerners (from already developed countries) say that the real secret of development or happiness is in wanting and doing with less, as advocated in Buddhist philosophy, for example. But these do not seem to be popular ideas in Southeast Asia at the present time. The achievement of development—or the things done in its name to bring it about—have also often been controversial.

DEVELOPMENT AND MAKING PEOPLE VISIBLE

The pursuit of development is based on classification, "making people visible," learning things about them, and putting them into categories—also

Photo 12.2.   Starting up the engine of a homemade truck taxi to take guests from a festival in the Akha village of Nam Dat, Muang Sing, northern Laos, 2005.

sometimes referred to as mapping. In his book *Seeing Like a State* the Southeast Asian specialist and political scientist James Scott (1998, 83) makes the argument that one of the crucial features of the modern state is a need to make more things visible:

> Any state intervention in society—to vaccinate a population, produce goods, mobilize labor, tax people and their property, conduct literacy campaigns, conscript soldiers, enforce sanitation standards, catch criminals, start universal schooling—requires the invention of units that are visible. The units in question might be citizens, villages, trees, fields, houses or people grouped according to age, depending on the type of intervention. Whatever the units being manipulated, they must be organized in a manner that permits them to be identified, observed, recorded, counted, aggregated, and monitored.

Just how much a government needs to know about its peoples and why and how well it classifies them depends on its goals, including what it needs from them, what it wants for them, or how it wants to change them. In Southeast Asia, the need for such knowledge varied considerably from precolonial to colonial and present-day governments. Some of the traditional states of Southeast Asia achieved massive accomplishments in engineering and architecture but otherwise had fairly simple needs and goals. The main goals of warfare were to capture or sack an enemy's capital and thereby destroy its symbolic structure of power, and to capture its population and relocate it to places nearby where it could be controlled and made useful to the state. Such governments do not appear to have cared a great deal about just who their subjects were in ethnic terms or about their local customs and personal religious beliefs and practices—nor did much need to be known about the highland and interior peoples on the margins so long as they did not cause trouble. They were sources of trade goods and slaves and perhaps of information about other states. But this did not require much knowledge about how the peripheral peoples lived, who they were in specific ethnic or linguistic terms, what their customs and religious beliefs and practices were like, or how they got their food.

During the early phase of colonial rule, governments had limited goals and therefore limited interest in counting, categorizing, classifying, or mapping things beyond their immediate strategic and economic concerns. But this changed in the nineteenth century as colonial projects expanded. The value of much broader interests can be seen in the ethnological "histories" produced by Thomas Stamford Raffles, John Crawfurd, and many other scholarly works and published reports. As colonialism progressed and the development of plantation agriculture, mining, and lumber extraction became important, the availability and quality of laborers of local and immigrant ethnic status became a matter of considerable interest. Efficient taxation also required knowledge of land, crops, forms of cultivation, and exchange. Beyond this, the later colonial regimes sought to exercise greater police, military, and administrative control over the peoples of the interior and highland regions who had previously been of little concern. The aims here included the reduction or elimination of tribal warfare and (where it was practiced) headhunting and the establishment of some degree of loyalty to the centralized regime. All of this required familiarity and some comparative knowledge, all the more so where sources of revenue, such as the opium and timber trade, were involved. And where there were important archaeological sites, these also needed to be explored, mapped, classified, and in some instances protected and restored by departments of antiquities. In some places, especially in Indonesia, customary law (*adat*) became an important topic that required collection and classification. Not all colonial scholarship was practical. Some of it was a matter of knowledge for knowledge's sake, and some of it combined practical and genuine scholarly interests. And over the course of the twentieth century, as colonial regimes became more concerned with the development of the countries and peoples over whom they ruled, they needed information to guide such processes.

DEVELOPMENT AND CLASSIFICATION

As the Southeast Asian countries became independent, development moved to the forefront—at least where wars were not being fought—and this required further knowledge. Development concerns and priorities differed and so therefore did research and classification. As we have seen, in socialist Vietnam, land reform was regarded as the beginning of agricultural development. And land reform required detailed knowledge of landownership and tenancy on the ground, at the village level, and for every village. This meant the creation of a series of uniform categories into which every village farmer or household could be placed, with the reallocation of land (and other rewards and punishments) to follow accordingly—from landlords (further subdivided) to landless workers.

As discussed earlier, development for Indonesia has included having a proper religion, and this has required a set of categories for different types of religion. The basic principle—deriving from the Indonesian constitution—is that becoming developed means having a monotheistic religion. Indonesia does not pursue development according to ethnic criteria or classify its peoples according to their ethnic status or ethnicity. However, it has classified some people as "isolated customary-law communities" (or PKAT), which usually meant ethnic populations that dwelt in forests, lived by hunting and gathering or shifting cultivation, and did not adhere to a monotheistic religion. The general purpose of this designation is to focus government attention on such groups so they can be developed into modern citizens with ways of life more like those of civilized peasant farmers (Duncan 2004a, 86–87).

Beyond Indonesia, efforts to classify people in relation to development are widespread. All of the other Southeast Asian countries appear to have some form of ethnic classification. The general purpose of such schemes of classification falls into the category of creating "citizenship," though economic and social development is involved as well. While a full review of the ethnic classification practices of the Southeast Asian countries is not possible, we can usefully consider some examples. (See the collection of case studies in Duncan 2004b.)

Malaysia

Malaysia does classify its population in ethnic terms but has a somewhat complicated way of doing so that reflects the formation of the country in two stages—the initial Federation of Malaya in 1957 (which included only the states of the peninsula) and then the creation of Malaysia in 1963 (which added the British Borneo colonial states of Sarawak and Sabah and, for a brief time, Singapore as well). As a result of these developments, the official (and popular) ethnic classifications used in peninsular Malaysia are somewhat different from those of the Borneo states. In both instances, the present-day categories are rooted in part in colonial ones. In peninsular (or west) Malaysia, there are four main ethnic categories, including Malays (at the time of independence about 50 percent of the population), Chinese (about 37 percent), Indians (about 11 percent), and Orang Asli and others (about 2 percent). In the Borneo states of Sarawak and Sabah, the population is generally divided between native and nonnative peoples, especially Chinese. Many different native groups are recognized, but in Sarawak these are usually grouped into five categories, including Malays, Bidayuh (formerly Land Dayak), Iban (formerly Sea Dayak), Melanau, and Orang Ulu ("Upriver Peoples," a composite category).

For the purposes of directing development, the most important countrywide distinction is between Bumiputera and others (Chinese and Indians). Bumiputera (or "native sons") includes Malays (defined according to several criteria including adherence to Islam), Orang Asli of peninsular Malaysia, and the natives of Malaysian Borneo. This category has had wide governmental and popular use since the 1970s in association with the New Economic Policy. The general purpose is to differentiate the Malays and other native peoples from immigrant communities of Chinese and Indians and to provide Bumiputera with certain advantages and opportunities for employment, university admissions, and the ownership of capital in corporations, all intended to reduce their economic inferiority to the Chinese.

Thailand

Thailand does not officially recognize any category of indigenous peoples as deserving special protection or assistance, although the royal family has made the highland minorities a focus of paternalistic efforts of charity, education, and development. The people living in highland areas of northern Thailand are identified as hill tribes (*chauw khaw*), but such groups are not regarded as being the original inhabitants of the regions they occupy (Gillogly 2004, 116–17). Many have had difficulties in establishing citizenship. Some of them, especially the Hmong and the Mien (Yao), are considered recent immigrants from China or even more recent refugees from Laos and Burma. No official distinction has been made between these fairly recent arrivals in Thailand and others such as the Karen, some of whom have been in Thailand for centuries or more. Most of the groups that have arrived more recently tend to live at the highest occupied elevations in the mountains because land was available there. Recognition of the hill tribes as an issue for the development of Thailand gained importance only in the second part of the twentieth century. Before this time, the highland peoples were mainly overlooked by the government. Most of them lived in areas marginal to the central government and to most lowlanders. The forests they occupied and cleared for their fields were of little interest to the state except where there were valuable stands of teak. The opium grown by the Hmong and some other groups was mainly consumed locally or traded into China. The concern that initially drew attention to the hill tribes was their possible role in the communist movements that were developing in Indochina and spilling into Thailand. The Hmong and some other groups had ties with China and Laos. The security of border areas became an issue, and some Hmong villages were attacked and bombed. The arrival of large numbers of Hmong, Yao, and other refugees after the communist takeover in Laos in 1975 helped to diminish the view that hill tribes had ties or sympathies with the communists. But by then opium production in the mountains had come to be seen as a problem, especially as a result of international concerns and pressures to eliminate poppy growing (Gillogly 2004). The development of forestry, environmentalism, and the need to protect watersheds added to the problems attributed to the hill tribes—all of which were further exacerbated by the arrival of many more of them as refugees from Laos, Vietnam, and Burma, along with lowland Khmer and others escaping the Khmer Rouge in Cambodia.

Vietnam and Laos

The socialist countries of Vietnam and Laos take a somewhat different approach to ethnic classification than the other nations of Southeast Asia. Both place a greater official and ideological emphasis on equality, solidarity, and cooperation. However, there are important differences between ethnic definitions and categories in the two countries.

The contemporary Socialist Republic of Vietnam recognizes and classifies all people living within the borders of the country formed after unification in 1975 as citizens. The older term, *moi* (savage) for tribal peoples is now considered derogatory and is not used in official or political contexts—nor is the term *montagnard* (meaning "mountain people") that the French created to designate the ethnic minorities living in the highland areas, especially those of the central highlands in southern Vietnam. This term continued to be used in the Republic of Vietnam (South Vietnam) until its fall in 1975. It is also still used in the French and other external ethnological literature. In Vietnam, the term *montagnard* is considered unacceptable because of its colonial ethnological roots and associations. Instead, the term used is ethnic minorities. No special status or rights to homelands or autonomous territories are accorded to indigenous minorities, however. The emphasis is on equal rights, and political demonstrations (as took place in the central highlands in 2003) against government policies, such as permitting the migration of lowland ethnic Vietnamese into highland tribal areas, are viewed with strong disfavor.

The Vietnamese communist party and government have always taken the ethnology of ethnic minorities seriously. The present-day Vietnamese classification of ethnic groups has developed since 1945, when national independence was first proclaimed. The process of naming and classifying was to be done according to principles of scientific ethnology. An Institute of Ethnology was created in 1968, to both identify and classify minority ethnic groups and do research on the social and economic problems of these groups. Such research was confined to the northern half of the country until after unification in 1975, after which it was extended to the south, especially the central highlands. Initially (in 1969), the government decided there were sixty-three main groups plus numerous subgroups. In 1973, this number was reduced to fifty-nine. The final classification reached in 1979 placed the total at fifty-four.

The final official classification of fifty-four groups includes four (nonofficial) types: the Vietnamese or Kinh who occupy most of lowland Vietnam and form about 87 percent of the total population; the highland ethnic minorities of northern Vietnam, most of whom are Tai-Kadai-speaking non-Buddhist peoples, but they also include Hmong, Yao, and others; and the indigenous groups of the central highland and other parts of the Annamite Cordillera, which include a large number of different Mon-Khmer and Austronesian-speakers. The official list also includes two lowland minorities: the Austronesian Chams (those left after many moved to Cambodia following the Vietnamese incorporation of the kingdom of Champa in the fifteenth century, some of whom are today Muslim) and the Khmer of the Mekong Delta (the remainder of the former Angkor state, including the delta). The final category also includes the Chinese or mixed Chinese descendants of immigrants (McElwee 2004, 184–89).

The government of Laos (Lao People's Democratic Republic [PDR]) has developed a rather unique approach to classifying its highly diverse population. The members of all indigenous ethnic groups in the country are defined as "Lao" to emphasize common citizenship, equality, and cooperation. But in order to recognize diversity and address the different issues of development facing different types of people, the government divides Lao into three different categories according to geographical elevation. This principle carries forward the widespread official or nonofficial ethnological distinction between lowland and highland peoples but adds a further middle category. The three resulting categories are Lao Lum (lowland or valley dwellers), Lao Theung (slope or mountainside dwellers), and Lao Sung (summit or mountaintop dwellers; Ovesen 2004, 221). This threefold classification was created at the end of the French colonial regime and

Photo 12.3. Currency in Laos showing national symbols. Lao currency note (2003) shows three women dressed in traditional costume representing Lao Lum or lowlanders (center), Lao Theung or "midlanders" (on the right), and Lao Sung or highlanders (on the left). To the right of the women is an image of the Pha That Luang near Vientiane, a Buddhist stupa and the national monument of Laos.

adopted by the socialist government (see photo 12.3). It was intended to be a way to avoid discriminating either for or against any particular ethnic group. It was also intended to reflect differences in ecological adaptation found at different altitudes and to provide strategies of development accordingly. Valley dwellers, who are wet rice farmers, are assumed to have different problems and needs than slope dwellers, who are traditionally swidden farmers. Summit dwellers in turn are supposed to face yet different challenges than slope dwellers. But since summit dwellers are also swidden cultivators, such differences are less obvious.

The categories of Lao Lum, Lao Theung, and Lao Sung have some ethnic and historical basis, and there are differences in prestige. The prestige ranking is the reverse of altitude. The lowland Lao Lum have the highest prestige, while the highland Lao Sung have the lowest. The three categories also embody ethnolinguistic differences. The Lao Lum are all Tai-speaking peoples, including the ethnic Lao, the Lue, the Black Tai, the White Tai, and various other groups. The prestige of the Lao Lum reflects especially the status of the ethnic Lao as wet rice cultivating, literate, Buddhist, state-organized groups that are distributed along the Mekong and other rivers of the country. The Tai peoples are generally not considered the earliest of the ethnic groups to arrive in Laos, but they became the politically, economically, and culturally dominant group. The midlevel-dwelling Lao Theung are Mon-Khmer speakers. In the northern part of Laos, most of these people

are ethnic Khamu, while in the southern part the Mon-Khmer are fragmented into many smaller, linguistically distinct groups numbering only a
few thousand each. The Mon-Khmer are generally considered the original
or oldest group to occupy Laos. The Khmer are ritually acknowledged in
some traditional Lao state ceremonies to have special status. Some Mon-
Khmer groups have changed their classification from Theung to Lum by
adapting Tai customs and language (Ovesen 2004, 224).

The highland Lao Sung are also ethnolinguistically and historically different from both of the other two categories. These people include both
Tibeto-Burman (especially Akha) and Meo-Yao (that is, Hmong and Yao)
speakers. As in Thailand, these groups are regarded as the most recent arrivals, and the assumed reason they live at the highest elevations is again that
this was where land was available. While the highland Lao Sung are shifting
cultivators like the midland Lao Theung, there is an important difference.
The farming activities of some of these groups, especially the Hmong and
Yao, included the growing and sale of opium. The development issues involving the Lao Sung who were commercial poppy growers has been finding suitable substitute cash crops. Many Lao Sung villages have also been
moved to lower locations.

DEVELOPMENT AND POVERTY

The reduction of poverty and the improvement of standards of living (as
defined and measured by governments, aid agencies, and other NGOs) are
at the heart of notions of development. Poverty has various implications,
including food scarcity, poor prospects for improvement, powerlessness,
lack of prestige, and a high rate of mortality. Poverty is in some sense relative to wealth and culturally defined. It is one thing to be materially poor if
everyone else is also and quite another if they are not. A group of hunter-
gatherers living in relative isolation in the forest cannot be meaningfully
called "poor" for several reasons, including their own cultural standards,
their autonomy, and their control over their daily lives—though unfortunately, as we have seen, such conditions no longer exist for most hunters-
gatherers in Southeast Asia.

The relationship of poverty to hunger has become ambiguous, at least
in developed countries—where it is pointed out that the poor are more
apt to be fat than are the affluent, in part because fattening foods are
cheaper than nonfattening ones. But poverty is still linked to hunger in
some regions of Southeast Asia. For example, the government of Vietnam
calculates both an overall poverty rate and a food poverty rate, the latter
below the former. The technical term used by specialists in development
is "food security," meaning certainty in having enough to eat throughout

the year or from one harvest to the next; people who live with food poverty do not have food security. In the poorest province of Vietnam, which is that of Hoah Bin in the northwest, the official general poverty rate for 2004 was 54.4 percent, and the food poverty rate was 25.4 percent, meaning that a quarter of the population may suffer hunger, not merely a "low standard of living" (Rugendyke and Nguyen 2010, 88–89). In mainland Southeast Asia, such rates (or higher ones) are probably now found in parts of Laos, Burma, and Cambodia as well. Anthropologists, geographers, and others familiar with Southeast Asia will point out that extremes of economic poverty here are historically much lower than in China or India.

RESETTLEMENT

Resettlement has also been an important dimension of development in Southeast Asia, though also a highly criticized one. Not all resettlement has been to improve the lives of those affected. Civilian populations are displaced in times of war and, at other times, for reasons of "security," as it is usually put. As discussed in chapter 4, an estimated three-quarters of a million rural Chinese in Malaya were resettled into "New Villages" during the communist insurrection that began under colonial rule—the purpose being to cut support to the insurgents rather than to improve the lives of those who were resettled. Resettlement may also be necessitated by natural disasters such as volcanic eruptions, typhoons, or tsunamis. Our concern here is with resettlement related to development. But such deliberate resettlement also varies. It may be occasioned by either a direct effort to make improvements or as a means to an end that has no immediate benefit to those moved—when a dam is being constructed, for example. Also, resettlement as a tactic to promote development does not necessarily leave the people involved better off. Some resettlement efforts have had better results than others. Those that target individual families in need of land or other economic opportunities appear to be more successful than those that move people regardless of their need; also, those in which individuals or villages seek or agree without pressure or coercion to be relocated seem to have better outcomes than involuntary ones; and not surprisingly, resettlement efforts that are adequately financed in terms of startup support for those moved do better than ones in which poor people are left to cope on their own. Finally, it is necessary to look at resettlement programs from the perspective of those already living in areas to which people are moved as well as those who are moved in. The following cases of resettlement reveal some of these issues.

Resettlement in Laos

The resettlement of village populations in Laos has been going on for a long period of time. Stories are common in rural Laos of villagers moving into caves to escape destruction during the Vietnam War, when Laos was heavily bombed. And in more recent decades, resettlement has been an important development strategy. As in mainland Southeast Asia, most resettlement in Laos has been "vertical," that is, from a higher to a lower elevation, which is another way of saying it involves moving highland peoples to lower places, though doing this is not the point. In a recent account, development specialists Ian Baird and Bruce Shoemaker (2005) provide a critical overview of what takes place and why, and with what consequences. Their purpose is to make the NGOs and other aid agencies that have initiated or supported most of the programs and projects involving resettlement aware of the consequences. Most resettlement, they argue, is initiated by the government rather than by the villagers involved. Villagers themselves are supposed to initiate or at least agree to resettlement. But most have been pressured to move by the government, or forced to do so as a result of various development programs deemed important by the state. Aid agencies have therefore frequently been complicit in resettlement projects. However, some have become increasingly concerned with the problems linked to resettlement.

Based on their own knowledge and experience, and on studies by others, Baird and Shoemaker conclude that policies and programs involving resettlement (especially the program of very rapid opium eradication) may have been well intended. But for those resettled, the results have been mainly misfortunes or disasters. The many highlanders forced to resettle—either as a matter of deliberate policy or as a consequence of government efforts to achieve some other purpose—have been subjected to long-term poverty, food shortages, and increased rates of disease and mortality.

The government and aid agencies have favored (or justified) resettlement for several reasons. Security was an early reason. After the current government came to power, many former opponents among the highland ethnic groups remained to operate as resistance guerrillas. The presence of such holdouts (a few of which have been reported to still exist) formed powerful reasons for resettling villages that continued to support them. The Hmong, who are known to have often supported America military efforts in Laos, have, in particular, been liable to resettlement. Resettlement for security reasons is now mainly a matter of previous rather than ongoing resettlement.

The recent or current reasons for resettlement include the effort to eliminate opium growing in the highlands of Laos. Opium eradication began with an international campaign by the United Nations, led by the United

States and supported by other foreign governments and development NGOs. But it became a crusade for the government of Laos, as a matter of genuine concern, as a justification for forcing highland resettlement it wished to accomplish for other reasons, or because aid dollars are involved. Opium eradication may involve moving cultivating villages out of remote and secluded highland areas to lowland sites where they can be more effectively prevented from raising poppies. Resettlement may also result from the economic difficulties experienced by former producers unable to find alternative sources of adequate income. Laos is now, according to the UN task force, mainly opium free (United Nations Office on Drugs and Crime 2008).

Another reason for resettlement is the reduction or eradication of swidden cultivation as a general practice. The belief that swidden farming is both harmful to the environment and a cause of poverty to its practitioners has been around for decades. In Laos, the idea probably originated by NGO-aid agencies rather than the government, but it was embraced by the government and became a major reason for resettlement. The reduction or abandonment of swidden cultivation involves a limited number of alternatives. One of these is a shift to wet rice farming, which is viewed as more productive, permanent, environmentally friendly, and civilized. The problem is that land suitable for wet rice is scarce or nonexistent in highland locations, hence resettlement if the change is to be made. Another is the shift to cash cropping—the cultivation of fruits and other crops to be sold in markets. This can be done in highland locations, but access to markets is often a problem; if not overcome, the result may be impoverishment and pressure to resettle. The government has also restricted access to land through the Land and Forest Allocation Program. The result of reducing access to land is the shortening of fallow periods to only a few years, which is counterproductive in that it brings the loss and deterioration of soils. As do most anthropologists, geographers, and others familiar with current swidden practices, Baird and Shoemaker argue that, given the population densities that prevail throughout most highland areas of Southeast Asia, including Laos, swidden cultivation can be sustained without harm to forests. They also argue that, from the perspective of the swidden cultivators, the alternatives usually do more harm than good—and therefore, while one of the purposes of reducing or eliminating swidden practices is to reduce poverty, the opposite has been the case (Baird and Shoemaker 2005, 3, 6–7).

A further reason or justification for the resettlement of highland people is an effort to provide better access to markets, schools, medical care, and other services. Doing this makes resettled villages more easily governed and administered. Relocating remote villages to more accessible locations is an alternative to creating roads to them (as has been done in northern Thailand, for example). Moving villages to places with better access is done in two somewhat different ways. One is to simply move a single village to a place along or near a road. Another is to move several villages to one location where services can be dispensed and markets formed—and, thus where there is a road as well. Laos has had two different programs for creating such complex settlements. Both types may (and frequently do) combine villages of different ethnic types, for example, Hmong and Khamu, although in such cases, the groups tend to be separated—for example, the Khamu on one side of the road, the Hmong on the other. Sometimes, highland villages facing resettlement resisted being moved into multiethnic settlements because of concerns about their religious practices being different (Baird and Shoemaker 2005, 12–13).

The creation of new multiethnic settlements has also had a cultural purpose. Such resettlement is intended to promote acculturation, nation building, and citizenship. Laos is a country made up of diverse ethnic groups. As we have seen, the government has sought to reduce this complexity by labeling everyone as Lao and then creating subcategories according to altitude. The creation of multiethnic new settlements is seen as a further step toward cultural unification. The government's goal is not to promote mutual acculturation among different upland ethnic groups but rather to encourage the highland peoples to become more like (and mixed with) the lowland ethnic Lao—by adopting wet rice cultivation and the Lao language, clothing, housing styles, religion, and other customs (Baird and Shoemaker 2005, 11). Like most of the governments of mainland Southeast Asia, Laos officially values ethnic diversity as reflected in ethnic costumes, festivals, and beauty contests, for these are entertaining and a tourist attraction. But like most of the other mainland Southeast Asian governments, officials are mainly people from the dominant lowland ethnic groups—in this case Lao Lum. Such people tend to equate civilization with Lao speech, culture, and Buddhism.

Resettlement in Indonesia

The government of Indonesia has also made extensive use of resettlement as a development strategy. However, there are major differences with what has occurred in Laos and mainland Southeast Asia generally. In Laos, resettlement has been local in the sense that resettled populations have usually not been moved a long distance. In Indonesia, some resettlement has also been local—as when interior, forest-dwelling villages are moved to the coast and for some of the same reasons that highland villages in Laos have been moved to lowland sites. However, Indonesia's major effort at resettlement has been the *transmigrasi* (transmigration) program, which has involved resettlement between islands, often over great distances (Hardjono 1977). A further difference is that resettlement in Indonesia has been undertaken to readjust what the government has viewed as serious imbalances in population—too many people in some places and too few (or at least more available room) in others. This has not been a reason for resettlement in Laos where, if anything, the areas to which resettled people have been moved are more crowded than those from whence they came.

Indonesia has a large population (currently nearly 250 million, the fourth largest in the world). Moreover, much of the population is concentrated in the relatively small islands of Java (40 percent of the country's total population) and Bali, which together have often been referred to as Inner Indonesia. For a long while, part of the solution to the problem of overpopulation in Inner Indonesia was to move some of the people to the larger islands of Outer Indonesia, including Sumatra, Kalimantan, Sulawesi, and Irian Jaya (Indonesian New Guinea) where (it was supposed) there was abundant, empty land for settlement. The movement of Javanese and Balinese was also intended to have a secondary benefit. These peoples would be spreading their highly productive techniques of intensive wet rice cultivation and their civilized culture to areas of shifting cultivation and more backward cultural ways—a win-win plan, at least in official theory. The *transmigrasi* program was first conceived and begun by the Dutch. Their interest was in both providing land for the landless in Java and in increasing the labor supply in some of the outer islands. The program was continued after independence by the Indonesian government under President Sukarno, and its greatest development occurred under President Suharto. It was discontinued after the departure of Suharto in 1998 because of its failures, though the problems it caused continued after this time.

The transmigration program often did badly for several reasons. One was the assumption that the intensive forms of wet rice cultivation followed by the Javanese and Balinese could be practiced equally well, or even at all, in the areas to which the migrants were sent. In fact, there were good geographical reasons that wet rice cultivation had historically developed mainly in Java and Bali and that shifting cultivation, sago growing, mixed cultivation, fishing, and hunting and gathering had developed elsewhere in those "empty" regions that were targeted for *transmigrasi* schemes. If the areas to which migrants were sent had the soil types and other geographical features that favored intensive wet rice cultivation, it would already have been in practice. Some transmigrants left their schemes, returned home, and took up other occupations. Another related problem is that there were already people living in the regions chosen for resettlement. These people did not agree with the government's view that they had more land than they needed, even if they changed to more intensive forms of cultivation, and they did not always appreciate having their land occupied by peoples from faraway islands with very different religious and other cultural practices.

Transmigration in West Kalimantan and Halmahera

Kalimantan Barat (or Kalbar), the west coast province of Indonesian Borneo, became a place of ethnic conflict and, at one point, serious violence. The conflict that developed in the rural areas of Kalbar was not simply a consequence of government-organized resettlement. Indonesians from elsewhere also came on their own to a place that offered various opportunities beyond acquiring land for cultivation. Among those who came both as sponsored transmigrants and as independent settlers were many Madurese, Madura being a densely populated, agriculturally poor island off the northeast coast of Java. Many Madurese gravitated to small-scale trade and developed a niche below or beyond that occupied by the Chinese, peddling fruits, vegetables, and other items on the streets or from house to house and opening small shops in rural villages. Fair or not, Madurese men developed a reputation for abrasiveness in dealing with Dayaks in rural areas. Eventually, incidents of conflict took place, and Dayaks began to attack Madurese living in vulnerable locations, killing some and burning shops and houses. The Madurese fled in large number to more secure towns and cities where they became refugees.[1]

The ethnic attacks on the Madurese did not occur because the Dayaks were hostile to all ethnic outsiders engaged in trade. Normally, Dayaks get along well with the Chinese, who are seen as playing a useful economic role. In the towns, Dayaks work for Chinese. In western Borneo, the Chinese communities are often very old and have become socially and culturally compatible with the Dayaks. In the rural areas and small towns, the Chinese, who have no restrictions on drinking alcohol and eating pork, attend Dayak festivals and, in turn, invite Dayak friends and acquaintances to their own celebrations. Chinese-Dayak intermarriage and persons of mixed descent are both common. The local Malays, who as Muslims are not free to openly eat pork or drink alcohol, do not participate in Dayak festivals but nonetheless generally stay on good terms with Dayaks.

As to elsewhere in Indonesia, the anthropologist Christopher Duncan (2002, 2004a) has discussed what occurred as a result of transmigration and resettlement on the island of Halmahera in North Maluku Province, eastern Indonesia. He focuses on its effects on the Forest Tobelu, an interior people of northern Halmahera who traditionally lived by hunting and gathering, processing sago, and occasionally by planting swidden gardens. Over the years, the postcolonial government made various efforts to resettle and civilize the Tobelu as part of a wider scheme to promote the development of isolated peoples: "Once groups were chosen to be the object of this program they became subject to (often forced) resettlement in more manageable locations. In the process the government tried to intervene into virtually every aspect of their lives, changing settlement patterns, agricultural techniques, religion, and even trying to change eating habits" (2002, 349).

Transmigration from Java and Bali to the Moluccas began in the 1950s. Eventually, a total of eighteen transmigration settlements—with a total population of more than twenty-eight thousand—were established on Halmahera. In turn, a new form of logging accompanied the expansion of transmigration: clear-cutting for the purpose of developing timber plantations where a single species of tree would be planned, to fit with the government's plan to develop and civilize the Forest Tobelu. They were to become laborers on the timber plantations. Serious religious and ethnic violence with an extensive loss of life took place on Halmahera as elsewhere in the Moluccas in 1999–2000, leading to the forced removal of thousands of transmigrant settlers (Duncan 2004a, 105).

LAND ENCLOSURES AND THE ASSAULT ON SWIDDEN CULTIVATION

One of the most important development issues for highland and interior people in Southeast Asia is the reduction and transformation of traditional practices of shifting cultivation. The closest historical parallel to what is now happening over large regions is the enclosure of lands in medieval and early modern Europe. The enclosure movement in Europe involved the breakup of communally held village lands into private, often fenced, parcels.

Less the fencing, the enclosure of lands in Southeast Asia is occurring in a number of ways and for various reasons. These include the transformation of lands formerly controlled and used by swidden cultivators into national parks, nature reserves, watershed forests, and other protected zones. These and other state projects thus involve resettling some or all shifting cultivators to areas outside the protected zones, as well as moving lowland peoples into highland and interior forest areas formerly occupied exclusively by shifting cultivators and hunters and gatherers. Some of this resettlement has been organized and directed by the state, as with village relocation and consolidation efforts in Laos and the transmigration program in Indonesia. Some of it has been enabled by other state projects, such as road building and extending military and police control into formerly remote areas.

One of the alternatives to shifting cultivation is the creation or extension of industrial plantations of tea, rubber, coffee, oil palm, or monospecies timber, of the sort first developed during colonial rule. These developments include direct state projects, private ventures, and joint projects with international corporations. Creating large plantations is the opposite of protecting natural forests. The development of plantations requires clear-cut log-

Photo 12.4.   Resettled Akha village of Adoo in northern Thailand was moved several years before from inside a national forest, Chiang Mai Province, 2006.

ging, land grading and draining, and road building. Both state projects and private ventures reduce or bring an end to shifting cultivation and foraging, although plantations do so more radically and with greater finality than the creation of state-protected forests, nature preserves, and watershed areas.

The changes that involve the reduction or transformation of shifting cultivation have occurred under both capitalist and socialist regimes—though, by the end of the 1980s, this distinction lost much of the significance it formerly had. Both the socialist and the capitalist countries of Southeast Asia have extended state protection over large areas of forest occupied by shifting cultivators and foragers. Both types of regimes have resettled shifting cultivators out of protected regions and dam sites and sometimes permitted or enabled the resettlement of lowland peoples in need of land into other areas already occupied by shifting cultivators. The governments of both the socialist and capitalist countries have logged forests to create plantations. Some countries have done these things in a more authoritarian and aggressive manner than others.

Developing and transforming land use has affected highland and interior-dwelling ethnic minorities and lowland majorities in different ways. As noted in chapter 5, Sellato argues that new, post-Suharto policies of decentralization in Indonesia have left the Punan hunter-gatherer-collectors of interior Kali-mantan potentially better off than they have been in a long time—though he notes also that whether they will be able to take good advantage of their new opportunities remains to be seen. Other such examples can perhaps be found, but many accounts suggest that highland and interior minorities are more often adversely affected by development projects.[2]

Dams and National Parks

Dams, national parks, and other protected areas are good examples of development projects. Laos's plans for development prominently include building dams to supply hydroelectric power for sale to surrounding coun-tries. As elsewhere, the dams are being built in highland areas, both because these regions provide the maximum technical opportunities and because lowland regions are more densely settled. Large dams in developing coun-tries are built with international aid. The decision to build a dam and where to build it is also based on the relative costs and benefits. The benefits in-clude flood control, water storage for irrigation and other purposes, as well as the generation of electric power for local use and sale. The human costs include the number of people and communities that will be displaced and resettled. A dam built in an area remote from developed centers of popula-tion is deemed to be less costly in human impact than one built in a more densely populated area.

But in Laos, as also with the Bakun and Batang Ai projects in Sarawak—where hydroelectric developments have been paramount considerations—the costs and benefits tend to vary locally within the country. Dams built in forested mountains provide an opportunity for logging and therefore for those who gain economically from logging, for there is little reason to submerge and destroy valuable timber that can be saved. And since roads have to be built to the dam sites anyway, these can also be used for log-ging purposes. The need to resettle populations may also in itself be an attractive consideration to the government if it desires to relocate a local highland population for other reasons. And while the costs of dam building are heavier for the highland minority populations that are displaced, the benefits go disproportionately to peoples located downriver. Water control and flood prevention are of little value to the people who live by hunting and gathering and swidden cultivation, and the electricity generated may not reach them at all.

The creation of national parks, nature reserves, and state-protected places is also an important element in development. The cultural reasons for such programs are well known. Lands still covered with old-growth forest or other valued natural cover, especially those that have spectacular natural features, will be protected and preserved for future generations. If national parks and reserves are characteristics of the land use practices of the United States and other developed countries, then they are things that developing countries desire to have as well. To be modern and developed is also to be green.

Beyond such environmentalist considerations, there are practical reasons for developing countries to create national parks. They attract tourists, and tourism figures prominently in efforts to reduce poverty and promote economic development. National parks offer tourists the promise of mature forests, spectacular rivers, mountains, gorges, and wildlife. They offer an enticing contrast to the teeming lowland and urban populations of some regions. And because of tourism, the creation of national parks and reserves is supposed to bring benefits in the form of opportunities for employment as maintenance workers, guides, snack and souvenir sellers, and providers of homestays. But there are also drawbacks, stemming in part from the original American idea that national parks should be places of wilderness, where nature is protected from human ravages. National parks were envisioned as places for trees, wild birds, animals, and the occasional archaeological site. The living human presence should be minimal, nondestructive, and carefully controlled. The presence of hunter-gatherers in and around national parks has been accepted in some places (for example, the Penan in Mulu Caves National Park in Sarawak), but that of shifting cultivators has usually been regarded as problematic and incompatible with the purposes of these places.

Who benefits from the development of national parks and nature reserves? Do the local peoples, who become part of the attraction for tourists, benefit, or do outsiders benefit more? In the case of national parks and nature preserves, the issue is more acute. Do the economic benefits of developing parks and reserves offset the losses of land and access to resources they bring to local peoples? A recent study indicates that developing Cuc Phuong National Park in northern Vietnam has negatively affected the Muong minority villagers who lived in and around it. Another study of the effects of a major national park on an aboriginal group in Taiwan published in the same volume (*Regional Minorities and Development in Asia*) reaches the same conclusion (Simon 2010; see also McElwee 2002).

Barbara Rugendyke and Nguyen Thi Son studied the local impact of the first national park created in Vietnam. The park was intended to protect the only remaining primary forest area in northern Vietnam and to attract tourists. At the time of its original opening in 1966, the Muong villagers then living within the park were permitted to remain. However, after this, the Muong, who live by swidden cultivation and by hunting and gathering, and whose population had begun to rise, were deemed a threat to the park's mission of forest preservation and renewal. In 1986, the government began to resettle the Muong inhabitants outside of the park. And as in other protected

areas of Vietnam, the use of forest resources became illegal, for locals or minorities are not given any special rights. The villagers removed from the park
and others living in the vicinity report that without being able to forage in
the park they cannot obtain sufficient food from subsistence cultivation. The
Muong have not done well with cultivation practiced in a fixed location, and
those resettled were moved to an area with poor soils.

Not all Muong were moved from the park, whose officials said that
perhaps about one thousand should remain, these being ones with a long
history of living within the park, though presumably over time, with population increase, some would have to be moved as well. The Muong living
outside of the park but on its peripheries continue to supplement their diet
with foods foraged and hunted within the park although they know that it
is illegal to do so. Those who are caught are heavily fined, and violent conflicts have occurred. Part of the government plan was that tourism would
bring economic benefits that would offset the negative consequences that
the park's development brought the Muong. Also, there was the hope that
the Muong would come to see the park as an asset rather than a liability
and would therefore be more inclined to protect it. By the time of the study,
such positive developments had not taken place, nor did it seem likely they
would (Rugendyke and Nguyen 2010).

DEVELOPMENT AND HOUSES

Houses are regarded as an important reflection of development. In parts of
Indonesia (especially Sumatra and Sulawesi), where some of the most striking customary domestic architecture in the world is to be found, traditional
houses are appreciated and have figured prominently in tourism—which in
turn has a prominent role in strategies of development. Traditional houses
are also often included in ethnological museum displays in architectural
gardens and theme parks, including Taman Mini near Jakarta; Sarawak
Cultural Village, outside of Kuching; and the National Museum of Ethnology in Hanoi. Villagers who have abandoned traditional houses sometimes
build scale models on their own, either as tourist attractions or so their
children and grandchildren will see how they used to live. Also, people who
build modern-style houses do not necessarily tear down or abandon their
traditional ones, at least before they have begun to fall apart. A common
sight in parts of Sarawak, Vietnam, and Laos is a new modern house sitting
next to (or joined with) a traditional one—the older one often occupied by
the elder generation, who will say that the old house is more comfortable,
and the new one a source of pride for everyone (see photos 12.5 and 12.6).

These and other qualifications are important. But the general trend in
house building today (among highland and interior minorities as well as

Photo 12.5.   Mnong household in Lieng village, central highlands, Vietnam, has kept their old longhouse after building a new, attached, national-style square house made of concrete, block, and stucco, 2004.

Photo 12.6.   In the Oi village of Kong Heng in Attapeu, southern Laos, a man sits on the porch of his old but comfortable traditional dwelling of thatch, wood, and bamboo, attached to which is a newly built, national style house, 2006.

Photo 12.7.   Using knowledge most possess, previously prepared local materials, and shared labor, village men in the Lue village of Pak Chaek (Luang Prabang Province, northern Laos) can build this small traditional house in one day, 2005.

lowland majorities) is toward modern or national styles and the use of modern, industrially produced materials—machine-sawn lumber and plywood, cement, cinder blocks, corrugated sheet metal, and glazed windows, in particular.[3] Houses in Southeast Asia are traditionally made from organic materials obtained from the surrounding fields and forests: grass, leaves, wood and bark, bamboo, and rattan.[4]

Traditional building materials (and methods of construction that are often based on labor exchange) are cheaper than modern manufactured materials. For example, Hmong or Yao houses in Laos (and Vietnam) are more often built of traditional materials and in traditional styles than are Hmong or Yao houses in Thailand, indicating differences in prosperity. Decisions about how to build a house are not simply a matter of development and the prestige of modernity, however. Government pressures and tourism and may also be involved in some places. Government ideas about development in Southeast Asia may include the belief that people should if possible live in the right sort of house or at least one made from the right modern materials. In Laos, for example, one resettlement project included building Lao-style houses for relocated highland villagers so they

Photo 12.8.   Lumber for houses in contemporary Laos is often sawn by hand, as here by Punoi men on the outskirts of Muang Sing, Luang Namtha Province, 2005.

would have a proper model to follow in constructing their own (Baird and Shoemaker 2005, 11).

As we have seen, multifamily longhouses in particular seem to raise problems for governments. Both postwar Vietnam and Indonesia disapproved of longhouses because they did not fit the correct form of house according to the preferences of the state, as different as these preferences were in the two countries.[5] But here tourism can add a further complication. We have also noted the architectural dilemmas faced by Iban tourist longhouses in Sarawak. Here, the choice has sometimes been between keeping an authentic-looking traditional but rundown longhouse that tourists want and expect or building a totally new longhouse that may cost them their tourist business altogether.

Longhouses in Borneo

Throughout Borneo, there have been two patterns of architectural change among longhouse dwellers. One has been to abandon longhouses entirely in favor of separate individual family houses, and the other has been to keep longhouses but modernize them in terms of both design and materials. In

Sarawak, the government has left the decision of keeping longhouses to the villages concerned and, in some instances, has provided assistance for repairing or renovating them—and Dayak political leaders with longhouse backgrounds generally extol their virtues.

By contrast, in Kalimantan (Indonesian Borneo), most longhouses were broken up as a result of government efforts during the Suharto era. Such efforts were part of broader campaign to modernize the peoples that the administration defined as backward and isolated. In the case of multifamily longhouses, the government objected on the principle that longhouses were dirty and prone to destruction by fire. Sometimes, missionaries also supported the dismantling of longhouses to promote conversion to Christianity (and therefore to spread a politically correct form of religion) or to separate the converted or the insufficiently converted from the pagans and their communal festivals. The staunchly anticommunist government objected to longhouses because they seemed to be communistic.

Not all Dayaks in the interior of Kalimantan acceded to government efforts to have them tear down their longhouses. Some longhouses survived throughout the interior, especially in the more remote areas where government authority appears to have been weaker, and among groups that were less inclined to accept it. The upper Kapuas River and its tributaries in West Kalimantan was one such region. Here, many Iban and Taman still kept longhouses into the late 1990s at least. The Iban in particular have a long history of what colonial governments regarded as troublemaking rebelliousness. These Taman and Iban are also situated near the border with Sarawak, from whence some Iban had come in the first place. Here, they trade and are well aware that people are free to keep their longhouse if they so wish.

Tourism also complicated the elimination of longhouses in Indonesia. The effort to get rid of longhouses in Kalimantan was under way at the same time that the architectural theme park Taman Mini Indonesia (Beautiful Indonesia in Miniature) was being planned and developed outside of Jakarta. The Disneyland-inspired architectural park was intended to display the beautiful, diverse, traditional houses built by the various indigenous peoples of the Indonesia Archipelago. Not all types of houses could be shown, since there were far too many different ones. Rather, one house type or a composite of several was chosen to represent each of Indonesia's provinces. In any case, the four provinces of Kalimantan were represented by the same longhouses that were regarded as unacceptable dwellings for their own inhabitants back home. Taman Mini became a great hit with both Indonesian visitors and foreign tourists. And this, plus the success of longhouse tourism in Sarawak, seems to have brought awareness that at least some longhouses should be preserved, if not necessarily with people living in them. In addition to those of the upper Kapuas and elsewhere that have remained as lived-in domiciles for villagers or parts of villages, some old longhouses have been kept preserved as empty relics. Other longhouses have been built as tourist attractions in the interior or as civic centers in cities including Pontianak in West Kalimantan.

DEVELOPMENT AND MOBILITY

If we leave aside the massive dislocations brought by the wars in Vietnam, Laos, and Cambodia, we can still say that the peoples of Southeast Asia are probably more mobile than ever before. Some of this mobility is still the consequence of ethnic conflict and political oppression—for example, the Karen and other ethnic minorities who have fled from Burma to Thailand, many to live permanently (it would now appear) in refugee camps strung along the border.

However, much of the mobility is linked to development as discussed throughout this chapter. And as with other dimensions of development, increased mobility has both positive and negative dimensions. Products grown or created in villages bring cash income for the inhabitants (which they certainly now desire and need). As with access to employment in towns and cities, opportunities for modern education and medical care are also things that rural peoples throughout Southeast Asia now value, and beyond an elementary education, these opportunities usually require movement to towns or cities. The United Nations regards personal mobility based on free choice as a positive factor in development; and the right to travel an important human freedom—taken for granted by most westerners but much more problematic for many people in the developing world.

Conversely, greater mobility is also linked to increased exposure to HIV/ AIDS and other infectious diseases; to increased prostitution in Bangkok and other Southeast Asian cities; to the spread of methamphetamines; and to the human trafficking of women and children. Mobility is also a force for acculturation (or deculturation), and the loss of culture or customs is widely regarded by Southeast Asian peoples as unfortunate. The desire for modern national-style houses, clothing, electronic appliances, motorcycles, automobiles, and pickup trucks are all very important in this respect. The recent (spring 2010) political conflict in Thailand has been attributed to the dissatisfaction of rural dwellers at being left economically behind in the development of the country. For better or worse, posttraditional mobility has probably been much more extensive among the lowland than highland peoples. For a number of decades, so many peoples have been working outside of villages (or leaving them permanently) that they may no longer be considered peasant societies. But while somewhat more recent, posttraditional mobility is now pervasive among the highland and interior peoples as well.

Increased mobility also means people coming into villages from the outside. The effects of tourism and missionaries have already been discussed. Government authorities, police and military patrols, and development workers now make their rounds. Traders are also more common. In some regions, such as the highlands of northern mainland Southeast Asia, traders have always come. But as dirt roads and motorcycle tracks have been extended to previously remote villages, and as cash crops have become more important, their numbers have grown. In the White Tai village of Bouammi in northeastern Laos, where we stayed for a few days early in 2010, a young couple from China arrived on a motorbike. They were regulars who were buying human hair, and they were well received. Selling their hair, along with weaving Lao sarongs, was one of the few ways young women could earn money without leaving the village.

Notes

1. INTRODUCTION

1. A more complicated but accurate designation of Southeast Asia that takes account of both countries and the distribution of ethnic groups and languages would be something like this: the countries noted above minus Indonesian New Guinea (Irian Barat), plus parts of south and southwestern China and the highland areas of eastern India and Bangladesh.

2. As followed, for example, in Tania Li's (1999) edited book on highland Indonesia.

3. Hildred Geertz (1963), for example, organizes her overview of Indonesian peoples in these terms.

4. Except for the Papuan speakers of New Guinea and the indigenous peoples of Australia, if the latter are included in Oceania.

5. See King and Wilder (2004) for a detailed study of the history of anthropology in Southeast Asia.

6. Ethnological compendiums have continued to be produced in recent years for certain countries, though not by professional anthropologists (probably in part because doing so requires assumptions of ethnological realism most anthropologists are now unwilling to accept). These works, by the French development specialist Laurent Chazée (2002) and others, are published by several presses in Thailand, especially White Lotus, a major publisher of reprints and new works on Thailand and northern mainland Southeast Asia. Some of these volumes are extensively illustrated with color photos of houses, villages, and people.

2. PREHISTORY AND LANGUAGES

1. Mon-Khmer is the language family of the Khmer or ethnic Cambodians, as well as of the lowland Mons and various tribal or highland-interior peoples of Cambodia, Laos, Thailand, and Vietnam.

2. Turmeric is a root in the ginger family that is also used as a spice, but it may have originally appealed because of its color as much as its flavor.

3. Some scholars classify Hmong-Mien as a Sino-Tibetan group.

3. EARLY STATES, CIVILIZATION, AND COLONIALISM

1. Given the importance of trade and the technical and cultural richness of Chinese civilization—systems of water control, scripts, religion, philosophy, forms of government, art, and architecture—there is no obvious answer to why Chinese influence did not develop in Southeast Asia outside of Vietnam as did Indic civilization.

2. In his recent book *The Art of Not Being Governed: An Anarchist History of Upland Southeast Asia*, James Scott provides a lengthy treatment of the long-standing situation in the northern mainland that would fit as well with that in the insular regions where coastal states and interior tribal peoples existed in some proximity as well.

3. A former colonial official and historian who studied with the social anthropologist Raymond Firth at the London School of Economics, Gullick described and analyzed the traditional Malay states from an anthropological perspective. His particular focus was on the states of west coast Malaya, but he included some consideration of others in the peninsula as well. His interpretation appears to also fit the Malay states of east coast Sumatra. It has been criticized for being functionalist, and it was insofar as he questioned how the different and incompatible interests of the rulers of the states and their chiefs of the districts were reconciled, at least to the extent that the states did not break apart. However, he does not deemphasize conflict, which is one of the main charges aimed at functionalism. In this regard, dismissing Gullick as a typical functionalist seems a bit wide of the mark. He also emphasized symbolism and meaning, though not to the extent of saying that nothing else mattered as some Southeast-Asianist scholars had come to do by the 1980s.

4. For an anthropological overview and the basis of what follows in this section, see Burling (1965, 121–31); for historical details, see Leonard Andaya (1992) and Barbara Andaya (1992).

5. The theme of sexual relations between white men and native women is central to British colonial fiction, for example, stories by W. S. Maugham ([1923] 1985) and *Burmese Days* by George Orwell ([1934] 1962). The general theme of such stories is that a lonely colonial white man serving in some remote outpost of empire takes a native woman as a mistress and fathers several children with her. Eventually, his white wife or sweetheart discovers what has been going on, and social disaster ensues—the hero in *Burmese Days*, for example, is driven to suicide.

6. The colonial economies of Southeast Asia have also been referred to as dualistic. This meant that they consisted of a large-scale, European-dominated, export-

oriented sector and a small-scale subsistence sector in the hands of the native population (Boeke 1953). Political rhetoric aside, this was an oversimplification. Between the native masses and the colonial elites there were middle economic groups. However, as in the case of the police and military, these consisted typically of nonnatives, specifically Chinese but also in some instances Indians and Arabs. In contrast to the immigrant "middle-man" merchant populations who could rise through business success, little upward mobility was possible within the native populations. In some regions of Southeast Asia, differences in economic status did develop within native communities, but these involved development of landlords and tenants based upon the sharecropping of rice.

7. The Philippines gained independence from the United States in 1946; followed by Burma, from Great Britain in 1948; Indonesia, from the Netherlands in 1949; Cambodia, from France in 1953; and Vietnam and Laos, also from France, in 1954, following a protracted war in Vietnam. After granting independence to Burma at an early point, the British released their other Southeast Asian colonies somewhat later—Malaya, in 1957; and Singapore and the northern Borneo states of Sarawak and Sabah, in 1963. After this, only several fragments remained. The oil-rich Malay kingdom of Brunei, also in northern Borneo, continued as a British protectorate until 1984; and East Timor, a Portuguese colony until 1975, when it was invaded and taken by Indonesia.

8. For a short version of these developments, see Burling (1965, 147–59); for a longer one, Stockwell (1992, 329–85).

4. ETHNIC COMPLEXITY IN MODERN SOUTHEAST ASIA

1. Both the Indians and the Chinese in Southeast Asia are still commonly referred to as "overseas" communities (as in Overseas Indians and Overseas Chinese) to distinguish them from the inhabitants of their home countries. It is interesting that this notion has not been applied to Europeans living in the Southeast Asia countries or who became settler colonists in North and South America, Australia, and elsewhere—none of these are ever said to be Overseas English, Irish, Germans, or Italians, and so forth. Also, it does not seem to matter how long a community has been established. The implication is that, while European (and other) immigrant populations to the United States, Australia, South Africa, and elsewhere become Americans, Australians, and South Africans, the Overseas Chinese and Indians continue to remain distinct ethnic groups over the generations—something that has occurred in some Southeast Asian countries but not others. But while it might seem to be a form of stigma, the term "Overseas" continues to be used in both scholarly and official discourse in the home countries. This is presumably in part because immigrants from China have long been successful in overseas business developments, while Indians in the United States and other Western countries have recently played a major role as engineers and developers in high-tech industries.

2. On the Indian communities in Malaysia and elsewhere in Southeast Asia, see Sandhu and Mani (1993).

3. There are far fewer Chinese in the east coast Malay states because the colonial economy did not need or therefore attract them—there were no tin mines and few rubber plantation or logging operations. Malay Reserves that restricted landownership to Malays were created in some areas such as the Kelantan Plain. Nonetheless, the same pattern of Chinese establishing themselves in rural areas as well as towns took place. In Kelantan, a subethnic distinction is recognized by everyone between the Chinese who came earlier and established trading and farming villages along the Kelantan River and those who came later and went into shopkeeping in the towns.

4. Squatting in Malaysia, especially in and around urban areas on the west coast by Malays, Chinese, and Indians has been widely tolerated and even supported by the government for a mixture of humanitarian, practical, and political reasons (and in fact it is an alternative to homelessness as found in the United States).

5. HUNTER-GATHERERS, REAL AND IMAGINED

1. Sellato (1994, 164–65) argues for the late arrival of such iron-based tools and weapons in the interior of Borneo—at most only a few centuries old and less in the more remote areas.

2. The original meaning of the term "Punan" itself was probably something like nomad or wanderer in the forest. All such terms were exonyms, that is, names for groups or types of people originally used by outsiders, rather than by the people of the group themselves (although they often eventually accept the term for themselves).

3. Here "Punan" is the equivalent of "Dayak," which is also used both for particular groups of swidden-cultivating, usually longhouse-dwelling, native groups, and as a term for all such groups. Since the problem with which we are dealing concerns equally all of the various hunting and gathering groups of Borneo, no matter what they are called, the use of the term Punan in the generic sense will do for our purposes as well—although I shall also refer to the Penan of Sarawak.

4. The full name is therefore a bit of a puzzle: if the Phi Tong Luang were spirits, why would they need or want to move out just because the leaves of their houses had dried up and changed color? Certainly, Thai peoples suppose that spirits like to live in houses. They themselves continue to build great numbers of houses for spirits, but unlike those of the Phi Tong Luang these are more on the scale of doll houses and much too small for people.

5. There are also "Mrabri" in Laos (Chazée 2001) that usually identify themselves as Yumbri.

6. The other concerned the Yanomami of South America.

7. See especially Brosius (2007; though he stresses differences between the western and eastern Penan) and Kaskija (2007).

6. SWIDDEN FARMERS

1. On shifting cultivation in Southeast Asia, see also Spencer (1966) and Conklin (1963).

2. In his account of the Iban, Derek Freeman ([1955] 1970, 73) uses the term tribe as a subethnic label to refer to the Iban of, or from, a particular river—for example, the Ulu Ai Iban from the Batang Ai who migrated to the Baleh River. These various river groups, which were more or less endogamous, formed a "loose tribal organization." States of feud involving headhunting frequently existed between these different river groups.

3. For an overview, see Victor King's (1993) *Peoples of Borneo*.

4. Discussed in my (2004a) *Architecture of Life and Death in Borneo*.

5. Because of their importance as the largest ethnic group in Sarawak, their historical importance in the founding and development of the country under the Brooke regime, and in part the quality and provocative nature of Freeman's accounts, the Iban have continued to attract a great deal of scholarly attention. We now have more recent ethnographic accounts that update Freeman's findings and cover new regions (Sutlive 1978). There are books on many more special topics including Iban shamanism and religion (Jensen 1974), Iban weaving, and Iban history under colonial rule (Pringle 1970). Much has by now been written about many specific topics including—but not only—Iban ethnobotany, material culture, and language. The Sarawak Museum in Kuching has a large collection of Iban and other Dayak materials including an extensive archive of photos and videotapes. The state government–run Council on Customary Law of Sarawak collects and publishes the customary law of the Iban and other indigenous groups. There is now also an Iban foundation (the Tun Jugah Foundation) that supports research and scholarship on Iban topics and has recently published a volume on Iban shamanism (Sather 2001) and a four-volume encyclopedia of the Iban (Sutlive and Sutlive 2001).

8. INDIGENOUS RELIGION

1. An example is the well-known book by Stanley Tambiah *Buddhism and the Spirit Cults of Northeast Thailand* (1970).

2. Here the active and regular veneration of family ancestor spirits is linked to unilineal descent as well as some specific marriage-residence rule. This usually means patrilineal descent and virilocal residence (with the family of the groom). But unlike the Vietnamese, a great many of the peoples in Southeast Asia neither reckon descent mainly or exclusively through the male line nor perpetuate male-oriented families through patrilocal residence.

3. Attagara (1968, 118) writes that

> sometimes the body is not cremated right away. For example, in the case of unnatural death the body has to be buried for a certain period of time before it can be cremated. For this type of death, the body has to be taken out of the house as soon as possible; otherwise the *phi ruan* [house spirits] might be offended. After the religious rite is performed in the temple, the body is then buried. If the relatives wish to have a cremation soon after, they can have a quick burial rite by placing the casket in a shallow grave and putting three lumps of earth over it. After that is done the body may be dug up for cremation.

4. The complete two-stage mortuary tradition in Southeast Asia is described below:

1. An initial funeral is performed, and the remains are disposed of, either by burial or placement in some aboveground receptacle or tomb.
2. The remains stay where they have been placed until only (or mainly only) the skeleton is left, or until resources for holding the final ceremony have been accumulated and the often lavish preparations completed.
3. The skeletal remains are then recovered, cleaned, and reburied or placed in a new container for permanent storage, or cremated.
4. The second phase of the funeral involving the recovery and reprocessing of the remains is typically larger than the initial one and often has an air of celebration and festivity lacking at the first. (Winzeler 2008a, 164)

5. His concern is only with Vietnamese practices rather than with broader comparisons. If he is aware of two-stage customs elsewhere, he does not mention them in his discussion, which is mainly concerned with the political context of religious activity. Among other things, however, the Vietnamese practice suggests again the likely antiquity of two-stage mortuary processes in Southeast Asia.

6. The Vietnamese scholars Nguyen Van Ku and Luu Hung (2002) have published a volume of photos of the ceremonies, the tombs and the statues that include a description of the mortuary sequence, and the beliefs involved.

7. This is the sort of explanation that Melford Spiro (1967, 194–95) gives of spirit possession and spirit mediumship among the Burmese in his account on Burmese supernaturalism:

> Within the Burmese framework, the exorcist is a religious practitioner, expelling harmful supernaturals from the bodies of their victims through the assistance of benevolent supernaturals. If, following the exorcism, the victim returns to his normal behavior, it is assumed that the ceremony has been a success, i.e., the harmful supernaturals have been expelled.
>
> . . . From the naturalistic point of view . . . the alleged victim of supernatural possession is mentally ill, suffering from psychological dissociation; the exorcist is a psychotherapist; and the exorcistic séance is a form of psychotherapy. Although modern therapists may be offended by this designation of Burmese exorcism, the exorcistic séance described in this chapter certainly satisfies the minimum definition of "psychotherapy" proposed by some psychiatrists.

8. Tambiah (1970, 331–33) states that the Thais in northeastern Thailand believe in and fear witchcraft, but he does not discuss specific instances. Gregory Forth (1998) reports that the Nage of Flores in eastern Indonesia have well-developed witchcraft beliefs and practices and discusses these at some length. For an overview of the anthropology of witchcraft (though concerning mainly Africa), see Lucy Mair's (1969) book.

9. Also, witch crazes are not mentioned in the volume edited by C. W. Watson and Roy Ellen (1993) on witchcraft and sorcery in Southeast Asia.

9. RELIGION, SOCIETY, AND THE STATE

1. Examples include those described at length by Stanley Tambiah (1984) as being of great importance for the modern Thai.

2. The main departure from the common anti-Geertz two-part view of Javanese religion has been Mark Woodward's (1989) assertion that the division is simply between two versions of Islam in Java. This could be taken to mean only that most Javanese identify themselves as Muslims, some as devout and some as syncretist and nominal. Woodward, however, deemphasizes the Hindu-Buddhist basis of Javanese mysticism and claims it is derived more from Islamic mysticism. He also asserts that the Javanese peasant animist and magical beliefs and practices are not all that different from those of other traditional Southeast Asia ones. When all the studies and their conclusions are taken together, we seem to mainly learn that more research in more places does not necessarily produce more certainty or more clarity. Or similarly put, we have the markings of a good contest of "will the real Javanese Muslim please stand up," in which case one, two, or three contestants might arise.

3. A series of scholars have recently discussed policy developments regarding religion in Vietnam, including Jellema (2007); Malarney (2002); Salemink (1997); Taylor (2007); Thien (2007); and Wells-Dang (2007).

10. RELIGIOUS CONVERSION ON THE ETHNIC MARGINS

1. Ethnographic accounts of religious conversion (especially to Christianity) and its consequences have become common. In addition to those discussed or cited in this chapter, they include the following: Aragon 2000; Hefner 1993; Hoskins 1987; and Keane 2007.

11. TOURISM AND LOCAL PEOPLES

1. Anthropological studies of tourism among the Toraja include Toby Volkman's (1987) work and a book by Kathleen Adams (2006) based upon long-term research. Anthropologists and other researchers have also made some effort to study tourists, that is, their reactions to their experiences and their interaction with local people (e.g., Edward Bruner [2005]).

12. DEVELOPMENT FOR BETTER OR WORSE

1. The anti-Madurese attacks by Dayaks in Kalbar drew a rather sensationalistic reaction from the Indonesian and international press, partly because, in some instances, the Dayaks had beheaded those they killed. This played into the broader Indonesian view of Kalimantan as a dark land of savages who still followed blood-thirsty pagan practices. There were gruesome photos of heads lying beside bodies or put on stakes with signs telling Madurese to get out. But gruesome though they may have been, the beheadings were more akin to modern terrorism than traditional headhunting practices in Borneo. The latter always involved taking the severed heads home, putting them through elaborate rituals of celebration to incorporate their spirits into the local community, and then hanging the skulls up in the longhouse

or men's house. Not taking the heads would be something like robbing a bank and not taking the money.

2. For example, see Ironside (2008) on the effects of development on the indigenous minorities in Cambodia.

3. In the 1970s, in Kelantan, Malaysia, the Malays divided houses into two general types: *rumah kayu* and *rumah batu*. *Rumah kayu* are houses made of wood, though not in any particular style. *Rumah batu* (which literally means stone house) were made of cement, cinderblock, brick, and stucco. (This twofold classification left out the many poor rural houses built mainly of bamboo and thatch.) The *rumah batu* houses were built in a more modern style, cost more, and were more highly valued. Building one was regarded as a sign of upward mobility. Here, as elsewhere in Malaya, the trend to such stone houses was probably a colonial innovation introduced by the British.

4. There are exceptions. Traditional longhouses in Borneo, which require the use of large amounts of timber, may be more costly to build that newer-style ones made of cement block and other manufactured materials, or the traditional materials may not be available at all if the local forest is gone.

5. There was an ideological objection to longhouses in both countries—and here there is an ironic conversion from opposite ends of the political spectrum. While the Suharto regime in Indonesia disliked longhouses because they seemed communistic, the communist regime in Vietnam objected to the longhouses of the central highlands and made some effort to break them up because they believed they inhibited the progress of socialism (McElwee 2004, 197, 201, 208; Winzeler 2004a, 141)

References and Suggested Reading

Abadie, Maurice. [1924] 2001. *Minorities of the Sino-Vietnamese borderland: With special reference to Thai tribes*. Bangkok, Thailand: White Lotus Press.

Adams, Kathleen M. 2006. *Art as politics: Re-crafting identities, tourism and power in Tana Toraja, Indonesia*. Honolulu: University of Hawai'i Press.

Andaya, Barbara Watson. 1992. Political development between the sixteenth and eighteenth centuries. In *The Cambridge history of Southeast Asia. Volume 1: From early times to c. 1800*, ed. Nicholas Tarling, 402–59. Cambridge: Cambridge University Press.

Andaya, Leonard Y. 1992. Interactions with the outside world and adaptation in Southeast Asian society. In *The Cambridge history of Southeast Asia. Volume 1: From early times to c. 1800*, ed. Nicholas Tarling, 345–401. Cambridge: Cambridge University Press.

Aragon, Lorainne V. 2000. *Fields of the lord: Animism, Christian minorities and state development in Indonesia*. Honolulu: University of Hawai'i Press.

Arasaratnam, Sinnappah. 1979. *Indians in Malaya and Singapore*. Rev. ed. Kuala Lumpur, Malaysia: Oxford University Press.

Atkinson, Jane Monnig. 1987. Religions in dialogue: The construction of an Indonesian minority religion. In *Indonesian religions in transition*, ed. Rita Smith Kipp and Susan Rodgers, 171–86. Tucson: University of Arizona Press.

———. 1989. *The art and politics of Wana Shamanism*. Berkeley: University of California Press.

Attagara, Kingkeo. 1968. *The folk religion of Ban Nai: A hamlet in central Thailand*. Bangkok, Thailand: Kurusapha Press.

Avé, Jan, and Victor King. 1986. *Borneo: The people of the weeping forest, tradition and change in Borneo*. Leiden, Holland: National Museum of Ethnology.

Baird, Ian G. 2008. Spaces of resistance: The ethnic Brao people and the international border between Laos and Cambodia. In *Living on the margins: Minorities and borderlines in Cambodia and Southeast Asia: Siem Reap, Cambodia, March 14–15,*

2008, ed. Peter J. Hammer, 19–44. Phnom Penh, Cambodia: Center for Khmer Studies.

Baird, Ian G., and Bruce Shoemaker. 2005. *Aiding or abetting: Internal resettlement and international aid agencies in the Lao PDR.* Toronto: Probe International.

Ballhatchet, Kenneth. 1980. *Race, sex and class under the raj: Imperial attitudes and policies and their critics, 1793–1905.* New York: St. Martin's Press.

Bateson, Gregory, and Margaret Mead. 1942. *Balinese character: A photographic analysis.* New York: New York Academy of Sciences.

Beatty, Andrew. 1992. *Society and exchange in Nias.* Oxford, UK: Clarendon Press.

———. 1999. *Varieties of Javanese religion: An anthropological account.* Cambridge: Cambridge University Press.

Bellwood, Peter, 1997. *Prehistory of the Indo-Malaysian archipelago.* Rev. ed. Honolulu: University of Hawaii Press.

———. 2004. The origins and dispersals of agricultural communities in Southeast Asia. In *Southeast Asia from prehistory to history*, ed. Ian Glover and Peter Bellwood, 21–40. London: RoutledgeCurzon.

———. 2005. *First farmers: The origins of agricultural societies.* Oxford, UK: Blackwell.

Bellwood, Peter, James J. Fox, and Darrell Tryon, eds. 1995. *The Austronesians: Historical and contemporary perspectives.* Comparative Austronesian Project. Canberra: Australian National University.

Bellwood, Peter, and Ian Glover, eds. 2004. *Southeast Asia from prehistory to history.* London: RoutledgeCurzon.

Benjamin, Geoffrey. 1979. Indigenous religious systems of the Malay Peninsula. In *The imagination of reality: Essays in Southeast Asian coherence systems*, ed. A. L. Becker and Aram A. Yengoyan, 9–27. Norwood, N.J.: Ablex.

Benjamin, Geoffrey, and Cynthia Chou, eds. 2002. *Tribal communities in the Malay world: Historical, social and cultural perspectives.* Leiden, Holland: International Institute for Asian Studies.

Bernatzik, Hugo Adolf. [1938] 1951. *The spirits of the yellow leaves.* London: Robert Hale Limited.

Berreman, Gerald. 1992. The Tasaday: Stone age survivors or space age fakes? In *The Tasaday controversy: Assessing the evidence*, ed. Thomas N. Headland, 21–39. Special Publication 28. Washington, D.C.: American Anthropological Association.

Bevis, William W. 1995. *Borneo log: The struggle for Sarawak's forests.* Seattle: University of Washington Press.

Blust, R. 1976. Austronesian culture history: Some linguistic inferences and their relations to the archaeological record. *World Archaeology* 8:19–43.

Boeke, J. H. 1953. *Economics and economic policy of dual societies, as exemplified by Indonesia.* New York: International Secretariat, Institute of Pacific Studies.

Boon, James A. 1977. *The anthropological romance of Bali 1597–1972: Dynamic perspectives in marriage, caste, politics and religion.* Cambridge: Cambridge University Press.

Bourdier, Frédéric, 2001. *Development and dominion: Indigenous peoples of Cambodia, Vietnam and Laos.* Bangkok, Thailand: White Lotus Press.

———. 2006. *The mountain of precious stones: Essays in social anthropology.* Siem Reap, Cambodia: Center for Khmer Studies.

Brosius, J. Peter. 2007. Prior transcripts, divergent paths: Resistance and acquiescence to logging in Sarawak, East Malaysia. In *Beyond the green myth: Hunter-gath-*

erers of Borneo in the twenty-first century, ed. Peter B. Sercombe and Bernard Sellato, 289–333. Copenhagen, Denmark: Nordic Institute of Asian Studies.

Brown, Lester R. 1970. *Seeds of change: The green revolution and development in the 1970s*. New York: Praeger.

Brown, P., T. Sutikna, M. J. Morwood, R. P. Soejono, Jatmiko, E. Wayhu Saptomo, and Rokus Awe Due. 2004. A new small-bodied hominin from the Late Pleistocene of Flores, Indonesia. *Nature* 431 (7012): 1055–61.

Bruner, Edward. 2005. *Culture on tour: Ethnographies of travel*. Chicago: University of Chicago Press.

Bunnag, Jane. *Buddhist monk, Buddhist layman: A study of monastic organization in central Thailand*. Cambridge: Cambridge University Press.

Burling, Robbins. 1965. *Hill farms and padi fields: Life in mainland Southeast Asia*. Englewood Cliffs, N.J.: Prentice Hall.

———. 1967. Tribesmen and lowlanders in Assam. In *Southeast Asian tribes, minorities, and nations*, vol. 1, ed. Peter Kunstadter, 215–29. Princeton, N.J.: Princeton University Press.

Burns, Peter M. 1999. *An introduction to anthropology and tourism*. London: Routledge.

Cady, John F. 1964. *Southeast Asia: Its historical development*. New York: McGraw-Hill.

Carey, Iskandar. 1976. *Orang Asli: The aboriginal tribes of peninsular Malaysia*. Kuala Lumpur, Malaysia: Oxford University Press.

Chambert-Loir, Henri, and Anthony Reid, eds. 2002. *The potent dead: Ancestors, saints and heroes in contemporary Indonesia*. Honolulu: University of Hawai'i Press.

Chazée, Laurent. 2001. *The Mrabri in Laos: A world under the canopy*. Bangkok, Thailand: White Lotus Press.

———. 2002. *The peoples of Laos: Rural and ethnic diversities*. Bangkok, Thailand: White Lotus Press.

Chinyong, Joseph Liow, and Nadirsyah Hosen, eds. 2010. *Islam in Southeast Asia*. 4 vols. London: Routledge.

Chouvey, Pierre-Arnaud. 2010. *Opium: Uncovering the politics of the poppy*. Cambridge, Mass.: Harvard University Press.

Christie, Clive. 1996. *A modern history of Southeast Asia: Decolonization, nationalism and separatism*. London: I. B. Tauris.

Clutton-Brock, Juliet. 1999. *A natural history of domesticated mammals*. Cambridge: Cambridge University Press.

Cohen, Erik. 2001. *Thai tourism: Hill tribes, islands and open-ended prostitution*. Studies in Contemporary Thailand 4. Bangkok, Thailand: White Lotus Press.

Condominas, Georges. [1957] 1994. *We have eaten the forest: The story of a Montagnard village in the central highlands of Vietnam*. New York: Kodansha International.

Conklin, Harold C. [1957] 1975. *Hanunoo agriculture: A report on an integral system of shifting cultivation in the Philippines*. Northford, Conn.: Elliot's Books.

———. 1963. *The study of shifting cultivation*. London: Routledge and Kegan Paul.

Connell, J., and B. Rugendyke. 2008. *Tourism at the grassroots: Villagers and visitors in the Asia Pacific*. London: Routledge.

Connolly, Jennifer. 2003. *Becoming Christian and Dayak: A study of Christian conversion among Dayaks in East Kalimantan, Indonesia*. PhD diss., New School University, Ann Arbor, Mich., UMI Dissertation Services.

Cooper, Robert. 1984. *Resource scarcity and the Hmong response*. Singapore: Singapore University Press.

Covarrubias, Miguel. 1937. *Island of Bali*. New York: Knopf.

Crawfurd, John. [1820] 1967. *The history of the Indian archipelago: Containing an account of the manners, arts, languages, religions, institutions, and commerce of its inhabitants*. 3 vols. London: Frank Cass.

DeBernardi, Jean. 2006. *Chinese popular religion and spirit mediums in Penang, Malaysia*. Stanford, Calif.: Stanford University Press.

Dentan, Robert K. 2000. The Semai of Malaysia. In *Endangered peoples of Southeast and East Asia: Struggles to survive and thrive*, ed. Leslie E. Sponsel, 209–32. Westport, Conn.: Greenwood Press.

Dentan, Robert Knox, Kirk Endicott, Alberto Gomes, and M. B. Hooker. 1997. *Malaysia and the Orang Asli: A study of the impact of development on indigenous peoples*. Boston: Allyn and Bacon.

Dove, Michael R. 1985. *Swidden agriculture in Indonesia: The subsistence agriculture of the Kalimantan Kantu'*. Berlin: Mouton.

Du Bois, Cora. [1944] 1960. *The people of Alor: A socio-psychological study of an East Indian Island*. Cambridge, Mass.: Harvard University Press.

Duncan, Christopher. 2002. Resettlement and natural resources in Halamahera, Indonesia. In *Conservation and mobile indigenous peoples: Displacement, forced resettlement and sustainable development*, ed. Dawn Chatty and Marcus Colchester, 247–361. New York: Berghahn Books.

———. 2004a. From development to empowerment: Changing Indonesian government policies toward indigenous minorities. In *Civilizing the margins: Southeast Asian government policies for the development of minorities*, ed. Christopher Duncan, 86–115. Ithaca, N.Y.: Cornell University Press.

———, ed. 2004b. *Civilizing the margins: Southeast Asian government policies for the development of minorities*. Ithaca, N.Y.: Cornell University Press.

Eder, James F. 1987. *On the road to tribal extinction: Depopulation, deculturation, and adaptive well-being among the Batak of the Philippines*. Berkeley: University of California Press.

Elizalde, Manuel, and Robert B. Fox. 1972. *The Tasaday forest people of Mindanao*. Rochester, N.Y.: BEE Cross Media.

Ellen, Roy. 1993. Introduction. In *Understanding witchcraft and sorcery in Southeast Asia*, ed. C. W. Watson and Roy Ellen, 1–26. Honolulu: University of Hawai'i Press.

Endicott, Kirk. 1970. *An analysis of Malay magic*. Oxford, UK: Clarendon Press.

———. 1979. *Batek Negrito religion: The world-view and rituals of a hunting and gathering people of peninsular Malaysia*. Oxford, UK: Clarendon Press.

———. 1983. The effects of slave raiding on the aborigines of the Malay Peninsula. In *Slavery, bondage and dependency in Southeast Asia*, ed. Anthony Reid, 216–45. New York: St. Martin's Press.

———. 1999. Introduction: Southeast Asia. In *The Cambridge encyclopedia of hunters and gatherers*, ed. R. B. Lee and R. Daley, 275–83. Cambridge: Cambridge University Press.

———. 2000. The Batek of Malaysia. In *Endangered peoples of Southeast and East Asia: Struggles to survive and thrive*, ed. Leslie E. Sponsel, 101–22. Westport, Conn.: Greenwood Press.

Endicott, Kirk, and Robert Knox Dentan. 2004. Into the mainstream or into the backwater: Malaysian assimilation of Orang Asli. In *Civilizing the margins: Southeast Asian government policies for the development of minorities*, ed. Christopher Duncan, 24–55. Ithaca, N.Y.: Cornell University Press.

Evans, Grant. 1990. *Lao peasants under socialism*. New Haven, Conn.: Yale University Press.

———. 1998. *The politics of ritual remembrance: Laos since 1975*. Honolulu: University of Hawai'i Press.

———. 1999. Ethnic change in the northern highlands of Laos. In *Laos: Culture and society*, ed. Grant Evans, 125–47. Chiang Mai, Thailand: Silkworm Books.

Evans, Grant, Christopher Hutton, and Kuah Khun Eng, eds. 2000. *Where China meets Southeast Asia: Social and cultural change in the border regions*. New York: St Martin's Press.

Firth, Raymond. [1946] 1966. *Malay fishermen: Their peasant economy*. London: Routledge and Kegan Paul.

Fisher, Charles A. 1964. *South-East Asia: A social, economic and political geography*. London: Methuen.

Forth, Gregory L. 1998. *Beneath the volcano: Religion, cosmology and spirit classification among the Nage of Eastern Indonesia*. Leiden, Holland: KITLV Press.

Fox, James J. 1973. On bad death and the left hand. In *Right and left: Essays on dual symbolic classification*, ed. Rodney Needham, 342–68. Chicago: University of Chicago Press.

Fraser, Thomas M., Jr. 1960. *Rusembilan: A Malay fishing village in southern Thailand*. Ithaca, N.Y.: Cornell University Press.

Freeman, Derek. [1955] 1970. *Report on the Iban*. London: Athlone.

Furnivall, J. S. [1939] 1967. *Netherlands India: A study of plural economy*. Cambridge: Cambridge University Press.

Geertz, Clifford. 1960. *The religion of Java*. Glencoe, Ill.: Free Press.

———. 1964. Internal conversion in contemporary Bali. In *Malayan and Indonesian studies presented to Sir Richard Winstedt*, ed. J. Bastin and R. Roolvink, 282–302. Oxford, UK: Clarendon Press.

———. 1980. *Negara: The theater state in nineteenth-century Bali*. Princeton, N.J.: Princeton University Press.

Geertz, Hildred. 1963. *Indonesian cultures and communities*. New Haven, Conn.: Human Relations Area Files Press.

Gillogly, Kathleen. 2004. Developing the hill tribes of northern Thailand. In *Civilizing the margins: Southeast Asian government policies for the development of minorities*, ed. Christopher Duncan, 116–49. Ithaca, N.Y.: Cornell University Press.

Glover, Ian, and Peter Bellwood, eds. 2004. *Southeast Asia: From prehistory to history*. London: Routledge/Curzon.

Goddard, Cliff. 2005. *The languages of East and Southeast Asia: An introduction*. Oxford: Oxford University Press.

Goffman, Erving. 1961. *Asylums: Essays on the social situation of mental patients and other inmates*. Garden City, N.J.: Anchor Books.

Goh, Robbie B. H. 2005. *Christianity in Southeast Asia*. Singapore: Institute of Southeast Asian Studies.

Golomb, Louis. 1985. *An anthropology of curing in multiethnic Thailand*. Illinois Studies in Anthropology 15. Urbana: University of Illinois Press.

Gomes, Alberto. 2007. *Modernity and Malaysia: Settling the Menraq forest nomads.* London: Routledge.

Goody, Jack, ed. 1968. *Literacy in traditional societies.* Cambridge: Cambridge University Press.

Gosling, L. A. Peter, and Linda Y. C. Lim, eds. 1983. *The Chinese in Southeast Asia.* 2 vols. Singapore: Maruzen Asia.

Grist, D. H. [1959] 1986. *Rice.* 6th ed. London: Longman.

Gullick, J. M. 1958. *Indigenous political systems of western Malaya.* London School of Economics Monographs of Social Anthropology 17. London: Athlone.

Halpern, Joel M. 1964. *Government, politics and social structure in Laos: A study of tradition and innovation.* New Haven, Conn.: Yale Southeast Asian Studies.

Halpern, Joel, and Peter Kunstadter. 1967. Laos: Introduction. In *Southeast Asian tribes, minorities, and nations,* vol. 1, ed. Peter Kunstadter, 233–58. Princeton, N.J.: Princeton University Press.

Hanks, Jane Richardson, and Lucian M. Hanks. 2001. *Tribes of the north Thailand frontier.* Monograph 51. New Haven, Conn.: Yale Southeast Asian Studies.

Hanks, Lucian M. 1972. *Rice and man: Agricultural ecology in Southeast Asia.* Chicago: Aldine-Atherton.

Hardjono, J. M. 1977. *Transmigration in Indonesia.* Kuala Lumpur, Malaysia: Oxford University Press.

Hayami, Yoko. 1996. Karen tradition according to Christ or Buddha: The implications of multiple reinterpretations for a minority ethnic group in Thailand. *Journal of Southeast Asian Studies* 27 (2): 342–449.

———. 2004. *Between hills and plains: Power and practice in socio-religious dynamics among Karen.* Kyoto, Japan: Kyoto University Press.

Hayami, Yoko, and Susan Darlington. 2000. The Karen of Burma and Thailand. In *Endangered peoples of Southeast and East Asia: Struggles to survive and thrive,* ed. Leslie E. Sponsel, 137–55. Westport, Conn.: Greenwood Press.

Headland, Thomas N., ed. 1992. *The Tasaday controversy: Assessing the evidence.* Special Publication 28. Washington, D.C.: American Anthropological Association.

Hefner, Robert. 1985. *Hindu Javanese: Tenggir tradition and Islam.* Princeton, N.J.: Princeton University Press.

———. 1993. Of faith and commitment: Christian conversion in Muslim Java. In *Conversion to Christianity: Historical and anthropological perspectives on a great transformation,* ed. Robert Hefner, 99–125. Berkeley: University of California Press.

———, ed. 1993. *Conversion to Christianity: Historical and anthropological perspectives on a great transformation.* Berkeley: University of California Press.

Heinz, Carolyn Brown. 2004. Hmong Shamanism (Thailand, Laos). In *Shamanism: An encyclopedia of world beliefs, practices, and culture,* ed. Mariko Namba Walter and Eva Jane Neumann Fridman, 806–10. Santa Barbara, Calif.: ABC–CLIO.

Hertz, Robert. [1907] 1960. *Death and the right hand.* Glencoe, Ill.: Free Press.

Hickey, Gerald Cannon. 1964. *Village in Vietnam.* New Haven, Conn.: Yale University Press.

———. 1993. *Shattered world: Adaptation and survival of Vietnam's highland peoples during the Vietnam War.* Philadelphia: University of Pennsylvania Press.

Hitchcock, M., V. King, and J. M. Parnwell, eds. 2009. *Tourism in Southeast Asia: Challenges and new directions.* Honolulu: University of Hawai'i Press.

Hoffman, Carl. 1986. *The Punan: Hunters and gatherers of Borneo*. Ann Arbor, Mich.: UMI Research Press.

Holt, John Clifford. 2009. *Spirits of the place: Buddhism and Lao religious culture*. Honolulu: University of Hawai'i Press.

Hoskins, Janet. 1987. Entering the bitter house: Spirit worship and conversion in west Sumba. In *Indonesian religions in transition*, ed. Rita Smith Kipp and Susan Rodgers, 136–60. Tucson: University of Arizona Press.

———, ed. 1996. *Headhunting and the social imagination in Southeast Asia*. Stanford, Calif.: Stanford University Press.

Howe, Leo. 1984. Gods, people, spirits and witches. *Bijdragen tot de Taal-, Land en Volkenkunde* 140:193–222.

———. 2001. *Hinduism and hierarchy in Bali*. Oxford, UK: James Currey.

———. 2005. *The changing world of Bali: Religion, society and tourism*. London: Routledge.

Huhua Cao, and Elizabeth Morrell, eds. 2010. *Regional minorities and development in Asia*. London: Routledge.

Ironside, Jeremy. 2008. Development—In whose name? Cambodia's economic development and its indigenous communities—From self reliance to uncertainty. In *Living on the margins: Minorities and borderlines in Cambodia and Southeast Asia: Siem Reap, Cambodia, March 14–15, 2008*, ed. Peter J. Hammer, 91–128. Phnom Penh, Cambodia: Center for Khmer Studies.

Iten, Oswald. 1992, The "Tasaday" and the press. In *The Tasaday controversy: Assessing the evidence*, ed. Thomas N. Headland, 40–58. Special Publication 28. Washington, D.C.: American Anthropological Association.

Izikowitz, Karl Gustav. [1951] 1979. *Lamet: Hill peasants of French Indochina*. New York: AMS Press.

Jain, Ravindra K. 1970. *South Indians on the plantation frontier in Malaya*. New Haven, Conn.: Yale University Press.

Jay, Robert R. 1963. *Religion and politics in rural central Java*. Cultural Report Series 12. New Haven, Conn.: Yale University, Southeast Asian Studies.

———. 1969. *Javanese villagers: Social relations in rural Mojokuto*. Cambridge, Mass.: MIT Press.

Jellema, Kate. 2007. Returning home: Ancestor worship and the nationalism of Doi Moi Vietnam. In *Modernity and re-enchantment: Religion in post-revolutionary Vietnam*, ed. Philip Taylor, 57–89. Singapore: ISEAS.

Jenkins, Peter, and Waveney Jenkins. 2007. *The planter's bungalow: A journey down the Malay Peninsula*. Singapore: Editions Didier Millet.

Jensen, Eric. 1974. *The Iban and their religion*. Oxford, UK: Clarendon Press.

Jonsson, Hjorleifur. 2005. *Mien relations: Mountain people and state control in Thailand*. Ithaca, N.Y.: Cornell University Press.

Kammerer, Cornelia Ann. 1990. Customs and Christian conversion among Akha highlanders of Burma and Thailand. *American Ethnologist* 17 (2): 277–91.

Kaskija, Lars. 2007. Stuck at the bottom: Opportunity structures and Punan Malinau identity. In *Beyond the green myth: Hunter-gatherers of Borneo in the twenty-first century*, ed. Peter B. Sercombe and Bernard Sellato, 135–59. Copenhagen, Denmark: Nordic Institute of Asian Studies.

Keane, Webb. 2007. *Christian moderns: Freedom and fetish in the mission encounter*. Berkeley: University of California Press.

Kedit, Peter M., and Clement L. Sabang. 1992. Tourism report: A re-study of Sekrang longhouse tourism. In *Tourism in Borneo: Issues and perspectives. Papers from the Second Biennial International Conference, Kota Kinabalu, Sabah, Malaysia, July, 1992,* ed. Victor T. King, 45–58. Borneo Research Council proceedings series. Hull, UK: Borneo Research Council.

Kennedy, Raymond. 1945. The colonial crisis and the future. In *The science of man in the world crisis,* ed. Ralph Linton, 306–46. New York: Columbia University Press.

Keyes, Charles F. 1977. *The golden peninsula: Culture and adaptation in mainland Southeast Asia.* New York: Macmillan.

———. 1987. *Thailand: Buddhist kingdom as modern state.* Boulder, Colo.: Westview.

———. 1993. Why the Thai are not Christian: Buddhist and Christian conversion in Thailand. In *Conversion to Christianity: Historical and anthropological perspectives on a great transformation,* ed. Robert Hefner, 259–83. Berkeley: University of California Press.

———. 2006. "The peoples of Asia": Science and politics in the classification of ethnic groups in Thailand, China and Thailand. In *On the margins of Asia: Diversity in Asian states,* ed. Charles Keyes, 89–132. Ann Arbor, Mich.: Association for Asian Studies.

Kiernan, Ben. 1996. *The Pol Pot regime: Race, power, and genocide in Cambodia under the Khmer Rouge, 1975–79.* New Haven, Conn.: Yale University Press.

Kiernan, Ben, and Chanthou Boua, eds. 1982. *Peasants and politics in Kampuchea, 1942–1981.* London: Zed Press.

King, Victor T. 1993. *The peoples of Borneo.* Oxford, UK: Blackwell.

———. 2009. *The sociology of Southeast Asia: Transformations in a developing region.* Honolulu: University of Hawai'i Press.

King, Victor T., and William D. Wilder. 2004. *The modern anthropology of Southeast Asia: An introduction.* London: Routledge Kurzon.

Kipp, Rita Smith, and Susan Rodgers, eds. 1987a. *Indonesian religions in transition.* Tucson: University of Arizona Press.

———. 1987b. Introduction: Indonesian religions in society. In *Indonesian religions in transition,* ed. Rita Smith Kipp and Susan Rodgers, 1–31. Tucson: University of Arizona Press.

Koentjaraningrat, R. M. 1975. *Introduction to the peoples and cultures of Indonesia and Malaysia.* Menlo Park, Calif.: Cummings Publishing.

Kroeber, A. L. 1919. *Peoples of the Philippines.* New York: American Museum of Natural History.

Kruse, William. 1998. Tourism, cultural change and the architecture of Iban longhouses in Sarawak. In *Indigenous architecture in Borneo: Traditional patterns and new developments,* ed. Robert L. Winzeler, 138–69. Borneo Research Council proceedings series 5. Phillips, Me.: Borneo Research Council.

Kunstadter, Peter, ed. 1967. *Southeast Asian tribes, minorities, and nations.* 2 vols. Princeton, N.J.: Princeton University Press.

Kwon, Heonik. 2006. *After the massacre: Commemoration and consolation in Ha My and My Lai.* Berkeley: University of California Press.

Laderman, Carol. 1983. *Wives and midwives: Childbirth and nutrition in rural Malaysia.* Berkeley: University of California Press.

Lambrecht, Curtis W. 2004. Oxymoronic development: The military as benefactor in the border regions of Burma. In *Civilizing the margins: Southeast Asian govern-*

ment policies for the development of minorities, ed. Christopher Duncan, 150–81. Ithaca, N.Y.: Cornell University Press.

Landon, Kenneth P. 1949. *Southeast Asia: Crossroad of religions.* Chicago: University of Chicago Press.

Laungaramsri, Pinkaew. 2001. *Redefining nature: Karen ecological knowledge and the challenge to the modern conservation paradigm.* Chennai, Thailand: Earthworm Books.

Leach, E. R. 1950. *Social science research in Sarawak: A report on the possibilities of a social-economic survey of Sarawak to the Colonial Research Council.* London: His Majesty's Stationery Office for the Colonial Office.

———. 1954. *Political systems of highland Burma: A study of Kachin social structure.* Cambridge, Mass.: Harvard University Press.

Lebar, Frank M., ed. and comp. 1972. *Ethnic groups of insular Southeast Asia. Volume 1: Indonesia, Andaman Islands, and Madagascar.* New Haven, Conn.: Human Relations Area Files.

———. 1975. *Ethnic groups of insular Southeast Asia. Volume 2: Philippines and Formosa.* New Haven, Conn.: Human Relations Area Files.

Lebar, Frank M., Gerald C. Hickey, and John K. Musgrave. 1964. *Ethnic groups of mainland Southeast Asia.* New Haven, Conn.: Human Relations Area Files.

Lee, Richard. 1992. Making sense of the Tasaday: Three discourses. In *The Tasaday controversy: Assessing the evidence*, ed. Thomas N. Headland, 167–71. Special Publication 28. Washington, D.C.: American Anthropological Association.

Lehman, F. K. 1963. *The structure of Chin society: A tribal people of Burma adapted to a non-Western civilization.* Urbana: University of Illinois Press.

Lewis, I. M. [1971] 1989. *Ecstatic religion: A study of shamanism and spirit possession.* London: Routledge.

Li, Tania. 1999. *Transforming the Indonesian uplands: Marginality, power and production.* Amsterdam, Netherlands: Harwood Academic Publishers.

Lieban, Richard. 1967. *Cebuano sorcery: Malign magic in the Philippines.* Berkeley: University of California Press.

Liow, Joseph, and Nadirsyah Hosen, eds. 2009. *Islam in Southeast Asia.* 4 vols. London: Routledge.

Maffii, Margherita. 2008. Changes in gender roles and women's status among indigenous communities in Cambodia's northeast. In *Living on the margins: Minorities and borderlines in Cambodia and Southeast Asia: Siem Reap, Cambodia, March 14–15, 2008*, ed. Peter J. Hammer, 129–40. Phnom Penh, Cambodia: Center for Khmer Studies.

Mair, Lucy. 1969. *Witchcraft.* New York: McGraw-Hill.

Malarney, Shaun Kingsley. 2002. *Culture, ritual and revolution in Vietnam.* Honolulu: University of Hawai'i Press.

Manser, Bruno. 1996. *Voices from the rainforest: Testimonies of a threatened people.* Petaling Jaya, Selangor, Malaysia: INSAN.

Maugham, W. S. [1923] 1985. *The Casuarina tree: Seven stories.* Singapore: Oxford University Press.

McCoy, Alfred W. [1971] 1991. *The politics of heroin.* Brooklyn, N.Y.: Lawrence Hill.

McElwee, Pamela. 2002. Lost worlds and local people: Protected areas development in Vietnam. In *Conservation and mobile indigenous peoples: Displacement, forced settlement, and sustainable development,* ed. Dawn Chatty and Marcus Colchester, 296–312. New York: Berghahn Books.

———. 2004. Becoming socialist or becoming Kinh: Government policies for ethnic minorities in the Socialist Republic of Vietnam. In *Civilizing the margins: Southeast Asian government policies for the development of minorities,* ed. Christopher Duncan, 182–213. Ithaca, N.Y.: Cornell University Press.

McKean, Philip Frick. [1977] 1989. Towards a theoretical analysis of tourism: Economic dualism and cultural evolution in Bali. In *Hosts and guests: The anthropology of tourism,* ed. Valene L. Smith, rev. ed., 119–38. Philadelphia: University of Pennsylvania Press.

Metcalf, Peter. 1982. *A Borneo journey into death: Berawan eschatology from its rituals.* Philadelphia: University of Pennsylvania Press.

———. 1989. *Where are you spirits: Style and theme in Berawan prayer.* Washington, D.C.: Smithsonian Institution Press.

———. 1996. Images of headhunting. In *Headhunting in Southeast Asia,* ed. Janet Hoskins, 249–90. Stanford, Calif.: Stanford University Press.

Michaud, Jean. 1997. A portrait of cultural resistance: The confinement of tourism in a Hmong village in Thailand. In *Tourism, ethnicity and the state in Asian and Pacific societies,* ed. Michel Picard and Robert E. Wood, 128–54. Honolulu: University of Hawai'i Press.

———, ed. 2000. *Turbulent times and enduring peoples: Mountain minorities in the South-East Asian massif.* London: Curzon.

———. 2006. *Historical dictionary of the peoples of the Southeast Asian massif.* Lanham, Md.: Scarecrow Press.

———. 2007. *Incidental ethnographers: French Catholic missionaries on the frontier of Tonkin and Yunnan.* Leiden, Netherlands: Brill Academic Publishers.

Mulder, Niels. 1996. *Inside Southeast Asia: Religion, everyday life, cultural change.* Amsterdam, Netherlands: Pepin Press.

Nash, Manning. *The golden road to modernity: Village life in contemporary Burma.* New York: Wiley.

Needham, Rodney. [1972] 2007. Penan. In *Beyond the green myth: Hunter-gatherers of Borneo in the twenty-first century,* ed. Peter B. Sercombe and Bernard Sellato, 50–60. Copenhagen, Denmark: Nordic Institute of Asian Studies.

Newell, William H. 1962. *Treacherous river: A study of rural Chinese in north Malaya.* Kuala Lumpur, Malaysia: University of Malaya Press.

Nguyen Van Ku and Luu Hung. 2002. *Funeral houses in the central highlands of Vietnam.* Hanoi, Vietnam: The Gioi.

Ong, Aihwa. 1987. *Spirits of resistance and capitalist discipline: Factory women in Malaysia.* Albany: State University of New York Press.

Orwell, George. [1934] 1962. *Burmese days.* New York: Time Incorporated.

Osborne, Milton. [1979] 2004. *Southeast Asia: An introductory history.* Crows Nest, NSW, Australia: Allen and Unwin.

Ovesen, Jan. 2004. All Lao? Minorities in the Lao Peoples Democratic Republic. In *Civilizing the margins: Southeast Asian government policies for the development of minorities,* ed. Christopher Duncan, 214–40. Ithaca, N.Y.: Cornell University Press.

Ovesen, Jan, and Ing-Britt-Trankell. 2004. Foreigners and honorary Khmers: Ethnic minorities in Cambodia. In *Civilizing the margins: Southeast Asian government poli-*

cies for the development of minorities, ed. Christopher Duncan, 241–70. Ithaca, N.Y.: Cornell University Press.

Peacock, James L. 1973. *Indonesia: An anthropological perspective*. Pacific Palisades, Calif.: Goodyear Publishing.

Pearse, Andrew. 1980. *Seeds of Plenty, Seeds of Want: Social and Economic Implications of the Green Revolution*. Oxford, UK: Clarendon Press.

Brac de la Perrière, Bènèdicte. 2009. An overview of the field or religion in Burmese studies. *Asian Ethnology* 68 (2): 185–210.

Pholsena, Vatthana. 2006. *Post-war Laos: The politics of culture, history and identity*. Ithaca, N.Y.: Cornell University Press.

Picard, Michel. 1996. *Bali: Cultural tourism and touristic culture*. Singapore: Archipelago Press.

———. 1997. Cultural tourism, nation building and regional culture: The making of a Balinese identity. In *Tourism, ethnicity and the state in Asian and Pacific societies*, ed. Michel Picard and Robert E. Wood, 181–214. Honolulu: University of Hawai'i Press.

Picard, Michel, and Robert E. Wood, eds. 1997. *Tourism, ethnicity and the state in Asian and Pacific societies*. Honolulu: University of Hawai'i Press.

Pookajorn, Surin, ed. 1992. *The Phi Tong Luang (Mlabri): A hunter-gatherer group in Thailand*. Bangkok, Thailand: Odeon Store.

Pringle, Robert. 1970. *Rajahs and rebels: The Ibans of Sarawak under Brooke rule, 1841–1941*. Ithaca, N.Y.: Cornell University Press.

Provencher, Ronald. 1975. *Mainland Southeast Asia: An anthropological perspective*. Pacific Palisades, Calif.: Goodyear Publishing.

Purcell, Victor. [1951] 1966. *The Chinese in Malaya*. 2nd ed. London: Oxford University Press.

Raffles, Thomas S. [1830] 1978. *The history of Java*. 2 vols. Kuala Lumpur, Malaysia: Oxford University Press.

Rajoo, R. 1993. Indian squatter settlers: Indian rural-urban migration in west Malaysia. In *Indian communities in Southeast Asia*, ed. K. S. Sandhu and A. Mani, 484–503. Singapore: Institute of Southeast Asian Studies.

Redfield, Robert. 1957. *The primitive world and its transformations*. Ithaca, N.Y.: Cornell University Press.

Reid, Anthony, ed. 1983. *Slavery, bondage and dependency in Southeast Asia*. New York: St. Martin's Press.

Richie, James. 1994. *Bruno Manser: The inside story*. Singapore: Summer Times Publishing.

Roff, W. R. 1984. Islam obscured? Some reflections on studies of Islam and society in Southeast Asia. *Archipel* 29:7–34.

Rosaldo, Renato. 1980. *Illongot headhunting 1883–1974: A study in society and history*. Stanford, Calif.: Stanford University Press.

———, ed. 2003. *Cultural citizenship in island Southeast Asia: Nation and belonging in the hinterlands*. Berkeley: University of California Press.

Rousseau, Jérôme. 1990. *Central Borneo: Ethnic identity and social life in a stratified society*. Oxford: Oxford University Press.

———. 1998. *Kayan religion: Ritual life and religious reform in central Borneo*. Leiden, Holland: KITLV Press.

Rugendyke, Barbara, and Nguyen Thi Son. 2010. Sustainable futures? Displacement development and the Muong. In *Regional minorities and development in Asia*, ed. Huhua Cao and Elizabeth Morrell, 79–96. London: Routledge.

Salazar, Zeus A. 1971. Footnote on the Tasaday. *Philippine Journal of Linguistics* 2 (2): 34–38.

———. 1973. Second footnote on the Tasaday. *Asian Studies* 11 (2): 97–113.

Salemink, Oscar. 1991. *Mois* and *Manquis*: The invention and appropriation of Vietnam's Montagnards from Sabatier to the CIA. In *Colonial situations: Essays on the contextualization of ethnographic knowledge*, ed. George W. Stocking Jr., 243–84. Madison: University of Wisconsin Press.

———. 1997. The king of fire and Vietnamese ethnic policy in the central highlands. In *Development or domestication: Indigenous peoples of Southeast Asia*, ed. Don Mc-Caskill and Don Kampe, 488–535. Chiang Mai, Thailand: Silkworm Books.

———. 2003. *The ethnography of Vietnam's central highlands: A historical contextualization, 1850–1990*. Honolulu: University of Hawai'i Press.

Sandhu, K. S., and A. Mani. 1993. *Indian communities in southeast Asia*. Singapore: Institute of Southeast Asian Studies.

Sandhu, Kernial Singh. 1969. *Indians in Malaya: Migration and settlement, 1786–1957*. Cambridge: Cambridge University Press.

Sather, Clifford. 1995. Sea nomads and rain forest hunter-gatherers: Foraging adaptations in the Indo-Malaysian archipelago. In *The Austronesians: Historical and contemporary perspectives*, ed. Peter Bellwood, James J. Fox, and Darrell Tryon, 245–86. Comparative Austronesian Project. Canberra: Australian National University.

———. 2001. *Seeds of play, words of power: An ethnographic study of Iban shamanic chants*. Kuching, Sarawak, Malaysia: Tun Jugah Foundation.

Sauer, Carl. [1952] 1969. *Agricultural origins and dispersals*. 2nd ed. Cambridge, Mass.: MIT Press.

Schebesta, Paul. [1923] 1973. *Among the forest dwarfs of Malaya*. Kuala Lumpur, Malaysia: Oxford University Press.

Schiller, Anne. 1997. *Small sacrifices: Religious change and cultural identity among the Ngaju of Indonesia*. New York: Oxford University Press.

Scott, James C. 1998. *Seeing like a state: How certain schemes to improve the human condition have failed*. New Haven, Conn.: Yale University Press.

———. 2009. *The art of not being governed: An anarchist history of upland Southeast Asia*. New Haven, Conn.: Yale University Press.

Sellato, Bernard. 1989. *Hornbill and Dragon*. Jakarta, Indonesia: Elf Aquitne Indonésie.

———. 1994. *Nomads of the Borneo rain forest: The economics, politics and ideology of settling down*. Honolulu: University of Hawai'i Press.

———. 2007. Resourceful children of the forest: The Kalimantan Punan through the twentieth century. In *Beyond the green myth: Hunter-gatherers of Borneo in the twenty-first century*, ed. Peter B. Sercombe and Bernard Sellato, 61–90. Copenhagen, Denmark: Nordic Institute of Asian Studies.

Sercombe, Peter B., and Bernard Sellato, eds. 2007. *Beyond the green myth: Hunter-gatherers of Borneo in the twenty-first century*. Copenhagen, Denmark: Nordic Institute of Asian Studies.

Sharp, Lauriston, and Lucian Hanks. 1978. *Bang Chan: Social history of a rural community in Thailand*. Ithaca, N.Y.: Cornell University Press.

Siegel, James. 2006. *Naming the witch*. Stanford, Calif.: Stanford University Press.

Simon, Scott. 2010. The hunter's spirit: Autonomy and development in indigenous Taiwan. In *Regional minorities and development in Asia*, ed. Huhua Cao and Elizabeth Morrell, 59–76. London: Routledge.

Skinner, G. William. 1957. *Chinese society in Thailand: An analytical history*. Ithaca, N.Y.: Cornell University Press.

Smith, Valene L., ed. [1977] 1989. *Hosts and guests: The anthropology of tourism*. Rev. ed. Philadelphia: University of Pennsylvania Press.

Smith, William Robertson. 1901. *Lectures on the religion of the Semites*. Edinburgh, Scotland: A. & C. Black.

Spencer, J. E. 1966. *Shifting cultivation in Southeast Asia*. Berkeley: University of California Press.

Spiro, Melford E. 1967. *Burmese supernaturalism: A study in the explanation and reduction of suffering*. Englewood Cliffs, N.J.: Prentice Hall.

Sponsel, Leslie E., ed. 2000. *Endangered peoples of Southeast and East Asia: Struggles to survive and thrive*. Westport, Conn.: Greenwood Press.

Stockwell, A. J. 1992. Southeast Asia in war and peace: The end of European colonial empires. In *The Cambridge history of Southeast Asia. Volume two: The nineteenth and twentieth centuries*, ed. Nicholas Tarling, 329–85. Cambridge: Cambridge University Press.

Stoler, Ann Laura. 1995. *Capitalism and confrontation on Sumatra's plantation belt, 1870–1979*. Ann Arbor: University of Michigan Press.

———. 2002. *Carnal knowledge and imperial power: Race and the intimate in colonial rule*. Berkeley: University of California Press.

Strauch, Judith. 1981. *Chinese village politics in the Malaysian state*. Cambridge, Mass.: Harvard University Press.

Stronza, A. 2001. Anthropology of tourism: Forging new ground for ecotourism and other alternatives. *Annual Reviews of Anthropology* 30:261–83.

Stuart-Fox, Martin. 1996. *Buddhist kingdom, Marxist state: The making of modern Laos*. Bangkok, Thailand: White Lotus Press.

Sutlive, Vinson H. 1978. *The Iban of Sarawak*. Arlington Heights, Ill.: AHM Publishing.

Sutlive, Vinson H., and Joanne Sutlive, eds. 2001. *The encyclopedia of Iban Studies*. 4 vols. Kuching, Sarawak, Malaysia: Tun Jugah Foundation.

Tambiah, Stanley. 1970. *Buddhism and the spirit cults in northeast Thailand*. Cambridge: Cambridge University Press.

———. 1976. *World conqueror and world renouncer: A study of Buddhism and polity in Thailand against a historical background*. Cambridge: Cambridge University Press.

———. 1984. *The Buddhist saints of the forest and the cult of amulets: A study in charisma, hagiography, sectarianism, and millennial Buddhism*. Cambridge: Cambridge University Press.

Tanabe, Shigaharu. 2002. *Cultural crisis and social memory: Modernity and identity in Thailand and Laos*. Honolulu: University of Hawai'i Press.

Tapp, Nicholas. 1989a. The impact of missionary Christianity upon marginalized ethnic minorities: The case of the Hmong. *Journal of Southeast Asian Studies* 20 (1): 70–95.

———. 1989b. *Sovereignty and rebellion: The white Hmong of northern Thailand.* Singapore: Singapore University Press.

Tapp, Nicholas, Jean Michaud, Christian Culas, and Gary Yia Lee, eds. 2004. *Hmong/Mia in Asia.* Chiang Mai, Thailand: Silkworm Books.

Tarling, Nicholas. 1992. The establishment of colonial regimes. In *The Cambridge history of Southeast Asia. Volume two: The nineteenth and twentieth centuries,* ed. Nicholas Tarling, 5–78. Cambridge: Cambridge University Press.

Taylor, Philip. 2007. Modernity and re-enchantment in post-revolutionary Vietnam. In *Modernity and re-enchantment: Religion in post-revolutionary Vietnam,* ed. Philip Taylor, 1–56. Singapore: ISEAS.

Thien, Do. 2003. *Vietnamese supernaturalism: Views from the southern region.* London: RoutledgeCurzon.

———. 2007. Unjust-death deification and burnt offering: Towards an integrative view of popular religion in contemporary southern Vietnam. In *Modernity and re-enchantment: Religion in post-revolutionary Vietnam,* ed. Philip Taylor, 161–93. Singapore: ISEAS.

Tong Tana: The Lost Paradise. 2001. DVD, directed by Jan Röed, Eric Pauser, and Björn Cederberg. Kungslingen, Sweden: Charon Film AB.

Trier, Jesper. 1986. The Mlabri people of northern Thailand: Social organization and supernatural beliefs. *Contributions to Southeast Asian Ethnography* 5:3–41.

Tsing, Anna Lowenhaupt. 1993. *In the realm of the diamond queen: Marginality in an out-of-the way place.* Princeton, N.J.: Princeton University Press.

United Nations Office on Drugs and Crime. 2008. Opium poppy cultivation in South East Asia: Lao PDR, Myanmar, Thailand. December. www.unodc.org/documents/crop-monitoring/East_Asia_Opium_report_2008.pdf (accessed August 9, 2010).

Volkman, Toby Alice. 1987. Mortuary tourism in Tana Toraja. In *Indonesian religions in transition,* ed. Rita Smith Kipp and Susan Rodgers, 161–68. Tucson: University of Arizona Press.

Wanasanpraikeo, Theera. 2008. Changes and challenges of community forest practices in forest-dependent communities in Kachin state. Master's thesis, Chulalongkorn University, Bangkok, Thailand.

Waterson, Roxanna. 1990. *The living house: An Anthropology of architecture in South-East Asia.* Singapore: Oxford University Press.

Watson, C. W., and Roy Ellen. 1993. *Understanding witchcraft and sorcery in Southeast Asia.* Honolulu: University of Hawai'i Press.

Weber, Max. [1922] 1963. *The sociology of religion.* Boston: Beacon Press.

Weinstock, Joseph A. 1987. Kaharingan: Life and death in southern Borneo. In *Indonesian religions in transition,* ed. Rita Smith Kipp and Susan Rodgers, 71–97. Tucson: University of Arizona Press.

Wells-Dang, Andrew. 2007. Strangers on the road: Foreign religious organizations and development in Vietnam. In *Modernity and re-enchantment: Religion in post-revolutionary Vietnam,* ed. Philip Taylor, 399–444. Singapore: ISEAS.

Wiebe, Paul D., and S. Mariappen. 1979. *Indian Malaysians: The view from the plantation.* Durham, N.C.: Carolina Academic Press.

Wiegele, Katherine L. 2005. *Investing in miracles: El Shaddai and the transformation of popular Catholicism in the Philippines.* Honolulu: University of Hawai'i Press.

Wilford, John. 2009. A tiny hominid with no place on the family tree. *New York Times*, April 28.

Wilkinson, R. J. [1906] 1957. Malay customs and beliefs. Papers on Malay Subjects. *Journal of the Malayan Branch of the Royal Asiatic Society* 30 (4): 1–87.

Winstedt, Richard [1925] 1961. *The Malay magician: Being shaman, Saiva, and Sufi.* London: Routledge and Kegan Paul.

Winzeler, Robert L. 1985. *Ethnic relations in Kelantan: A study of the Chinese and Thai as ethnic minorities in a Malay state.* Singapore: Oxford University Press.

———. 2004a. *The architecture of life and death in Borneo.* Honolulu: University of Hawai'i Press.

———. 2004b. Southeast Asian shamanism. In *Shamanism: An encyclopedia of world beliefs, practices, and culture,* ed. Mariko Namba Walter and Eva Jane Neumann Fridman, 834–42. Santa Barbara, Calif.: ABC–CLIO.

———. 2008a. *Anthropology and Religion: What We Know, Think, and Question.* Lanham, Md.: AltaMira.

———. 2008b. Religious conversion on the ethnic margins of Southeast Asia. In *Living on the margins: Minorities and borderlines in Cambodia and Southeast Asia: Siem Reap, Cambodia, March 14–15, 2008,* ed. Peter J. Hammer, 45–64. Phnom Penh, Cambodia: Center for Khmer Studies.

Wolf, Eric. 1966. *Peasants.* Englewood Cliffs, N.J.: Prentice Hall.

———. 1982. *Europe and the people without history.* Berkeley: University of California Press.

Woodward, Mark R. 1989. *Islam in Java: Normative piety and mysticism in the sultanate of Yogyakarta.* Tucson: University of Arizona Press.

Wyatt, David. 1984. *Thailand: A short history.* New Haven, Conn.: Yale University Press.

Zeppel, Heather. 1992. Getting to know the Iban: The tourist experience of visiting an Iban longhouse in Sarawak. In *Tourism in Borneo: Issues and perspectives. Papers from the Second Biennial International Conference, Kota Kinabalu, Sabah, Malaysia, July, 1992,* ed. Victor T. King, 59–66. Borneo Research Council proceedings series. Hull, UK: Borneo Research Council.

Index

Italic page numbers refer to maps, photos, and tables. When there are multiple identical note numbers on one page, they are preceded by the chapter number, for example, n3.2 refers to note 2 in chapter 3.